JUDGES, JAGS, and JOKESTERS

Judicial War Stories From the Workers' Judge

by Ronald Erickson

Dedication

I dedicate this work to those that are closest to me. With special dedication to my close companion and wife, Phyllis, who gave me love and encouragement. With further love and dedication to my children, Faye, Kyle, Lars, and Cameron. They are all exceptional. A special dedication to the grandchildren: Hallie, Matthew, Bill, Andrew, Evan, Nick, Griffin, and Ellen. A special tribute to my departed son, Kurt. I think he would have liked the book.

Lastly, this book is dedicated to those who have served and someday may serve this exceptional nation. This country is and always has been exceptional and mainly because of the people that have worn the uniform.

Acknowledgments

I would like to thank my wife, Phyllis, for the help and encouragement she has provided during this rather extended writing. There were times when I doubted myself and whether or not this work would ever come to fruition and without her support, this would not have been completed.

Thanks to Faye, Kyle, and Lars for helping out with assembling the photos and providing technical assistance. Their help was considerable. Cameron is creative and his special assistance was helpful. He suggested more sex be included in the book as "sex sells," but I will have to reserve that for my first novel.

I acknowledge the support and assistance I received from Russ and Patty Sherer. They are terrific people and I am grateful to have become acquainted with them. Their help on the Russ Sherer portion of the book was immense. I also thank "Dale Hartman" for his insights and assistance with the Gibberd investigation. Perhaps this book may perpetuate some renewed interest in moving this investigation to a closed case status.

Lastly I acknowledge the help and assistance of Dianne Swanson, Copy Editor and publication person. She helped me to complete the many steps necessary to get this work in print.

Author's Note

The conversations and events depicted in this book are as I recall them and are believed to be accurate. In the interest of preserving privacy, some individuals in the book were given stage names. For the most part, people who were attorneys, politicians, or judges maintained their own identity. Those who were public officials or public figures usually maintained their identity. I do not think anyone will be embarrassed by anything contained herein and many survivors will appreciate hearing about some of the accomplishments of their forbearers. I think I can say the same thing for the judges and other players identified in the workers' compensation system. Later on in the book when we get into the Gibberd trial, all of the witnesses were given new names. The party's names remained as reported in the system. No composite people were used. Everyone portrayed in this book was a real person, even that F-cking George.

This book is not intended to be a law book or a source of legal advice. Work comp attorneys are cautioned against citing this book as authority in their next comp case as it was never intended to replace "Larson on Workers' Compensation Law."

This work is not intended to be politically correct. The events portrayed and the language used accurately reflects the times and places. If you prefer a politically correct work, find something written by a politician and that may possibly satisfy your needs.

Table of Contents

Chapter 1 - It's a Start	1
Chapter 2 - City Attorney Days	11
Chapter 3 - Military Daze	41
Chapter 4 - Citizen Soldier	97
Chapter 5 - Getaway	113
Chapter 6 - Family Times	139
Chapter 7 - Inconsistencies	163
Chapter 8 - Death in St. Paul	177
Chapter 9 - Russell Sherer Lives	249
Chapter 10 - Police Business	259
Epilogue	275
Appendix	277

Chapter 1
It's a Start

This is a story about a kid from St. Paul who eventually became a judge. Not exactly a real judge, but the kind they call a workers' compensation judge. Some would say I am not a real judge, but I always counter, "I may not be a real judge, but I play one on TV." "Real judges" are on the district court or higher and those folks have managed to get up tight with a governor. I was once removed from that level as I got appointed by the guy who got appointed by the governor. I managed to hang together and do the job for twenty six years and believe I did a decent job. That later statement is what we in the law call "self-serving" and is to be ignored for that reason. I guess I could tell you a little bit about what I did and how I got to be a judge and let you decide if I did a decent job.

This first chapter will tell you where we are going. Please ride along. It's fairly painless and it's like the metro transit, nobody pays. Just get on the train.

Early on, I started out as a gumshoe lawyer trying workers' compensation cases when it was called "workmans' compensation." Gradually the "workman" began to undergo a sex change and the field of law evolved into "workers" compensation. Many who practice in the field simply call it "comp" or "workers' comp." Most of the folks over the age of 50 still call it "workmans' compensation." Old habits die hard. At times, the workers die hard as well, but more on that later.

I am older at this point, but when I started out the disability rate or "comp rate" was only sixty bucks a week and one-fourth of that (fifteen bucks a week) went to the comp lawyer representing the client. You had to hustle to make a buck, but if you got enough of the folks on disability, those fifteen dollars a week checks started to add up and you could eke out a living.

The bread and butter of the comp attorney has always been the back injury. It always has the potential to morph into a real long-term problem and for the lawyer that meant a continuing annuity. Your kids had a chance at a real college and not just Coon Rapids CC.

The hernia claim was another mainstay of the "Neanderthal" comp lawyer.

My typical client was always lifting a heavy box or machine or even a full coffee cup and felt a sharp pain in the groin area. Hopefully, he went to his doctor sometime before his exit physical and told the doctor a consistent story so we had the makings of a hernia claim. Mr. Injured Worker did not always tell his friends and coworkers the same story. If he was a backyard mechanic and was pulling an engine over the weekend and just happened to tell a coworker that he "strained himself" working on his 55 Chevy, then the insurance company came up with a denial and that meant litigation business for your friendly comp lawyer.

A standard hernia repair was a few hundred dollars in medical bills and six to eight weeks of disability. The insurance companies would fight these claims tooth and nail. The companies' main concern was if they gave ground on this claim, suddenly a giant salient or bulge in the defensive perimeter would develop and hernia claims would be multiplying like trial lawyers. To ward off this threat to the homeland, the insurance companies would deny many of the hernia claims and as a result, they went to trial. I was representing the injured worker and with a low comp rate it was hard to make any money, but the advantage was that to offset the paltry comp rate, the judges were liberal and the employee usually won. The lawyers tried the small case because they hoped the "Hernia Guy" would return if he later developed a more lucrative claim and in the meantime, tell his friends about his hot-shot lawyer. When I started, lawyers could not advertise as it was considered unethical so one had to build a practice slowly, one case at a time. Some of the lawyers had connections with the unions and they would funnel business to favored lawyers.

At the present time, I have not seen a hernia claim in years. Most of the heavy manufacturing is gone. Minnesota was formerly home to Whirlpool, Minneapolis Moline, Franklin Manufacturing, and a host of foundry and machine shops that supported those manufacturers. A lot of the people that worked in the manufacturing industry did rough, heavy work and experienced the hernia injuries that go along with that type of work. Most of those jobs have gone to Mexico or China and they have taken their hernias with them. The hernia claims were a great way for a young lawyer to get going and learn the business. The stakes were not real high so the case could be entrusted to a younger, budding trial lawyer and if the case was lost, it was not the end of the world.

The hernia claims have been replaced with repetitive motion claims and stress-related problems. The current work is often not very hard, but it can be repetitive and monotonous. The enterprising comp lawyer has learned to prosper with carpal tunnel claims and a host of positional and motion-related injuries. Many of the cases are functional over-lay cases. These are cases with a physical component but the actual injury is complicated by an adverse mental reaction. The physical symptoms may have even disappeared, but the mental problems remain and continue to sometimes disable the worker.

One of my first workmans' compensation cases as a trial lawyer involved an older, black gentleman called Mr. Gray. Mr. Gray had a routine back injury and by all appearances a fairly "clean" claim. He reported the injury, told his doctor about the injury, and his doctor reported it in the medical records. I could not figure out why the insurance company was denying the claim. It looked like a two-hour case and a slam-dunk victory for the home team.

Several weeks before the trial, as was my custom, I met Mr. Gray in my office and went over his testimony. I always stressed things like what happened on the date of the injury, when the injury was reported, and what facts he told his doctor about the injury. He also had to be able to relate the work days that he missed due to the claim. Specific dates are easy to forget, so I usually advised my clients to keep a log or notes on their calendar of important events and they could refer to it during the trial so that they could relate the events to the judge with some accuracy. In a pinch, I could use the first report of injury to jog a client's memory as to the date and time of the original event. Mr. Gray seemed on board with the plan and he asked me to write down some of the key dates for him and he would make sure this coincided with what was on his calendar at home. He would bring the "paper work" with him to the trial. He told me that he had "forgotten" his reading glasses and needed me to write things down for him.

At the trial, it began well, but when we got into the dates of injury and the dates of disability, Mr. Gray was faltering. He did not bring his calendar or any notes we had discussed. I showed him the first report of injury and that was no help. I finally showed him a copy of the notes with the supporting dates that I had penned out in my office. The defense attorney, Gene Brandt, was a nice guy and did not object. That was a smart move, as Mr. Gray was sinking himself with his sudden amnesia. I did what any panic stricken young lawyer should do, I asked for a recess. Judge Frank Haskell, a WWII vet, and normally a gruff fellow, buttonholed me on the way out and said, "Maybe you should settle this one."

I was still rattled when I met with Mr. Gray and asked him why he did not testify like we had discussed in my office and why he did not respond when I showed him the notes. His response was that, "I cannot read." I was stunned. Mr. Gray was used to fooling people and I was a pushover. In law school the clients always read. I settled the case with Gene and we moved on. I owed Gene one for that settlement.

I had failed to "read" obvious signs from my client, such as asking me to write everything down, and "forgetting" his glasses. These are signs that I should have read. I was the one who could not "read." This was not a lack of legal experience; this was my lack of real world experience. I had grown up in rural Ramsey County when farms and country schools dotted the countryside. Maybe I was still a country bumpkin. That evening, I climbed back on my turnip truck and, on my way home to the farm, gave the issue more thought.

After doing my thing with "comp," and although it seemed like heresy at the time, I determined that I needed a position with more variety. I accepted a position where I could get both civil and criminal experience. I moved to the Coon Rapids City Attorney's office as the first full-time city attorney. As city attorney, I advised the city manager, the mayor, and council on all legal and illegal matters, and also prosecuted for a thirty-man police department. I say "man" advisedly because there were no women in the department back in the cave-man days. I liked prosecution and soon found myself in court paired against my predecessor in the city attorney's office. The police had picked up his wife for speeding over on River Road and we met in a contentious courtroom encounter. The police had a great time watching the two city attorneys do battle and the city attorneys became friends after emerging somewhat scarred from the conflict. It was kind of like two kids fighting on the schoolyard, who later became best friends. I also soon became friends with the local building inspector named Al Flynn. Al was a WWII vet who served his country gallantly in San Francisco and came back to Coon Rapids after the war. He gradually acquired a million dollars in real estate while riding around in his old pickup truck. Al was a real estate "wizard" and also possessed the guile of a skilled trial attorney. I learned a lot from Al and others around City Hall.

I liked being city attorney. In fact, I liked all of my jobs. That seems rather unique as the modern work force seems to be less and less satisfied. The city attorney job was very time-consuming as it was characterized by endless meetings, either city council or planning commission or something else. To this day, I would rather be water-boarded than go to a council meeting.

At the time I was city attorney, I made a very unusual career move. I have always had a tendency to be unpredictable. My wife, Connie and I were having relationship problems. Sometimes a drastic change is needed to get two people back on track. The simple fix is not always best. I determined to join the Army Judge Advocate General's Corps (JAGC). I was commissioned with the understanding that the family and I would be stationed in Germany. I already had state and local law experience and I figured that becoming an Army JAG would round me out with federal law experience. Plus, I came to the realization that I wanted to serve. I had always tried to make safe career choices, but this one was more of an adventuresome choice. As a former prosecutor, I switched sides and went to the "dark side" as a defense counsel. As a JAG, I tried a ton of courts-martial and will tell you about a few. One court-martial involved a young private, Hull, who was sentenced to ten years, but the judge messed up big-time with the instructions and this JAG defense lawyer had to scramble to obtain an accurate record of trial.

As Captain (CPT) Erickson, I had two legal assistants, one of whom seemed to be impossible to motivate. Young Private First Class (PFC) George

It's a Start

Kowalski from the Bronx soon became known as that "F-cking George" and eventually I was forced to fire that F-cking George. I thought that George would just go quietly, as by all indications he did not like his job as a legal clerk or lawyer helper. In a surprise move, George ended up pleading with me to retain a job that I, and everyone connected to the office, thought he hated.

My Army days featured experiences as a line officer in addition to those as a JAG officer. This JAG was soon thrust into the role of pay officer and was entrusted with $44,400 in cold hard cash to dish out to the troops on payday. This was an experience that is no longer dreamed about in the modern cashless military. I also served as Staff Duty Officer (SDO) and desperately tried to think my way out of a fight with a drunken GI. I later switched jobs and became a law teacher. My Commanding Officer (CO) was Lieutenant Colonel (LTC) Swanson, who we called, "Starchy," the West Pointer with the oscillating ethical compass. Starchy cheated at push-ups and sent birthday cards to the general's dog. Starchy showed up at the physical fitness test decked out in shorts and running shoes. The rest of us dog faces were in the traditional PT-test wear consisting of fatigues and combat boots. Despite the two boot handicap, I managed to give Starchy a real match up in the mile run. He received no quarter.

Most of all, my time in the military served as a sound lesson for a maturing barrister in how the real world actually works. As a defense counsel, I represented soldiers from every possible race and ethnic background. This was Real World 101. I do not know where else one could get that sort of practical experience. These real world lessons were probably the best all-around training or proving-ground one could have for a later career as a judge.

Eventually all fun things must end and I was no longer CPT Erickson, but became the civilian CPT Erickson and remained in the reserves as a JAG officer for over twenty years. As the Air Force Reserve Recruiter says, "The adventure continues." The reserves yielded some additional courtroom heroics and you are ordered (not) to follow along as this reserve officer traveled both far and wide.

The civilian CPT Erickson remained in the reserves, but that only filled up one weekend a month and two weeks of the year, so it was necessary to obtain a day job. Unfortunately, things did not improve on the domestic front and a few months after returning to the States, CPT Erickson and his wife, Connie, were no longer together.

Civilian Erickson took a position as an unemployment referee with the State of Minnesota Department of Employment Security. This department changes names like some of us change socks so it is commonly known as the "unemployment office." The job as a referee did not feature officiating at fall football games, but did involve traveling throughout the state conducting unemployment hearings. Most of the hearings were without lawyers. When people represent themselves in legal proceedings, it is referred to as a "*pro se*" trial. A hearing was conducted on a frigid January day in Bemidji and the employee brought his attractive girlfriend along and she was soon bare-breasted as it was lunchtime for her infant. The referee struggled to maintain concentration and not let his mind wander from the hearing. It was a large distraction.

After remaining on the job for a few months, a colleague, Phyllis, emerged as a love interest. This attraction followed events at the famous annual bowling party held during the spring of every year. It is a statewide event for all state workers, but the litigation section hijacked the party and turned it into the spring prom. All sorts of office crushes and relationships suddenly emerged during this spring night. Most of the romances were short lived as third party relationships were involved. Phyllis soon departed on a trip with a boyfriend, but sent me a greeting card.

Phyllis and I eventually married and lived happily ever after. End of story. Not quite. I moved out of the unemployment office and went back to workers' comp. In a relatively short time, my friend from the reserves, Mick Hanson, and I were both appointed judges. The ink was hardly dry on our appointment when a disgruntled office seeker challenged the appointments in federal court. The appointment of the two Norwegians was upheld by a federal judge and the dynamic duo becomes the first federally "approved" comp judges. Hanson was emboldened by his courtroom triumph and decided he could solve the immigration problems of the United States and rode off to Florida to eventually become an immigration judge. I am not sure that one went as planned.

I had been a lawyer for twelve years when I was appointed a judge and believed I was well qualified. It is often difficult to evaluate your own qualifications, as I am sure General Custer never doubted himself. Every case is different, although there are always similarities running through most litigation. If you have decent experience, you can roll with the unexpected things that pop up in most courtrooms. For example, most folks would not take a recent law school graduate and stick them on the judicial bench. The graduate may be brilliant and likely know much more law than a graying barrister, but would they make a better judge? Have they ever represented a client who could not read? Have they ever watched a client go off to prison, despite the best efforts of counsel? Have they ever been directed out of court following a hard day of trial? Getting experience is not always fun and easy.

As a new judge, I had the advantage of varied experience and hoped that I may have acquired a small degree of wisdom. Wisdom is a tough commodity to find and is often achieved with a dose of pain. In some respects, wisdom is like common sense, it is not at all common. Hopefully more wisdom was found as I moved along, but it was not without cost.

Judges experience personal issues and problems just like any of us; this story is no exception. Phyllis and I decide to expand the Erickson network. Birth control and birth "un-control" issues are examined in almost too much detail. I had previously been "cut-off" from further propagation of the species, but later engaged a skilled physician to "putz with my nuts." The procedure was successful and another Erickson was added to the network. Nowadays the billboards say "Experience Vasectomy" "No Scalpel" and "No Pain." I am not sure how they can accomplish anything without cutting, but the physicians must have turned to lasers or drugs to do the deal. I have experienced a vasectomy and do not feel the need to undo what was already redone.

Life is not without tragedy and no one is immune from life's cruel blows. A beloved son is no longer with us. This is a memory lane that is not an easy drive.

Everyone needs an escape from the day to day world and I like to do what many Scandinavians do: fish or build stuff. I had a long running attachment to the Gunflint Trail in northeastern Minnesota and acquired a land-locked lakefront acreage and built my own cabin. Every stick of wood was ferried across Forlorn Lake by boat. This was not your routine weekend construction project. Sometimes, privacy and solitude are not easy to find. The Gunflint Trail yields many a story and I have been there long enough to share a few. New stories are still coming in and a recent tale involved a young man who netted suckers in exchange for a case of beer and the suckers were masqueraded as walleyes and passed off to a sucker public as Minnesota's prime fresh water fish.

Day to day life among the judges involves living and working with many diverse personalities. Judges do have bad days, and unfortunately a few of the judges have more bad days than good. Management gets complaints on judges and if they get too many, pretty soon a judge may have worn out their welcome. Management made the decision that a long time judge was no longer useful and a couple of his colleagues closed ranks and tried to outwit management. It worked for a time, but ultimately, it was like defeating the Big Green Machine. The wheels of big government continue to roll and a good judge is "forced" to retire. Most of the time, I agreed with management, but on this occasion, I ceased being a management shill.

Like it or not, life is full of inconsistencies. People say one thing and do another. "I am going to lose ten pounds, but first I will have a beer and plan my strategy." We all have a tendency to say one thing and do another. I slowly discovered over the years, that what one does is usually a more accurate indicator of what happened as opposed to what one said they did. For example, one may testify that they cannot lift a 2" x 4", but then be observed manhandling a 4' x 8' piece of sheet rock. One may claim to have serious limitations, but when one observes them lifting heavy building materials, then claims of such restrictions ring hollow. I have certainly seen some unexpected things pop up in surveillance films and I will share some of the most memorable scenes. Quite often, what is seen on film is inconsistent with what one claims in the courtroom. I devote a chapter to inconsistencies and mention several actual cases where inconsistencies are uncovered through the medium of surveillance film. One example is the "prevaricating preacher." He claimed not to have the strength to lift a pencil, but was seen on film, lifting a large TV out of his trunk and filling his gas tank and not wearing a neck brace that he favored for courtroom attire.

One may claim to have serious limitations, but when an attractive young woman is observed bouncing about on the water trailing behind a jet ski, then her claim of having substantial physical restrictions begins to seem at odds with her actions. The insurance companies and their attorneys are constantly searching for inconsistencies or inaccuracies within the ranks of the injured workers. If the employee is not reliable, and their testimony not accurate, then it becomes very difficult to award benefits to that person.

Over thirty years ago, my home town of St. Paul was normally a quiet and peaceful place. That was not the case on the evening of August 26, 1985. On that evening on Dale Street, an English gentleman named Raymond Gibberd was gunned down in daylight hours. Mr. Gibberd had come from Great Britain to work for Control Data Corporation (CDC) as a computer consultant. He was shot some 3-4 blocks from his office while on an evening break. Two hard-working police detectives relate in some detail their efforts to solve this case. Despite spending hundreds of hours of investigative time, no motive for the crime was ever found. A crime without a motive makes it more difficult to solve as the motive often leads the authorities to the perpetrator of the crime. Any first year law student knows that the government does not have to establish a motive for a crime, but cops, jurors, and judges love to have a motive for crimes as that makes their job easier.

Mrs. Betty Gibberd, the wife of Raymond Gibberd was seeking payment of workers' compensation benefits on behalf of herself and two minor daughters. CDC denied benefits contending that Mr. Gibberd was off premises and on his own time and the killing had nothing to do with his employment.

We soon learn that the shooting death of Mr. Gibberd was not the only crime that went down on that warm summer evening. It was discovered that within the hour and only a mile away, Russell Sherer, a William Mitchell Law Student, had been shot in similar fashion. Miraculously, Mr. Sherer survived the shooting.

The workers' compensation case took on elements of a criminal trial. My criminal experience as a city attorney and as a JAG lawyer came in handy. The case was concluded and appeals were taken as the case worked its way through the system and there still remained many unanswered questions. Years later, lingering questions encouraged a follow-up inquiry. I located the two detectives, both retired, and found out what happened after the trial. A trip to Texas yielded an expansive interview with St. Paul Police Sergeant Hartman. It turned out that both cases did not lack for suspects.

Russ Sherer survived the shooting and the reader will follow Mr. Sherer's rehabilitation and eventual return to work and law school. Without a doubt, it is a miracle he lived. Russ was successful both before and after this horrific event.

My family always took an active interest in politics. My Dad vacillated between the democrats and the republicans, but in later years he settled on the republicans. My older brother always tended to be conservative. As a lad of about 14, I rode my bike over to Lexington Plaza near Larpenteur Avenue in Roseville and saw a political rally of sorts featuring Adlai Stevenson. He was running for president for the second time around against President Eisenhower. Ike was just about unbeatable and certainly Stevenson with his intellectual demeanor was not going to unseat the former Allied Supreme Commander. Stevenson appeared on a hastily constructed wooden platform next to the Dairy Queen with Senator Hubert Humphrey, Governor Orville Freeman, and a couple other state politicians. There were not many young people in the audience; in fact there were not that many people at all. This political rally did not draw 100 people and I doubt if there were more than 75. My friend, Bruce, and I were two of the few onlookers that traveled via bikes. This was an old-time political stump speech rally. There were no TV cameras rolling. All of the Minnesota politicians gave their pitches and Stevenson took center stage. Stevenson spoke with an accent that struck me as sounding British. He certainly was not from Minnesota. As it turned out, Stevenson did not resonate with Minnesota voters as Ike carried the state with ease. That was the last time a republican presidential candidate prevailed in this liberal bastion, except for Nixon in 1972 against George McGovern.

I guess the political bug struck me at an early age. I have met Humphrey, Ventura, Quie, Carlson, and a cast of many. I describe most of those encounters as we move through the years.

The late Irving Younger said that trying a lawsuit is about the most difficult mission in the world that one could undertake. This is certainly true. When I did become a judge, cases in front of me were all tried to the court as there were, and there are no jury trials in workers' comp cases. That did make the case much easier to try for the lawyers as they did not have to worry about picking a jury and otherwise posturing and trying to properly or sometimes improperly influence the jury. In a jury case, many of the legal and evidentiary arguments have to be made out of the presence of the jury so that they are insulated from hearing improper evidence and argument. The necessary procedural safeguards inherent in the jury system do contribute to the time it takes to try a jury case. I functioned as judge and jury all rolled into one so that allowed the case to proceed much quicker than a judge-jury trial.

I am now retired, and at this point, I usually do not miss being a judge. I did miss it for the first five years. As one retires, one becomes less and less visible. I am damn near invisible at this point. When I was in the Army, Starchy told me that I was in a high visibility role. Before I totally fade from view, perhaps it is time to tell my story. This is my story and I am stuck with it. It is not my story alone, but a bunch of stories and tales of folks I have encountered, liked and disliked, throughout my travels through life. As you take this trip, you can commence your adventure just about any place. If you are most interested in the St. Paul shootings, then start with Chapter 8. Each chapter practically stands on its own, so start where you are most interested. This is almost like a Hebrew book; one could start from the back and read forward. Lastly, this book is not politically correct. If that is what you seek, even more than competence, there are many books written by political figures that should meet your needs.

Chapter 2
City Attorney Days

As a young lawyer, I succeeded in talking myself into a full-time position as city attorney for Coon Rapids, Minnesota, one of the ten largest cities in the state of Minnesota. My job was to advise the city manager as well as the mayor, council, and department heads on all city legal matters. In addition, I was also the city prosecutor for a thirty officer police department. The city population was about 30,000 and we were running about 1 police officer per 1,000 people, which was just about the recommended force size. I also represented the city in all civil trials. This was really a two-lawyer job, but somehow, I managed to do it myself for over three years. It did take its toll on me personally as it was very demanding. There was no doubt that it was too much for one person.

One of the first people I met as city attorney was the long-time Building Inspector, Al Flynn. Flynn was one of the most clever and shrewdest individuals I have ever known. He had a nose that was completely wired for money. He was the first town building inspector and got in on the ground floor of city development. As the city developed so did Al. He also had the luck of the Irish, which did not hurt. If you went to a party with Al, be prepared because he always won the door prize.

Al was a WWII vet and served as a mess sergeant (SGT) on the "Western Front" - San Francisco. He was at the Presidio, one of the most beautiful Army posts in the world, for the duration of the war. As mess SGT he got up every morning before the chickens, got breakfast ready for the troops, and was on the trolley at six a.m. and heading downtown to his other full-time job. He was head maintenance man at the Sir Walter Raleigh Hotel during his military days. Al finished up at the Hotel in the early afternoon and was back on the trolley and returned to the Presidio in time to prepare the evening mess.

Al told me that his officer in charge (OIC) knew he was working another job, but could find no fault with Al's Mess Hall so chose to look the other way. Was Al getting one over on the Army? He was putting in his time and putting out good food. There were no big gripes from the troops. Rather than spend his free time between meal preparation playing cards or drinking beer, Al took another job. The civilian labor shortage was acute, with all the able bodied young people in uniform, so Al did his part to alleviate the shortage by doing double duty. If paying your taxes is considered patriotic in modern day America, then certainly wearing the uniform and winning on the home front would have to be considered the model of patriotism in WWII America. I should point out that I have never considered it patriotic to do something that the law requires under penalty of jail time.

Al "won" the war in San Francisco and decided to come back to Minnesota. His boss at the hotel, begged him to stay and offered him more money, but Al's mother was getting on in years and he decided to come back home. Was that an easy choice? Who would pick minus 30 degrees in the winter and mosquito infested summers over balmy San Francisco? That was the only time I questioned Al's decision making.

After the war, the returning veteran wanted a woman, car, and house in that order. As usual Al picked up on the trend in a hurry. He sensed that the mythical woman was going to want more than a vacuum cleaner and a new set of pots and pans. Most of the vets returned to their original hometowns, although they had seen the world and were much less firmly planted than their parents had been. The hometown was often in the frozen north. Florida and California were still orange groves. The young nubile women of the frozen north were going to need more than GI Joe to keep them warm and Flynn concluded that real fur was often a better butt warmer than GI Joe. He returned to Coon Lake Township and bought a 40-acre tract in a remote part of the town and started raising mink. The Mississippi River was nearby and the mighty Mississippi provided an abundant source of cheap mink food in the form of carp. They were netted out of the river in droves and Al hauled them to his mink farm in his pickup truck. Years later, when my son, Kyle, fished near the Mississippi River Power Dam, he would catch carp in abundance. He did not have any mink to feed, but he would trade carp for a walleye with Vietnamese fisherman who coveted the native fish of their distant homeland. Carp must be a universal fish, as the Germans liked it as well. When I soldiered in Germany I never caught on to eating carp, but they had a sea bass that was pretty tasty. It was probably carp, but they just called it bass so they could sell it to gullible GI's, who would rave about it.

Al made some money with the minks as he rode the post-war fur boom. The boom topped out when the ads began to appear on TV and in the papers to buy your own little furry critters and make a fortune raising them in your basement. Chinchillas were the rage. Everyone would get a pair of breeding stock and pretty soon you had potential fur coats running all over the house. Not much thought was given to caring and feeding the furry friends and perhaps most difficult, killing and skinning the new family pet. Chinchillas were not very big and it must have taken a basement full of them to turn out a coat. As everyone with a basement was entering the fur business, Al sensed it was time to get out. He sold or skinned out his herd and exited the business.

Al had learned a lot about electrical and plumbing work while doing his time as a maintenance man on the west coast, and prior to the Army, he had dabbled in building and construction. He was well qualified to take the building inspection job at the newly formed City of Coon Rapids.

Al attended all of the council meetings and rode around in a city vehicle and inspected homes and construction sites. He was in a unique position to know everything that was going on in a fast growing town. If there was a lot for sale or a home to purchase, Al knew about it. When the power company put some homes on the market to purchase and move off site, Al put in a bid for the surplus homes. Northern States Power had a dam and power turbines located on the Mississippi River. The power company had company-owned houses in the area that they rented to local workers. When the plant closed the workers had to move. The power company probably wishes they still had the hydro plant as they have to get off the fossil fuel fix in a few years. Al found vacant lots near the surplus housing and put a lot and a house together and, "bingo" he was in the rental business. Then as now, there was a good market for single-family rentals and Al was able to feed into that market. If Al found a low lot in the area that was in need of fill, that was no problem. He would locate a high lot in the vicinity, arrange a bargain price, and pick up the fill in his truck. Dirt from the high lot filled in Al's low ground.

Al's biggest strike was the farm he bought in the middle of town. Prior to purchase, he got wind of where the new state highway 10 was probably going. This was public information and Al was shrewd enough to calculate the full import of this development. His farm was located on one of the major roads in town, Hanson Boulevard. He had property on both sides of Hanson Boulevard and right where he concluded the highway was going. He turned out to be correct; the highway ran at a diagonal right through his farm. Of even greater importance, Hanson Boulevard was right on an interchange. The highway department would acquire a substantial amount of Al's property including his house and barn. Some of the naïve local residents pictured "Poor Al" as losing his beloved home to the big, bad highway department. Al was well paid for his "loss" but of even greater consequence, was the property the department did not take. The highway department took enough property to accommodate the Hanson Boulevard/Highway 10 interchange and Al was well rewarded for the land taken. He was left with the former farm property located adjacent to the interchange. He had four lots on the busiest interchange in the area. Al knew what people wanted on highway interchanges and that was gas stations. Al sold his first interchange lot to an oil company in the early 60's for $75,000, which was a ton of money at the time. A couple of the other interchange properties went for fast food franchises at a generous price tag.

Just to illustrate how much money was involved, about that same time, I bought a three-bedroom rambler with a garage and finished basement located in Columbia Heights for $28,000. I bought it directly from the owner with no real estate commission and a modest down payment. That was a big step up for me as my first house was an old two story and cost me $9,600. I paid less than a $1,000 down for "this old house" and I was in the door. I did find a newer house that was a lot more money, but I could not come up with the down stroke and my parents refused to loan me the down payment so it was the old house for me. I liked the old house a lot. In those days, one could buy a decent house on a contract for deed, with a modest down payment and you could avoid the clutches of your friendly banker. I doubt if I made enough to qualify for financing with a bank. I think you can still find "deals" such as "my old house" out in the market, but they may not be in abundance and you probably have to look a little harder for them. If you do not have money, then you have to expend time in order to find the deal you can handle. Check with the small independent realtors as they are more likely to have some of the more modestly priced listings. If you can find a FSBO (for sale by owner) you are likely to make the best deal. Pay a lawyer to write up the documents for you, as it will be much cheaper than a realtor. Realtors always want a percentage of the cost of the house and a lawyer will work for a flat fee (usually much less than the 3 % a buyer's realtor will want). The local city assessor is a very good source of information on prospective real estate and make sure you use that source of information. Just the other day, I needed information on a piece of property I own in a distant state and I called the local assessor and came away with a treasure trove of useful information. Perhaps you can find the information online and you can save yourself a trip to City Hall.

Al also found himself with an old church building located near the interchange. The religious edifice had long since ceased to function as a church, but Al liked real estate, no matter its lineage, so he rehabbed it into an office building. It did not take very long and he had a real estate company renting the old church property. Al did obtain, through the mail system, a cleric's license. Al probably had some scheme to leverage his church and newfound cleric license into some sort of tax exemption for his church property, as church property is exempt from local real estate property taxes. He did not have quite the *chutzpah* to pull that one off as he was still getting a paycheck from City Hall.

When Al's farm was being acquired by the Highway Department, he understood the condemnation system from his time hanging around City Hall. The state typically sent out an appraiser to view the property and come up with a value. If the property could be purchased at the appraised value, that was the end of the line. If the property could not be bought at the appraised value, then it went to condemnation. When it went to condemnation, the government

City Attorney Days

lawyer headed for the courthouse and got their order for condemnation and the court picked three appraisers. In point of fact, the court usually picked the three appraisers that the government's attorney recommended. The court-appointed appraisers would view the property and check on recent sales and then assign a value. If either party did not like the value provided by the court-appointed group, then it went to trial in the court or venue where the property was located.

Al turned down the original state offer on his farm property, sensing he could do better with local appraisers. For one thing, Al knew everyone in the real estate business. The court-appointed appraisers were usually local realtors, and all of the realtors knew that Al owned considerable property and thought that there may be a listing and commission out there in the future for them. In my experience, the word *commission* is the holy grail of realtors. That drives the train and moves the cattle. Nothing would be done to jeopardize a current or future commission.

After Al turned down the state's offer he knew he had some time to get his property looking its best before the court-appointed appraisers were involved. He painted his house and barn. He planted flowers and shrubs. Al knew what sold property and that was curb appeal. The same thing drives appraisals. The better the property presents, the higher the value as reflected by the court appraisers. When the court appraisers contacted Al and asked to view the property, Al insisted on stalling them for a few days. In the meantime, Al noted areas where his property could be improved. He went out and purchased plastic flowers and "planted" them in strategic areas where the real ones died or were not previously planted. He correctly concluded that no one would notice the fake flowers and they would present his property much better for the appraisers. He was well served and received a generous award. Even more important, were the four corners he was left with that were reserved for oil companies or fast food places.

Al had a real nose for oil stations. He somehow picked up a lot adjacent to a local service station. The proprietor, Mel Schulte, was also on the city council. His campaign slogan was "Tell Mel." I am not sure what you were supposed to tell him, but you must have some gripe with City Hall, most people did. Mel's wife, Doris, was the political maven in the family and she probably should have run for council instead of telling Mel to do it. She would have been ecstatic over the job and Mel would have been happy fixing transmissions. One day Al was in talking or "telling Mel" about things in City Hall and mentioned that he may sell his vacant lot to a car wash. Mel replied "It might be nice to have a car wash in town." Al then responded, "They are going to sell gasoline." That was not what Mel wanted to be told. That same afternoon Al got a call from the real estate department of the oil company that Mel was affiliated with. Al sold his lot for a nice price at an early date. He knew how to push the right buttons. He also knew when to sell his properties and sensed that if one could get a nice price now, it was better to part company with cozy acres, rather than holding out for the last dollar.

Mel's wife, Doris, nudged him into the political ring, but he was not the only one to enter politics because of a not so gentle shove from a spouse. The Mayor, Bob Voss, was a reluctant candidate, but his wife persuaded him to run. He was a good and dedicated mayor, but I do not believe he ever enjoyed the job. Spending your weekends and evenings doing something you do not like is drudgery. Carolyn Voss later ran for council and was successful and served two terms. The council was actually loaded with members with ambitious wives. Dave McCauley, another council member, had a politically active and attractive wife named Lonnie. Dave eventually left the council and then went on to run for county commissioner. He won and served a term or two. His wife, Lonnie, ran for mayor and won in a walk.

Al could have succeeded in a number of fields. He bought Winnebago stock at low levels and then sold before the gas prices rocketed up and gas lines formed in the 70's. He had the natural instincts of a good personal injury lawyer. A lawyer I knew had a personal injury case involving a young boy with a scar on his face. One day he was taking some pictures of the scar to send on to the insurance company for settlement purposes. Al happened to be in the office on other matters and was watching the photography session. The boy was getting photographed and happened to have a smile on his face and Al told the boy, "Don't look so happy." It made perfect sense and the lawyer did not pick up on it. The message he wanted to send was that the boy had not had a happy moment since the accident and resulting cursed scar.

I have had a number of scar cases and a frequent problem for the lawyer is that scars heal quite fast. Over time what starts as an ugly scar, often heals beautifully with barely a hint of a prior slash. Al devised his own remedy to thwart the healing process and achieve a courtroom recovery. He related to me that he had been a passenger in an automobile and he sustained a cut to his chin during an accident. Al retained counsel and the matter was placed in suit. When the case was set for trial, he spent the day before the trial date, working the scar by vigorously rubbing it with his knuckle. The following day, when he showed up for court the scar was still red and prominent on his face. The defense counsel looked him over and was heard to say, "That looks bad" and came forward with a generous settlement offer.

Al used three or four different lawyers, depending on what was at stake. He liked to use Ed Coleman in Anoka for real estate matters. Ed related to me one day that he represented Al on a complex real estate matter and they concluded the transaction and Ed gave Al his bill for services rendered. Al paid him and also included a gratuity or add-on. Ed related that was the only time in several years of practice that he had received a "tip." Ed was said to be one of the best ball players to ever come out of Anoka. Years later when he prosecuted for the City of Anoka he was rumored to have a plug in his ear tuned into the ballgame during a slow trial. I prosecuted in front of Ed and thought he was a great guy.

Shortly before I got up to Anoka County, the municipal or local judges were all part-time. They all had local law practices in addition to acting as a local judge. When I was first admitted to practice I tried my first case in front of Judge Knutson, a part-timer in Anoka. The local judge in Coon Rapids was Tom Forsberg. Forsberg lived in town and practiced with a local firm. One of Tom's former partners was Bill Merlin who was the part-time city attorney for Coon Rapids and my predecessor in the office. One of the current partners in the firm was Wyman Smith. One of my friends was awaiting his trial in the local municipal criminal court and Forsberg was the presiding judge and Merlin was the prosecutor and the defendant was represented by Wyman Smith. They probably made a disclosure on the record and got everyone's permission and proceeded with the trial. Years ago, we did not spend all of our time worrying about conflicts of interest. They were hard to avoid in small communities. Forsberg was a fair guy and had I been prosecuting the charge, I would not have worried about it.

I thought the local municipal courts were great because the filing fee was low and for the small cases you did not have to waste all your time on discovery. You went in and tried your dispute and you did not have to spend thousands in discovery to dispose of the small case. Currently, if you have a small case, you end up in district court and those folks are so high and mighty they spend their free time figuring out how they can toss you out of court so they can get in a round of golf or go back in their chambers and sit on their ass. My good friend from the Army Reserve, Jack Elmquist, told me that the judges in Ramsey County make every effort to toss your case or run you out of court if you dare darken their courtroom with a case claiming under $100,000. I took a small case into Ramsey County district court and had the same experience as Jack dealing with an arrogant and lazy judge that could hardly wait to bounce you out of court. It is a damn shame that the district judges have become so regal that they cannot take their "precious" time and spend it doing what they were elected to do. By the way, never give up your right to elect district judges. Do not fall for the so-called Quie Plan or any other scheme to take away your franchise. The politicos will tell you it is judicial reform. It is as close to reform as reform school, a former device used to train juveniles in bigger and better crime techniques.

Al made it a point to use Tom Forsberg for at least some of his legal matters. As building inspector, Al also issued tickets or citations for zoning and building violations and it did help to have a sympathetic judge. Later on, Wyman Smith also represented Al. Bill Merlin was critical of Al and did not think he did a decent job in court. Merlin was closely aligned with the prior mayor and Al did not particularly like the prior mayor so that was another problem between the two city officials.

Wyman Smith was a clever and gifted lawyer and had a unique way of resolving disputes. One of his clients owned some property along Coon Creek in town and owed some back taxes on the creek property. Much of the property was too low for building purposes so that did put a limit on the property value. Still, it was nice wooded creek-side property and certainly had some value. His client had become embroiled in another dispute with the city and Wyman had a claim with the city he wanted to resolve. Wyman proposed that the city take the Coon Creek property and he would dismiss his other suit. I had so many things to do that I was glad to get rid of the lawsuit and moreover the creek property had great potential for a city park. The finance director was not real excited about the deal, but the city manager agreed with me that the property had nice potential for a park and the council went along with the acquisition and settlement. The city eventually developed the property into a very nice park. It is called Coon Creek Park.

By the time I was city attorney, Forsberg was a full-time municipal court judge. One reason the judges went full-time was to eliminate some of the conflicts as previously pointed out. Tom gave me some good advice along the way. I was initially reluctant to charge people with bad checks or N.S.F. (non-sufficient fund) checks as I thought we were turning into a collection agency. Part of the problem was that previously if the check was paid prior to the court date, the case was dismissed. I made the mistake of initially advising the police department that we were not going to prosecute checks. Tom took me aside and advised that I could not do that or the big stores would jump on me and the local bar owner, Ray Swanson, was a county commissioner and could make things very uncomfortable for me. That was good counsel from Tom and I quickly got back into the check collection business. I did make one big change in policy. I would no longer dismiss the case if the check was paid and I expected the clerk who took the check to be present in court for trial. The manager of the local Red Owl asked me why I would no longer dismiss a N.S.F case when the check had been paid. I asked him, "If someone came into your store with a gun and robbed your checkout and later returned the money, would you still want that person prosecuted?" He responded in the affirmative. "There is no difference in the check situation; the crime is already committed by the time the case gets to my office and subsequent restitution is for the judge to consider in determining a proper sentence." I was trying to think longer term and if a bad check could be resolved by paying it when you felt like it, that did not seem like a strong enough sanction to avoid recidivism.

I used to frequently prosecute cases in front of Forsberg. Early on, I finished up with court around lunchtime and Forsberg invited me to lunch. I was young and occasionally liked to have a Manhattan or two at lunch. Forsberg

City Attorney Days

was a WWII vet and liked to have a totty or two. I learned a lot about the local political scene and got a lot of legal tips during those lunches. Tom had a huge St. Bernard dog and the dog would frequently get loose and run in the neighbor's flowerbeds. Tom would go down to City Hall and pay a fine for having an unleashed dog running loose in the city. I appreciated that gesture or I would have been in the very uncomfortable position of swearing charges against the local judge. This was the first and only time I have ever heard of a judge charging himself, finding himself guilty, and paying a fine. I was not about to challenge the legality of such a move.

When I took over as city attorney, I replaced Bill Merlin who was the previous long-time city attorney who did the job on a part-time basis. Bill did not believe in working for free and did charge the city on an hourly rate. Some of the City Fathers came to the conclusion that they could save some real money by hiring me on a salary and just using Bill as a consultant. One of the council members told me when I was interviewed that, "We can get three of you for what we are paying Merlin." Merlin was a large corpulent man and I was thin in those days, so I was not sure if they were speaking of physical appearance or money. I concluded it was money.

Shortly after I took over from Merlin, we had lunch with the city manager. Merlin wanted to sell me his law books, but I did not care much for his library. Plus, he wanted a rich price for his books. I tried to discretely get some idea if his price was firm, but he responded tartly, "Ron, what are you saying?" I said, "I am saying I will have to think further about your books."

It was not long after I started as city attorney when Merlin's wife, Mary, was cited for speeding over on the River Road. Officer Donald Gorder picked her up on radar. By this time, Bill was starting to feel the pinch from losing his biggest client and neither he nor Mary were thrilled with the prospect of a diminished lifestyle. There was no doubt in Mary's mind that I was directly responsible for cancelling her trip to Bermuda.

Bill and Mary were an intriguing couple. Bill was a large man and weighed in at north of plenty of pounds. Mary was an attractive and full figured woman, but looked like Twiggy compared to Bill. She had gone to law school at one time, but had apparently come to her senses, and departed. According to Tom Forsberg, Bill and Mary had a lively relationship and were sometimes at loggerheads. They certainly presented a united front in the courtroom during the morning of the speeding trial, as they were moving as one, unified against a common threat and enemy - me.

Bill had been an effective prosecutor for the city. The Police Captain, Bill Morris, told me, "Merlin took the police department and picked it up and shook it by the neck." Morris relayed that the *Miranda* case had just come down and the cops did not know how to handle it. The *Miranda* case was new and revolutionary for your average small town P.D. Merlin was impatient and blustery, but he was not stupid. The message gradually got around, that anytime the cops had a suspicion that John Citizen had done something wrong and when he was not free to leave (in custodial circumstances) the *Miranda* rule was triggered and a warning was required. Many times, a lack of *Miranda* warning has no bearing on the outcome of the case because you do not need the defendant's statement to secure a conviction, but Merlin wanted the officers doing it right and jumped on their asses when they did not follow the law. He was correct, because a big part of any good prosecutor's job is educating the department. The next case may hinge on whether or not the defendant's statement or admission could be used against him and Merlin was trying to instill sound practices. I tried to do the same thing, but according to most of the cops, I was more diplomatic in my approach to the education process. For example, when the accused is sitting in the back seat of a squad car and there were no door handles available to open the car door, then the accused is likely in custodial circumstances. The *Miranda* rule was triggered and for a police officer or prosecutor to argue otherwise was pure folly.

    Mary's speeding case came on for trial on a nice spring day before Judge Joe Wargo. Wargo was a blustery and boisterous fellow with a large white mane of hair. He certainly looked the part of a distinguished jurist and could have nicely played a judge in any Hollywood rendition featuring a courtroom drama. Wargo owned a lot of property in Anoka County and had founded a formidable law firm. He liked to move all trials along as he generally had lunch at the Edgewater in Minneapolis and liked to have a Manhattan in his hand by noon.

    On the morning of the crime, Mary Merlin had been on her way to the local community college where she worked as an instructor in the English Department. She may have been late and in a hurry, which was always a stock question on cross-examination, by any prosecutor pursuing a conviction in a speeding case. Before I got a shot at Mary, I had to present my own case.

    My first witness was Officer Donald Gorder. He was sworn in and tells the court, "he was working that morning with Officer Anderson." He set up the radar at 7:30 am at East River Road and Foley Boulevard. Gorder then relayed that, "I had Officer Anderson drive through the radar area at 30 mph and I observed the speed on my radar screen as 30 mph." "Objection" Merlin bellows, "No foundation." "Sustained" rules Judge Wargo, looking very judicial with a large flowing mane of white hair and a bulbous reddened nose.

    I plod ahead and change the question slightly and Gorder persists with the same story. Merlin shouts, "Same objection." Wargo bellows, "Same ruling." I prepare to head back to the bar for a third time, but Judge Wargo senses that this courtroom drama could extend into his lunch hour unless Erickson starts to make some headway. Wargo is not about to miss the first round of Manhattan's because of some snot nosed prosecutor so he thunders from the bench,

City Attorney Days

"Approach the bench." Merlin and I make our way forward. There is no jury to worry about so Wargo gets right to it in his courtroom baritone. "Look Erickson, you can't have Gorder telling us how fast Anderson was driving. He just saw Anderson's car go through and observed the radar screen at 30. Gorder cannot know what the hell is on Anderson's speedometer. Anderson may have been sailing through the damn area at 50." Wargo is deferential to Merlin but glares at both counsel and advises to, "Get to your damn point." Sounds like good advice to me.

I re-load for a fourth time and move ahead with Gorder. Gorder has also had the benefit of the Judge's evidentiary lecture and testifies that he had Anderson drive through and observes the speed on the radar screen at 30 mph. Gorder does not attempt to testify to the speed on Anderson's speedometer as Anderson will be called later to testify how fast he drove through on the drive-through and when his speedometer was last calibrated. A statute allowed the prosecution to put in the calibration record and it was at least prima fascia evidence that the officer's speedometer was accurate. I sense slow, but steady progress in this epic battle. Gorder gives a rudimentary description of the radar device and we offer records of the care and feeding of the devise. "No objection," responds Merlin as he senses he may be irritating Wargo.

I then proceed into the commission of the crime itself. Gorder describes the date and time of the offense and describes Mary's car as a green vehicle approaching the area in the west-bound lane. I ask him, "Did you observe the speed of the green vehicle on the radar screen as it passed through the area?" "Objection," blares Merlin "No Foundation." I respond to Judge Wargo that the testimony is offered subject to further foundation. "I will call Officer Anderson and lay further foundation for the accuracy of the radar on the morning in question." Wargo is thirsty and no longer interested in lawyer sport. He realizes that I cannot call two witnesses at once and the only alternative to receiving the testimony subject to further foundation, is to excuse Gorder subject to further recall and then call Anderson and excuse him subject to recall and put Gorder back on. Merlin would have the right to cross-examine every time on what was covered on direct examination and meanwhile the musical chair game of witnesses would continue well into the afternoon. Wargo would be lucky to make evening happy hour. "Objection overruled," responds the now impatient Judge.

Merlin's objection, although overruled has thrown me off the track. Gorder has forgotten the question. I backup and start over, "Did you observe the speed of the green vehicle on the radar screen as it passed through the area you described?" "Yes" is the brief and proper response. "What was the speed you observed?" "It proceeded toward me and I locked in the radar at 48 mph." "What is the posted speed in the area?" I asked. Gorder responded, "40 mph." I asked Gorder what he did next and he continued that he described the green vehicle including license number over his radio to Anderson, and Anderson stopped

City Attorney Days

Mary's car.

I called Officer Anderson and he related going through the radar set-up in the morning and observing his speed on his speedometer at 30 mph. He also did the same procedure at the end of the morning when Gorder's supply of tickets was exhausted. I had testimony that the radar was accurate at the beginning and end of the day so it must have been accurate when Mary burst through the area. I offered Anderson's calibration card without objection from Merlin. Lastly, Anderson testified that he received the description of the vehicle from Gorder via his radio and stopped the described vehicle and lo and behold, it was driven by none other than the Honorable, Mary Merlin. Gorder had issued the ticket (citation) due to a statutory rule providing that officers could only arrest and issue citations for misdemeanors committed in their presence. Anderson may or may not have seen the actual offense. He just stopped the vehicle that Gorder told him to pull over. Things were quite a bit more particular or specific in those days and under current practice, Anderson would likely issue the citation. The concept of "presence" has become more stretched out so that either officer, as long as they are in the general area of the offense, could issue the citation.

At this point, I had the four corners of my case nailed down. One of the toughest lessons for any young lawyer and particularly an inexperienced prosecutor is to avoid over-proving your case. The rookie barrister wants to prove every minute point beyond a shadow of a doubt and consequently calls every conceivable person that may have even a passing knowledge of the subject matter of the litigation. The problem is that invariably the questionable witness will recall some remote fact that will damage the prosecution's case. There is no point in fouling your own nest. At this distant time there were not a lot of formal rules governing discovery or sharing of information with the defense, although I made it a practice to usually share the information I had with the defense.

Judge Wargo did not appreciate a lot of extra testimony or baggage so I soon learned to get my case in chief presented as quickly as possible. If any bullshit was necessary, Wargo was more than able to provide that commodity. Most of the time, written briefs or case citations were not needed in Joe's courtroom as he relied on common sense and a lot of life experience to carry the day. Usually he turned out to be correct. Most of the cases turned on fact questions and Joe had a lot of experience to draw from.

We took a recess before the defense started and Lieutenant (LT) Morris met me in the hallway and told me I was doing well. I had begun the process of establishing credibility with the police department.

We returned to the courtroom and I rested and Merlin was on his feet and moved for a dismissal. Merlin launched into a long speech on why the case should be tossed, but Wargo was not in the mood, and cut him off with a gruff,

City Attorney Days

"Let's get on with it Merlin." Bill led off by calling his star witness and spouse, Mary Merlin. Mary spoke with a crisp New England accent and with no hesitation. She was overweight by modern skinny standards, but not obese. Her hair was close-cropped and thick. She presented herself well in the courtroom. Bill was out of the south and still spoke with a southern dialect in contrast to Mary's succinct speech pattern. Bill and Mary were speaking as one on this particular morning.

There was no doubt that the City of Coon Rapids was Bill's biggest client and he had billed the city substantial sums during the previous year and the loss of much of this business was going to smart. I suspect that Merlin had billed the account somewhat low in the initial stages, but got to the point where he wanted to get paid and began to bill the account more aggressively later on in the game. He maintained a satellite office in the area and had two associate lawyers and staff, so he had to bill to cover his overhead. Mary had done some work for the firm and some consternation was created at City Hall when some of the invoices reflected charges for "legal clerks" time. The legal clerk turned out to be Mary. In this day and age paralegals are common and a paralegal charge being billed at less than a lawyer rate would cause no consternation whatsoever.

Mary began her testimony by relating that she was taking a leisurely trip to school on the morning in question. She left early, and had plenty of time; she had no reason whatever to be in a hurry. When she got to the point where she was going to testify to her speed, I objected "No Foundation." Wargo sustained my objection. Wargo smiled wryly as he realized that Merlin had given me a rough time when I was on direct and now it was my turn. The speedometer in Mary's vehicle had not been calibrated to determine its accuracy and unless it could be established as accurate, there was no foundation for testimony based on the device.

Merlin had a sheepish grin and asked to approach the bench and whined to Wargo that, "he could not be expected to have his speedometer calibrated as he did not require that of the defendant's when he served as prosecutor." Wargo reminded Merlin that, "You were damn fussy about the calibrations of the squad cars on that morning." I kept quiet as Wargo was doing the punching for me. Merlin realized he was on the spot as without speed testimony, Mary was dead in the water. Merlin was terrified that he would be hearing about his "blown defense" over the next millennium. I had a hunch that there was no statute of limitations at the Merlin house when it came to Bill's transgressions. I have never experienced the benefit of such a mythical statute either. Merlin told Wargo, "I will get the speedometer calibrated as soon as possible and send the calibration into the court." I objected as, "Not timely, we are supposed to be ready to try the case today and not sometime in the future." Wargo glared back at me and said "overruled." Merlin had given me a tough morning and I was doing what I could to give it back to him.

Mary resumed her direct testimony and related that her speed was well under the lawful limit. She added rather gratuitously, "I always drive with one eye on my speedometer." That was all Bill needed and he declared, "No further questions, your witness."

Cross-examining Mary was like catching a barracuda with your bare hand. I had the impression that I was a household word in the Merlin house, but usually preceded by a pejorative starting with f or s. I started out by asking her what time she left the house and where she went. It turned out she had to drop the kids off at school before she headed for her teaching assignment. Merlin objected to relevancy. Wargo over-ruled as Joe knew I was trying to show she was running late and in a hurry. The question was also relevant because Mary had testified earlier on direct that she was taking a leisurely drive so this was certainly reasonable cross-examination. I established where she lived and about how far it was to the college. I asked, "What time was your class due to start?"

The date and time is always on the ticket (military time) so it was evident that Mary was in a bit of a hurry on the fateful morning. I had enough testimony to put the time line together for final argument and show she was in hurry and not doing a leisurely drive as she had testified. I asked her to describe the traffic that morning. "Objection, vague and indefinite," injected Merlin. "Overruled," replied Wargo. I took her through the trip again and asked about the traffic. "How would you describe the traffic on East River Road during the morning in question?" Mary hesitated and then answered cautiously, "The traffic was not unduly heavy, and it was a fairly ordinary day of traffic." Mary knew she had to be careful with this answer as I had two cops that I could recall to impeach her testimony if she went off the deep end and described the morning traffic as "heavy." Heavy traffic would make it harder to speed. Mary had testified on direct that she was sure she was not speeding as she always kept one eye on the speedometer. The ticket was issued for speeding on East River Road and Foley Boulevard, so I asked Mary what her speed was at East River Road and 75th Street. She could not answer. "What was your speed at East River Road and 85th Street?" Merlin objected, "Relevance your Honor, the ticket was issued twelve blocks removed from 85th Street." Wargo smiled and responded, "Overruled, she testified that she always had one eye on her speedometer, so I suppose she can be questioned based on her testimony." Merlin countered, "Your Honor, it was simply a figure of speech." "Mr. Merlin, this is cross-examination, over-ruled," responded Wargo. Mary had to admit that she could not remember the exact point prior to Foley Boulevard when she last checked her speedometer, although she quickly added, "I know I was not speeding." I moved to strike the last part of her testimony as "non-responsive," but Wargo let it stand.

The case was concluded and Merlin said he would waive final argument if I agreed to do likewise, and I agreed. I figured that Joe had heard enough from the two of us for one morning and he was not going to pay much attention to what the lawyers said, in any event. Joe said he would take the case under advisement and this concluded the day. Taking a case under advisement is an old ploy used by judges when they do not want to advise the parties in person of the results of the trial. I had stood up to Merlin and given a good account of myself. The police department was happy with the way I had battled and whether or not I won was not all that important.

Two or three months later a brief note on a printed form showed up in the office. "In the matter of State of Minnesota vs. Mary Merlin, the Court finds the defendant, not guilty." The result did not shock me. Joe decided to cut a break to a fellow lawyer's family, and why not?

Prior to the big trial, Bill had been rather curt with me, but never antagonistic. After the trial, our relationship improved and we started to get along on a personal level. He invited me over to his place for a poker party with some of his business cronies and his new law partners. Bill entered into a new partnership with three younger lawyers on the make and jettisoned his two junior associates. Bill must have concluded that I was going to stick around as city attorney, at least for the immediate future. Tom Forsberg was also invited to the poker party and it turned out to be a fun evening. Tom played very conservative poker. He said that, "I don't gamble." I'm Norwegian so I can understand not wanting to lose money. My wife, Phyllis, is a better gambler than me, so I leave most of the betting to her.

It turned out that Bill's new law partners were, Allen Oleisky, a fine fellow, who went on to join the Hennepin County Bench and Bill Starr. Bill ended up doing a fair amount of comp work and appeared in front of me on several occasions. He always did a nice job.

Unfortunately, after I had been city attorney for a couple years, Bill Merlin was diagnosed with cancer and was dead in a matter of weeks. I attended Bill's funeral and was sad to see him depart. The police "brass" showed up, but not too many members of the rank and file. Officer LeRoy Anderson was still heard to complain, but in a good hearted fashion "about losing that damn Merlin case."

Years later, after I had left the city attorney's office, I ran into Gorder in a bar and we reminisced over the Merlin case. After our discussion and before I left he told me, "You're the best prosecutor this town ever had." That may have been the beer talking, but it was still nice to hear.

Several years later, after my first wife and I separated, I joined a single's tennis club, but was usually too busy to attend. Friday night was "hustle tennis" but I was not much of a hustler. One evening, out of the blue, I received a call from Mary Merlin. She was a member of the tennis club and had seen my name on the membership rolls. We had a nice conversation and she asked me to look for her at the tennis club, but I never made it to the club. I was busy when she asked me and never did get around to seeing her or calling her back. Who knows, if I had gone out with her, there may have been another chapter to this story.

When I initially started as city attorney/prosecutor I had already had a fair amount of courtroom time and had done some criminal work. I was no Perry Mason, but I could frame a question, state an objection, and introduce a document. I could make noise like a lawyer. One of the first people I met was Bill Morris, a lieutenant with the police department. Morris was a resourceful fellow and had crafted himself a job as liaison between the police and prosecution. He made sure there was some sort of file put together and we met once a week before trial day and went over each case and Morris made sure I knew the strengths and weaknesses of each case. It saved me a lot of time as Morris knew I was very busy and frequently told me, "You're as busy as a whore keeping two beds." I had not been in the prostitution business, but many believed lawyering was close, so I think I knew what he meant.

Morris had been with the police department, practically from the start and knew all of the officers quite well. He related that, "Officer Beiner is not a very good courtroom witness as he is too passive." Beiner was also passive on the street as the patrol sergeants were frequently on his ass to write more tickets. Pressure to write more tickets was always present. The city manager pressured the police chief and the chief pressured the lieutenant and so forth down the line. I was doing the prosecution so I told the chief to not write so many damn tickets. I do not believe that the patrol officers had any "quota" as far as number of tickets to write, but there was no denying that there was pressure to perform. In current times we have tracking devices that can keep track of where a given squad car is at all times, but in previous days, one of the best ways to keep track of what the patrol was doing, was to count how many tickets were issued and note the times. They had radios and the police band was the only means of communication between the squad car and headquarters. When the officer was out of the squad, he was on his own.

Morris had his favorite officers and some that he did not like or trust. "Officer Rumchek has a tendency to exaggerate in court so be careful." Morris believed that Rumchek had gotten a little rough on an individual he had stopped and had me dismiss the case or at least plead it down to a lesser offense. Rumchek was a little bummed out toward me, but I told him to "talk to the lieutenant." I liked Rumchek, but I figured Morris was his boss and if he wanted me to deal the case, that was good enough for me. In current times, there would likely have been a huge civil case over allegations of "police brutality," but no one was seriously hurt so this was the end of it.

Morris was a big guy and overweight, but not sloppy fat and he was possessed of a natural scowl. The "cops scowl" was extremely handy and likely

City Attorney Days

made Bill's job easier. The scowl served as a visual warning to angry drunks or wife beaters that Morris took his job seriously. If the boisterous drinker was not careful, that scowl might be followed up with a nightstick moving swiftly from Bill's left hip.

Around me, Morris was always affable and had the smooth speech and manner of a good old boy southern sheriff. Bill's speech pattern may have endeared him to the southern cops as one day he related to me that he had been to a cop's convention and ran into some good old boys from Louisiana and asked them, "What do you guys do about search warrants?" The Bayou cop had no problem with warrants and in fact reached into his pocket and pulled out a piece of paper marked search warrant. "We just have the judge sign a bunch of these things in advance and then we just fill in the blanks when we need them." Bill replied that, "The judges up my way are a bit more careful than that." Indeed, that was correct and one thing Bill was always alert to is that if the warrant was to be served late in the evening that you "nightcap it." In other words, have the authority to serve it at night if that proved necessary. We had to show some reasons in the supporting affidavit as to why it may require evening service.

Morris was a veteran of two wars, WWII and Korea. He said, "I volunteered for the first one, but they came and got me for the second one." He stayed in the National Guard following the Big War and got called back when Truman activated the 47th "Viking" Infantry Division. He spent a year in Korea and was "never so damn cold in my life." I recall when I was just a kid and the Minnesota Guard was activated and they drove in formation past my home on Highway 10 on the road to their mobilization point at Camp Ripley. My brother was older and told me what was going on. I remember that most of the soldiers were not smiling or waving and looked grim. Many of those soldiers had already served in one war and were not happy with the prospect of fighting another one. They were not tossing chewing gum or candy for the kids. The drawdown following WWII was so severe and swift that when the Korean War broke out, President Truman had little choice but to activate the guard and reserve soldiers.

Morris had acquired a good share of wisdom and sense after serving in two wars and wearing a badge for many years. The city had recently passed a qualification requirement for new police officers requiring two years of college as a minimum requirement. Morris had zero college in his background and resented some of the new "college boys" who lacked street smarts. "Hell" Morris would say, "Our best cop is Buck Sheppard and he ain't got a day of college." The former Chief of Police, P.H. Nelson had instituted the college requirement and had created some stir within the ranks. Nelson reasoned that the college crowd could write better reports and communicate more effectively with the department and the public. In current times, a college degree or at least two years of college is a requirement in many departments, but fifty years ago, it would have been a decided exception to the rule.

Buck Sheppard frequently worked "undercover" in that he ran around at all hours of the night in civilian clothes and maybe did some smoking. He was quite effective and made his share of busts. One evening when Buck was on the prowl he came upon a burglary in progress and proceeded to take down the perp himself without back up. The next day, Morris crowed, "There you go, our best officer, Buck Sheppard brings down a burglar without backup and Buck doesn't have a day of college." Morris never missed a chance to take a shot at what he viewed as the misguided college policy.

Morris had a good nose for local politics and told me about certain "City Hall Hanger Outers." Those were folks who hung around City Hall and BS'd with people and kept current on the latest goings on. In the process they gathered information on what was happening and sometimes got information on a business deal or a land venture that could be profitable. One such person that Morris identified to me was a local insurance agent, one George White. White was an affable sort and a retired Air Force enlisted man. He lived in the neighborhood of Mayor Voss.

Shortly after I arrived in City Hall, one of my first adventures dealt with the city's new insurance contract. The city had a lot of employees and getting them all under a health insurance plan was a fairly lucrative deal. Before I arrived, the city had put the insurance contract for its workers out on bids. George was one of the bidders, but did not turn out to be the low bidder. I had just arrived and Bill Merlin was still attending council meetings and advising the council. Merlin correctly told the council that servicing the policy was a big part of the contract and that would probably justify not awarding the contract to the low bidder. It had become clear in the council's discussion of the issues that the mayor wanted to award the contract to his neighbor. The mayor justified his support for George by stating, "We should give the business to the local man." Generally, the bid had to go to the lowest "responsible bidder." The mayor reasoned that White was the most responsible bidder. Actually it turned out that the lowest bidder was also a local agent.

The mayor ended up with egg on his face and likely needlessly so. The mayor wanted to help his friend and there is nothing wrong with that. George was in the community and able to do a lot of administrative duties connected with the policy, and in so doing, he could take a lot of the load off the city staff. That is the way the contract should have been sold as actually saving the city money instead of favoring the local.

After the meeting, Merlin told me that they probably did not have to put the contract out on formal bids in the first place. They should have just asked for proposals. The contract was more than just cost, as service was a big part of the equation. Service contracts usually do not require bids. Merlin then added

City Attorney Days

that they should not have solicited formal bids if they were not going to follow the bidding procedure and go with the lowest bid. In other words, this was a political mistake. Merlin gave me similar advice on straw votes. Many times when an issue is hotly debated, someone in the crowd will come up with the idea of taking a straw vote. Merlin told me, "Never agree to a straw vote unless you are prepared to follow it." Sage advice, because the crowd will feel betrayed if you do not follow the vote. Straw votes are not fair to the people that stayed home that night and had no idea there was going to be a straw vote on an important matter at City Hall that evening. Moreover, the council was a representative body and not a democracy. The representatives are charged with the responsibility for making decisions and they cannot delegate their duties back to a few straw voters. A savvy mayor will simply state, "We do not do straw votes." If an explanation is demanded, then the mayor will have to get into the civics lesson.

Mayor Voss managed to lose the mayor's office in a close race the next time out. The so-called "insurance issue" likely played a part in the mayor's political slide. Mayor Voss had done nothing illegal or wrong, but oftentimes how something is handled can make all the difference in the world.

As it turned out, the mayor and council were facing a much bigger political powder keg in the form of a potential gas rate increase. This was a hot potato political issue and was much bigger than the insurance issue as it involved just about everyone in town. The local gas company had decided to seek a rate increase. In those days the local gas company operated under a franchise with the city and the city council had authority to grant or deny gas rate increases. In later times, the state pulled the ratemaking authority from the local councils and gave it to the State Public Utilities Commission. Rate increases were always controversial as it affected the most sensitive nerve in the human body, the one running down your hip in the vicinity of your wallet. A former council member named Don Erlandson was leading the charge against a rate increase. Don was active in the police reserve and it was apparent that he was laying the groundwork for a run at the mayor's office.

There are always a few veterans around City Hall that can tell you who is going to be running for mayor or council and who will win. Around our City Hall, Bill Morris and Al Flynn had the best view and could normally tell me who was running and who was winning. They both told me that Erlandson was running for mayor and he would likely win. This was definitely a word to the wise.

The gas company filed a petition with the city for a gas rate increase. The council set a public hearing on the rate increase. The matter came on for hearing and the council chambers was packed. I was doing the council meetings myself at that point and I knew this meeting was going to be hot. After the gas company presentation, it was time for the public to speak. Don Erlandson was one of the first to speak and spoke long and eloquently against the proposed rate increase. His words were well received and his campaign was successfully underway. Erlandson's speech closed on a cautionary tone. He warned the council that if they granted a rate increase, that he was going to seek a referendum on the issue and put it to a city-wide vote. There was no doubt as to how that referendum would turn out as most of the ordinary folks in the city thought the gas company were the biggest gougers in town. Maybe, even bigger gougers than the politicians.

The city council listened to the presentation by the gas company and they laid out in an eloquent and professional manner just why they needed more money from the rate-payers in Coon Rapids. This was a non-partisan council, but the way it went down is that the mayor and three republican colleagues voted to allow the rate increase while the lone democrat, Joel Jacobs voted against the measure. Joel was a calculating politician and quickly realized that there were more voters in town against the gas company than for it. Joel went on to serve in the state legislature for several terms and got back in the utility business at a later time as a member of the state public utilities commission (PUC). In one of life's ironies, my wife, Phyllis, would later be appointed by Governor Ventura to succeed Joel on the PUC. Politics is sometimes a small world. The ordinance granting the rate increase became the law of our little land.

The gas company made a case for a rate increase before the council, but no one had much of any idea what was behind the numbers they presented. The utility did not want us looking at their books and in any event, the city could not afford to audit their books and as a result, we had only a vague notion as to where their money was going. The officers could have been going to Fiji every year for board meetings or all driving Jaguars. This was one of the shortcomings of city control. We lacked the resources to really look behind the numbers they presented. Looking back on it, the council should have demanded some sort of independent audit and charged it back to the gas company. We all concluded we were stuck with the numbers they presented, but maybe there were alternatives. Other alternatives were never proposed to me nor a request for a legal opinion on any other options. With the benefit of experience, I probably would have suggested an independent audit or at least a review of the books at gas company expense and if they did not go along with it, then deny the request for a rate increase.

One person who did not believe the numbers presented by the gas company was Don Erlandson. True to his word, Erlandson quickly secured the necessary signatures on a petition asking for a referendum on the city ordinance granting a rate increase to the gas company. Our city charter allowed for a referendum on city ordinances.

I was on the spot because the council had voted the matter in and did not want a referendum on the matter. They obviously believed that the gas company had demonstrated a need for the rate increase and if they were to continue offering service in the city, they had to be paid. On the other hand, Erlandson was showing political strength and if I wanted to stick around as city attorney, I better not cross him. I had to walk a political tight rope by not angering my current or possible future bosses. Two of my smarter associates, Flynn and Morris, had advised me that Erlandson would soon be my boss.

After the referendum came in, the city clerk had first crack at it and checked the signatures and crosschecked against city records such as utility bills to determine if the signatures appeared to be legitimate. The clerk gave it a blessing and the issue then worked its way to my desk. It was on the agenda for the next meeting. I made it a point to talk to Judge Forsberg and also to Bill Merlin. Merlin reminded me that not every ordinance is subject to the referendum process, especially those ordinances that require judgment or mimic the legislative process.

At the council meeting, the chambers were packed and other than the city manager, no one knew what I had decided to do. The referendum issue was one of the first on the docket and the mayor asked me what the next step should be on the gas company issue. I gave a fairly long response and reminded the council that not every issue is subject to a referendum because some involve the resolution of conflicting values and opinions and thus boil down to the council's best judgment. On the other hand, the city charter provided for a referendum process and it was important to follow the proper legislative process. Because there was doubt as to how we should proceed, I had decided to seek an opinion from the Attorney General (AG) of the State of Minnesota on how to proceed with the issue. I told the council that I recommended we seek an attorney general's opinion. I got done with my presentation and the mayor asked me, "Aren't you going to ask for an attorney general's opinion?" Fortunately, Councilman Larson had been awake and reminded the mayor that I had recommended an AG opinion. The council passed a resolution directing me to seek an attorney general's opinion as to whether or not the rate ordinance was subject to the referendum process and that was the end of that issue for the evening. The crowd disbursed and gathered around Don Erlandson outside the council chambers. Erlandson said, "Let them get an attorney general's opinion. We can still take them to court if we have to." The battle lines were drawn.

I contacted the attorney general's office and was referred to Mick Gallagher, the Special Assistant AG, who handled municipal legal matters. I knew Mick's brother Dan Gallagher from my workmans' compensation experience so felt better knowing that the matter was going to be reviewed by someone with competence and experience. Mick was very business-like and told me what I should present to him with my request for an opinion. He needed our city charter and all the ordinances relating to the referendum process. The gas company had a franchise with the city and he needed that document and any other ordinances relevant to the gas company. He also wanted a copy of the ordinance the council passed granting the rate increase and the completed petition for referendum. It took me the better part of a day to get all of the documents together and frame my letter of request to the AG and get it dispatched.

This was not the simplest request the AG's office received, so most people realized it was going to take some time. After a month or so had gone by I called Mick Gallagher to make sure he had all the information he needed and to also ask, "By the way, how are things progressing with the opinion?" He told me he was working on it and it would be a "couple weeks or so" before it came out.

In the meantime, I met Al Flynn over lunch as I wanted to get some idea what was happening on the street with the gas issue. "Erlandson is going to court." Flynn added, "You knew the AG was going to deep six the ordinance when you sent it for an opinion." I told Al, "Hell no, I did not know what he was going to do, but I am glad there was someone else to make a ruling on the matter other than me." Al again reminded me that Erlandson was going to be my new boss after the next election.

The days did stretch out and a "couple weeks" moved closer to a month. The delay did serve to quiet people down and cut down on some of the emotional energy generated by the issue. The council requested that I check again on the status of the opinion. I did and was told by Mick that a senior AG or the Big AG was reviewing it and it would be out shortly. If I recall correctly, the Big AG at that time was Doug Head.

In a matter of days the opinion reached my desk. It was directed to me because I was the requesting party. The citizens request for a referendum was found not to be proper. The rate-making ordinance was not subject to the referendum process. Setting rates involved the council weighing conflicting opinions and facts and reaching a legislative decision based on judgment and reason. This is what the council was elected to do and you could not substitute their judgment by simply setting aside the ordinance. We had representative government and not a democracy and the people had given the council rate-making authority and it was unconstitutional to pull that authority and give it to another group. It amounted to an unlawful delegation of authority.

The council voted to accept the AG opinion and deny the referendum. The only dissenting vote was, once again, Joel Jacobs who voted no. Joel had a good knack for picking up the political winds. Don Erlandson was at the meeting and made it clear he disagreed and was going to court. The effect of denying the referendum was that the original ordinance authorizing the gas company rate increase, stood as passed and there would be no referendum.

As things worked out, Erlandson became seriously ill and did not challenge the council's decision. No one else had the passion or the political will to mount a judicial attack on the denial of the referendum. Erlandson did get

City Attorney Days

better and did run for mayor and won rather handily. Larson, who voted for the rate increase and against calling for a referendum, was also defeated by a large margin. The gas company got their increase, but it was not without cost.

As things worked out, Don Erlandson became a very good mayor and a friend. He took a reasoned approach to problems and generally treated people well. He was active with the Police Reserve Unit and there was some fear that he was going to turn the city into a "police state" with excessive power to the police. As the city prosecutor, I did not notice any change in attitude or approach by the police. The Police Reserve Unit did afford Don a good political base and he was able to draw on it for probably a couple hundred votes. In a local election where a lot of folks do not bother to vote, that is a big voting block.

Mayor Erlandson remained opposed to the rate increase, but made no attempt to interfere with the prior decision on the referendum. I think that was a wise decision as he viewed it as "What is done is done and let's move forward and take care of the city's current problems." Don made it clear that he did not agree with the previous decision, but he did not dwell on it and did not waste a lot of time blaming Mayor Voss. I believe that politicians can and do dwell too often on the mistakes of their predecessors. A politician can only play the "blame game" for so long and finally people began to ask, "What are you going to do about the problem?" It is an excuse for not solving a current problem and not a very good excuse. Most leaders soon realize that they have milked that cow dry and move off that angle.

Mayor Erlandson did give up on the referendum, but he by no means gave up on his opposition to the gas company. He was convinced they were exploiting the public. Don got word that the gas company had filed a petition with the Federal Power Commission (FPC) for a rate increase (the FPC later morphed into the Federal Energy Regulatory Commission FERC). As I recall, this was based on an increase in the cost they were paying for gas in the wholesale market. In other words, their suppliers were charging them more, so they wanted permission to increase their tariffs so they could pass the gas cost plus other "handling charges" on to their retail customers. Most of the local franchises had a provision that provided that if the utility's wholesale price went up, they could pass that on to their customers without coming before the council with a rate increase. Don saw a rate increase coming and the council was not going to be able to do a thing about it. Don reasoned that the gas company was already overcharging the city customers so that they should absorb some or all of the cost of any wholesale price bump.

Don contacted several of the mayors in the metro area and did find some support for opposing the rate increase. They collectively decided to do what they could to block the proposed increase. Don directed me to look into it and see what I could do. I got ahold of one of the staff lawyers with the FPC and had him send me copies of the filing papers and pertinent documents. The staff lawyer advised me that the rate petitions were usually based on rather dire projections by the utility of what their costs were going to be so that they could get as large a rate increase as possible and thereby protect themselves from the worst case scenario. One can understand why they would take that approach as it served to give them a generous increase and cover unknown contingencies. My position was that the utility had inflated their costs and potential liabilities and the utility should be prepared to absorb at least a portion of the rate increase. I took Don's argument and ran with it. The staff lawyer for the FPC did not know what position the staff would take and I asked him to keep me informed of all developments. He assured me that he would keep me in the loop.

I put together a brief in opposition to the proposed increase and petitioned to intervene as a party. Our petition to intervene was granted so we were assured of getting copies of all pertinent filings. In fact, the paper began to flow at a brisk pace. Trees were dropping everywhere.

Don liked my brief in opposition to the increase and indicated he wanted to testify before the FPC. I must confess, I knew very little about utility regulation and the volume of the filings were daunting. I found a few things in the filing that looked unreasonable and tried to focus on those items.

Time moved on and eventually we received news from the FPC that the rate increase hearing was to commence on a certain day. Don got busy organizing his group and told me that he wanted me to go with him to Washington, D.C. Don also made it clear that he was going political. Don had good contacts with the democrats and intended to use his political strings. I was as green as grass and was surprised that politics would play a role in a rate increase. I had a lot to learn.

Out our way, our Washington Congressman was a long-time democrat from Minnesota's Eighth District named John Blatnik. John had been in Congress forever and through seniority had risen to Chair of the powerful Labor Committee. John was an Iron Ranger and the hub of his district was Duluth, some 150 miles to our north. Blatnik had one of the biggest districts in Congress as it stretched from the northern Minneapolis suburbs all the way to the Canadian border. It was easily 275 miles from north to south. It struck me as an odd shaped district and I wondered what we shared in common with the miners of the Iron Range or the trappers from Grand Marais.

The next time I had lunch with Judge Forsberg, I asked him if he knew John Blatnik. He knew Blatnik, but did not seem to be overly impressed. I asked him about the odd geographic configuration of the Minnesota Congressional Districts. As usual, Forsberg knew the story. "Historically the metro area has always had three congressmen and there have been five from out-state. The population has shifted and the metro area should have been given another congressional seat, but the Legislature did not want to take away one of the rural seats. They shifted the lines and gave each of the five out-state congress-

City Attorney Days

man a share of the metro area." Forsberg continued with his lesson in practical politics, "Blatnik ended up moving all the way down to Coon Rapids plus a few other northern suburbs." He added that Blatnik had a lot of seniority and power and the move may work out pretty well for Coon Rapids. My political education continued unabated. I had majored in political science in college, but I must have read the wrong books. I had read about gerrymandering, but this was a new dimension on that age-old concept. In the out-state area the republicans usually held the two seats in southern Minnesota and Blatnik held sway in northeast Minnesota. The seat in western Minnesota and also the seat in northwest Minnesota were always pretty close races with the western Minnesota seat slightly favoring the republicans and the northwest territory going with the democrats. Each side must have concluded that there was no reason to rock the boat. The thinking was perhaps we could pick up a seat in the next election.

Don Erlandson was obviously well connected and he spoke of John Blatnik as an old friend and also planned to see Senator Hubert Humphrey when we were in Washington. I usually tended to vote conservative and thought of Congressman Blatnik as a wild-eyed liberal. When I met him, he was level headed and could not have been more gracious. He was anxious to meet with us and very attentive to our needs. Don spoke to him concerning his concerns over the rate increase and included some background information concerning prior rate and referendum issues. Coon Rapids was new to his district and John was anxious to do what he could to please his new constituents.

As I thought back on this experience, I could not help but compare how graciously we were treated, in contrast to how Blatnik's successor in that seat, Jim Oberstar treated some of his constituents. When Obama Care was hotly debated in congress, Chip Cravaack and some of his neighbors showed up at Oberstar's district office in North Branch and wanted to talk about health care. Oberstar was in his office, but refused to see Cravaack and his neighbors. Cravaack became irritated with this callous treatment and told his friends that "someone should run against this guy." Cravaack turned out to be the guy. The Eighth District has always been a stronghold for the democrats. They had held the seat since the great depression. Cravaack ran a strong, hard campaign and unseated Oberstar. Oberstar ran a terrible campaign. This was the first time he had been vigorously challenged in over 30 years in the House and he obviously had no idea how to mount a campaign. He went negative and he featured Cravaack in his TV ads. My impression when I saw Oberstar's attack advertisement was here sits this doddering old man telling us we should support him over this good-looking energetic pilot. I thought it was a Cravaack promotion, but later toward the end of the misguided missile I saw it was Oberstar's attack ad. Oberstar should have gotten on a bike and put on a helmet to cover a head of dwindling gray hair and told us about the marvelous bike paths and other federal goodies and plunder he had garnered for the district. He went negative and it backfired in a big way. Years ago, politicians never mentioned their opponent's name. The thinking was, why provide free advertising for the enemy camp. Oberstar would have been smart to dust off the old playbook and concentrate on himself and not his adversary. Oberstar turned sour grapes after his defeat, but he only needed to find a mirror to figure out why he lost. He started out as John Blatnik's legislative assistant, but unfortunately for him, he forgot one of the main things that John taught him. Don't forget where you came from. Oberstar had gone native. He was buried in Maryland.

Senator Hubert Humphrey did not meet with Don and I individually, but arranged to meet with our little group at day's end. Our group consisted of mayors and other public officials from the metro areas who were affected by the proposed rate increase. Senator Humphrey had been Mayor of Minneapolis, a long time U.S. Senator and Vice President under Lyndon Johnson. He lost by a whisker in 1968 to Richard Nixon and had recently regained his senate seat. I had grown up with Humphrey as my senator and all of my experience with him had been watching him on television. My impression was that he frequently sounded like a used car salesman. I recalled his statement describing the Vietnam War as a "great adventure" and thought he was simply shooting off his mouth. His son was not a participant in this wonderful adventure that he was promoting. The Vietnam War was not a great adventure as characterized by Humphrey, but serious business and beset by problems way beyond the scope of this book to solve. Unfortunately, those who served in Vietnam were not revered as prior veterans had been honored, but were looked upon as losers, baby killers, or even "chumps."

My grandfather was a long-time Humphrey advocate. Grandpa told me that when he would run into Humphrey on an infrequent basis, that the senator remembered his name. My grandfather worked on the line at Minneapolis Moline putting together tractors so he was hardly a big donor or cigar smoking union leader. He was a working stiff. He had been a banker until his bank was closed in 1924. He probably blamed Calvin Coolidge for the closing of the Willow River State Bank and cast his lot with the democrats. The bank closing certainly played a big role in my father's life and may have been one of the biggest family events of the 20th century. My father's chances of going to college pretty well went out the window along with the bank. My Grandmother Goring knew my grandfather and said that he was probably too generous. He was reluctant to say no and loaned money to people he should have turned down.

My cousin Duane had a different version of why the bank went down. He related that my grandfather had loaned money to his brother-in-law, Milton Pederson, who ran a bank in Hope, North Dakota. Milton had advised grandpa that the bank examiners were coming through and he needed a quick infusion of capital or he would be shut down. He got his transfusion, but in the meantime, the bank examiners decided to check out The Willow River State Bank

City Attorney Days

and grandpa had a bad case of the capital shorts and was shut down.

Humphrey was obviously plenty smart and had a memory like an elephant. Our delegation of 25-30 people gathered in a spacious conference room in the Old Senate Office Building. His staff people got us grouped together in a corner of the room near the windows and the senator made his entrance. He began by calling out a number of people that he recognized for an individual greeting. Don was obviously pleased when he was one of the chosen few. The senator had been prepped as to who was in attendance, but it was still an impressive display of name recognition.

The senator began his talk with some background information on one of his favorite topics - himself. We were local officials and he pointed out that he began his political pilgrimage as the Mayor of Minneapolis. He recalled that position fondly as it was "on the front lines of real problems and much closer to the people" as contrasted with his current gig in Washington. He had "wrestled with gas rates" when he was the mayor. He knew how difficult those decisions could be.

Senator Humphrey continued with his talk and I felt myself become very captivated by his discourse. He wore a nice blue suit and black shoes and moved before us with obvious grace. He was taller than I had imagined, as he was around six feet. He used no notes and there was no teleprompter in sight as he glided back and forth before our eyes. His voice was sure and powerful and not the sometimes high-pitched version I had heard on television.

He finished his talk by reminding the delegation that his office was our office and we should not hesitate to ask for help. He bade us leave as he advised that he had another group to meet. He probably wanted to go home as it was already past 7:00 p.m. He took his leave, but did linger to shake hands with everyone as we filed out of the conference room.

After the senator left, I was stunned by how effective and personable he was. Most of the delegation came away with the feeling Senator Humphrey had sat down and spoken directly to them. How different this impression was from the TV persona we had become accustomed to seeing. He did not strike me as "genuine" or "forthright" when I saw him on television. His voice seemed to go up an octave or two and at times it bordered on shrill. My friends sometimes referred to him as "flannel mouth." He was not a flannel mouth, but unfortunately for the senator, I think he was just one of these people who was not very good on TV. Had he been more effective on the box, there does not seem to be any doubt that he would have defeated Nixon. He was saddled with the Vietnam War and certainly most of those connected with that questionable effort were under growing suspicions regarding our leadership out of Washington.

Years later I happened to encounter Hubert H. Humphrey Jr., better known as "Skip" Humphrey. Skip was very personable, but he lacked the magnetism or spark of his famous father. Like his father, I did not find him effective on television. Apparently, there were others who shared my view. Skip ran for governor with the DFL endorsement in 1998. The republicans ran Norm Coleman who went on to knock off the great Walter Mondale and capture the senate seat held by the late Paul Wellstone. Humphrey and Coleman were busy taking jabs at one another and did not seem to notice the emergence of Jesse "the body" Ventura as the third party candidate. Humphrey insisted that Ventura be included in all of the television debates. As a former professional wrestler and sports color commentator, Ventura was in his element when he was in front of a television camera. In one of the debates, the candidates were asked if the school lunch program should be curtailed. Ventura piped up, "They feed the prisoners don't they?" Ventura showed up at the debates by himself and the two opponents showed up with delegations mindful of the Mohammed Ali crowds. Ventura pointed out that he did not have "people" like his opponents and he could handle the debates himself without a room full of political people.

When Phyllis and I went to the polling place the evening of the governor's election, the number of young people voting stunned us. It was obvious that a lot of first time young voters had turned out. This was the first time that Phyllis' nail person, Trisha DuCharme, had ever voted. Trisha was only in her twenties and has probably not voted since, but she correctly pointed out that Ventura was going to win. Trisha is smart and was spot on as Ventura won with 37 percent of the vote and Coleman finished second with 34 percent and Humphrey a distant third, not even securing 30 percent of the vote. When it was said and done, I remarked to Phyllis, "Who would believe that someone named Hubert Humphrey could not pick up 30 percent of the votes in this state." Television still calls the tune in most political battles.

After our rapt audience with Senator Humphrey, Don and I grabbed a beer and thought back on the senator's talk. Don was clearly energized by the senator and I could not help but feel he had put a bounce in my step. As it turned out, the FPC did go on to allow a rate increase, but it was less than they had asked for in the original filing, so at least to some extent, I am sure Don felt vindicated by our efforts. I was not too sure if we had made any headway, but this trip did feature an experience I would never forget.

Before I left the city attorney's office, the city took steps to get rid of Al Flynn. They reorganized his department and put him under the administrative control of someone else. They kept him on a tight leash and finally Al reached the end of his rope and had to leave city hall. He was honored by the city and a park located next to city hall was renamed "Al Flynn Park." Al stuck around the city and kept track of his real estate. He ran for mayor but did not prevail. Al and I remained friends after I left City Hall, but I wished I had seen more of him. He passed away when I was out of town in Reno. What a guy.

Don Erlandson was re-elected mayor, but passed away before finishing his next term. He was a dedicated and hard-working mayor. A park over by Coon

Creek is named in his honor.

Bob Voss's wife ran for council and served two terms. My friend, former Police Chief Jerry Nelson, served on the City Council with both Carolyn Voss and Lonnie McCauley. Jerry is still on the Charter Commission and has been serving the city in some capacity since 1962. That is 54 years at last count. The city used to run a municipal liquor store when I was city attorney and the city was putting out a private label liquor and solicited names for the brand. I put in an entry and suggested "Voss Sauce." Somehow my entry was not successful. Too bad. It may have been sufficient to perpetuate the Voss political legacy. The big problem with most of the municipal liquors was thievery or mismanagement and sometimes both. Coon Rapids and most other municipalities have exited the liquor business. The only people that seem to make money from these operations are the people running the place.

CHAPTER 3
MILITARY DAZE

My days as city attorney were full and busy. I was working hard during the day and frequently attending council or other meetings at night. I was also doing some law practice on the side and began to get involved with real estate ventures.

I lived in Anoka County, but not in Coon Rapids. Being an absentee city attorney had some advantages as I could flee the city, even briefly, to escape the pressures of the job.

As city attorney, I was up early and frequently out the door at night for a council or planning commission meeting. When I did not have these burdens to bear, the city manager was good at finding other dinners or gatherings for me to attend. I belonged to the Anoka County Bar Association and that was another evening a month. I was still underpaid, but with some extra money earned by a part-time law practice, I was able to pay off some debts and buy a decent house in a working class neighborhood and even bought a new car. I got caught up financially, but on a personal level, I was falling behind. Connie and I were not getting along well. When we did speak, the conversation usually got around to what I was missing out on and how I was never around. I knew I was gone a lot, but honestly did not know what to do about it.

One evening, my cousin Duane came over for a visit and an evening meal. Duane had just returned from a tour in Vietnam where he had served as a platoon leader. He was a 1st lieutenant (1LT) and had been in combat with the Americal Division in the central highlands of Vietnam. The central highlands were host to some of the toughest fighting in Vietnam and I was captivated by his stories. Years later, I would read Karl Marlantes account of the central highlands fighting in his novel *Matterhorn* and be equally fascinated. Duane asked me if I thought about serving and frankly I had not given it a lot of thought. He said, "You should think about the JAG Corps." We spent some time talking about military law and how it worked. Duane revealed that he had been detailed as a junior lieutenant to act as defense counsel for soldiers accused of crimes before courts-martial. He did relate that this had changed and now the military was using lawyers or JAGs at courts-martial.

I recalled a story that had been relayed to me by my Uncle Harland. Harland had served in WWII and started as a private and worked his way up to major. Harland had no college background, but was a smart guy and had done well in the quartermaster branch. He learned how to bake and was a successful baker in civilian life after the war. Harland told me that during the war he had been detailed to act as defense counsel for a young enlisted soldier who was charged with some sort of crime. Within a few days he found himself before a court-martial. A court-martial was and still is a board of officers who act as jurors in determining guilt or innocence of the soldier and then mete out some sort of punishment, often jail time. Harland related that the procedure went very fast and the man's company commander and another soldier came in and testified against the accused soldier and he was quickly found guilty and dispatched to the local stockade and eventually back to the States. After the conclusion of the matter, the president of the court-martial, (senior officer on the court) asked Harland what he thought of the procedure. Harland was no shrinking violet and responded, "I do not think this was fair and I think the kid got railroaded." The president was somewhat taken aback as the response was not the school solution and a bit of a surprise coming from an ambitious officer. Harland was obviously not interested in an extended military career. The president regained his composure and responded that, "This kid will never serve the 5 or 6-year sentence, but will likely be released in a few months and may even end up back in the lines if the war continues." Harland did not know if the officer knew what he was talking about, but it made him feel a little better about the whole procedure.

My Brother, Craig, served in the Army as a lieutenant in the aftermath of the Korean War. Craig was an ADA (Air Defense Artillery) officer serving in El Paso at Ft. Bliss. A knife fight took place on post and Craig was detailed to serve as the knife wielder's defense counsel at a forthcoming court-martial. Craig was a smart guy and did some investigation and found some guys who may help in a self-defense argument for the accused soldier. Craig relayed that his CO (Commanding Officer) cautioned him against "wasting too much time on this thing."

Craig proceeded ahead despite the warning and gained an acquittal for the soldier. Craig was successful and he was never again detailed as defense counsel. He must have persuaded the board that the accused was merely brandishing the knife to scare off would-be attackers. Craig's courtroom heroics were likely more the exception than the rule. Craig did not stay in the military and perhaps his prowess as a defense counsel may have had something to do with it.

I later learned that Duane was correct in his description of the Army Justice System. Washington's Revolutionary Army relied for its disciplinary code on the British Articles of War. The military is often slow to change and continued

Military Daze

with the Articles of War right through World Wars I and II and the Korean Conflict. By the 1950's and 60's many of those who had been citizen soldiers during WWII and had some experience with the Articles of War, decided changes had to be made to the military justice system. Many vets had been elected to congress so they were in a position to make changes. Some of the elected vets no doubt had experienced courts-martial in much the same fashion as my Uncle Harland and Craig and realized that they had to make the system more fair to the accused soldier. Without a trained lawyer representing the soldier, it was hard to see how much of a defense could normally be mounted. The result was the passage of the Uniform Code of Military Justice (UCMJ) in 1965. Among the changes it provided, was detailed defense counsel at all major courts-martial. Defense counsel had to be certified lawyers (JAGs).

Duane had spent three years on active duty with one year in Vietnam. After he finished active duty he entered the Maryland National Guard and had been promoted to captain and was serving as a company commander. He liked being in the guard and plus it provided him with some extra money that he could definitely use. The idea of being in the guard or reserve did appeal to me but to get to that place it seemed necessary to serve on active duty and really learn what the military was all about. I had always wanted to serve, but previously the time never seemed to be right.

At first blush, going in the Army seemed totally crazy, but as I thought about it in more detail, it began to make some sense. Perhaps if I had some time and a decent opportunity, I could make things work out with Connie. The military offered 30 days of paid leave per year and that was vastly more vacation than I had now and it would be nice to have some time and opportunity to see the world. My friend, Gene Enstad, suggested that I should tell the Army to send me to Germany. He figured they would do it to entice me into the corps. Gene had been a Marine and knew something of the military ways.

Gene did prove to be correct and after some contacts with JAG Personnel they agreed to send me to Germany if I would commit to serve. I ultimately agreed to go and was rather reluctant to tell a lot of people about my plans. I knew it seemed like a crazy plan, but I had my reasons and had determined to see it through. Connie was initially in favor of this scheme, but she was apprehensive about such a big move. I determined to make the move and left the city attorney's office and moved on to the Judge Advocate General's School (JAGS) at Charlottesville, Virginia. The JAG School was located on the campus of the University of Virginia. It is a beautiful campus and was founded by Thomas Jefferson. Jefferson's stately home, Monticello, is in the Blue Ridge Mountains and overlooks the campus. Jefferson claimed the founding of the University of Virginia as his greatest accomplishment. He designed the famous "serpentine wall" that snakes through the campus and also designed the old main building. The old main edifice features a round dome and looks a lot like the dome on

Jefferson's Monticello. If you cannot recall what Monticello looks like, reach into your pocket and pull out a nickel and look at the back side of the coin. The University of Virginia had originally been a boy's only school and was not co-ed until sometime in the 60's. The women were around by the time I got down there.

I hit Charlottesville and did not know the least bit about the military. I had picked up a copy of the Officer's Guide and was frantically pouring through the book trying to figure out how to wear the uniform and some of the protocol such as whom to salute. I did not have to go to basic training, but the downside was that I was going to have to self-teach myself on how the Army works. I soon made friends with another captain named Bill Miller. Bill had previously been an enlisted member and had been in an armored unit at Ft. Hood. I believe it was the Second Armored. Bill knew a lot about the nuts and bolts of the Army and showed me how to salute and who to salute. Essentially one salutes all who outrank you and also all you outrank. It other words, if they did not wear the railroad tracks (captain's bars) you saluted them. Miller was big on wearing the proper uniform and looking like an officer. "Never get caught out of uniform." At the JAGS we always wore the Class A uniform (military dress uniform). The dress uniform in those days was the "dress greens" plus the khaki or summer uniform. The dress green uniform consisted of wool blend green pants with a black stripe up the side (stripe for officers only), a light tan shirt with black tie, and a green dress coat with stripes on the sleeve. It was springtime in Virginia and everyone was wearing the khaki or summer uniform. This was the greatest uniform ever designed by any military. The pants looked like regular khaki slacks and the shirt was a short sleeve with the *epaulettes* on the shoulders. Your unit designation was on the shoulder and your rank on the right collar and your branch of service on the left collar. The best feature was that wash and wear was authorized and this made it easy on the JAG. I was a little heavy when I started, but soon found some time to start getting in shape and by the time I left Charlottesville, I did look decent in the uniform. The khaki uniform was eventually phased out in the late 70's and that was a sad day. I think one reason for the phase-out was that many of the officer and senior enlisted people put on too much weight and displayed fat wrapping around their belt. About that same time, the military launched a weight control program to slim us down. They should have launched the weight control program earlier and saved the khaki's.

No military uniform is complete without a hat or as the military calls it "headgear." The green uniform featured a round hat with a cab driver bill and everyone called it the flying saucer. The other hat was a green or khaki-folding hat. This is the same style hat that one always sees the legionnaires wear when they are at a drunken convention. The cap with the fold was properly called a garrison cap or by the GI's, the *cunt* cap. The garrison cap was very easy to

Military Daze

wear and I soon got in the habit of storing it on my belt, so that if I went outdoors, I had ready access to the headgear. Miller made it clear that you always had to have your cap on your head when outdoors or you had committed the offense of being out of uniform. Miller was right about that point as there were enough things in the Army to worry about without adding uniform problems to the list. Another problem to contend with in the Army was the shoes, although one did not have to worry about the color as that was always black. Shoes had to be well shined. I took my cousin Duane's advice and got a pair of plastic shoes. They were called corfams and were popular with the indolent JAGs. Later on I learned that the infantry looked upon them with distain. The corfams did stay shiny and looked decent, but the downside was that your feet sweated. You could wring your socks out at day's end. I had shiny shoes but wet feet throughout much of my military career. The military referred to the dress shoe worn with the dress uniform as "low quarters." It sounded like a description of my abode. Later on in my military career, when I was in the reserves, we were in formation and the Old Man (colonel) was conducting an inspection of the troops and he looked me over and I was wearing Rockport's with some sort of dim shine and he said, "You should get these corfam or shiny shoes and you will look better." I responded, "They make my feet sweat too much Sir!" He frowned but moved on down the line. By this time in my career I coveted dry feet more than a glowing efficiency report.

The "uniform issue" was something that seemed to always be cropping up in the military. Most of the rest of the military was not too excited about JAGs as the lawyers frequently were perceived as coddling trouble makers or telling commanders not to bomb churches. The uniform was one thing they could catch us on and extract a small measure of revenge. When I got to my active duty site, an infantry LTC soon told me that I could not wear the garrison cap unless I was in a travel status. I had to dig out my flying saucer and wear that around the post. Actually I was getting tired of wearing greens every day and went over to the military clothing store and bought myself a set of work or fatigue uniforms including the combat boots. My duties took me all over the place and greens were not practical on a dusty post. The Community Commander, LTC Tom Ziek saw me in fatigues and when he recovered from the shock said, "I like that." He liked the idea that I had chosen to look more like a soldier than a lawyer. The Army does have an insidious way of slipping into your veins.

A very important part of the uniform is the belt. Without the belt you will find that any progress is guarded. The belts are all web type belts. The fatigue or duty belt features the black web and a black buckle. Your web belt comes in a roll and you put it around your middle and find a razor knife and cut the webbing to size and clamp the buckle in place. If you gain some weight, then you may have to pitch the webbing and head for the clothing store and get some new webbing. By that time, you probably need new webbing anyway as it does tend to fray from sliding it in and out. The black duty buckles last forever.

The dress belt had the same black webbing but substituted a brass buckle for the duty buckle. The buckle was supposed to be shiny or well-polished at all times. I found (by accident) if you keep the plastic film on the buckle it will remain shiny for quite some time. The air takes the shine out of the brass and turns it dark. When I was in Germany, I ran into an ex-Marine named Thorpe Nolan and he told the story about his former gunnery sergeant who was frequently shining his belt buckle (A Gunnery SGT in the Marine Corp. is like a Sergeant First Class (SFC) in the Army). The enlisted personnel simply refer to him as "gunney." Gunney would frequently serve in the role of platoon sergeant. Nolan's gunney eventually wore a hole in his brass buckle, but apparently kept wearing it and kept shining what was left of it. I am sure that Nolan noticed my dingy belt buckle and commented, "You have barnacles growing off that belt buckle Erickson." "Those are not barnacles, but Zebra Mussels." I got the hint and located some Brasso and started to polish my buckle. Once you get into that "spit and polish" stuff there is no end to it. I also started polishing my brass. The brass is your branch insignia, the U.S. pin, and your rank. The rank "brass" was easy because it was not brass, but the two parallel silver captain bars. They were made out of steel plate and never dulled. The JAG branch insignia was a wreath with a crossed sword and quill pen. The pen crossed the sword, indicating that the pen was mightier than the sword. That was sometimes true, although if I was in a sword fight, I would take the sword over the pen or preferably a 9 millimeter. The branch insignia was hard to polish because the wreath was rough and you polished the top of the wreath, but could hardly get in the seams. The U.S. pin was small and easy to polish. One advantage to the fatigue uniform is that there was no brass to polish as everything was in black. The black boots did require polish. I gradually perfected the "spit" shine. The Army later switched to the desert boots and that eliminated the saliva-shined boots.

The Army used to be big on social functions and that required another uniform called "dress blues." Dress blues had a navy blue coat and royal blue pants. The pants had a gold stripe and the coat had gold stripes. The brass was the same as on the dress green uniform, but the rank on the shoulder featured clip on boards that were called "shoulder boards." Some of us used to refer to this costume as the "bell hop uniform." When I was at Charlottesville I inquired as to whether or not to buy dress blues and the consensus seemed to be, wait until you get to your duty station and find out if you need them and you can always buy a set. Some of the officers told me that they had dress blues and had never put them on.

When I was at Charlottesville, I lived in a small house that I shared with two other captains. None of us had cars, so we walked back and forth to school.

Military Daze

Charlottesville was beautiful in the spring with the pink dogwood in bloom. Rain is a frequent occurrence during that time of year. One morning it was raining hard and a couple of us grabbed an umbrella and headed out the door. We made it to class and had barely warmed up the seat when the class got a memo from the Deputy Commandant advising us that under a long-standing military tradition, officers do not use umbrellas. I did not get court-martialed but did decide it was time to buy a jacket. A green short-waisted coat was authorized with the summer uniform. The rank was worn on the shoulder *epaulettes*. Later on in my time, the green jacket went out and the Army switched to a black jacket. The black jacket was much more attractive and one could wear it as a civilian jacket (take your rank off) and look somewhat decent and not like a total nerd. I still have the black jacket and also my khakis up in the attic and hope to get back in them one of these days. A fellow Comp Judge, John Jansen, (JJ) was also in the Army Reserves and used to frequently wear the khakis to work and I used to advise him that "the crease in those pants does not meet regulation." He would respond in a proper military way and tell me to "go to hell."

Before we left Charlottesville, we were given our orders for our active duty assignments. My orders came in for 1st Armored Division with duty station at 7th Army Training Center at Grafenwohr. Everyone in the Army called it "Graf." I knew I was going to Germany, but had to run for a map to find out where Grafenwohr was located. It's located in Bavaria about 140 kilometers east of Nuremberg. Many of the JAGs in my class at Charlottesville had prior service in another branch, and had later gone to law school and came back in the service as JAGs. They already had at least 5-6 years into retirement and some officers had close to ten years of service so it made sense to go back and try and make some rank and build toward a retirement at the conclusion of twenty years. One of the JAGs named Frank John Wagoner had been to Graf and described it as, "a pit or maybe an arm pit." Frank had been a company commander in Vietnam and had spent his share of time out in the bush. Frank and I got to be friends, probably because he was one of the few guys who was older than me. Actually, there were several guys around my age. We had no women in the class. Frank was a real warrior as he had an airborne patch on his garrison cap. I was a bit envious, but was not sure I was ready to start jumping out of planes. Frank told me that when he had a company in Vietnam that one day in morning formation, one of the troops was drunk, giggling, and making lots of noise. Frank remained calm and walked over and decked the troop in front of the entire company. Later, after he had been in the field with his company for quite some time, he returned to the cantonment area and determined that he needed a drink and found the local class 6 or whiskey store and wanted some booze. The clerk gave him some sort of lame excuse as to why he could not be served and Frank leveled his M-16 at the clerk and service quickly picked up. Lots of things happen in a war zone that do not occur in a quiet state-side post.

When I got to my duty station at Grafenwohr, Germany, I soon found out that I would indeed need dress blues. The Training Center Commander was an "old Army" type, Colonel (COL) Lodge. His nickname was "Bud." He was a gruff appearing guy, but in reality he was sensible and fair minded. He liked the formalities of the old Army and one thing he retained was the New Year's Day Reception at the officer's club. About three weeks before New Year's Day, all of the officers on post including Captain (CPT) and Mrs. Erickson received an invitation to attend the Commander's New Year's Day Reception. Any military invitation is very complete. It advises you who is to attend and where and when to show and what to wear. Dates are always expressed as 1 January 1972 and not January 1, 1972. The military uses the 24-hour clock and thus noon was 1200. (8 p.m. would be 2000; midnight becomes 2400) The time thing makes a lot of sense and avoids having to fool with a.m. and p.m. Most police departments also use military time so I hope you paid attention as later on in this book as we get into the police testimony the matter of military time will again surface. The date at the front of the month makes sense as it does not get confused with the year. The military invitation always specifies the uniform. The invitation for the New Year's Day Reception provided: "Uniform: Dress Blues with four in hand tie." I had to run around and find out the military translation of "four in hand tie" It meant a regular black tie with a Windsor Knot. This was contrasted with a regular black bow tie, which was sometimes required for evening functions.

The first of January rolled around and I was prepared as I located a warrant officer who was getting out and he had a pair of dress blues that I picked up on the cheap. The coat fit well, but the pants were a bit snug. I would have to "suck it up" for a couple hours. I got out my "new blues" and cleaned my corfam shoes and polished my brass. My warrant officer friend did not have a blue saucer hat and I could not wear my green saucer or garrison cap as one cannot "mix uniforms" or wear a green hat with the dress blue uniform. Connie wore a brown dress and was overweight, but still looked attractive when she got fixed up. We lived right next to the officer's club so I took my chances and moved out without headgear and route stepped to the club, out of uniform. We got in the receiving line and I watched as some of the officers clicked to attention and then greeted COL and Mrs. Lodge. I was not up to that but gave him a handshake and "Happy New Year." COL Lodge seemed content with that protocol since I was a JAG. Standing next to the COL was a first lieutenant (1st LT) who was keeping track of who showed to make sure that everyone who got an invitation showed or at least had a decent excuse. I lived next door to a dentist I named Dr. Molar and he was a captain like me, but he never showed for anything. It was like pulling teeth to get him to any military function. I asked him if he heard about the New Year's function, and he said no. I suspect he

Military Daze

knew about it, but his commander, a dental major, may have chosen to ignore it or make up some lame excuse for being AWOL. Years later I found myself in the small Oregon town of Coquille and walked by Dr. Molar's dental office and was tempted to stop and say hello, but was afraid Mr. Molar would not want any reminders of his military career so I did not stop in and give him a grim flash back to his blissful time in Graf.

After we greeted the colonel, we moved on into a dining room and had a glass of champagne and some *hors d'oeuvres* to celebrate the New Year and mingled with the other folks on post. Connie had gotten to know a woman named Nancy Schumacher and her husband was an armor officer named Ed. We spent some time making small talk with them and then eventually moved back to our quarters. I did not need an overcoat as German winters were much easier than Minnesota winters as there was not that much snow and the weather seldom got below 15-20 degrees Fahrenheit.

I was accustomed to brutal Minnesota winters with the mercury frequently plunging to well below zero. During three winters in Germany, I could only recall one or two evenings when it got below zero. That does not mean it was not cold as it was a wet winter. It was always damp. The North Sea kicked up plenty of winter winds and moisture that blew south and usually hit my way in the form of mist, light rain, or a cold damp wind.

Graf was the largest European base in free Europe and most of the career soldiers had memories of spending time at one of Graf's spartan training camps. Camp Aachen was one such camp and it was primitive. Graf was a training base and there were a lot of tanks and artillery and that meant a lot of dust and mud. Most of the regular grunts who had been to Graf only remembered the dust and mud.

One of the best parts of being at Graf was the nice quarters. Our building was practically new. We had a spacious three-bedroom unit with a separate room that they called a maid's quarters. We did not have a maid so I used it as an office. We had a nice balcony on the back that was a nice place to keep your grill and have a beer at night. It did not take me long to discover German beer. The City of Grafenwohr was a small town of perhaps 2000 people and was located right outside the gate from our post. The post was secure in that it was fenced and the gate was manned by armed guards. A big sign announced that cars were subject to search. The guards were MP's (military police) although they also used Polish vets who were former Polish military who worked as civilians for the Army. They wore their Polish military uniforms so there were many who pondered "who the hell are these guys?"

Beer was a big deal in Germany. They had strict brewing laws that dated back to Bismarck's time as to how the stuff had to be brewed and only certain ingredients were allowed. Just about any decent sized town had its own brewery and Graf had a decent sized complex. The Germans were fussy about their brew as that was usually their drink. In the old days, the water was not always reliable, but beer was always safe. The Germans made a pretty good white wine, but it was not produced in sufficient quantities to satisfy a large thirsty population. The Germans liked bourbon, whisky, or scotch, but it was all imported and was too expensive for the average working stiff. Brandy was available, but also expensive. The German was left with beer and consequently wanted a good beer. No self-respecting German would drink a Miller, Bud, or similar swill.

    If the Germans were on a construction site and planning on putting up a building or other project, the first thing they constructed was a small hut or building to house their beer. When they had a break it was not a coffee break, but a beer break. Beer was delivered to the beer hut at least once or twice a week. When I saw the Germans working on a project on post, it did not appear to me that they moved too fast. I suspect when they were off post and not on a government job, they drank less and moved a bit faster. Former Marine, Gene Enstad, worked at Hamm's brewery back in the 60's and they were allowed to drink beer whenever they felt like it. Gene said he frequently "felt like it." He had a glass and filled it right from the production line. Nice work if you can get it. The work comp rates must have nudged up in that place.

    If you wanted a beer on post, you went to the officer's club and got one over the counter or you located a whiskey store. On a military post, the whiskey store was called a "class 6 store." I think it referred to a regulation number as in authorized by Class Six of AR (Army Regulation) number six. The store was not self-service, so you would tell the clerk (German civilian employee) what you wanted and presto it would emerge and you would show your ID card, and maybe a ration card, and get your booze. Booze was cheap as we were not paying any tax or import dues. When I first got to Graf, I bought a 6-pack of Pabst one night and it cost me 60 cents. At a dime a beer it was about the same price as a coke. I could also buy German beer at the class 6 except it did cost more than a Bud. The Grafenwohr Brewery had a beer that they called "Grafenwohr Export." As the name suggests, it was brewed for export purposes and labeled as such. It probably had to be labeled as an export because it managed to avoid payment of export tax or perhaps it was to avoid a local tax. I also found out from veteran beer drinkers at Graf (not a scarce individual) that one could go to the Grafenwohr Brewery and buy a case of beer direct. They featured beer in the re-capable lid that snapped off. The GI's called them "snappers." The local beer in the snappers was much better than the export. I was convinced that if the brewery had a beer batch that was sub-standard that they bottled it up and labeled it export and shipped it off to the Americans. The Germans assumed that the dumb-kauf Americans would not know the difference between a good beer and bull piss. That has all changed with the advent of all the craft breweries and Americans can finally obtain a decent beer.

The average GI was still doing a lot of drinking in those days (Vietnam War wind down period). Drinking and driving was still a problem. On post, the MP's dealt with the problem driver and turned the individual over to his commander for some sort of punishment. When we were off post, we were subject to German law and the German police were fairly serious about enforcing drunk driving laws. One area that the GI sometimes got into trouble with was the black market laws. Our booze and cigarettes were shipped over to Germany without paying German import duties. The exemption was predicated on the end product only being used by American troops or dependents. Your wife and kids were designated as "dependents" because they were not in the country on their own hook; they came with you along with your couch and other personal property. The soldier was responsible for making sure his family members did not get into trouble. Occasionally they would get into difficulty and some were sent home. The military paid to get them over there and was providing a roof over their heads and educating them. The military took the position that they could send dependents home if they got out of line. I was never asked for legal advice on the matter, but the Army did send dependent trouble makers home and no one questioned their authority.

If there was a violation of the black market laws, many of these violations did not end up as courts-martial, but were resolved with company punishment or some sort of administrative punishment. All soldiers had a ration card to buy booze. Rations were large and you had to be real thirsty to run dry. If you made improper sales or transfers to Germans, you would likely lose your card. If you were an officer or senior enlisted, you would likely be offered a field grade Article 15. This would be the kiss of death for any officer or senior non-com (enlisted).

Article 15 draws its name from Article 15 of the UCMJ. It is also called non-judicial punishment. If the Article 15 is handed out by the company commander, the punishment is usually a fine or sometimes a reduction in grade, depending on the rank of the soldier on the receiving end of the punishment. A field grade Article 15 is administered by a field grade officer (major or higher) and is usually reserved for infractions by more senior NCO's (NCO translates to non-commissioned officer or more senior enlisted personnel). Before a soldier accepts Article 15 punishment, the soldier has the right to consult with a JAG. If the Article 15 is without merit, the JAG will likely advise the soldier to demand trial by court-martial. If the commander has good sense, they will contact the trial counsel (JAG advising the Command) and be told the case is shaky and withdraw it. There may be administrative action that the commander can take, without resorting to an Article 15 or court-martial. For example, if the problem relates to an off post incident, the commander could administratively restrict the soldier to the post. In other words, pull his pass privileges.

During about half of my time at Grafenwohr, my principal duty was as defense counsel. One afternoon I was in my office and a military policeman (MP) enlisted soldier came in and had been given an Article 15 for improper discharge of a firearm. At that time, the standard sidearm for the military was the 45-caliber pistol. This weapon put out a large shell and could do some damage, although it was hard to maintain accuracy except at close quarters. The MP initially gave me some story about cleaning his weapon and the weapon accidently discharged and blew a hole in the floor. I asked him how the weapon would be pointing down as most people clean their weapons at a table or desk. He then said he was clearing the weapon, prior to cleaning when it discharged. I asked him if he minded talking to my legal assistant, Roy Butts. Roy had been an MP so I figured they would talk the same language. There was a large barrel of sand located outside the MP station with a sign "Clear all Weapons prior to entry" and I thought it odd that he had not unloaded his 45 at that point, but maybe that did not apply to MP's. About ten minutes later, Roy was back in my office with the recalcitrant young MP and a new story, the truth. It turned out that the military policeman was at his desk and practicing his quick draw and the 45 discharged. The charge was proper and the MP had committed the offense so I advised him to accept the Article 15. If it went to court-martial, the government would certainly add a charge of destruction of government property and they could prove that charge without a doubt. It was no secret around the company that he was the one who blew a hole in the floor. In advising soldiers on Article 15's, I was usually hesitant to advise the soldier to demand trial by court-martial, because then they were at risk of going to jail. Moreover, the government is not limited to the charges listed on the Article 15 form. For example, the soldier had improperly discharged a weapon and in addition, had seriously damaged government property. He also may have violated a regulation or local rule by even having his weapon out of his holster in an office setting. I did not have time to research that point, but would not have been surprised to find additional infractions. It illustrates the old saw, "Be careful what you ask for, you may get it." `

    I was the first defense counsel the Army had ever had at Grafenwohr. That meant I had to set up my own office and get all systems in place. Having been city attorney, I was used to working on my own. I was not used to asking for help and the Army was not too anxious to help out defense counsel. My Commander, LTC Sieve Anders, was located in Ansbach. I was a long way from the flagpole.

    The state of the Army when I got into it was not good. About half of the soldiers were still draftees and they did not want to be in the Army. Drug use was rampant. A lot of the barracks were unsafe at night and some of the commanders and NCO's were not doing their best to make them safe. The volume of courts-martial was unending. I was routinely trying two to three courts-martial per week and it was wearing me down. When I was in the office, I was consulting with soldiers on Article 15's and did not have time to prepare for court. Most of my trial preparation was in the evenings.

I was responsible for a battalion at Bayreuth and another battalion at Amberg, and I was traveling to each place once per week to consult with soldiers. We also had an Air Defense Artillery (ADA) battalion that was headquartered at Graf, and they had another detached company down at Regensburg. Grafenwohr was the 7th Army Training Center and 7th Army had a considerable cadre of soldiers who were necessary to run the base. For example, there was an MP Company and a small hospital they called a dispensary. Vilseck was a sub-post of Graf and they had a school located there and also an ordinance company. I had troops that I was responsible for scattered all over West Germany. Years later, I went back to Graf and they had three defense counsels doing what I was doing. They were serving a volunteer force that wanted to be there. I was serving angry draftees that could hardly wait to get in trouble.

I had two assistants to help me. One of these assistants was Roy Butts. Roy had worked as a Baltimore City Cop, but returned to the service and resumed MP duties. Roy eventually became a warrant officer and had been a Criminal Investigative Department (CID) Officer for several years. Warrant Officers were specialized officers who did not serve as commanders but were senior people who worked in a specialized area. He had a lot of experience and gave me a lot of good advice. He knew the Army and was a good source of general information on how the Army worked. He was also good at digging out information from the commanders and NCO's as he knew the ropes and spoke the language. My other assistant was a young enlisted draftee from the Bronx named George Kowalski. George was a bright young person but hated the Army and was preoccupied with going back to New York. George was into trains and most of the time was wishing he were on a train or at least looking at one. I found it very difficult to get George motivated or committed to our cause. George had gone off the track.

Military trials were bifurcated or split into two parts. The first part of the trial dealt with the "findings" part of the case and that portion determined whether or not the soldier committed the crime. If he was found guilty then the trial moved to the sentencing portion. One thing we were always doing was trying to get background information on accused soldiers. If a soldier had been a good troop and had some friends among the NCO's in his company, then we would usually call them during the sentencing portion of the trial to endeavor to get a lighter sentence. They were called witnesses in extenuation and mitigation (E and M). Most of the soldiers were going to be convicted so we needed E and M testimony in order to try and get a lighter sentence. There were times we negotiated a plea of guilty and tried to negotiate a light sentence along with the plea of guilty. For example, we may negotiate a plea of guilty together with a limit of confinement to four months. We would then plead guilty but before sentencing the soldier could enter testimony in extenuation and mitigation. If we had a good soldier we may be successful in gaining a sentence of only two months of confinement. We then "beat the deal" and the troop only got the two-month jail sentence that was adjudged. If the troop was sentenced to six months in confinement, then he only served the four-month term as limited by the pre-trial agreement.

Butts and I were continually perplexed at George's lack of interest and motivation. Butts began to refer to George as that "F-cking George." Around the office, George had acquired a new name. I still called him George. One day I had to run some errands and gave George a list of two or three things to do. It was a very modest request. George did not get any of the things done that I had asked. I got back late and had to do the items myself. I was not happy when I spoke with George the next day. I asked George what his problem was and he said, "CPT Erickson, I find that most of these people we are defending are just no goods and I do not feel like helping them out." I replied that he was right that many of them were no goods and perhaps not worthy people, but that they still deserved decent representation. That was the way the system worked. "Some of these soldiers are good people, who have just been caught up in the system or made a poor decision and they certainly deserve our help." I gave him the example of a young soldier who was a good guy and probably did not deserve to go to jail and we were able to mount a solid defense on his behalf. "George, for a lot of these people, we are all they have. They deserve a fair shake from us." I told George that he would have to step it up or I would have to replace him. I do not think that George took me seriously. I knew George's First Sergeant (1st SGT) and did speak to him about George. The 1st SGT is the senior enlisted person in the company and is often called Top or Top Sergeant by the troops. Top told me he would "tighten him up." I spoke to Butts and suggested that maybe George was not smart enough to do the job. "Oh no, CPT Erickson. I went over and looked at his file and his test scores are high." The Army tested all the enlisted personnel and George had a high GT score, which corresponded to intelligence quotient or IQ. I should have known that Butts had checked out George.

George made slight progress over the next couple of weeks but showed little drive or enthusiasm. Once again I gave him a couple things to do and when I got back he had not accomplished anything. George had not taken me seriously, but I was not kidding. I concluded he was no longer an asset and maybe even a negative, because I could not count on him to perform a given task. It was getting late, but I was disgusted with George and wanted to move him out without delay so I called his 1st SGT and told him, "Hi Top, I am afraid PFC Kowalski is not working out so you will have to send him back where he came from." "Okay, CPT Erickson, I will ship him on the next boat." I knew Top and was confident he had done what he could to motivate George. George had been with "Old Ironsides," 1st Armored DIV Headquarters out of Ansbach and he would return within the next 24 hours. Later that evening I was in my quarters and it was after dark and George showed up at my doorstep. He was visibly upset and asked to speak with me. I had worked late and was still in fatigues so I grabbed my field jacket and headgear and went out in the cool fall air to find out what George would spin. "Captain Erickson, Top told me that you are sending me back." "That is correct, George." He pleaded, "But CPT Erickson, you have all these cases and they have to be worked up. How are you going to get it all done?" I told George, "I will get it done just the way I have been doing it. I will do it myself. Nothing will change." George was no fool and he was taken aback by my blunt response. He tried sympathy. "If you send me back to Ansbach, my buddies there will know I got fired and I will be totally mortified." "That is too bad, George, but haven't I given you plenty of warning and a fair chance to perform?" George conceded that he had been warned. "Well then, what is your complaint?" George gave me his final shot. "I have no complaints with the way I was treated, CPT Erickson, but give me one more chance and I will not disappoint you." George was begging to keep a job, that I believed, he hated. I thought he would be relieved to return to his old unit and vegetate through the balance of his two-year draft obligation. George did show me in that cool German night air that he did have pride and did give a shit enough about the job to at least make an effort to keep it. I told George that I would give him one more chance. "I promise you CPT Erickson, that you will not be sorry. Can you please call Top and tell him I do not have to leave as he has me slated to move out tomorrow." I told George I did not have Top's number, but if he were in his quarters, I would walk over and tell him you could stick around for a while. George thought he was in quarters as it was getting late.

The next day George was in the office bright and early and ready to work. I gave him some people to contact in a unit and see what he could dig up to help Private Schmedlap. After George left, Roy came into my office. "I got a call last night from that F-cking George and he sounded very upset and said that CPT Erickson fired me. Why would he do such a thing?" Butts was a cop and not a diplomat and gave it to George right between the eyes. "CPT Erickson fired you because you were not doing the job. Doing the job is not sitting around and bullshitting with Lee and Brady (two other enlisted men)." George was taken aback and asked Butts what he could do. Butts said, "Probably nothing at this point." George was stunned by the response and realized that Roy was not going to help him get his job back. "Do you think I should talk to CPT Erickson about my job?" Butts told him, "If you want to stick around, you better try and persuade CPT Erickson to change his mind." George admired Butts and when Butts told him he was inadequate that hit George like a kick in the ass from a mule.

George did stick around and he did make significant improvement. He shifted over to the asset side of our small office. George was always bright; it was just a question of getting him to apply himself. George finished his enlistment and even made Specialist 4 (SP4) before he departed. After George's revival, he approached me one day with a request to fill out an enlisted evaluation so that he could be promoted to SP4. George revealed that if he returned to the Bronx as a PFC, he would never hear the end of it from his buddies. I gave him a good report card and he made SP4 shortly before his ETS. (End Time in Service)

Roy Butts was in kind of a unique position. He started as an MP and eventually moved up to CID. He had been to Vietnam and worked as a CID. He had been there during the Tet Offensive and told me that he was pulled off CID during the Tet Offensive and functioned as an MP. Like many other MP units, he was actively engaged in combat during the Tet as the enemy had moved into the south in such numbers that the war knew no boundaries. Roy's wife was a beautiful Danish woman named Karen and she and their son spent a year in Denmark while Roy was in Vietnam. His son went to Danish schools during that time.

Roy rotated out of Vietnam and was stationed in Germany. Karen spoke German, so they got along fine outside the gate and lived in a German rental home. Roy was super busy as a CID as the drug problem had snowballed during the Vietnam period. It was a drug bust that provided Roy's downfall as a criminal investigator. Roy had made a drug bust and somehow the pipe that was seized was lost. Roy found that his credentials had been pulled. Without credentials (badge, papers, side arm) he could not work as an investigator. To begin with, he just stayed home, but after a short time, he soon realized he could not just sit in Germany and do nothing. He started traveling to Nuremberg every day and working as a legal assistant in the JAG office. He assisted the defense attorneys with investigation and trial preparation. Roy did not think it would be proper for him to help the trial counsel (prosecution) as he thought there might be some sort of conflict. I am not sure I understood the conflict, but I was glad Roy had chosen to help the defense.

Roy showed up at my doorstep shortly after I arrived at Grafenwohr. He concluded he would rather commute 5 miles a day rather than drive 170 every day, back and forth to Nuremberg. Roy was an excellent investigator and was resourceful at digging up background information on various troops. Roy had an excellent vocabulary, but his only drawback was that he was not much of a writer and he was reluctant to write up some of his findings and preferred to give me oral briefings. That worked out okay, but I did not always have time to get oral briefings. Roy taught me a lot about police work and investigation work in general.

Roy liked a coffee break from time to time and we would hike over to the snack bar and take a break. He always sat toward the rear of the hall and kept

Military Daze

his back to the wall and his eye on the door. A few years ago, I saw where a Minneapolis patrolman had violated that rule and paid for the infraction with a slug in the back. To this day, I usually take a seat in a restaurant where I can watch the room and the door. I am not a fanatic about it like Mitch Rapp, but it is one small personal security step that I usually take. Phyllis thinks I am nuts. Roy had been in the Army over seventeen years and was biding his time and hoping to reach eighteen years before someone decided to take some administrative action against him. The eighteen-year mark of service is significant in that you receive that very important letter that says, unless you screw up big time, you are on track to get a retirement. You are going to get a retirement unless the Secretary of the Army says otherwise or you are court-martialed. I recall years later, what a relief it was when I was in the reserves and got my twenty-year letter and was told it looks like I was going to get my retirement.

One spring day Roy came into the office and showed us his "way to go letter." He had eighteen years in and looked to be a lock to get his twenty. A month or two later Roy received his orders for his next assignment indicating it was a terminal assignment (last duty station) at the Presidio in San Francisco with duty at the SJA office. Roy had some friends in high places inside the MP Corps that took care of him. About three years later, I saw Roy in San Francisco and he had left the Army and was getting a retirement and had been unable to get a job in law enforcement due to gender quotas, so he opened an antique shop in Larkspur, across the bay from San Francisco. It was an interesting concept. He leased out small spaces to local collectors and he watched the store and made sales when they were not around. This concept became popular in Stillwater, Minnesota and other places around here.

One day before Roy departed he was in Nuremberg and he checked with the SJA and he advised them that I had too many cases and was spread too thin. Their records in Nuremberg indicated I had less than ten courts-martial on my calendar whereas in reality, I had around fifty. Head Quarters (HQ) was really in the know.

One of my most interesting cases involved a young troop I will call Private (PVT) Hull. Hull was charged with arson in trying to burn down the barracks. He lit someone's door on fire during the evening. I do not know if it was a prank that went awry or whether some sort of grudge motivated the fire. I think it was a prank, but the commander did not think it funny as Hull could have burned down the barracks. Hull had been drinking heavily that evening and could not recall starting any fires. The prosecution had a decent circumstantial case, but had no direct eyewitnesses. A critical piece of evidence was an admission he allegedly made to another soldier.

I thought about a defense of intoxication or drunkenness. The problem with such a defense is that I would have to put the defendant on the stand, and I doubted he would hold up on cross. The instruction by the judge on a drinking defense starts out by saying that drunkenness is no defense, but could be asserted if the crime required proof of a specific intent. In this case it was the intent to willfully and maliciously burn or set on fire an inhabited building. I was concerned that his recollection may be greater than he had told me and he would likely incriminate himself. Private Hull readily agreed with my decision. It worked out to be a good move. I gradually learned (sometimes the hard way) that it was best not to give the government any help in proving its case and attempting to lie your way out of a tough spot in front of a military jury was a sure way to get a stiff sentence. I was very careful, as a military defense attorney, not to suggest any testimony, but simply elicited the facts from the accused and avoided asking him directly whether or not he had committed the crime. If the facts indicated he had committed the crime, I would counsel the accused to plead guilty, but before he did, I would try and work out a deal with the government.

PVT Hull did not testify and we only had a limited defense. When the evidence was concluded and the lawyers had argued, the military judge instructed the panel of officers who functioned as the fact finders or jury. During the instruction, I was very tired, but thought there may have been a mistake of some kind in the instruction. The defense counsel seldom raises a mistake before the trial judge because he will simply make a correction in front of the jury and the mistake is corrected and there goes any appellate issue you may have. In this case, the military judge droned on and continued, "That you must presume the defendant is GUILTY." This was obviously a slip of the tongue by the judge, as the defendant is always presumed innocent. The jury likely knew what he meant, but what he meant is not what he said. If the trial counsel had alerted the military judge, the correction would have been made and there would not have been much of a case on appeal.

Unfortunately, the military court was not sympathetic to PVT Hull and he got ten years. I felt terrible and felt I had let PVT Hull down. George tried to cheer me up by declaring that the government had a strong case against me. A few days later, I got a call from MAJ Cuthbert, the assistant SJA, and a fair minded individual who asked me if I "heard something wrong with those instructions." I said I was not sure, but "tell me more." I went and spoke with SP4 Lee Aitkin who was assigned to help the trial counsel and worked for him. Lee was a very sharp enlisted person from Idaho who had been drafted right out of college. I did not want to put Lee on the spot, but I discretely asked him if he heard a problem with the instructions. "What do you mean?" I told him it would have something to do with the presumption of guilty or innocent. Lee candidly told me that I was correct; the judge had said he was presumed guilty.

It was about that time that I got the typewritten record of trial. The record had been cleansed and the printed record was that the accused was presumed "innocent." I had to contact the reporter and see what she had to say. The re-

Military Daze

porter was a seasoned Department of Army civilian. I drove to Nuremberg and went to her office. I was very polite as I usually was and asked her if the judge had not in fact said that the "accused was presumed guilty." She admitted that he had said that, but "I knew what he meant, so I changed it." I reminded her that "it is not your job to try and figure out what the judge meant, but it is your job to record what he said." She gave me no argument, but did a certificate of correction and shipped it forward. She gave me a copy for my records. I knew that Hull was going to be let out.

About a year or so later, the reviewing court set the conviction aside and ordered a new trial. I was in my office one day and got a call from the SJA, LTC Anders and he proceeded to tell me they were going to send the case back for a new trial, but they intended to introduce the prior testimony of the witness who had given the testimony as to Hull's admission. He made it sound like a routine deal and I was supposed to give him some sort of assurance that the government could use the prior testimony. He was getting no such assurance from me. I told him that I disagreed with his analysis and believed that the prior testimony was not admissible. I assumed the problem was that the main government witness had ETS'd and was gone. I had already planned to withdraw if possible or advise Hull to ask for another attorney if the case came back. The new lawyer could argue that I had done a lousy job cross-examining the main witness and the government had to bring him back for live testimony rather than introducing his prior testimony. Further, I was not going to be around that much longer and it made sense not to give the case to a short timer. By this time, LTC Anders was not my favorite person, and I was determined not to give him anything positive from me that he could later use to ship Hull back to Leavenworth. I later found out that Hull's lawyer back in the States had worked out some sort of plea where Hull got credit for time served and was released. I was glad to hear that news as I always thought the sentence was too stiff.

I had been at Graf about a year and the workload continued to be grueling. I managed not to work very often on weekends, but put in long days during the week. Connie objected to the hours I was working and she was very despondent. There was a time that I seriously contemplated sending her home and she would have gone in a heartbeat, but that "solution" was not practical as I had sold our home and she had no place waiting for her in Minnesota. Besides, one of the main reasons I undertook this adventure was to spend more time with my kids. As things worked out, Connie eventually started to get acquainted and became very fond of our foreign home.

In addition to doing courts-martial on a regular basis, I was also occupied with administrative board actions. At that time the Army was boarding soldiers out for a variety of reasons and usually that meant a less than honorable discharge and sometimes a loss of veteran's benefits. Usually a lieutenant prosecuted the government case. I had good luck with boards and never had a case where a soldier was eliminated when he did not want to be.

During my first year in Graf I tried probably close to a 100 courts-martial. Most of the trials were special courts, but a few were general courts. The special courts were more comparable to a misdemeanor or gross misdemeanor that one finds in civilian courts. All courts-martial are "convened." Convened means ordered into existence to haul Private Schmedlap into court. The Army needs an order to move or do just about anything including dispensing jail time. The maximum sentence in special courts was six months' confinement, forfeiture of all pay and allowances and reduction to private. Special courts were convened at the brigade level (full colonel or O6). Certain special courts were also empowered to adjudge a bad conduct discharge and they were affectionately called BCD Specials. The super-duper BCD Special was convened by a general officer. A general officer also had to convene a general court. General courts were empowered to dole out big time punishments. The authorized punishments of all courts-martial were limited by the Table of Maximum Punishments, as found in the UCMJ. General courts are like the felony courts found in the civilian world.

One of the main advantages to being tried by a court-martial is that before one can be charged by a general court, there must be an Article 32 investigation. This means a senior officer is appointed to investigate the crime and report to the convening authority or commanding general. The investigation is formal and most of the testimony has to be taken under oath. The accused and his attorney are present and cross-examination of the government witnesses is allowed. It does give the defense counsel a free discovery session as they get to hear the testimony of the witnesses, ask questions on cross, and get a pretty good feel for the government case. The defense counsel can call the accused to testify, but usually I did not call my client to the witness stand. The only time one would call the accused is when you are convinced they did not commit the crime and the government has a weak case and maybe you can get the case tossed at the investigation level and save putting your client through the trauma of a court-martial.

One case that did get dismissed at the Article 32 investigative level was a rape charge. The accused was a Staff Sergeant (SSGT, E-6) and was charged with raping a German national. The German woman was an attractive brunette who had met the SSGT in a bar and claimed she had been taken to a German apartment and forced to have intercourse. The SSGT happened to be black and this created much uneasiness with the German woman. Her father was present at the hearing and I could tell she was very reluctant to testify. She testified that he hit her and forced himself upon her. The SSGT told me that it was a totally consensual act. I did not call him at the hearing as I thought the woman was a weak and reluctant witness. Moreover, there were no pictures of any bruising or marks and there was no medical evidence indicating bruising or force in the pubic area. A damaging aspect of the case was that she did not report the crime until almost two days later. The timing of the charge closely correlated with her father finding out she had been with a black man. The case was dismissed by the government. I suspect that the German woman made it known that she was not particularly anxious to pursue the matter.

After the rape case was dismissed by the government, Butts confided in me that when he was with the CID, he investigated a similar charge against the Staff Sergeant. The claim had been made by a German national and the allegation was that the SSGT had used force, but there was no significant physical evidence. It looked like there may have been a pattern developing. Fortunately for the SSGT this was before the computer age and the government did not get wind of the prior matter and attempt to use it to show a common scheme or plan. If the German woman had been the daughter of the local *burger meister* the case may not have been dismissed. Although, if the complaining witness is real weak and wants to back out, the government does not have too much to work with.

I had one murder case when I was at Graf. A Puerto Rican kid was charged with stabbing to death another GI. The Puerto Rican kid got beat up by another GI in a bar fight and went back to his apartment in Vilseck and grabbed a knife and returned to the bar and stabbed the GI in the chest. The accused lived off post with his wife. Our best shot on the case was to try and get a manslaughter plea. We would have to convince a military jury that the crime was committed in the "heat of passion" and consequently the accused did not have the requisite intent to be guilty of murder. Our problem with the heat of passion argument was that 15-30 minutes transpired between the fight and the stabbing. The government would certainly argue that he had sufficient time to "cool down" and if anything, this was pre-medicated murder. After the stabbing, the military ambulance picked up the victim and initially took him to Vilseck Post, but there was no medical facility at Vilseck so they had to move on to Grafenwohr. Precious time was wasted and the victim managed to choke as his lungs filled up with blood. He may have survived if he had been taken directly to Graf.

Both the accused and the victim were known in the unit and the crime was witnessed by several other troops. There was not much doubt that the government could establish the original fight and the time lapse and my client stabbing the other soldier. My only shot was the manslaughter claim. The accused was put in to pre-trial confinement and held at the confinement facility (stockade/jail) in Fuerth located in the Nuremberg area. I went down to see him within the first few days. He spoke English, but not very well and was not at all articulate and did not seem like the smartest kid on the block. I made a mental note to think about requesting an interpreter for the trial.

George and I spent a night in Vilseck and went to the bar and spoke with the bartender and tried to find some witnesses. It was a difficult order as most of the Germans did not want to get involved. It was a couple of American soldiers fighting and why did they care? We spoke with the medic that drove the victim back to Graf. He thought there was a doctor at Vilseck, but then had to turn around and head for Grafenwohr. He thought the victim was still alive when they got to Graf. Whether or not the delay was a factor or not, I would not be able to determine until I had spoken with a doctor.

The problem I had with the case is that I had a huge work load and little help and my Stabber was tucked away in Nuremberg and that was almost a two-hour drive from Graf and another two hours back. Getting in and out of the slammer took time and I was trying a couple cases a week so, had little time for client contact.

I finally found the time to get to Nuremberg and I got a call that PVT Stabber had obtained civilian counsel. I was not surprised. I had been working the case, but did not have time for my client. Civilian lawyers were doing fairly well in Germany during that time as the Army was saddled with an abundant amount of troublemakers and drugs were plentiful on the civilian market. A number of the military lawyers were convinced that the SJA (Big JAG, LTC Anders) was making better deals with the civilian lawyers than he was making with us ordinary grunts. It struck me that Anders was giving a better shot to the civilians. They probably took him out once a month and bought him a schnitzel and beer and told him he had pretty blue eyes. As it worked out, the young Puerto Rican soldier got a deal on a plea to manslaughter. It was a good deal and I am not sure whether or not I would have been offered the same deal. The civilian lawyers were not under military control and they could take more leeway and chances in the courtroom than military lawyers. The civilian lawyer did not have to worry about his next efficiency report or their reputation in the corps. Later on, the JAG Corps moved the defense attorneys to a separate department or sub-branch so the efficiency reports were all inside the defense side of the house. I am not sure how several years in the defense side would affect your future assignments. The personnel gurus used to like some trial counsel (prosecution) experience in your background.

I was pretty well strung out with the work-load, and the trial counsel named Jake told me to call LTC Barney Brannon if I had any trouble. What the hell, I decided to call Barney. Barney was the big personnel honcho in Germany. Maybe I should have called LTC Anders first, but I did not think it was a big deal and called Barney. Later, I suspected the trial counsel told me to call Barney directly as that would get me on the wrong side of Anders. Many JAGs were cut throat. Barney asked me if I was interested in teaching and I said I was and he said I could go over to Vilseck and teach at the school. I did not have to relocate and could commute back and forth. I told him I did not mind commuting. In fact, I preferred to commute so I did not have to force my kids

Military Daze

to change schools. Within a week or so, I got orders assigning me to 7th Army Training Center and I was off to a new assignment. A PCS (Permanent Change of Station) was not authorized and the Army did not have to spend the money to move me and I wanted to stay put anyway. George departed for the Bronx about the same time and he sold me his VW staff car. It was not a VW Beetle, but looked like the German staff car seen in WWII movies. The car transaction was like everything else involving George, a little different. George set a price for the car and I told him it was too low and offered more. I was trying to out-bid George, but I was the only bidder. George convinced me that I was not taking advantage of him and I bought his car. I drove that thing all over the countryside for the next couple of years and sold it when I left the country.

"Vilseck" or "Vilsuck" was considered a sub-post of Graf, but they did have their own post commander, a full colonel. The main activity was a school that taught various courses to NCOs and officers. For example, the school had a Company Commanders Course and a 1st SGT Course. My job would be to teach the legal subjects offered as part of the curriculum. For example, the U.S. government and the West German government had hammered out an agreement governing the legal rights and obligations of American soldiers stationed in Germany. It was called the North Atlantic Treaty Organization/Status of Forces Agreement (NATO/SOFA). The salient point was that the U.S. military retained jurisdiction for offenses committed by service members on post and also off post and out on the German economy. For off post crimes the German Prosecutors could recall jurisdiction and prosecute in a German court if they notified us of their intention to do so within a certain limited time frame. (I think it was within 30 days of the date they were notified of the incident) If the Germans did not recall jurisdiction, then the Americans were free to proceed with a court-martial. The German courts did not have jury trials but cases were heard by three judge panels. That was the way their system worked for all accused. The soldier did have a right to a lawyer and they were provided a German lawyer and this was courtesy of the U.S. taxpayer. We also detailed a JAG to observe the proceedings and make sure things were done fairly.

The German courts had a reputation for dishing out stiff sentences so many of the company commanders were not too sad to see one of their young trouble makers tried by a German court. Depending on the type of crime, occasionally a GI actually caught a break by being tried in a German court. The Germans were big on psychological testing and their courts were much more receptive to insanity or lack of criminal capacity defenses based on mental problems than American courts. The "I did it but I was crazy" defense sometimes worked in a German court whereas it was a very tough sell in any court-martial or in most civilian courts in the USA. Also, the Germans did not necessarily automatically try someone over 18 as an adult like they do in the States. Immature GI's over age 18 could find themselves being classified as juveniles by the German courts and treated with the same kid gloves and restraints found in the American kiddie court system.

Perhaps one of the gristlier cases and an example of a GI "lucking out" in a German court involved a young American lieutenant who murdered a German woman and cut her up and dumped her body parts in trash cans along the autobahn. First Lieutenant Gerald Werner was with the Second Armored Cavalry Regiment (2ACR) at Bayreuth. He had an exemplary record and was about to be promoted to captain. He lived off post, but his roommate happened to be in the field. His former German girlfriend showed up at his doorstep and she brought news that she had become pregnant by another man. LT Werner was apparently willing to help, but first they had sex and then took a bath together. He drowned her in the bath tub. He later claimed that something snapped in his head and he held her underwater. He tried to cut her up and force her body parts down the toilet but that did not work so he loaded the body in his car trunk and made several distribution stops along the autobahn.

LT Werner went back to his apartment and cleaned the apartment with the vigor of a German "*putz frau*" (maid). He did such a complete job of cleaning that the *putz frau* who came through shortly after the crime, noticed nothing out of the ordinary. Only four days after the crime, on March 17, 1964 the German Politzi and the American CID showed up at his doorstep. They knew that his friend, Ms. Schamel had taken the train to Bayreuth. LT Werner denied that she had arrived. The Police searched his apartment and found no clues. Just on a hunch, the authorities checked his car and a small drop of blood was found on his license plate. This time they searched the apartment again and took out all the drain traps and found body hair and blood linking him with this gruesome crime.

The Germans asserted jurisdiction of the case, but LT Werner remained in the American Confinement Facility at Fuerth. The Germans conducted a whole battery of psychological exams. In November of 1966 Werner was tried in a German criminal court in Bayreuth. Werner was found not guilty because of a total lack of mental responsibility. The German court ordered him held in a German *Bezerk Kranken Haus*. The case was appealed by the German prosecutor and the acquittal was upheld by the German appellate courts. In April of 1967 Werner was transferred from the American prison at Fuerth to the German mental facility. His military pay had been stopped back in November of 1964.

It turned out that Werner's parents were both of German heritage. His father went to Germany and attended the court proceedings. He was a professional photographer and spoke perfect German. Some folks may have speculated that Werner received lenient treatment in the German courts because he was an American German. He was one of theirs.

On December 2, 1971 Werner was released from the German hospital and came under American control. The following day an Army Medical Review

Board determined he was not fit for duty and disabled and he was retired on a 100 percent disability.

After Werner was released and retired he returned to Minnesota where he was promptly taken to Dakota County Court where he was civilly committed and sent to the Veterans Administration (V.A.) Hospital in St. Cloud where he was kept in a locked ward. They later determined he was sane and he was released. He remained under a guardianship with his father as the guardian. He did not like the idea of his father controlling his assets (Army disability pay). As a disabled veteran and in a pay status, he was entitled to legal assistance at no cost.

My friend, CPT Tom Armstrong, was pulling legal assistance one Saturday morning at Ft. Snelling when LT Werner showed up and announced that, "You may have heard of me, I was called the Beast of Bayreuth. I killed a German woman and dumped her body along the autobahn." At the same time, the legal clerk announced, "CPT Armstrong, I have an appointment for lunch and I have to leave." Timing is everything.

Tom ended up representing Werner in the local probate court and managed to terminate the guardianship. He eventually got to know Gerald Werner and slowly some of the story came out. It so happened that a week or so before the murder, LT Werner had been detailed as Staff Duty Officer (SDO). The SDO acts as the eyes and ears of the commander and typically pulls duty in the evening or on weekends when the commander is not available. He is authorized to act for the commander.

When LT Werner was pulling Staff Duty Officer a young sergeant came in to see him and told him about some personal problems he was having. Werner blew the thing off and was not sympathetic to the plight of the young SGT. He probably should have arranged for the troop to speak with a chaplain. Later that evening, the young SGT was found hanging from a basketball backboard in the post gym. LT Werner felt personally responsible for the suicide as he did not help the young soldier. This may have been a contributing factor to his sickened mental state.

When he killed and cut up his former girlfriend, he related that it did not seem like he was doing the act, it was more like watching an earlier TV show. It was not him committing the act, it was someone else. Suddenly, his victim was like garbage to be flushed down the toilet.

When the Army took him off the payroll, the lieutenant general (LTG) that acted had done so in response to an article in the "Over-Sexed Weekly" (Overseas Weekly) that featured a headline declaring that "Looney Lieutenant still on Military Payroll." The problem was that the LTG acted in haste and in response to publicity and before a JAG review. The general should have known that you can barely breathe unless you have a JAG review.

Tom filed a claim for back pay on behalf of LT Werner. He was claiming

1st LT pay for almost seven years from 1964 through 1971 when he was placed on disability pay. In a ruling by the U.S. Court of Claims on February 25, 1981 they found that his pay was not properly administratively stopped by the LTG and that his almost seven-year absence was through no fault of his own as he had been found not guilty by the German court. He had not committed a crime in the eyes of the law so how could his absence be his fault? The so called "Looney Lieutenant" had almost seven years of back pay coming. Many folks would properly argue that it is "morally wrong" to reward an individual such as Werner with a monetary windfall following the commission of a heinous murder. On the other hand, taking away someone's pay is also serious and the Court of Claims rightly pointed out that the Army has a procedure for doing that task and they should follow their own rules (The case is reported as Werner v United States, US Court of Claims, Feb. 25, 1981). When the local German paper in Bayreuth got news of LT Werner's monetary award, they ran a headline that proclaimed, "The Beast Strikes Again."

Tom ran for a district judgeship at about the same time that he was representing LT Werner. His Aunt Elizabeth had loaned him some money for his campaign and he was able to pay her back. Tom defeated an incumbent judge who had been censored for misconduct. Thankfully, we had judicial elections and Tom prevailed and displaced the incumbent with the tarnished record. Tom was later re-elected for several terms until he retired. Most of his JAG buddies helped him out with time and money during his run for the district court bench. The reserves does work that way.

Before he was on the bench, Tom managed to keep track of LT Werner and attended Werner's wedding at the Ft. Snelling Chapel. It was a military ceremony with dress white uniforms. Dress whites were popular in the pacific theatre, but were seldom worn in the frozen north or in Europe. Werner's wife had a son that was pulling a life sentence for murder. Later on, the couple was divorced. Rumors surfaced that there had been domestic abuse. Werner was not a man to fool with.

He died in March of 1999 and his gravestone says Vietnam vet although he spent most of his time during Vietnam in a German *Bezerks Haus*. He died alone in a townhouse and in the company of his two dogs. He was dead for quite some time and the dogs got hungry. It was a cruel and harsh ending. Some would consider it to be a proper closure.

One of the first things that followed when I got to Vilseck was they put me on the duty roster for SDO. Army Europe had a regulation that provided that JAGs were not to get extra duty such as staff duty. The reason being that JAGs had to be available to consult the command and provide defense counsel duties at odd hours and they could not provide that service if they were serving as staff duty officer. I was off for the evening and enjoying some nice German weather when Jake, the local trial counsel, came over and gleefully informed me that I was AWOL as I did not report for SDO. My boss at that time, at the school was an MP captain named Rackovich and I got ahold of him and told him about the Euro-Regulation and he suggested I pull the duty at this point and tell the staffing people about the rule to prevent future problems. I said, "Roger that," and jumped in my trusty staff car and headed for Vilseck.

I had no idea what to do as SDO and when I got over there I found another officer to tell me what the hell I was supposed to be doing. I was expected to be in fatigue uniform (which I usually was) and was given a shoulder marker with the identification of SDO. I was supposed to feel a surge of power as suddenly I was running the post. I had an NCO assigned to assist me and I also had a jeep. I did not have a military vehicle driver's license so I was not authorized to operate the jeep, although I did have a GI license, which authorized me to operate a POV (privately owned vehicle) on post or on German roads. It turned out that neither the NCO nor the jeep were particularly useful.

I did talk with the NCO and get his take on what we were doing and we agreed that every couple hours or so we would ride around the post and make sure everything was okay. He confided in me that he was trained in the martial arts so I thought that may help in the event the Russians decided to come across the border or if an unruly GI caused trouble. I did not draw a side arm, although I probably could have asked for one. The NCO told me that we could usually grab a couple hours sleep late in the evening, but one of us had to be awake at all times. When we were not out in the jeep we were supposed to be at our post located in the Post HQ as we were also charged with taking any important phone calls.

At about 10 or 11 o'clock we took our first run around the post. It was already quiet and very dark on post and Vilseck was spooky during the day, but really took on an eerie feeling after dark. We were functioning much like a civilian police patrol, checking the area and making sure there were no break-ins or high crimes being committed. We did get a call from a custodian or some civilian telling us that one of the buildings had not been locked so we ran down whoever was in charge of the building and called the officer out of quarters to come down and lock the place. He was not happy and some NCO or junior officer caught some hell the next day.

We were in the HQ building around midnight when we got a call that some drunken soldier was raising hell down in the snack bar. We went down to check the snack bar and you did not need Dick Tracy to find our drunk. I approached the soldier and was met with a barrage of profanity. I looked around and Bruce Lee had deserted me. My first thought was this buffoon is going to take a swing at me. I tried to recall what Butts had told me about right and left arms and if the watch is on the left wrist then the right arm is dominant so get closer to his right side so that he does not have room to unleash a hay maker. I told the GI that it was foolish to get into all sorts of trouble over this and the best thing for him to do was to go back to the barracks and sleep it off. We managed to find someone sober enough to scoop him up and drop him off at the barracks and that seemed to end that problem. We saw him off and I was happy I avoided a fight. I did write up a report and a statement and sent it over to his CO (Commanding Officer). I spoke with the company commander a couple days later and asked him if he did anything about the incident and he said, "I told the 1st SGT to talk to him and he probably took him out in back of the barracks or whatever." CPT Cossey was not about to take any action because of an affront to a JAG officer. Most line officers figure we had that coming. There was no formal action taken and that was just as well.

I did manage to grab a couple hours of sleep as SDO and I did report for my regular teaching duties the next morning. Fortunately, I was not on the platform that day, so I did manage to get home early in the afternoon and catch a nap.

It was not long after pulling SDO that I was designated as Pay Officer. News of the Euro Regulation was traveling very slowly as it was having a hard time reaching Camp Swampy. I got the same argument from Rackovich as I previously got, so once again I marched off to be Paymaster Ron. We had two people detailed to act as pay agents. One officer was detailed to pick up and pay with checks and the other officer paid with cash. I was Ronnie Cash. We were detailed two NCO's as pay escorts.

The big day arrived to pick up the cash and the first stop was the Company Arms Room where we all drew 45's plus ammo clips. We were dealing with money and this was serious. We all piled in a jeep and took a freezing ride in the direction of Ansbach. I went to Army finance and was handed a check. The check was for $44,400. The strange part of it was that I had to go all the way back to Graf to cash it. My recollection is that I went to American Express at Grafenwohr to cash the check. Myself and the NCO counted out the money before we left the facility. It was all payable in $20 Jackson's. The money was placed in a paper bag and I walked out with over $44,000 under my arm like it was a sandwich. Being somewhat of a practical sort, I wondered why they did not just mail me a check. I had just spent five hours in a freezing jeep and all I had to show for it was a piece of paper. They probably did not trust the Army mail system and for good reason. The mail clerks always seemed like they were getting in trouble for filching mail. Playboys or Penthouse magazines always seemed to have trouble getting through the system and anything that smelled like money was in trouble.

Payday was the next day so I still had to figure out what to do with the money overnight. I suggested that I keep it under my pillow. The NCO was an experienced pay guy and he told me, "We take the money back to the company and put it in the company safe." We went on to Vilseck and surrendered the money to CPT Cossey. He assured me that the money would be safe, but I slept

Military Daze 69

uneasy as I would be in the Army over the next 5 or 6 years to make up that deficiency. My brother was in the Army stationed in New Jersey and he told me about going to Philadelphia to pick up cash in a rather sleazy neighborhood and some of the local residents were not too prosperous and eyed him carefully. He realized that some of those guys were ex-GI's and knew exactly what he was doing and could smell the cash. It was unnerving.

We had managed to secure the cash and the checks. Showtime was in the morning, right after formation. The genesis of this whole operation was that the Army still offered the option of payment in cash. The soldier could pick up a stack of $20's or choose to pick up his paycheck. The pay officer handling the checks had it easy. When the soldier wanting the check reported in, the paymaster simply matched the name with the check and handed out a piece of government paper.

As Officer Cash, the soldier would report in to me and announce his name and rank and state he was reporting in to the pay officer. By "reporting in" the officer or enlisted soldier came to attention and saluted and announced, "SGT Jones reporting to the paymaster, Sir." I returned the salute and paid the reporting soldier. I did have a major who was still getting paid in cash and I proceeded to count him out over a thousand in $20's and he took the money and saluted and departed. The major had most likely started out as an enlisted person and preferred staying with the cash method. Most of the officers on post including myself had shifted to check to bank. I figured with the moving around that I was doing, that made the most sense. I had a master list and that indicated how much each of the soldiers was to receive. The soldier likely had a paper voucher that he surrendered and I kept the paper voucher and gave him the $20's. I am using the male "he" advisedly as I do not remember paying a single woman soldier on that fateful day. That is just the way it was forty plus years ago.

The soldiers reported-in dressed in fatigue uniform. In former days, I am told, they had to change into Class A uniform (greens) to get paid, but at least in "Vilsick," that was no longer the case. I wish I could recall the name of the major who took a sizeable cash payment, as he had a DSM (Distinguished Service Medal) and that was issued for very uncommon valor. It was right under the Medal of Honor, for the most distinguished award for valor in combat. I was pretty sure he did not get that kind of a medal for defending courts-martial.

One advantage of not paying too much attention to the Euro-Regulation that would exclude me from duty was that I was learning more and more about the Army. The post had a closing formation once per week, so unless you died or were on the platform, you were expected to fall in for formation. Our little group of fifteen or so instructors would form a squad as far in the back as possible and the post commander would advise our company to report and CPT Cossey would advise the brass that, "all present and accounted for, Sir." It was always the same report. Someone must have snuck off, but it was never reported. The flag would come down while retreat was played and you would remain at attention. You remained at attention until you heard the command "Dismissed." The officers would sometimes stick around and BS, but generally it was back to our work area and in the cars and on the way home. Retreat at Graf was at 4:30 and I did not observe it at one point and was correctly called out on it by a senior enlisted man who reminded me, "Retreat is for officers too, CPT." He was correct as I had tried to avoid it by scurrying into the building. The next day, I was reminded of my breach of protocol by MAJ Kaiser, the Post Range Officer. I apologized and told him it would not happen again. It never did, for even if I was in my car and heard that bugle blow, I would stop my car and get out and face the HQ and salute.

CPT Ed Schumacher was a Kentucky farm kid who had played football at Kentucky U. and had been in the ROTC (Reserve Officers Training Program) and had gone on active duty and eventually served in Vietnam. Ed was an armor officer, but his passion was shooting and for two summers he went back to the States and spent the summer touring with the Army marksmanship team on team shooting events held all over the place. Some of the events featured international competition. His wife, Nancy, stayed at Graf and Connie spent a lot of time with her and they became good friends. Ed told me the story of when he was competing in an international meet and one of the teams was from Cuba. The Cubans happened to be competing right next to the Americans. A Cuban shooter was firing next to Ed and was having some problems on that particular day and a more senior person approached the Cuban shooter and whispered something in his ear. Ed said, "I wish I could have understood what he said, but from that point on the Cuban could not have shot his foot if he had a 12 gauge; he completely fell apart." The U.S. Army destroyed the Cubans in that particular struggle. Anytime we defeated the Red Menace it brought joy to my olive drab (OD) heart.

Ed's Marksmanship Training Unit was in Europe to provide range training with the M-16 rifle and 45 sidearm for the units assigned to USAREUR (U.S. Army Europe). His unit sometimes fired on weekends and Ed invited me to shoot one Saturday. I spent a day shooting and was instructed by some of the best shooters in the Army. This skill served me well as our reserve unit always fired for qualification once per year. By qualification, captains and below had to demonstrate shooting proficiency with the M-16, and field grade officers had to qualify with a 45-caliber pistol. It was not too hard to qualify and I did qualify as a sharpshooter on at least a few occasions. Officers did not wear a sharpshooter designation badge as we were all supposed to be sharpshooters.

Ed was a fight fan and several of the officers followed the major boxing events on German TV. The "Thrilla in Manilla" and other fights featuring Ali and Fraser were all on German home TV. Don King was promoting the fights

Military Daze 71

and he was taking the fights offshore and showing them in movie theatres back in the USA There was no home TV in the States and cable was not even a glimmer in Don's eye. The German's had the fights live, but not on prime time. We got up at around two or three in the morning and went over to Ed's quarters and huddled around the TV and watched some to the greatest fights of the century.

We also had "American TV" via the Armed Forces Network. Almost all of the programs were taped in the States and sent over for programming in Europe. Most of the programs we saw were a week or two old. There was one advantage to the delayed programming as the shows were uninterrupted and without commercials. For example, we got Johnny Carson and the "Tonight Show" and at that time it was an hour and a half show and we saw it in exactly one hour. A third of the show was ads.

Armed Forces TV (AFTV) also featured some of their own programming. They put on the news at least twice a day. The military ran AFTV and their newscasters were constantly rotating in and out of uniform. When we got over there they were giving us the news in civilian clothes and shortly after, they put on greens or blues. The routine varied throughout my tour. Some people would write in and advise the station that they looked at uniforms all day long and did not want to look at them at night. Others would respond, "These folks are in the service just like I am. Order them to wear the uniform every day just like I do." And so the argument raged on. I have never been a TV fanatic, but occasionally I would stay up late and catch a show featuring some scantily clad or no clad females on German TV. The Germans would provide TV without a lot of interruptions and then bunch the commercials for 10 or 15 minutes and then resume programming for another 45 minutes or so without a break. When my friend, Joe Rehyansky found out he was going to Vilseck, the first question he asked was, "Do they have television there?" When he found out we had American television then everything was cool.

Later in our tour, Ed Schumacher took over command of the Headquarters Company at Graf. The HQ Company ran the post mess hall which fed enlisted soldiers in HQ Company, but also a couple of companies of ADA soldiers stationed at Graf. We were located near the Czechoslovakian and the East German border so their mission was to protect us against air attack and knock down some Russian MIGs in the process.

Ed confronted a problem with soldiers from the ADA not busing their dining dishes when they were done eating. A group of 6-8 soldiers got in the habit of eating and leaving and someone from the mess crew had to clean up after them. Ed found the solution. The next evening when the troops came into the mess hall to dine, they were told that they would be fed, but they were not allowed to use the mess hall dishes. There was a protest and of course the cry was made, "You have to feed us, what are we going to eat?" Ed's response was, "We will feed you but not on my china. You all have been issued TA-50. Go

Military Daze

get it and we will fill your mess kits." (TA-50 is personal gear issued to every soldier and includes mess kits, canteen, cold weather gear, etc.)

It was not long after that incident that Ed received a call from the battalion commander, an officer, some called, LTC Porky. "Hello, CPT Schumacher, this is LTC Porky. I understand you are not feeding my troops." Ed responded, "That is not true, we are feeding them, but they got in the habit of leaving their dishes behind for my people to pick up and we do not have the personnel to provide busing service to your troops or my troops either. Since your troops are not going to clear their dishes, then they are not eating on my china." LTC Porky was obviously irritated and took another tack. "Those mess kits may not be sanitary. My men could get sick." Ed had an answer for that one too. "Do not worry Sir, I will have my Mess SGT inspect the mess kits prior to meal time to make sure they are squeaky clean and if they are not clean, we will not feed them until they are." Porky had a short fuse. "CPT Schumacher, why don't you just give the troops an Article 15?" "LTC Porky when was the last time you saw a troop receive an Article 15 for not busing a dish? Moreover, I cannot give these troops an Article 15 because they do not belong to me. You have the authority to hand out an Article 15, but that is up to you."

When I think back on that incident, I wonder why LTC Porky did not jump on his own troops with both feet, because clearly they were slothful and inconsiderate. He likely was told that his people were not getting fed and he ran with that story. Once he got the facts from CPT Schumacher, he should have taken his own troops to task. Maybe he did, when he got the truth and I hope he did. We had two company commanders that lived in our building that were serving in LTC Porky's battalion. One day they were complaining about "Porky" and I knew exactly who they were talking about as he did bear a striking resemblance to that lovable cartoon character.

Ed and his Mess SGT ran a good mess hall and took a lot of pride in their food. One Thanksgiving they opened the mess to families and our crew went along with Ed and his bunch to the mess hall for a Thanksgiving meal. It was very good. I frequently ate at the mess hall when I was traveling. Officers paid for the privilege, but it was inexpensive and always very good. I never had any squawks with the mess halls.

One family activity I got into was "*Volks* Marches." They were German sponsored hikes. They were usually 5 or 10 Kilometers and were sponsored by a local town or civic group. They were usually in the fall, and at the end of the march one received a decent medal. Graf had a *volks* march and I think I still have the medal lying around with other forgotten lore. The military liked to promote the activity with the Germans as it supposedly fostered German-American relations. "German-American relations" seemed to be the magic words that allowed troops to sometimes be excused from duty early or obtain some sort of privilege. My good colleague, Rick Luis was in the Army in Germany as a drafted enlisted person and stationed near Frankfurt. The Germans were having a local festival and the GIs were encouraged to attend. In fact, they were released from duty early so that they could join in the merriment. Rick and his buddies made their way downtown and soon found the beer tent. The beer tent was a mainstay of any German celebration. It was the first thing to go up and the last to come down.

After the beer tent, Rick and his friends made their way to the midway. One of the rides at the midway was the dodgem or bumper cars as the Americans call them. These are the small electric powered cars that are operated in an enclosed area about the size of a basketball court and are popular at state and county fairs in this country. The American way of operating the cars is aggressive and the primary object is to crash into the other cars. Cultural differences showed up in the operation of the bumper cars. The Germans operated the cars orderly and carefully and proceeded in a clockwise direction without bumping or jousting. Rick and his crew quickly introduced the Germans to the American version of dodgem cars. They proceeded to bang into the Germans and slam them from the front and back. The German drivers did not take to this lesson in cultural diversity and reacted in an irate manner. It was not long before a couple of the GI's and the Germans were engaged in fisticuffs. The German Politzi were quickly summoned, but fortunately one of the hard driving Americans spotted them and sounded the alarm and most of the American youths quickly abandoned their enterprise. The two pugilists were apprehended by the German police while Rick and his buddies scurried off. The two American fighters were quickly hauled off to the German slammer. Rick's battalion commander (the colonel) had to drive some twenty miles in the dark of night to the German klink near Meinz and bail them out. The colonel was not pleased. Rick "laid low" at the base for a time, but it did not take the colonel long to issue a stinging memorandum. The conduct was described as "deplorable" and by their actions "they have undermined German-American relations and sought to destroy years of effort in building harmonious relations between the Americans and our German hosts." It was not exactly the bombing of Dresden and eventually things quieted down and Rick and most of his buddies avoided any disciplinary action. The two battling GIs were given an Article 15 or some sort of punishment. So ended another failed attempt at promoting German-American relationships.

I got to know a few of the Germans, but it is difficult to make a lot of foreign friends. We probably would have made more friends if we lived off post, but with a larger family, my housing allowance would not have gotten me anything close in size and scope to the place I had on post. Most of the GIs who lived off post seemed to get along fine with their German neighbors, but sometimes there were problems with the landlord wanting them to transfer American cigarettes or ice cream to the Germans. That was sometimes a potential black market problem.

One of the Germans I got to know pretty well was named Guenther who ran a German *gast-haus* or *pension* in town. Guenther had been in the German Army during WWII and had the dark dot on his bicep of the German SS. That was the top German force. Guenther had served on the Eastern Front and said, "We ran out of everything. Gas, food, warm clothes, you name it, we were short of it. War is *scheiss*" he concluded. My limited German extended to knowing what he meant. Guenther had somehow made it out of the Russian Front alive and surrendered to the Americans. He liked Americans and he appreciated our service in his country.

Another German I met was Mickey Griener. Mickey ran the local dive and strip club properly called "Mickey's." Mickey was a mason and I went through the order when I was in Germany. I usually saw Mickey at lodge meetings. His bar was outside the fence and featured over-priced drinks and nude women. It was a hit with many of the GIs. Most of the officers did not spend too much time in the place. One night I was in there and the stripper was attractive and she was playing around with a dildo. Graf never lacked for class. I was there with a couple of other captains and our wives so we did not linger on that evening.

Years later, I returned to Graf when I was in the reserves and located "Mickey's Coffee Haus" on Main Street. It was a small and gracious coffee shop which featured coffee and pastries, but you could get a "bump" if you wanted a liquor or *scholle* as the Germans called their white lightening. Mickey had closed the strip joint because the draftee soldier had disappeared and the volunteer soldier was not all that interested in wasting his time and money. Mickey was glad to see me and I introduced him to MAJ Jack Elmquist and Mickey gave me a big hug. The three of us spent the balance of the evening talking about everything going on in Germany and the States. Mickey liked to go to the US and had made the traditional German stops at New York, Miami and San Francisco. Unfortunately, Mickey had cancer and did not make it back to the States. He gave me some information on a Mercedes to sell for him over here, but he was gone before I could close the deal.

Shortly after I got to Vilseck they reorganized the department and put the little legal department under administrative control of a section called Command, Training, and Management Department. (CTMD) The head of the department was LTC Swanson. He got the nickname "Starchy." Starchy was a West Point grad and had the starchiest fatigues in the U.S. Army. He also had a wandering eye so that it was hard to tell if he was looking at you or someone in the next room. I did not mean he was a skirt chaser, but he just had eyes like Ben Turpin, who was featured in the Laurel and Hardy movies. Not too long after arriving in Graf, I became friends with Dr. Allan Brown who was also a captain and lived in the next building. Dr. Brown had been reading up on aerobic exercise, a concept made famous by an Air Force Doctor, Ken Cooper, and set forth in his book, "Aerobics." At that time, jogging or running was something you did if you were late for happy hour at the club, but you did not do it for exercise or even fun. I located an old pair of sneakers and started in. I stuck with it until my knees gave out, many miles later. One day we were jogging and Allan said that he had given a lecture on jogging at Vilseck and this "guy who had the starchiest uniform, I had ever seen kept asking me all sorts of questions. Do you know that guy?" "I certainly do. That had to be Colonel Swanson." Dr. Brown continued, "This colonel, whatever his name is, Starchy or whatever, monopolized the whole session." I replied, "Yes, no doubt about that one, that was certainly LTC Swanson or Starchy, whatever you want to call him."

At Vilseck, I started out teaching Article 15s, UCMJ (criminal law) and NATO/SOFA to First SGTs who came to Vilseck to drink beer and incidentally take the First SGT's Course. They spent a week or two at Vilseck and took a whole raft of courses preparing them to succeed as a First or Top SGT in Europe. I gave them the legal outline. I had never done any teaching and was still new to the Army so there were some rough spots in my teaching. It takes some time to learn a new craft. Sometimes you would click with a class and sometimes not.

The life and death of the whole department hinged on the student comment sheets. If you got any bad comments, then you were doing a bad job. It did not make any difference if you were actually pounding some knowledge into those khaki-colored brains.

One afternoon when I had been at Vilseck maybe a month or two, I was called into Starchy's office and he said, "We are really worried about you." I asked why? He simply repeated, "We are really worried about you. Do you have any problems or is there something wrong?" "Everything is fine," I replied. I certainly would not have shared any problems or concerns with Starchy. Last I looked, he was an infantry officer and not a chaplain. I told Starchy, I would improve and took my leave. Frankly I was a bit annoyed, but not angry, because I knew I would get better. Later on Starchy approached me and said, "You have really improved." It was a nice comment and I thanked Starchy.

At the school we had frequent guests or dignitaries. Henry Kissenger taught there after the war, but we did not see him return. Henry did happen to be in Weisbaden when Butts and I were there for a JAG conference located at the American Hotel. We were in the same hotel with Henry. The CID was helping with security, and of course Butts knew the people doing the heavy lifting. The Army controlled all of the rooms around Henry's suite. The CID and MPs had drawn M-16s and manned the rooms above and below Henry and on both sides of his room and across the hall. Since Henry seemed safe, Butts and I took our leave and walked down to Weisbaden and found the local casino.

European casinos are a bit more refined than the American version. At that time, men had to be attired in a coat and tie. Butts lost some money, but I do not like to gamble so I grabbed a drink and enjoyed the atmosphere. Weisbaden is a lovely place and the soft lights of the city and the cool November air made for a beautiful evening.

One distinguished visitor that came to Vilseck when I was there was Alexander Haig. He had recently been named SHAEF Commander and was essentially the boss of NATO forces. Haig looked fit and alert and presented well in fatigues. I was alerted that the Big General may be visiting my class that day. At the start of the class, I told the class that he may show so be ready and don't throw anything at me. He did arrive, but it was not my job to call everyone to attention so I just kept firing. After a short time, the SGT called everyone to attention and we all stood and braced and the general took center stage. He told us, "Be at ease" and began a twenty-minute talk. He was a top-notch speaker and he gave the Top SGT's a big pep talk and told them the future of the free world was on their shoulders. He concluded his remarks and everyone stood up and he took his leave. We all seemed somewhat relieved when he left, although at his level, if he saw something he did not like, he would not have dealt directly with the offending party. He was an impressive figure.

When I was at Graf, we were visited by James R. Schlesinger, The Secretary of Defense. Schlesinger looked like an intelligent sort and part of his persona was he smoked a pipe. He was an economist and theory guy and somehow got appointed Secretary of Defense by President Nixon. Later he moved on to serve as Secretary of Energy under Jimmy Carter. Schlesinger was making his rounds through Graf and had even gone out to one of the field camps. Somehow or another, word leaked out that the secretary has lost his pipe. Word went down the line to find the secretary's pipe. A search party was quickly organized. It was not long before a couple platoons of troops were organized to find the damn pipe. Colonels and majors assisted in this vital mission. Somehow I escaped getting recruited for this venture. When I heard about this futile effort, my thought was that it was a pointless mission, because if a GI spots it, he will either step on it or place it in his pocket as a souvenir. I was beginning to understand how the Army worked. For all we knew, it may have been a cheap corncob pipe such as favored by General MacArthur. In fairness to Schlesinger and COL Lodge and the top command, they likely did not order a full-scale search; this was probably the doing of more junior officers who were trying too hard to please the brass. They never did find the errant pipe and Schlesinger got along just fine without it. I am sure he carried a spare or two.

GEN Creighton Abrams also came to Graf when he was Chair of the Joint Chiefs. He was probably desperate to get out of Washington. He was still a rough and ready guy and he liked to tell war stories, drink a whiskey, and schmooze with the troops. One of the best stories about Abrams was when he was the Big Commander in Vietnam and one of his subordinates was trying to impress upon him the importance of winning the "hearts and minds of the Vietnamese people" and Abrams responded, "Hell, get them by the balls and their hearts and minds will follow."

Our legal office at Vilseck featured a senior JAG, CPT Bushwhack, and he was the Officer in Charge (O.I.C.). I was the other officer and there were three enlisted persons. Bushwhack had been around the JAG corps for quite some time and had been to Vietnam. He was originally drafted and served as an enlisted soldier until he applied for a commission and moved into the JAG corps. Bushwhack struck me as a bit peculiar, he seemed quite effeminate, but I had no big problem with him.

When I first got to Vilseck, CPT Bushwhack had been there for a couple months already. One day, one of the line officers named Jim Nance took me aside and said he wanted to talk with me. Nance related that he had been recruited by Bear Bryant to play at Bama, but he had heard too many stories of how Bryant worked his players, damn near to death, and Nance said, "I did not want any part of that shit." He went to "Old Miss" and played football against the Bear instead of for him. Nance warned me about having another captain writing my report card (Officer Efficiency Report or OER), and told me he griped to the powers that be (Starchy or someone before him) and got his rater changed to a field grade. He told me it might work out with Bushwhack, but "you two are the same grade and you may be competing for the same assignments and jobs. There is too much chance that Bushwhack may want to cut down on his competition." I should have taken Nance's advice to heart because Bushwhack did not do me any great favors with my report cards. I was naïve to the cut-throat ways of the officer cadre.

One of the enlisted people in our office when I arrived was Corporal "Bobby." Bobby had known Bushwhack at a prior duty station and tagged along with him to Vilseck. It was obvious that Bobby had a poor attitude and made it sound like he was moving Mt. Olympus if you asked him to do something. Bobby was married to a Vietnamese national and they fought like the French and the Viet Minh. I suspected Bobby was either drinking a lot or smoking something as he did not seem real alert at work. One day, Bobby did not show up for duty and he was gone. Where he went, I never did find out. Bobby had kept all his TA 50 at the office. It sat around the office for a couple months waiting for Bobby to return and one day I was in the office with SFC Halloran and we decided it was time to "dispose of Bobby's shit." We divided up his TA 50 and moved it out. I got a warm sleeping bag and some winter choppers and the rest of it was dispersed. I suppose we should have waited for the company commander to come down and inventory the stuff, but we just decided the Army already had its chance for Bobby's stuff and now this was our chance.

After Bobby went AWOL, we had about given up on a replacement, and one day PVT White appeared. In a bit of irony, White was black and also had reddish hair. White was ambitious and worked out quite well for the first couple months. I started going to the gym every day to play basketball and White started going along. SFC Halloran took a liking to White and spent some time trying to mentor the young soldier. White obtained a leave to go back to the States to take care of some alleged problem and never returned. He was AWOL and followed in Bobby's boots. Later, I was talking with the company commander one day and he told me he was awful close to busting White on drug charges for distribution and that may be one of several reasons why he failed to return. The junior enlisted personnel did not seem to be over-worked or abused so I was having difficulty understanding why they kept going over the hill.

Halloran was a terrific guy and I took a liking to him. He was a product of the "old, brown shoe Army" as he liked to put it. Halloran did like to drink a beer now and then and mentioned that in the old Army it was practically required that you show up at certain times such as Friday evening at the NCO Club. I ran into him one night in Vilseck at a local *gast haus* and he was already into a few beers. He said he talked to COL Creighton (post commander and good guy) one night about me and told him I was doing fine and would continue to improve. He said COL Creighton asked him how he knew I would improve and Halloran responded, "Because he is a lawyer." I took that as a compliment. I asked him where that conversation took place and he said, "Right here." The guy that ran the place was named Kris or Kristian, but I cannot recall what he called the place. Probably Joe's Bar. He made one of the best schnitzels in Germany and the French fries were hard to beat. There was a spot in Graf that made great fries and one night CPT Nolan told me that they threw their potatoes in a rain barrel for a couple hours before they cut them up and that was the secret formula for their success.

Halloran had married a German National and she was nice and still attractive. Halloran told me they were not getting along all that well, but I suspected he was spending too much time at the local *gast haus* talking to Kris. Halloran told me that he had to lobby hard to get a tour in Vietnam. He was a career soldier and he realized that to get promoted he had to have a patch on his right shoulder (When a soldier has served in a war zone they are allowed to wear the unit patch on the right shoulder. In other words, if you had served in the first infantry in Vietnam, when you rotated out you could move the unit patch from your left shoulder to your right shoulder). Halloran told me that he wanted to go to Vietnam to satisfy himself or prove to himself that he had the right stuff for combat. He said he contacted some people he knew to get himself sent to Vietnam. He ended up taking a slug in the shoulder for his effort. He would not be the first person I would encounter who lobbied to go to Vietnam.

Halloran was not overworked as he was the NCOIC of the office and supervised an E-5 named SGT Dix and the legal clerk who was usually AWOL.

He also taught a course in the 1st SGT's Course. I think his course was mostly war stories and it was always well received. He had great rapport with the 1st SGT's because he had been to Vietnam and knew his way around the "old Army." The Marines called it "the old breed." A great read on WWII in the pacific is "With the Old Breed" by Gene Sledge, an enlisted Marine.

Halloran had two sons and they were in high school at Nuremberg. The kids boarded down there at that time. Both of his sons were polite and proper young people. His oldest was into mountain climbing and got an ROTC scholarship to go to the U of Washington. He picked Washington because it was a good school and had an ROTC program and because of its proximity to mountains. Some kids pick a school because their girlfriend goes there, but this kid had more sense than that. Halloran was rightly very proud of his son as he was going to be a college grad and an officer in a few short years.

One day we were in the office and Halloran asked me if I would do him a favor and take him over to Graf as he wanted to go to the *Bundes* Post and call his kid. He had not heard from him in a while. I thought the world of Halloran and this was a small favor to ask. We went over to Graf and Halloran was able to get through and got his son on the phone. He was crying quite profusely. He relayed to his son that he had heard about a climbing accident in the Washington Mountains and was concerned for his welfare. When he composed himself he said to his son that he should write or call more frequently. He got off the phone and was still trying to settle himself and apologized for breaking down. I told him there was no need to do that as obviously he was justifiably concerned over the welfare of his son. We found a coffee shop and took a break before going back to Vilseck. I did not think too much of it at the time, but am now rather flattered to think that Halloran asked me to go with him to receive some of the most important information of his life.

Halloran loved to tell war stories. One day he relayed to me that when he was in Vietnam that a new company commander came on board and he was very enthusiastic and "gung ho." Apparently he started "volunteering" his unit for extra missions or "ambushes." This was not a popular decision with the troops because they realized that this eager young captain may get a good report card and even a promotion, but that they may die over that promotion. This was the Post Tet Offensive Vietnam and the war was losing popularity both at home and in Vietnam. Halloran related that there was a lot of grumbling among the men over the extra time in the bush. They were concerned about getting back home in one piece and not in a body bag. The next time they went out on an "extra" mission the company 1st SGT took an M-16 round in the leg. "The company commander got the message." The 1st SGT also got the message as someone strongly believed he was not looking out for the troops.

The "volunteering company commander" was an extreme example of a career soldier attempting to ingratiate himself with "The Boss" or the "Old

Military Daze

Man." Just plain sucking up is a way of life for many in the military. When I was at Graf, GEN Will Persons was the TJAG USAEUR and that meant he was the top JAG in Europe. This was an important slot as it usually meant you were on track to be TJAG. TJAG is number one JAG world-wide. Kind of like the WWA champion. Persons must have been exceedingly bored or anxious to get away from his wife, but in any event he showed up in Vilseck and wanted to have dinner with the local JAGs. The local trial counsel, Jake, told me to be ready by 1800 and we would be joined in Vilseck by CPT Dan Dandy who, at that time, was the teaching JAG at Vilseck. Dandy was a fairly senior captain who was serious about making major. He tossed so many compliments at GEN Persons that toward the end of the evening Persons was almost starting to become embarrassed. He was not a guy to run about tooting his own horn. Dandy portrayed Persons as the greatest warrior since Patton and the smartest JAG since John Jay. Jake and I sat through this immense suck up and probably uttered about 3-4 sentences during this suck up session and the rest of the evening was dominated by Dandy Dan. Jake shot me a couple looks of disgust, but Dandy marched on and continued to suck up without pause.

After a couple hours of this torture, Persons finally got up and announced that he had to leave. In a military function, protocol dictates that one does not leave a social event until the senior officer departs. Usually everyone fawns over the old man until he and his spouse or companion depart and then everyone still standing makes a mad dash for the exits. As soon as Persons announced his departure we lingered for a minute or two and took our leave. Jake and I had heard enough from Dandy to last us for a long time so there was no point in lingering and absorbing any more bullshit.

Jake got in the car and his first comment was that he had never seen such a suck up in all his life. "Why in the hell didn't he just blow him and get it over with." Jake did have a way of getting to the point in a hurry. Jake continued, "Just blow the guy and end the damn evening." I did not agree with Jake very often, but on this particular night he was spot on.

Persons was a decent guy and I am sure he was embarrassed by Dandy's fawning. Later on I encountered Persons at a JAG conference. One of the speakers was a Major Pain that majored in bragging about his great trial skills. Major Pain was equally skilled at client contact and for one thing did not allow his clients to smoke in his office. I for one did not object to smoking in my dump as it killed the smell of mold and mildew in my lousy office. Following this Painful lecture, I encountered General Persons at the break and we were discussing some of the speakers. Persons commented that "Major Pain has one approach to defending GIs and I am not sure how I would describe it but it seems to work." I replied, "It sounded to me like the Mohammed Ali approach. I am the greatest." Persons did prove to have a sense of humor as he got a grin out of that. I was tempted to ask if he had heard from CPT Dandy, but I decided to not push my luck. I lost track of Dandy and considered myself lucky, but luck does not always hold and later I encountered Senior Bullshit at Ft. Hood. He did make major.

When it came to the art of the suck up, there was no one better than Starchy. He sent a birthday card to the general's dog. I heard that from two independent sources so believe it to be true. One of the sources was CPT Robert Arthur who taught at the school and also worked for Starchy. A few years after I got off active duty, I was in Reno to attend the Judges Course and was wasting my money at the MGM Grand Casino. One of the security people walked by me and I recognized him as Bob Arthur from Vilseck. Arthur had gotten off active duty and gone to work for MGM. People with a military background are usually in demand for any security type of work. For one thing, they have had extensive weapons training and have undergone background checks. They usually have had some sort of security clearance. Most civilian police or security forces are organized along military lines. They have patrol people who act as foot soldiers and sergeants who act as line supers and lieutenants and captains who operate at a higher level. Ex-military are used to this type of command structure. Arthur advised me that he had gone back to school when he got off active duty, but he ran low on funds or interest and took a job at MGM. He related that the security force at MGM was larger than the Reno police department. The MGM was a huge place and at one time was the second most expensive building ever built. It was exceeded in cost by the "new" senate office building in Washington.

I asked Arthur what happened with his military career after he departed Vilseck. He had left around the same time I did. He landed in a stateside assignment and I believe it was at the Presidio. In any event, he got to his new assignment and one of his first missions given to him by his superior officer was to send a birthday card to the general's dog. Arthur accepted the assignment matter of factly and without comment. The officer asked Arthur, "Don't you think it is rather strange that I am sending a birthday card to a dog?" Arthur responded, "Oh no sir, my last supervisor also had me send cards to the general's dog. No problem." Arthur did confide that the stupidity of the dog birthday cards did have something to do with his departure from the military. Whether or not that was the truth, I had no way of knowing. There are lots of reasons that one departs from the Army. Sometimes it is the Army's reason and sometimes the soldier's.

Starchy did manage to find time for other pursuits besides birthday cards to dogs. Bushwhack related that he was at a meeting with Starchy and his superior, COL Cole. Army posts are always a favorite target for scam artists selling one thing or another at inflated prices. Apparently someone showed up and was selling land in some remote place in the States at exorbitant rates. Cole retorted, "Who in the hell would be dumb enough to buy land they did not even look at." Apparently Starchy fell into that category as he admitted to buying some Florida swamp without a peek. Cole's response was "Oh."

Starchy always saluted when he was in civilian attire. I saw him salute COL Cole one day when they were both in "mufti." Mufti is when military folks don civilian clothes. The uniform of the day is then referred to as "being in mufti." That is again one of those strange military expressions that leave me wondering where in the hell someone came up with that one. I was in civilian attire one day and spotted Starchy and I waved and he gave me a salute, so I quickly popped one back. We were both in civilian suits so I am not sure if he would have saluted if we were going to the PX (Post Exchange) dressed in jeans and a tee shirt. I imagine he would have obliged.

One task that all in the military must accomplish on an annual basis is to take the physical training test (PT Test). Our little section planned to take it together as a group. We fell in at the appointed place and most of us were wearing the regular fatigue uniform which included the regular Army black combat boot. We were surprised to see Starchy and the SGT Major show up in gym shorts and running shoes. Apparently, there had been some change in the PT regulations that allowed running shoes during the mile run and Starchy had "forgotten" to pass the news on to the rest of us gobs. I had been running for quite some time and was determined to beat Starchy, even with a two shoe handicap to boot. We were running on hard cobblestones on a route that one of the captains had marked out. I let Starchy take the lead as I slogged behind him and listened to Jim Nance moan, "I have never seen a mile run done in anything but combat boots." "The colonel does not give a shit what you have seen, CPT Nance" came the retort from CPT Pallos, the Greek MP captain from Jersey. Starchy kept moving out but I continued to dog him. I kept within a hundred yards of those running shoes. As we neared the finish the course took a dog leg to the right and I spotted Starchy looking back on the field as he rounded the bend and headed into the last couple of football fields. I had plenty of gas in the tank and gave it a kick. I caught up to Starchy with about 50 yards to go and blew by him and gave a wry smile as he responded with angst. This was not going to do wonders for my next OER.

The next event was the push-ups and sit-ups. Starchy related that he had a bet with CPT Drinkalot that he had made at the club last night that said he would do more push-ups and sit-ups than Drinkalot. Starchy was determined to get that free round. We paired up and Starchy conveniently matched up with the SGT Major. I was paired with Bushwhack and right next to Starchy. The protocol is that your partner counts the repetitions and when you are tired out or reach the end of two minutes, the counter announces the final totals and the parties switch positions. I looked over at Starchy and the SGT Major was dutifully counting out the repetitions. The procedure for an Army push-up is pretty simple. The counter places his hand on the ground or floor under the pusher's chest and the pusher comes down and touches the hand and then pushes up until his arms are fully extended and the counter gives a "one" and the repetitions continue. If the pusher does not go all the way down and all the way up, then he is not doing a push-up and is fudging the test. I looked over at Starchy and the SGT Major was dutifully counting out the repetitions. Starchy was barely moving his arms. He was leaving 6-8 inches of daylight between his chest and the SGT Major's hand on every repetition. He was not extending on the other end as well. I motioned with my arm in a downward manner to indicate he was not going down far enough. Starchy chose to ignore me and just as well. Starchy reported an amazing 50 plus repetitions on his push-ups and collected his beer, but he should have recorded a zero. Officer integrity was AWOL on that particular day in Vilseck. My OER headed much lower than Starchy's push-ups on that fateful day.

Officer integrity was often talked about, but sometimes hard to find. It was hard to find when we took the PT test. Later, COL Cole and Starchy had a general or colonel come in for an officer call and speak to the local cadre on "officer integrity." Following our lecture and on the way out, I heard CPT Pallos remark that "there is more integrity in a whore house than there is in the officer corps." There were brothels in Germany, but I avoided.

One thing I did accomplish during my Army career was to achieve a decent level of physical fitness. I got in the habit of working out every day at noon. It was a great stress reliever and a good way to take off a few pounds. I had never been much of a basketball player, but I started playing the game and would often find a half-court game or just play one-on-one against anyone who was around. The company clerk was a kid from Dubuque called "pinky" and a tall black kid named Washington, were frequently around the gym and I played one-on-one with one of those two. Pinky suggested I come out for the Company team, but I knew better than to try and compete with those kids. Starchy started showing up at the gym and we would occasionally play one-on-one, usually to 21. We played a variation of the regular 21 called "make it take it" in that if you scored, you kept the ball and kept shooting. This enabled you to catch-up if you got far down. This was half-court ball. I was not real fleet of foot so I was pretty good at the half-court game as I did not have to get in a track meet such as was prevalent with the young speedsters in full court service ball. Starchy and I got into some grueling matches. I was not the SGT Major and was not about to cut him any slack. I played as hard as I could and usually had the upper hand with Starchy. He did not show up quite as often when that began to happen. Starchy did not do me any great favors when it came to report card time and perhaps I would have fared better if I had simply allowed him to prevail on the track and on the court.

One of the people that worked in our little section was a civilian named Karen who did typing and clerical duties up in the office with the SGT Major.

Military Daze

One day we were riding the bus together and struck up a conversation. She lived in Graf as did I, and she frequently rode the military bus going back and forth between Graf and Vilseck. I usually took my car, as my work times were unpredictable. Karen was lamenting that Starchy did send the general's dog a birthday card. She thought it completely idiotic and I remained sullen and quiet. The PT test had done enough damage to my career. She related that Starchy had engaged in some braggadocio over his apparent prowess with the PT test. After Starchy had departed, SFC Newman grumbled that, "The colonel should do more mattress push-ups."

Karen's husband was a Staff Sergeant and was with the ADA unit at Graf. I recalled that COL Porky had given him a field grade Article 15 for some perceived transgression that seemed kind of petty. Her husband "Rick" did not want to take a chance on a court-martial and had accepted the punishment. I had counseled him on the matter and lamented the charges as they seemed trivial, but it was too big a chance to take to risk a trial by court-martial. LTC Porky had enough clout that he may have been able to get Colonel Lodge to convene a special court.

In any event, Rick had taken his punishment, which was not real severe and was supposedly prepared to take the consequences. Karen related that they soon would be getting their next assignment and moving on. I was rather surprised to hear the news because a field grade Article 15 with a Staff SGT was usually career ending. The Article 15 regulations provided for filing a copy of the final adjudication of the Article 15 in the NCO's permanent file at Department of Army (DA). Any sort of negative like that at DA seemed to me to be poison. Karen must have sensed my dismay as she responded, "Oh that Article 15. Everyone knew it was bullshit so the people in the office gave it the deep six, it never got sent on to DA." Rick had some friends who stuck their neck out to give him some help when they knew that the commander had gotten off the track. Rick picked up his 201 file (local personnel file) when he left Graf and he purged the file copy of the Article 15 and that put the matter to rest as there was no copy at DA or in his 201.

I was slowly getting my military education. There was a difference between what the Army regulation said and how things actually worked. Face it, I was a boy scout and was getting a real world education.

I had been around Vilseck for about a year and Bushwhack moved on. Bushwhack managed to get himself a military judgeship. He went back to Charlottesville and took the Military Judges Course and then returned to Germany to start hearing courts-martial. Bushwhack was succeeded by a tall, skinny drink of water, named Joe Rehyansky. Joe had served as an enlisted soldier in Vietnam so he had the advantage of having a war unit patch on his right sleeve. He had gone to law school in Florida on the GI bill and then came back in the Army as a JAG. He entered the Army from the state of Florida so he retained his state of Florida residence and also thereby insulated himself from state income taxes. Florida is like Texas, South Dakota, and Washington that do not have a state income tax. I entered the Army from Minnesota so was stuck with the Minnesota tax even though I was thousands of miles from home and not enjoying any of the marvelous services offered by my beloved home state.

The first time I met Joe he had just stopped in to listen to my class. I was pitching the 1st SGT's class and after I got off the platform he came up to me and stuck out his hand and introduced himself. The first thing he said to me was, "You're not as bad as everyone says you are." I replied, "Thanks for the compliment, I think?" I guess I had not been wowing my colleagues around the place. The comment sheets drove the train and I had gotten some negative comments.

Joe had learned the ins and outs of the military and was able to maximize his military experience. He had written awards when he was enlisted so he knew what to put in the proposal for an award to get it approved at higher levels. He promised me, "I will get you a Congressional Medal of Honor before you get out of here." I replied that I did not know there was a war going on. "Never mind, I know how to do it. I'll convince them you were under fire."

Joe overlapped with Bushwhack by a week or so while Bushwhack showed him the ropes. It was clear to me that they were not going to be corresponding when Bushwhack departed. Joe confided to me that, "Bushwhack is strange. He is going to end up in a rubber room." Bushwhack confided to me, "Rehyansky's right wing political views may not go over here and may get him in trouble." Joe was an outspoken political conservative and was not bashful about sharing his views with others. Joe also soon told me that he was in MENSA and that took an I.Q. of over 130 and they accepted his Army G.T. score as a basis for membership. I told him that I was fortunate not to be bogged down and burdened by the demands of MENSA membership. I hate meetings.

Joe had not been at Vilseck too long when he came in one day and showed me an article he had written about his experience on a border tour. He had submitted the article to National Review and they had accepted it for publication. The Army sponsored tours of the border and you were able to experience, first hand, the Iron Curtain that had been dropped across Europe by the Russian Bear. The "Iron Curtain" had been aptly named by Winston Churchill in his famous post-war speech delivered in May of 1946 at Westminster College in Fulton, Missouri. Churchill had a knack for spotting charlatans and scoundrels among world leaders, as he knew what Hitler was up to in Europe long before most folks had even heard of the maniac. Winston caused a bit of a stir in world circles as Stalin called him a war monger, but the phrase stuck. Joe was elated with his writing success and told me that he had been invited to have lunch with Pricilla Buckley on his next trip through New York. Joe became a fairly regular contributor to National Review and eventually worked his way up to lunch with the "main guy" Bill Buckley. Joe can still be found writing guest contributions to the American Spectator and other conservative publications. I got interested in Buckley when I was in college and read his first book that he had written while at Yale called "God and Man at Yale." Buckley's point was that Yale was founded on religious principles, but God was now AWOL at Yale. In fact, he had been dropped from the rolls (DFR).

    Not too long after Joe started, we got caught in a funding shortfall and the Army cancelled most of our classes. There were no travel funds available and consequently if the students could not get paid to get out to Vilseck, then we did not have any students. Congressman Les Aspin of Wisconsin (later Secy. of Defense under Clinton) was always a lightning rod for any adverse or unfavorable publicity about the Army. He was regularly featured in Stars and Stripes or the Overseas Weekly. The headline screamed, "Instructors at Vilseck Doing Nothing." The article then went on to describe how the instructors at Vilseck were lounging around with no students to teach and nothing to do. They did not bother to explain that the reason we were not busy was because there was no travel money for the students. The article as written was totally true in that we did lack for students at Vilseck and most of us did not have much to do. What the story conveniently omitted was the reason for our leisure: lack of funds. Aspin had developed a "pipe line" during the Vietnam War of soldiers that would regularly funnel information to him and he would act as their spokesman. We obviously had a whistle blower or one of Les Aspin's informants running around Vilseck who had funneled information about the work slow down on to Les. The incident clearly illustrated to me how a factually correct story can totally mislead the public, simply by omitting a couple of pertinent facts. Joe and I thought the story was hilarious.

    I never have been a big fan of sitting around so I simply expanded my practice of law. We had two companies of full-time troops at Vilseck. We had an ordinance company and the headquarters company. That number was pretty close to 500 souls and they had their share of legal problems. I put out the word to the company commanders that if their troops needed routine legal matters addressed that they could send them over to me. Formerly, they were all being transported to Graf. This way, they could walk over to see me and did not need a driver to escort them to Graf and waste half a day.

    I was always pretty familiar with income tax law, as I had been a revenue agent and soon built up a mushrooming tax practice. I could do most GI returns in 5-10 minutes so it was not that gigantic an undertaking. I also got involved in some divorce work. Some of the civilian attorneys were willing to have us negotiate with them on behalf of the service member. This usually worked out for everyone as it saved on attorney's fees and we tried to work out something that was reasonable for everyone. Some attorneys played hard-ball and sued it out and they would insist that the soldier retain local counsel. I was only admitted to practice in Minnesota and could not represent PVT Schmedlap in a Mississippi court so my role in that case was to write to the court and the other counsel and make sure that they were aware of the Soldiers and Sailors Civil Relief Act. The Act provided for appointment of local counsel, to make sure that the soldier's rights were protected under the Act. This practice was not always followed, even though it was mandated by federal law. I had one judge write me back and advise that they did not have any funds to pay lawyers and consequently he could or would not comply with the requirement. I wrote him back and told him he should simply assign a local member of the bar to assist the sued soldier, but he failed to respond and presumably felt okay about violating federal law.

One day, I had a young troop stop in my office and he had some questions on a divorce. I gave him some sound advice on what he could do and how I could help him and he seemed satisfied and went out the door. The main thing I told him is that he did not have to do what his wife or her lawyer wanted done, but that he had a say in the matter and I would be glad to assist him in negotiating with his wife's lawyer or helping him get a lawyer back in the States. About 15 minutes later, the SGT Major and COL WallBoard showed up at my doorstep. Wallboard was the deputy commander of the base and had been through an acrimonious divorce and decided to be the public defender for young troops going through the same gauntlet. Joe came into my office and he was not happy. He took this as command influence or interference with an attorney-client relationship. Joe was correct. For some reason Wallboard decided he was the public defender and came down to give me hell. I asked him what PFT Schmedlap had told him and essentially he related that I told him he was screwed. I asked the colonel, "Do you believe I told him that?" The colonel responded with a shrug. I told him to send Schmedlap down here and we can talk things over, but that is not at all what I had told him. Wallboard slowly realized that he had been fooled and he and the SGT Major took their leave. Joe said, "If he pulls that shit again, let me know right away."

Wallboard was not the most tactful officer I encountered. One day I had been talking with CPT Cossey, the HQ Company Commander, and Wallboard came along and started to grill him about his weekend commitment to the troops. Wallboard asked him, "How much time are you spending on the weekends with the company troops?" Cossey replied, "I try and get down to the company every weekend." Wallboard replied that he had been in the company area last Saturday and had not seen him. Cossey related that he and his wife had done some family things on Saturday. Wallboard retorted, "You have to spend more time in the company. The troops have things to look after that can sometimes only be addressed on weekends. You have to show a command presence." Wallboard left and Cossey and I resumed our conversation as though nothing had occurred. Company commanders have one of the most difficult jobs on earth. They are in the company area before 0600 and seldom leave before 1800. Weekends are spent with the company or you have some jerk like WallBoard asking you what in the hell are you doing with your spare time? If you have a friend or relative who is a company commander, that person is underpaid.

Meanwhile, Starchy moved on to some sort of other pasture and he was succeeded by LTC Virgil Dietrich. Dietrich was a much more regular guy than Starchy, and like Wallboard he also had a much younger and newer wife. One day Dietrich and I were engaged in our noon basketball one-on-one game and Dietrich caught one of my hips as we were scrambling for a rebound and he ended up on crutches for a few days with a badly sprained ankle. I felt bad about that one and told him so. I wished it had been Starchy.

For some reason, Dietrich and I got in a conversation about COL Wallboard. Dietrich had known Wallboard in Vietnam. Wallboard had been a battalion commander when Dietrich ran across him. Dietrich told me, "Wallboard would analyze a new mission and relate that we would lose several troops in the encounter, but we would take out more of the enemy so somehow or another that made it worthwhile." Dietrich did not like the idea of losing any American troops so did not approve of the way Wallboard did his cost-benefit analysis. Wallboard had only recently managed to make full colonel, so perhaps his method of battle analysis had proven to be the school solution.

Bushwhack had been absent from Vilseck for about six months when we got a strange report through the JAG vine that Bushwhack had been relieved as a military judge. Bushwhack had been serving his apprenticeship as a judge and had been hearing special courts-martial throughout the German countryside. It was truly a bizarre chain of events. Bushwhack had been presiding over a military trial and the trial had featured a trial by members. Members meant that it was a military jury that had convicted the young troop. He was waiting around to be sentenced and Bushwhack approached the troop and suggested some sort of meeting or get together. The troop told his lawyer about it and his lawyer reported it up the chain and Bushwhack was relieved of duty and shipped back to the States for discharge. I have no idea what Bushwhack was proposing, whether he was looking for a date or merely some companionship, but in any event, he had no business communicating ex-parte with a defendant. If he had anything to tell the accused, he could do it in open court or preferably communicate through defense counsel. It looked like he was hitting on the kid.

Word of Bushwhack's demise traveled like wildfire throughout Germany and worked its way down to the backwater of Vilseck. LTC Dietrich managed to get back on his feet after I derailed him and we were engaged in our noon workout and the subject of Bushwhack came up. Dietrich suggested that I write the DA and advise them that Bushwhack had been writing my OERs and had

Military Daze

not been unduly complimentary, but he has now left the Army in disgrace and some sort of entry should go in my file indicating that my rater (Bushwhack) was not very reliable. Dietrich understood the Army and he was a good guy, but writing something like that could work two ways. It could help, but it could also make me look like a whiner. I elected not to do anything, but that may well have been a mistake.

    I have no idea whatever happened to Bushwhack. He went back to the States and I am not sure whether his ethical breach ever got back to his local bar licensing authority. I really was not interested in narcing him out to his local bar and do not know if anyone else gave a rip or not. My information was only second or third hand news and that was certainly no basis for filing a complaint on another lawyer.

    I had about eight months left in the Army and I decided it was time to return to the courtroom. There were two trial counsel (prosecutors) jobs at Graf and I was to get one of these slots. I put my paper work in to go back to 1st Armored Division at Graf and join the prosecution team. After I put my paperwork in, LTC Anders backed water and put me back on the defense team. I talked to him about it and I got some BS telling me how highly qualified this dude named DeBarry happened to be. Anders was still mad about me speaking with Brannon about a transfer to Vilseck.

    When I had first gotten to Graf, we had a staff meeting in Nuremberg that I got roped into attending. Anders conducted the meeting and for some reason decided to tell us about his background. He was commissioned through ROTC into the infantry and served as an infantry officer for a few years until he applied for a funded program to have the Army pay his way through law school. This was a program that allowed officers to take a three-year holiday at taxpayer's expense and go to law school. The "student" received full pay and allowances and performed some sort of summer work for the Army, but otherwise was a well-paid civilian student. Most of these lay-abouts also collected on their GI education benefits so the money rolled in without pause. The Army did start their own medical school because they were having trouble getting qualified medical graduates to enter the uniformed services. There likely was a shortage of doctors in many parts of the United States. I have never believed for a second that there ever was a similar shortage of lawyers in any part of the U.S. The funded law school program was eventually junked, but not before Anders got his fill of it.

    I told Butts that it was kind of strange that Anders had given us his speech about his background. Butts said that he gave that speech because "most people around Nuremberg did not think he was a lawyer." Butts usually had most things figured out. Anders was already a major when he finished law school and matriculated into the JAG branch and consequently he never really had any courtroom experience, as most of the trial work was done by the captains.

He had never functioned as a civilian attorney and was really thin on lawyer experience but like him or not, he was the boss.

Not long after I left Grafenwohr, the trial counsel job was filled by Thorpe Nolan. Nolan had been an enlisted person in the Marine Corps and had gotten out and became a civilian cop in San Diego and had gone to law school at night. Nolan had a ton of stories and it was hard to separate the wheat from the bullshit, but it was interesting stuff so I just listened and enjoyed the show.

When I got back to Graf in the fall of 1975, I was stunned at the transformation that had occurred in the U.S. Army. Most of the criminals and draftee mal-contents had gone off to the stockade or been boarded out of the Army or if they were lucky, had simply hit ETS. Much to our shock, people were voluntarily joining the Army and they were good people. They did not have to be in the service, but they were there because they wanted to serve. The popular theory floating around the Army when the draft ended was that no decent person would voluntarily join the Army, but that only losers and near-do-wells would voluntarily join the ranks. As it turned out, that popular theory was just that, a popular theory that had no factual basis, but somehow has persisted even to this day. A current off-shoot of the "loser" Army theory is that the Army is filled with poor kids and is not a cross-section of our society. Actually, it is a middle class Army and studies have shown that to be true.

Meanwhile, back at Graf, part of my old work-load had been cut up and given to another defense counsel. We now had two defense counsels at Graf. I had been doing the work of two or three lawyers during my first tour at Grafenwohr. Most of the trouble-makers had returned to the streets of Gotham City and I finally had time to properly counsel people and mount a defense in the few courts-martial on my schedule.

Nolan was not unduly busy and he had installed a dartboard on the back panel of a door and he grew fond of playing darts. One day there were three captains and a sergeant major playing darts in Nolan's office and he remarked, "I wonder how much this dart game is costing Uncle Sugar." Nolan had some smart enlisted people working in his office and that made his job a lot easier. One of his legal clerks was named Mike and was from Boston. He had volunteered and came in the Army mainly for the education benefits. Mike had come from a big Irish family and there was not enough money for college. His father was a lawyer and did mostly criminal work and practiced out of their house. I am sure they learned to lock up the silver before one of Dad's clients came over to the house. During the time Mike was in Germany, he had taken advantage of the college courses offered to GIs through the University of Maryland and he had completed well over a year's worth of college credits. He had his GI bill left and was looking forward to finishing college when he got back to Bean Town.

The University of Maryland, as well as a Texas Junior College out of

Military Daze

Killeen, were busy offering college courses to GI's stationed in Europe. Their curriculum featured courses in law enforcement and business areas that would appeal to GIs. I was recruited to teach in the legal area and also taught a business course for a group called City Colleges of Chicago. Nolan also got in the teaching business and taught a criminal law course.

In one of my first terms, I was teaching a criminal law course down at Amberg, a small community about 45 kilometers south from Vilseck. We had an armored battalion down that way at a small post called Pond Barracks. My buddy, Rackovich, was a veteran MP and was teaching a course in law enforcement. We decided to car pool down and back as it was a bit of a drive and we could save ourselves some time and fuel. It was my turn to drive and I was driving my little VW German staff car. I stayed at Vilseck after normal duty hours and spent an hour or so doing some last minute preparations for the class. When I left our old horse barn (our office was located in an old cavalry horse barn) I noticed that we had a light snow in the works, but being from Minnesota, I did not give it much thought. I picked Rackovich up at his quarters and headed down to Amberg. We were on the back roads as in those days there was no autobahn in the area. The back roads took us through the small German bergs that dotted the countryside. The small German towns were picturesque and most of them still featured cobblestone streets. The terrain was hilly and we had just come down a rather steep grade and were entering one of those quaint cobblestone streets when I realized I was going a little fast and should slow down as we descended into the center of town. I tapped my brakes and suddenly realized that those snow covered cobblestones had become very slippery. We went into a skid and I braked and suddenly we did a complete 360 as we descended down the hill. We came to a stop in the middle of town. I asked Rackovich, "Are you okay?" "Ya, I am fine," came the reply. Rackovich had been in Vietnam and all over the world but I could tell he was a bit shaken. I was somewhat embarrassed that I had made such a stupid mistake. Since I was from Minnesota I should have known better. The car was very light and I was not used to such a light vehicle in bad weather. I was damn lucky my little car did not flip.

Amberg featured some nice crystal factories and one could visit them and shop in the crystal room following a short tour of the factory. Usually the crystal room featured new glassware but also "seconds" that looked new but had a small flaw. Fine German glassware and plates could be purchased for a German mark or two. The Officer's Wives Club in Graf frequently sponsored trips to the crystal factories. They also went to the Nutcracker and the Christmas plate factory and lots of other shops in the area. We acquired our share of all of those items at a buck or two an item. We bought European items such as porcelain plates made in Denmark that feature a winter or Christmas scene and a caption such as "Jule 1975." I have four or five of those plates hanging from the soffit in our kitchen.

I also taught a criminal law course up in Bayreuth. Bayreuth is one of these out of the way German towns that tourists seldom see. It was home to Wagoner, the German composer. I cannot recommend Wagoner, but I can recommend Bayreuth. One of the worst nights I have spent is when Phyllis dragged me off to an opera that featured the "music" or sounds of Wagoner. It was like a long drawn out funeral. Unfortunately, the experience soured me on opera and Phyllis has not been able to drag me back. Just last summer we took a Baltic Cruise and we spent time at St. Petersburg and she did get me back to the ballet. The ballet house was a splendid structure and the women were lovely and I could repeat that activity, but I am afraid my opera days have been permanently scorched.

The crown jewel of Bayreuth is the opera house or *Festspielhaus* located in the *stadt mitte* (downtown). It features hand carvings everywhere covered with gold filigree. A domed ceiling is adorned with gorgeous frescoes. Bayreuth was largely untouched by the war. It was a small town and was not tactically important for any reason. I thought it was important before I rotated home that I see the opera house. I parked my staff VW right by the front door and went in and took a look. The place was not even locked. At that point it was still a work in progress, but I could still appreciate the place. That ingrate Wagoner supposedly never liked the place, but I got even with him, I did not like his music.

Shortly after we got to Germany, we took an evening trip to Bayreuth and visited the Hermitage. It is a beautiful park and features a palace and English garden. It was built for Frederick the Great's sister, Wilhelmine. We managed to get up there in a small German VW Beetle that I bought from a GI from Minnesota for a couple of six packs. I had my car shipped from the States but needed something to run around with on a temporary basis. We went to Bayreuth for a band concert that was put on by a small college band out of the state of Washington. We were surprised to find a few other Americans up there for the concert. We encountered a young couple who were backpacking and spent some time providing them pointers on things to see, although we had barely been in country for more than a month. In those days, it was always easy to spot an American by the way they dressed. They were almost always, in jeans and frequently a sweatshirt on top. If the person sported a short haircut, that was always a sure sign of an American GI.

We lived close to Weiden and that was a beautiful city with an old wall around the *stadt mitte*. They had a farmer's market in the *stadt mitte* on Saturday mornings and that was an enjoyable interchange. One thing you did learn in a hurry was to be assertive. If you were standing in line to make a purchase, the Germans did not hesitate for a moment to step in front of you. We quickly learned how to say *"entshulagen bitte"* which means excuse me please and give the German a scowl and they usually backed off. This was a common

Military Daze

experience for all of the GI's and their families so it was not personal with us. Early on, we all made it a point to speak German when we went off post. It was their country, and at that time I had the radical idea that one should speak the language of the country you were living in. My German was never very good, but at least I made the effort to use it. One day Nolan and I were having a beer off post and when we finished I motioned to the waiter and said, "*Herr Ober, tzsalin bitte*" (waiter, check please). Nolan was easily impressed and referred to me as a "fluent bastard." I guess I was neither fluent or a bastard, but I did learn to get a beer and find the right *gleis* (track) at the *Bahnhoff*.

My broken German did not always serve me well out in the community. Sometimes the Germans would make a deliberate effort not to understand you. I went in a butcher shop one day to buy some cheese and they pretended not to understand me. It was *Kase* or *Kas'e*. One is cash the other cheese and I still do not know the difference.

We were on a trip in northern Germany and the clerk took a German customer ahead of me and then gave me a hard time with the transaction. All I wanted was a damn ice cream bar. I got the bar and as I left the store I deposited the wrapper on his front steps. I looked back and he was not happy, but I felt a little better.

The Germans are good people and I had a few that I got to know that I considered friends, but the Americans had been there for damn near thirty years and the Germans were getting tired of us and it was mutual. How would we like it if the Germans occupied our country for generations on end? On the other hand, the Germans liked the American dollar and the great boost to their economy provided by the free spending GI and his even more generous Uncle Sam. The U.S. military was probably the biggest employer in the country. The Germans loved working for the Army because the pay was good and they got great benefits including a holiday practically every week or two. Out at Graf, the German civilians got all the American holidays off because the Americans were not around to run the show, but also got all the German holidays as well. They even got some Bavarian or local days off that the rest of the country did not enjoy. The Americans also were good about paying for any damage to the German's property. When we had maneuvers or training, the tanks were always tearing down some German farmer's fence or running over a chicken. The Americans not only paid for the chicken, but all the eggs the thing was due to lay over the next ten years. I guess the German was not able to take the money for the damn chicken and run out and buy a replacement chicken.

The Germans were enjoying a good standard of living and one of the main reasons is that the U.S. was paying for their defense. They had all of the social welfare benefits including medical care. Butts said that he could afford a lot of things if the guy next door was paying half his bills. The Americans were the rich guy living next door to the Germans.

Everyone had a favorite story of their own encounter with "rad." Rad was simply short for "comrade" a common GI term for the German. The GI always has a term for the local civilian populace. In Vietnam it was often "Charlie" or "gooks." In Iraq it was "hajji." Hajji did this and Hajji did that. Another favorite term of the GI was referring to the USA as "back in the world." That was a carry-over from Vietnam where the GI was in a third-world country or simply "out of this world." The States was back home and back to the world. One day, Lee Aitkin used the expression "back in the world" and I asked him "where in the hell is this?" Lee was almost apologetic as he realized Germany was a civilized place with many amenities and pretty far removed from being in Vietnam.

Nolan had a lot of stories and one evening he told me about a bar fight that he got into one evening at one of the local gast houses. Nolan had bounced a couple rads around and apparently word got back to COL Lodge, but he chose to ignore it. Nolan was given to hyperbole so I never did find out whether it was a true claim or not, but it did make for a good war story.

Friday night at the officer's club was a long standing tradition in the officer ranks and I started to follow it during my later time at Graf. Most of the time we just wore fatigues and generally the women did not show up. One evening Nolan and I and another defense lawyer named Randy were enjoying a beer or two at the club and Nolan popped for our dinner. The evening wore on and Nolan got the bright idea to go to Portugal. In those days, service people could travel on a military ID card and a passport was not required. I had a passport anyway as it sometimes avoided problems. It seemed like a splendid idea to head to Portugal and we were walking back to our quarters to implement this great plan when Randy got sick and started to heave. Our trip to Portugal vanished in a second and Nolan and I said good night and headed to our quarters without another word on the subject. I never did get a chance to find out how Connie felt about my pending trip.

The Friday night ritual at the club has pretty well vanished from the modern day Army. Starting in about the mid-80's the Army began to crack down on drinking on post. Gate checks of sobriety began to spring up at military posts. All it takes is one drunk driving to ruin an officer's career. The crack down on drinking did not do anything to stimulate the business down at the friendly officer's club.

Back at Grafenwohr, our daily noon workout was carefully observed by Nolan and I. We went over and played basketball and I got involved in the martial arts. It was a good work out and kept me in good shape. Some of us who were noon regulars scheduled an informal game with a local German team. We played once at Graf and once at their home gym in Weiden. Basketball was still somewhat new in Germany and we were no stars but we managed to win both games. I even managed to get some points. In our road game at Weiden, we found a local gast house after the game and joined the Weiden team in a

Military Daze

fun evening of merriment. I found out about a beer they called *"radler* beer." It translated to "bicycle beer." It was a combination of lemon aide and beer. I guess you could get healthy and drunk at the same time.

We only had a few courts-martial and Nolan and I managed to settle most of them. I had one kid named Johnson who had been charged with some sort of crime, but who had been held past his end term of service (ETS) without obtaining the approval of a general officer as required by the Army regulation. This was a technical defense and was a good one as there was no doubt that the Army had failed to follow the directive and had not obtained permission from division level to keep Johnson around. The issue was: Does the Army effectively lose jurisdiction of the soldier when they do not get proper approval and he is still being held beyond his ETS? If the Army did not lawfully hold him, then Johnson was now a civilian and the Army lacked jurisdiction to try civilians. I did not believe the Army could go back and get the approval at this point, because the regulation said they had to secure the approval before he reaches his ETS in order to hold him beyond that date. I submitted a motion to the court and sent my copy to Nolan and said that the only way to effectively enforce the regulation was to dismiss Johnson because otherwise the Army could hold people over for traffic tickets or all manner of petty crimes without paying any mind to a soldier's interest in completing his time and going home as he is entitled to do. I was surprised when Nolan walked into my office one day and said I was getting my Christmas present early as he was dismissing the Johnson case. I was not sure what Nolan was thinking, but I must have impressed him with my legal argument and I was not going to quibble as a win is a win, any way you slice it. Nolan may have uncovered a case that supported my view, but kept it quiet.

Nolan had been an enlisted Marine (drafted) and for some reason he decided to go back to the Marines, so he put in for a transfer back to the Marines as a JAG. The Marines were probably glad to get a trained officer who understood the Marine Corps and they did not have to pay to send him to the Basic Course at Charlottesville. I did not think the Army would release him as they had paid money to send him to Charlottesville and had shipped him and his wife and twin daughters all the way to Graf. Nolan had been in Germany for almost two years so that was in his favor. He left for the Marine Corps shortly before I hit my end of service and headed back to the States.

When I was writing this book, I decided to look up Nolan and see if he had any follow-up information for me. I somehow located him in California and it looked to me that he had returned to the practice of law. I found it strange that he had no email address, but I shot him an old-fashioned letter and received an email from one of the twins, Jenna Nolan. Thorpe had passed away about fourteen years ago from throat cancer. I did not remember him smoking, but I guess he had gotten back into the habit when he lived in Washington D.C.

Thorpe had been briefly stationed back in the States after leaving Graf, but only remained in the Marine Corps for a short time. I think he was at Quantico, VA, but it was a short tour. He got out of the Corps and drove a bus for a time and then worked for the government in the Washington DC area. Eventually he migrated back to California where he returned to the practice of law.

Thorpe and Alice remained together until he died. Thorpe was very witty and smart. His father was recruited from Ireland to work on the Manhattan Project and Thorpe spent time as an infant in the dessert near Los Alamos. He said he still liked the dessert and enjoyed that part of California. He called himself a "desert rat."

Over forty years have passed since I served in Germany. Almost all of the people I knew in Germany are no longer part of my life. Joe Rehyansky is the only person that I maintain some contact with. I have shared some of these stories with Phyllis and Cameron as they came into my life during the post German era. I finally got an opportunity to take them to Germany and show them around the area where I served for three years. I showed them Graf, Vilseck, Amberg, Weiden, and Bayreuth. This was the epicenter of my world for three years. Before we plunge into that story; my time in the Army Reserve probably deserves some attention as that was a big part of my life. We can route step to the next chapter. No need to march.

Chapter 4
Citizen Soldier

After I got back to the States, I decided to stay in the reserves as I liked being a JAG and I also needed the extra money that came with the reserves. I caught on with the State of Minnesota and being in the reserves had a special benefit as when I went on my two weeks of annual training, I got paid by the State and also got my military pay. I was a "double dipper" and did appreciate it.

I did complete my twenty plus years in the reserves and qualified for a reserve retirement commencing at age 60. I ended up as an 05 or lieutenant colonel (LTC). You do manage to form fast friendships with the people you see month in and month out while in the reserves and many of those folks are still my best friends to this day. In fact, as I sit here, I am reminded we have a reunion dinner in Stillwater tomorrow evening.

Early in my reserve career we went on annual training to Texas each February. It was nice to get out of the frozen north in the winter and Ft. Hood was a lot warmer than Bemidji.

Ft. Hood is a vast place and was home to two divisions and the third corps. The 1st Cavalry was based at Hood as well as the 2nd Armored Division. The 2nd Armored DIV was referred to as "Patton's Own Hell on Wheels" named after the infamous field commander George S. Patton. In a bit of coincidence, the 2nd AD was later commanded by George S. Patton Jr. I happened to be at Hood after George Junior had taken charge. Junior had managed to carve out a good career despite being in the shadow of his famous father. He had served with distinction in Vietnam and had been in Germany during part of my time over there. At Ft. Hood, I had been assigned to the prosecution team with the 2nd AD for my two week reserve stay and the JAG office was located across the street from the mess hall and Division HQ. One day we had been quite busy working on courts-martial preparation and instead of chasing down to the club or elsewhere, we went to the mess hall. We got in the mess line and were waiting our turn when we turned around and there was GEN Patton right behind us in the chow line. I do not recall being yelled to attention when he entered the building. He probably preferred to let his soldiers eat in peace. We made some small talk with the general and we approached a female MP who was serving as some sort of lunch monitor. I remember that she was tall and attractive and was holding a traditional black night stick. Patton approached her and asked, "Who have you been beating on with that thing?" The startled MP responded, "No one, Sir." Patton added, "You ought to be able to find someone around here that needs a smack on the head." Patton was a law and order general.

I found that I hit it off very well with the young captains that were in the prosecution section. I enjoyed the company of a young captain from Mississippi named Robert Logan. Logan was a soft-spoken kid who was smart as a whip and very knowledgeable in military law. He soon gave me some hard luck story about being jilted by his girlfriend from back home. He related that his social life was in the dumper. I took one look at him and countered, "Was she the last girl on the planet? Look at you. You are no movie star, but you certainly are respectable looking and are smart and well spoken, you should not have any difficulty in having a good time around here. I have seen plenty of attractive women in the short time I have been here so I cannot imagine you having a problem. Quit feeling sorry for yourself and get moving forward." I told him that we had some single women in the unit that would be dying to meet him. A day or so later, Logan advised me that they were having a party at his off post house and our little group was invited. Logan soon met up with Rosalind, an attractive and personable enlisted person in our unit and by the time we went back to Minnesota, Logan had put his old romance in the lost loves file and moved ahead. Everyone gets dumped over the course of time and it is difficult for a few days, but I made up my mind years ago not to let a jilted relationship ruin my life or my future. I have certainly made mistakes along the way so it was best to try and learn something from the experience and live to love another day.

Logan and I put together a couple courts-martial while I was down there and I was given a couple to try. He second-chaired me on an AWOL case involving a young Hispanic soldier who had gone home on leave and failed to return. The case was defended by a young JAG from Virginia that everyone called "Hog Body." Hog Body had played football at Virginia Tech and fancied himself a hot shot defense attorney. He shot me a lot of braggadocio and bravado prior to the trial so I thought I was dealing with the next F. Lee Bailey. He asked to have PVT Alvarez' mother come to the trial as a potential witness. I could not imagine mom helping his case along, but under recent case law, the military had the obligation to produce requested defense witnesses even though the request was based on the flimsiest of reasons. We dutifully sent off a travel voucher for Mother Alvarez.

The day of trial soon followed and Hog Body had requested a board of officers (like a civilian jury). The judge asked the board some routine questions and the lawyers followed up and then each side got one preemptory strike. This means the prosecution and the defense can each strike one panel member for any reason whatsoever. Logan helped me on this one and about all he could tell me was, "This board is a real candy ass bunch. They have not been passing out any significant jail time." The board members were detailed to courts-martial for a period of time and may hear several courts-martial before their time is up. What Logan was telling me was, good luck, you are on your own, trust your intuition. What most military prosecutors looked for were officers who had experience dealing with troops. They loved those who had been in command. Commanders had experience dealing with trouble-makers and would have little tolerance for their hard luck stories. Hog Body had first strike and he picked one of the officers with a command background. I looked over the board carefully and noticed one officer who appeared reluctant to make eye contact. Very unscientific reasons, but I asked Logan about striking MAJ No Look and he agreed. The president of the board is always the ranking soldier, regardless of branch. Sometimes, it may be a matter of days separating the senior officer from one of their peers. I made my choice and then gave it to the judge to announce who was leaving. The judge had been around awhile and the JAGs had given him the nickname, "The Bear." Apparently he was fond of giving JAGs a tough time in the courtroom. There are judges of that ilk, but it was never my style. I gave the board a very short opening statement and sat down and proceeded with my case. In the pre-computer days, one established an AWOL with the morning report. The morning report was the attendance sheet for each company. It was kept in the ordinary course of the business of running a company and was admissible as a business record would be in a civilian case.

PVT Alvarez, in addition to going AWOL had also committed a small-time barracks theft. He had stolen his barrack mate's radio. I put the victim on the stand and victim related that he knew Alvarez because they were both in the same barracks and his radio turned up missing. Later that day he confronted Alvarez in the day room and Alvarez was drinking a Coca Cola and admitted he had taken the radio and did not seem to be the least bit upset about it. He simply continued to drink his Coca-Cola. I then put in the morning report to establish the AWOL and sat down. Hog Body blew a lot of wind, but did not put Alvarez on the stand and had no defense to offer.

The judge instructed the members on the law of AWOL and theft and they went into deliberation and quickly found Alvarez guilty of the two offenses. We then proceeded to the sentencing phase of the trial. This was the crucial part of Alvarez' trial as he had no real defense to the AWOL as he had gone over the hill and taken a stolen radio with him. I offered his military records and that showed where he had served and what he had done and also any awards or punishments. After putting in those items, I sat down and reserved my rebuttal rights. Hog Body called Mrs. Alvarez as his witness. She testified to what a good boy he was and relayed some of his so called problems that prompted him to go AWOL. On cross-exam, I realized I had to be very careful as no one wants to see someone pick on a mom. I asked her who else was in the family and apparently Mr. Alvarez was part of the family unit. I asked her if her husband was a vet or if he had served. Mr. Alvarez (senior) was an Army vet. I asked her if she and her husband had talked to junior when he was home AWOL about returning to the base. She confirmed that they had discussed it with Junior. I then took a bit of a chance, but since her husband was a vet I thought he would understand the serious consequences of Junior's actions so I asked her, "Did you and your husband advise your son to return to duty when you found he was AWOL?" Her response was a simple, "Yes." Alvarez not only defied the Army, but even worse, he defied his parents.

In my final argument, I argued that Alvarez knew he was AWOL but simply chose to ignore it. He broke the Army's code and moreover did not even obey his parent's directive to return to duty. He paid no attention to the Army or his parents and he needed to go away for at least six months and think about it. Also, he showed no remorse over the radio theft as he simply "kicked back and had himself a Coca-Cola."

The Board was out for deliberations all of a half an hour and sentenced Alvarez to six months of confinement and forfeiture of all pay and allowances for six months. Alvarez got the maximum sentence one could receive from this court and this was the first maximum sentence meted out at Ft. Hood in months. The SJA dubbed me "Maximas Ronaldis" and I was a local hero at Ft. Hood.

I tried another court-martial the following week and got another maximum sentence so all was good in the "Hood." General Patton was thrilled as he liked the idea of bad guys getting a ticket to jail. I got a Certificate of Appreciation signed by General George S. Patton and it hangs with some pride on a wall in my remote cabin.

The following year I went back to Hood and put a few more soldiers behind bars and they did not know what to give me so I got a "Certificate of Non-Appreciation." I have reproduced it and it's a total hoot (it is found as Appendix Exhibit No.1). The SJA, Colonel Lewis was a great guy and very bright. The certificate contains phrases and quotes from actual officer efficiency reports (OER's). COL Lewis went on to become SJA at West Point but somehow got caught up in one of the cheating scandals and that cut short his illustrious career.

I still correspond with Logan and he has a successful law practice in Newton, Mississippi. We stopped in and saw his family a few years back and had a great evening telling war stories. He has an annual *soiree* out in the woods and I may just go down to Old Miss and join him for the annual "Tanglefest in Mississippi." It sounds intriguing. Logan still credits me with pulling him out of the doldrums while at Ft. Hood and getting his life back on track. It probably had a lot more to do with Rosalind, the young attractive SP5 that we brought with us. Rosalind pulled a lot of people out of the doldrums.

The Ft. Hood times were all spent when I was recently released from active duty and still a young man (In my 30's). In many respects, being a captain in the Army is the best rank that an officer will have. The captains in the JAG corps still do most of the litigation and 80 percent of the other work load. In the "real" Army the captains run the companies and the company is still the heart and soul of the military. Later on in my career, I was promoted to major and eventually to lieutenant colonel (LTC). When I was an LTC most of my duties in the reserves consisted of supervising junior officers.

I did manage to get out from under the supervisory role on a case involving a full bird (colonel) who had made sexual advances to an enlisted woman. A Board of Officers had been convened to determine if the colonel should be kicked out of the reserves or be retained. The sexy colonel case had elements that may seem like a court-martial, but was not a criminal case. The colonel was from Iowa and had somehow managed to get Colonel Tom Reavely to represent him. I got to know Reavely when we were on reserve duty at Ft. Hood back when we were junior officers. Reavely was a fine officer and all around good guy. He still runs a very successful trial firm in Des Moines. There were not many JAGs in the Army Reserve Command (ARCOM) that could handle Reavely and I got the appointment. COL Frazee was the ARCOM SJA and he proceeded to fill me with fluff about how important this case was to my career and if I wanted to step-up, this was my chance. The truth of the matter was that I had gotten a bad report card (OER) along the way and that ruled out any promotion to full bird (colonel). I could get the Congressional Medal of Honor and still not make 06. I knew I was going to retire as an 05, but I did not want to go out with a loss.

Shortly before the trial, I was at weekend drill and ran into COL Clark Iverson and he asked me, "Do you think you can handle Reavely?" I responded in the affirmative and went on my way. Clark must have had his doubts, or why would he have asked me about it? It sounded to me like Iverson and Frazee had been talking. Years later, after we had all retired, I was on a Mediterranean cruise and encountered Reavely and Iverson and their spouses on the same ship. There seemed to be different spouses than the ones I previously recalled, but that was not that unusual in the military or the civilian world and we arranged a shipboard get together. We all showed up without spouses and we spent a couple of enjoyable hours talking over old times.

Actually the sex-craved colonel had two field grades representing him. He had COL Tom Reavely and also LTC Mick Hanson, my former associate at the day job. Mick was acting as co-counsel. How this guy had two field grade officers representing him, I am not sure. Maybe I should have raised some objection, but frankly I did not care if he had a battalion of lawyers. I was going to get him kicked.

When we commenced the proceeding, Hanson and Reavely moved to have my assistant, Tom Armstrong, removed from the proceeding. Tom was also a field grade officer and was simply helping me line up witnesses and move the proceeding along. Tom had a lot of experience, but I was trying the case and on this one, Tom was along for the ride. I pointed out to the board the obvious absurdity of this motion. The sexy colonel had not one, but two senior grade officers representing him and I was the only one representing the military and I needed help to line up witnesses and get my case presented. The President of the Board was the senior officer and he ruled in my favor. If I had lost that motion, then it would have been a long day, because it would have warned me that the Board was not seeing things my way at all.

The complaining witness was a young E-5 enlisted woman that had been part of the colonel's staff. She testified that she was cornered by the colonel during a movie and there had been digital penetration, but she denied intercourse. She testified that she was totally scared and intimidated and did not scream. She told her friend that evening and they did report it to the chaplain within 24 hours.

The colonel testified and denied the whole thing. The E-5 held up quite well and said that she was totally intimidated by his rank and authority and also completely stunned. The fact she did not scream and yell was their best defense. In the final analysis, there was no real reason given to explain why the E-5 would make up this story. She had no motivation to concoct this story or at least none was shown. The colonel was kicked. I believe he retired a lieutenant colonel and not a bird colonel as he had planned. I made sure his retirement date was moved up.

Mick Hanson went on to become a Federal Immigration Judge serving in Florida. My daughter, Faye, and her family lived in the Miami area so we made it a point of getting together with Mick and his future second wife when we were in town. We met Mick and Bonnie at their luxury condo overlooking North Miami Beach and had a drink and then went out to eat. Mick was looking good and Bonnie was decked out in a cocktail dress. Phyllis and I looked decent, but not so dressy. When the night was over I mentioned to Phyllis that "Mick and Bonnie were really decked out tonight." As usual Phyllis had picked up on everything and she responded, "That was Mick's way of showing us he is doing well and things are okay. He knows we will give a report to other folks from the JAG Unit and he wants to make sure it is a good one."

The reserves provided training, part-time employment, and a social life. We had a fairly steady diet of parties and social events during my time in the Army Reserve. You got to know your fellow soldiers well and also their wives, husbands, and significant others. When someone got married, you went to the wedding. When a couple split, it was soon common news. We got to know a reservist I will call Martin and his wife, Jody, quite well and liked them both. One evening we saw them at one of the unit parties and for some reason we did not spend too much time talking to them. The following day, Marty was served with divorce papers. He had no idea it was coming. Jody said that "Marty was no fun." I passed that on to Phyllis and followed with "What the hell is Jody talking about. Martin is a barrel of fun."

Phyllis gave me an incredulous look and responded that Marty was a product of a hard-working Scandinavian couple who dedicated themselves to instilling a work ethic in Martin. "They were very successful in that mission, but there is more to life than work and you have to remember that as well." It was a good zinger, but absolutely true. My parents did not provide me with love or affirmations, but did manage to bestow to me the Scandinavian work ethic and a sense of responsibility. To the Scandinavian parent, your self-worth is wrapped up in how hard you work. Martin's idea of a good time was planting a few hundred trees at his tree farm in northern Minnesota. My good time was building a cabin or a three-season porch. As the Scandinavian works, he accomplishes a lot and builds his self-worth, but others in the family may not appreciate it as "fun." Learning to have fun is still a chore for all Scandinavians, but we are "working at it."

I was in the reserves for almost twenty years and most of the time I was with a JAG unit. I did manage to spend three years with the 205th (Sep Lt) Infantry Brigade as the SJA. The commander of the unit was a one-star general. He was relieved of duty for having a relationship with one of the enlisted people in his office. Another woman with whom he had been close blew the whistle on the general. The general had been very firm about enforcing the rules against fraternization when he was dealing with subordinate officers in his command. Once this relationship came to light, justice was also swift and fast in dealing with the general. He was out the door within a matter of hours. A two-star came in from Iowa and pulled the plug. The Army moved as fast on that one as I have ever seen them travel.

One advantage of being with a JAG Unit is that you do associate with smart people and they are people that can read and understand regulations. Occasionally that can work to your benefit.

Our JAG unit managed to get ourselves "capstoned" to the JAG office in Frankfurt, Germany. The capstone concept was that each reserve unit had an active duty unit that you were married to and in the event of mobilization, the reserve unit would be reunited with your capstone unit. The reserve unit would run the store for the capstone unit while they went off to win the war. The regulation provided that the reserve unit should train with their active duty counterpart so that they could actually prepare for mobilization. That was the doctrine prior to the advent of the perpetual war. Annual training was two weeks of training during the year when you were back on active duty. Our reserve headquarters was the 88th U.S. Army Reserve Command (88th ARCOM) and they controlled our purse strings or annual budget. In typical military fashion, they made sure there was plenty of money for headquarters trips and training, but they were parsimonious when parceling money out to downstream units and particularly lawyers. Headquarters was taken aback when we advised them that we expected to have annual training in Frankfurt. Overseas travel was expensive. We not only wanted to train in Germany, but we produced Army policy to back up our position. It was based on either a FORCECOM (Forces Command) or TRADOC directive (Training and Doctrine Command). It did not seem fair when we had a regulation to back up our demands. The initial 88th HQ response was, "We do not have the funds for foreign travel." Our response was, "The regulation does not say anything about if funds permit, or any such limiting clauses, find the money." They grudgingly found the money and I ended up with at least three trips to Germany during my last 3-4 years in the reserves. The regulation made a lot of sense and I never felt like I was "getting over."

    I was the OIC (Officer in Charge) of one of the first trips our unit took to Germany. Jack Elmquist and I were with a group of officers assigned to Frankfurt. The trip was shortly after the wall had come down in 1989 so it was a fascinating time to be in Germany. We had rented a vehicle as it saved government money because we could pile a bunch of us in a car and avoid cabs which were costly. It was exhilarating to drive out in the German countryside and observe old guard posts standing empty and only fragments still remaining from that miserable wall. The eastern zone was decrepit looking and drab after 44 years of oppression, but we were confident it could only improve.

    I could not help but think back to my prior experience in Germany and experiencing the forbidding wall and the divided Germany. I had been to Berlin and traveled beyond the wall and into the eastern zone. Berlin has always been a huge sprawling place and when I was there it was still occupied by the four war powers. The American military operated a train through the eastern zone of Germany and on to Berlin. They continued to operate the train for freight transportation and troop movement because it was solid transportation and if we stopped running it then the Russians would claim that the Americans had abandoned the line. We had some sort of JAG conference scheduled for Berlin and we caught the train in the evening not too far from Frankfurt and very slowly crawled through the eastern zone. We had sleepers provided so I managed to catch a good night's sleep. At one point in the middle of the night, the train stopped for almost an hour and it was boarded by East German soldiers. They made a big deal out of marching up and down the aisles like they owned the train, but they did not bother us as we were all half asleep in any event.

    After the train adventure, we made it to Berlin without an international incident and found our way to the American Hotel. I located some of my friends from Charlottesville and we had a great visit. In those days, if you were in uniform, soldiers could ride the subway and trolleys without charge, so we availed ourselves of that opportunity. We visited the British and French officer's clubs and were welcomed in each venue and served splendid dinners.

The border between the American and the Russian zones was still featuring Checkpoint Charlie. As part of the occupation agreement the American and Russian forces had free and unfettered access to each of the respective zones. The Army encouraged us to go back and forth across the border and through Checkpoint Charlie, but we made sure to do it in class A uniform.

I made sure my uniform was in peerless condition and unaccompanied by any of my associates I made my way through the checkpoint and into East Berlin. I was on communist soil. The Brandenburg Gate was in the eastern zone and I made my way in that direction. I could not help but notice all of the bombed out buildings. This was a rare sight in the western zone of Berlin. I found the famous gate and took my time walking around the massive structure. I was glad we had not blown this thing sky high along with the rest of the city. As I was completing my tour of the gate, I approached a Russian Army Officer and I popped up a salute and he responded with a crisp return. Maybe the cold war was thawing?

As a drilling reservist, in addition to the two-week annual training, we had one weekend drill a month and that was at home station (Fort Snelling, MN). As I got more rank, I found myself chasing out to the base two or three times a month to pick up materials for the next drill or do some administrative function. One did not get paid for extra time spent on government business, but I looked upon it as a necessary part of the job. If you could keep up with that schedule as well as doing your course requirements, you were on track to qualify for a reserve retirement at age 60. Most of the people get washed out for not completing their course requirements. I recall sitting around Phyllis' swimming pool one weekend and working on finishing the Advanced Course.

As I write this portion, I have been retired from the reserves for twenty years. I miss seeing the guys on a regular schedule. It is nice to get the retirement check and I feel I earned it. The West Point cadets have a saying that the cadet gets a $100,000 education, however they do pound it up your ass a quarter at a time. I do not feel like the sore-assed cadet, but I do believe I earned what I received. I did everything a full-time JAG would do at a fraction of the cost. When I got off active duty, I had over three years of service and I had discovered that I liked the Army. I probably would have stayed in, with or without the retirement, but do not tell anyone about that secret.

I am no longer drilling, but we do maintain some contact via email and several of us attend the monthly session of the World War II History Round Table held at Ft. Snelling. The History Round Table was started over twenty years ago by a fellow reservist named Don Patton. If I have a hobby, it would have to be military history.

One night, about four years ago, after the Round Table, we were at the officer's club (I still belong but it recently closed) and five of us were sitting at a table and having an adult beverage and I asked the table who was in favor of the current War in Afghanistan. We all concluded it was a waste of money and more important, a lot of good troops were getting gut shot for nothing. This group cut across all party lines. The war was bleeding us financially and through loss of personnel. We continued to regularly take between 100-150 casualties per week. The 92 billion we spend on an Afghan "Pentagon" will not win any wars for the Afghan government and will either get blown up or end up in Taliban hands (Army Times June-July 2012 issues). Currently we are diving back into Iraq and have engagements pending in Syria and Lebanon. Reserves and guard members will have to be activated for these continuing wars as the active component is too small to manage such a wide front.

The Fort Snelling Officer's Club met its demise over three years ago. It was a great place and I usually used it for important events such as birthdays and retirements. It had a great history. One evening I was at the club with Cameron and he was probably age 12 and he soon struck up a conversation with a woman who had been at the club in 1937 for a special party. She was escorted to the party by her late husband who had recently been commissioned through the ROTC program. She said the active component seemed to approach the reserve officers with some distain, but that changed rather quickly as we approached a war time footing. The Army greatly expanded their pool of reserve officers as it correctly read the war clouds. She described a beautiful pool in the back of the club and a rolling 18-hole golf course located on what was now MN Highway 5. Horse barns were not far away and many of the officers rode and some played polo. It was no wonder that Ft. Snelling was known as the Country Club of the Army. The officer's club was the last vestige of that era to go.

The difficulty with the local officer's club was clearly illustrated a few years ago when I visited Ft. Riley, Kansas. Ft. Riley is a large post and the home of the infamous 1st infantry division (The Big Red One). My nephew, Erik Dean, was attending graduate school at Kansas State in Manhattan, Kansas and I drove down for a visit. We saw the Wildcat basketball team play Oklahoma on Friday evening and the following day visited Dwight Eisenhower's boyhood home in Abilene, Kansas. Ike's museum or library contains a lot of information and memorabilia from his presidency, but it is his boyhood home that is the highlight. It is his actual home and was moved on site and restored and furnished to reflect how it existed near the turn of the century when Ike, his brothers, and parents resided there. It is a modest two story frame home. Ike's father was a custodian at the local school so the family was of limited means. Ike was not the most brilliant president we ever had, but he had great common sense and a good sense of history. His common sense kept us out of Vietnam when the French asked us to come in and bail them out at *Dien*

Bein Phof. Ike had the good sense to realize that we did not want any part of a land war in Asia. The sheer numbers of foreign troops would eventually wear us down and out.

When Ike ran for President, he promised the American people that he would go to Korea and visit the fighting zone and if at all possible, end the war in Korea. Ike was true to his word and shortly after his election he went to Korea and in the process managed to get word to the North Koreans of his terms. I do not know this, but I strongly suspect his message to the Chinese and their agents, the North Koreans, was, "Either stop this war or we are going to nuke you back into the Stone Age." The message was received.

Erik and I left Abilene and Ike's boyhood home and moved on to Ft. Riley. Erik had joined the Kansas Army National Guard when he got to Manhattan so he knew his way around Riley. Erik had previously been in the Minnesota Guard so it was easy to transfer to the Kansas Guard and he did not miss a drill. At Riley we encountered a small military museum. It was a fascinating museum, but the most incredible part of this small edifice was that it housed two original Remington's. One was a small painting and the other a sculpture. As we left the museum I pointed to a small hasp and a master lock as the museum security system. I asked Erik how long it would take us to break that lock. Erik said, "Maybe a couple minutes if we do not hurry." We left the museum and it was getting close to dinner time so I suggested we go to the officer's club for some food and libation. It took us some time to find the place and we found an MP who gave us directions, but then added, "It is closed." "What do you mean, closed?" we asked. "It is shut down and they may try and re-open the place, but for now it is closed." I went by the club and sure enough there was no sign of life. The current version of the military officer spends their Friday evenings reading FM's (field manuals) or jogging and if they want a drink, they do not want to take a chance and have it on post. They may get pulled over for a spot check at the gate and if that happens after a trip to the club, there may be a problem.

For a long time, I had wished to take Phyllis and Cameron to Grafenwohr and show them my old post. During the summer of 2012 we got the chance. Prior to going to Germany, I contacted the military guest house at Graf and priced out a room to accommodate the three of us. I was shocked to get a quote of $155 per night for a small suite with two beds. I was not interested and tried to call the guest house at Vilseck, but never got an answer or a reply to my messages. Things were still asleep at Vilseck, almost forty years after I left.

We located a picturesque German guest house in a small German town called Kaimling, located 12-14 kilometers from Weiden. I had thought the Gasthof am Sonnenhang was in Vohenstrasse, but when I stopped and asked for directions in my halting German, I was directed to Kaimling, some 13 kilometers down the road. I was somewhat surprised that I could still conduct basic communications in German.

We reached Kaimling and soon realized it was a little "one horse town" but quaint and charming like the many small towns I had visited decades earlier. We soon found the Gasthof am Sonnenhang and I went into the office and greeted Maria in German and she responded in perfect English. I announced that I preferred to speak German while at the hotel, but she politely countered that "I will speak English." Maria was an attractive German woman in her late 20's and she and her husband Jon were running the place. Her father-in-law still owned the house and did most of the cooking. Maria showed us to our room and it was a lovely room with sky-windows and a large window looking out on a pasture complete with baying sheep. Phyllis and Cameron were even impressed.

That evening we went downstairs for dinner and dined out on a lovely patio. Maria was our waitress and she had her usual smile and good cheer and English. I ordered a schnitzel and it was incredible and under ten euros. The house wine was delightful and the beer on draft was hard to beat.

We took a short walk and returned to the Gasthof after dark and went to bed early. They offered no air conditioning, but a nice breeze was even better. We had a fabulous *fruhstuck* the following morning and went on to Weiden. Weiden still has the old wall around the *stadt mitte* (old town) and the old *rathouse* (City Hall) is beautiful. The *rathouse* was converted into shops and eating places and is no longer used for governmental affairs. A new *rathouse* stands toward the outskirts of town and is devoid of personality and charm but functions well as the modern faceless voice of local government.

We moved on to Graf and I drove up to the old entrance near the colonel's house and the officer's club and were turned around and dispatched down by the old rail yard and advised that the entrance was down that way. I reached the new destination and drove to the gate and presented my ID card to the guard and I was asked for my "travel papers or documents." I told him, "I used to be stationed here and I wanted to show my wife and son the place." For some reason the guard waived me through. The first thing that struck me was how much bigger the post housing area had become. Forty years earlier, many of the married soldiers lived off post or "on the economy" but I could see that many of those folks had been brought back on the reservation. Graf had 2-3 times as many troops as when I had been stationed there. The Army had closed down many of the old posts and kasernes in Europe and had consolidated in four major posts. Graf was obviously one of the few survivors. The number of grunts in Europe had declined to around 40,000 from over 200,000 back when I was fighting the Russians. The Russian Bear had been neutered and the pressure of America fighting the perpetual Mid-East Wars had compelled a reduction in force in US Army Europe. It was a change that was long over-due. It was about time that the Europeans started to pay their own way. WWII ended over seventy years ago.

The officer's club was closed for the 4th of July holiday, although this was the 5th. The club was totally changed from as I remember it. The bar area used to be huge with a large dance floor. The dance floor was smaller and had been chopped up into a couple smaller rooms. The old bar had been dark and expansive and always reminded me of an Iron Range bar in northern Minnesota. In keeping with the range tradition, some of the older officers liked a "beer and a bump." A whiskey with a beer chaser.

The tennis court outside the club had been replaced by a day care center. As I moved on to the post I noticed that the golf course was also MIA. It had fallen victim to post expansion and a shift in Army values away from what some deemed a time wasting game. I played my last round of golf at Graf and gave up the game. I sided with the Army on that one.

The modern Grafenwohr featured a huge Post Exchange that was close in size to a Target Greatland back in the world. The old library was where I usually read the Wall Street Journal during my time in Graf. The building was still there but housed some kind of post communications center. They put out a weekly publication featuring what the Army was doing at Graf as well as community activities both on and off post. They also put out a monthly or quarterly publication covering much of the same ground. There was obviously lots of money spent on keeping the troops informed, but whether or not the average GI was reading all of that information is another question. In the near future, I suspect much of the information will go out to the troops via smart phone. When I was in the Dark Age Army, reading skills among the soldiers were hit and miss. At Graf, we soon noticed a huge comic book section found in the PX. My kids were in heaven and assumed the section was for the local kids, but soon discovered that the GI's were the biggest customers of the comics.

I tried to get back on the post at Vilseck, but did run into a tougher guard. He did tell me that I could get on post and get a pass and come back and get Phyllis and Cameron, but it was late in the day and I wanted to show them Amberg. Amberg is an old walled city and features the Vils River running through town. The bridges over the Vils showcased flower boxes as did most of the house windows and it was picture perfect. We found out about a German festival up on the hill so we somehow found the correct bus and took it to the beer festival. The two breweries in Amberg had competing beer tents right next door to each other and we choose the one with an open table. Cameron was old enough to drink in Germany so he and I enjoyed a liter of beer in a large clay mug. I did not know whether or not this was some sort of promotional mug or not, but I did clarify that they wanted the mugs back. This would pose a challenge. We had not eaten for an hour or so and consequently we dispatched Phyllis to get us some food. I wanted a *brat mit kraut*. Phyllis was gone a long time. She finally returned with two skinny brats and a bun for me. In typical

German fashion, she bought the brat in one location and then to get a bun, she had to go to another vendor and stand in line once again and buy a bun. The Germans have never heard of a hot dog or an efficiency expert.

The Americans used to have a post in Amberg called Pond Barracks. We had an armored battalion that was part of the 1st AD at Pond Barracks. We did go by the old post and it had been converted into civilian housing and it was hard to tell the military had ever been near the place. We had a great time at the beer fest, but I did want to get going before dark. We decided to play the part of the Ugly American, so Phyllis put a beer mug in her purse and we did bring it back as a souvenir. I would have paid for it if the payment plan was available, but that did not seem to be an option. When I was in Germany, if you liked a glass or mug you could usually buy one. I still have a couple of beer mugs from Graf that I somehow grabbed. I think I paid for them, but maybe not.

We got back to the Gasthof Sonnenhang just as it was getting dark. Naturally, Cameron was already hungry again and despite the fact that the kitchen was probably closed, Maria prevailed on her father-in-law to cook us another delightful meal. Phyllis and I shared something light as we usually do at late meal times. We are trying to eat less as our metabolism slows to a crawl.

I topped the evening off with a cognac and a walk and rare cigar before bedtime. Cameron accompanied me as we walked down the hill and headed down the main street. We walked by a house with the barn attached and chickens in the yard and I pointed that out to Cameron. This is the quiet rural Germany that I remember. I told Cameron that I was glad he got to experience a little portion of the Germany that I had experienced so many years ago. It was hard for Cameron to imagine that years before I had lived in Germany with another woman and his half brothers and sister.

The next morning, we awoke to the tune of the lambs braying in the pasture right out our window. We had a wonderful breakfast. In typical German fashion, they had our table assigned with our name tag. In typical American fashion, I ignored the sign post and sat where I felt like sitting (we were late, everyone had eaten). The House *Fater* cooked us breakfast to order and that was on top of a wonderful table of breads, cereals, and fresh fruit. Coffee was almost as good as at Caribou. I wanted to do something for Maria when we left, so I left her a John Sandford novel. I finished it on the trip so I thought she might enjoy reading it. He is a Minnesota author and I wanted to make some connection with my home state. My book was still a long way from fruition. Maria and Jon had been to the States, but their experience coincided with the typical German trip. They saw New York, Miami, and San Francisco. That is the States for most Europeans.

On the way to Berlin we stopped at Bayreuth. This is a beautiful place and I wanted to make sure that we saw the opera house and also the Ermitage. The opera house or *festspielhaus* was a work barely in progress when I was there forty years earlier, but at this point it had been restored and they did a splendid job. The tour guide told us that Wagner never did like the place, although I thought he had a major role in its construction. I was not on that job so we will have to rely on the guide.

Princess Wilhelmine was Frederick the Great's sister and she constructed the opera House. The *schloss*, or castle, and a lovely outdoor park called the Ermitage are located a few miles outside the Bayreuth city limits. The castle was constructed by Fredrick Margrave and presented to his wife, Wilhelmine, as a gift. He must have forgotten their anniversary or something more serious. She must have been quite the babe. I had previously been to the Ermitage, but it is such a beautiful place that one wants to go back. When you come into the Ermitage you walk down a long tree covered walk way. I saw a couple unaccompanied small children running about and thought to myself, one seldom sees that in the States. It was common when I grew up as it was not necessary for parents to supervise their children 24 hours a day. If someone spotted me doing something I should not be doing, then they normally would speak up and make an on the spot correction. My parents would not consider that intrusive or unnecessary because if they found out about it, they would reprimand me a second time. It was the same way if I acted up in school, as the teacher was always right.

We did sign up for a tour of the Ermitage and caught the last one of the day. They took us through a grotto or old time bath. I was fascinated with the water pressure generated by a fountain because there was no pump and they followed the original plan. It was all powered by pressure and gravity. The original builders used wooden pipes and kept forcing the water through smaller openings and the ensuing pressure powered by a gravity fall created amazing strength.

The outdoor fountain features beautiful sculptures and incorporates the same methods used in the grotto to generate water pressure to highlight the wonderful sculptures. We found a table at a restaurant adjacent to the fountain and contemplated whether we had time to watch the show. I asked the waitress, "Was hour ist de wasser programe?" She responded "achtzen hour." At first I thought that was 8 o'clock but then I remembered my military time and realized it was 6 o'clock and that was right around the corner. We stayed for a few minutes and watched a beautiful water floor show.

Our little troop moved out smartly and headed to our ultimate destination, the great city of Berlin. Phyllis was still a commissioner and we were accompanied by a number of politicians. The main purpose of the trip was to check out German progress in energy efficiency. Most of the invited guests brought spouses along and they were able to attend most of the events on a space available basis. Spouses were sur charged for any expenses.

One of the guests on the trip was Kim Reynolds, the Lieutenant Governor of Iowa. Kim was most pleasant and very bright. She and her husband were accompanied by an Iowa State Patrolman who also brought his spouse. The patrolman's job was to provide security for the LT Governor. He was armed and ready for the task. Years earlier, back in 1989 he had been a young MP with duty station at Checkpoint Charlie. The Army put some of their best troops in Berlin as it has always been a friction point. The young MP received a phone call from one of his buddies telling him, "You have to come down here, you will not believe it." He moved out quickly in the direction of his duty station and when he arrived people were streaming back and forth. His MP friends told him that there was a large crowd that formed on the eastern side and they moved en-masse toward the west and the East German guards did not shoot or resist, but lowered their weapons and the gate was breached and freedom won. The wall went down without a shot being fired which was no small miracle.

 As I get further and further away from an active connection with the military, my knowledge of the current events and the latest point of emphasis may fade. I have never fired the M-4 but was very familiar with its predecessor the M-16. Weapons and equipment may change, but the basic structure and the strengths and weaknesses of the Army endure. I probably have a much greater sense of what the military cannot do as a result of my service. Sometimes it is better to know your limitations as opposed to your strengths. I gained much more from my service than I contributed. I am grateful for the experience.

Chapter 5
Getaway

My getaway or hiding place has always been the Gunflint Trail in northeast Minnesota. The Gunflint Trail starts in Grand Marais on the shores of Lake Superior and extends in a northerly direction some 44 miles to almost touch the Canadian border. I first went up there with my boyhood chum, Bruce Johnson, when I was 14. Bruce and I camped out on an Island located on Lost or Forlorn Lake. Bruce's father, Milton Johnson, had some connections with the local game wardens and they let him use the game warden's cabin located near the end of the Gunflint Trail. At the time of my first visit the Gunflint Trail was little more than a trail. It consisted of a gravel road and was hill and dale all the way. Bruce frequently got car sick. He would get out of the car and jog along the trail for a short time and that would alleviate his symptoms. The game warden's cabin was a necessity given the state of the Gunflint Trail as it could easily take the better part of a day to travel to the end of the trail and back to Grand Marais. That did not allow much of any time for game and fish enforcement or keeping an eye on Mother Nature. Milt made some cabinets for the kitchen and contributed some other comforts of home so that all who used the cabin made out fine. Milt most likely had a hiding place for a bottle of sour mash and the wardens were able to sleuth that one out without a great deal of effort. Milt had a fall-back position which meant a super safe position for the second bottle.

On one of my first trips to the Gunflint, I met one of the local game wardens named Earl Nelms. Earl had served in the Marines and had fought at Iwo Jima. He was wounded at Iwo and was full of shrapnel. He periodically would go back to the VA and have more shrapnel removed as it continued to work its way to the surface as the body naturally rejected this foreign substance named after the French lieutenant.

Bruce and Earl got along well and they took a canoe trip together and Bruce even got to accompany Earl on some of his patrol duties. One evening, they were near a lake or river and looking for fishermen who may be jumping the gun on the season. Fishing season opened at midnight of the opening day. It did not open at 10 or 11:00 p.m. on the evening before. Bruce heard one of the fishers ask, "What time is it?" The reply came back, "I don't know, ask the game warden." Little did they know, the game warden would later provide them the time and a citation for illegal fishing.

Bruce was with Earl on another occasion when Earl was checking on a hunter or fisherman and the guy took a swing at Earl. Earl reacted like a coiled spring. That guy was flat on his back in a millisecond. Bruce said, "I never saw a guy move that fast." Earl had learned a thing or two in the Marine Corps.

When I was a young lawyer, Earl and I used to have some spirited discussions relative to what the game warden could legally accomplish. The warden had the right under state statute to stop or detain a fisher or hunter "in the field." Did that extend to a motor vehicle? If the hunting party still had their guns stacked outside the car and were sitting around, certainly they were in the field. If they were in the car and everything was put away, they likely were no longer "in the field." I had a couple game and fish cases when I was a young lawyer and they usually turned on the constitutionality of the original stop and the subsequent search. The statute gave the apparent authority for a stop, but the constitution still applied and there had to be some lawful basis to get beyond the stop and into a lawful search. It helped if the warden had some independent reason for the stop in the first place and that may be to check a license, but to go beyond that and conduct a search required some further reason or basis. Frequently the warden would ask if he could take a look in the hunter's trunk or bag and if the response was affirmative then there was usually a valid consensual search.

I had gotten a game case tossed on a search issue out in Litchfield and news traveled fast as Earl and the other wardens soon found out about it. The game warden corps was a small fraternity in those days and any adverse decision was treated with urgency. The game wardens got even with me as when I billed the county after the trial for the public defender fee they stiffed me and said it was a private client. That was news to me, but in any event I did not get my county fee of $35.00. That was $35.00 for a bench trial. I even did a memo on the search issue.

Earl ran into a problem on a hunting trip to Canada. His hunting party came out of the woods and they had one too many ducks. This was easy to do with a group of dispersed hunters firing fast and furiously at whatever flies over the blind. Earl claimed one of the birds was a merganser and did not apply to the bag limit. I am not sure what happened up in Canada as far as the legal stuff goes, but when Earl got back to Minnesota, he was soon terminated. I called the governor's office and spoke with a contact that I had in the LeVander administration, but it was to no avail. They were convinced that Earl had to leave. The republicans are always boy scouts. I have talked to many old timers up on the Trail and to this day, they all agree that Earl got railroaded.

Getaway

At that point in time, Earl teamed up with an old friend from the Marine Corps named Chuck Carver. Chuck also had a background in law enforcement and had served as sheriff in Rice County. Earl acquired a small lodge on a remote lake called North Fowl Lake. Earl and Chuck started a hunting and fishing service and flew sportsmen in and out of Fowl Lake on fishing trips. Earl and Chuck also used their backgrounds in law enforcement to start a security service, wherein they monitored cabins and homes located in northeast Minnesota. Arrowhead Security would check on your cabin every month to make sure there was no break-in or disturbance and that everything was in working order. Such a business would thrive today, but fifty plus years ago, crime was not nearly the problem it is today. A rural residence is likely to be busted into in these times.

Earl and Chuck seemed to do fairly well with the lodge business, but I am not sure how many clients they had in the security business. Bruce had an Arrowhead seal tacked up on his cabin for many years, but I don't know how long he paid the bill. Bruce and I had been up to Earl's Lodge at Fowl Lake and even shot some ducks up that way. One evening we were passing a bottle around the table and a local yokel, who was offered a bump, responded, "The only time I say no is if you ask me if I want to quit." That became a famous phrase re-uttered on many a later adventure.

I only met Chuck on one occasion, but I did come away with a favorable impression of the man. One brisk fall day, sometime in October of 1971, Chuck was at North Fowl Lake Lodge and was going back to Grand Marais with Richard Ossana, whom we knew as "Frenchy," the bush pilot. One other rider, a guide named William Bushman was scheduled to be on board. I am sure they were in the same Cessna 185, a float plane that we had seen on our earlier trip to Fowl Lake. They took off from North Fowl with visibility of about a half mile and their destination was Devil Track Lake about five miles north of Grand Marais. It was a short flight; it was only around 30 miles by air. Neither Chuck, Frenchy, nor the other passenger was heard from again. They literally disappeared. Most folks who have never been in the Arrowhead Country, that part of northeastern Minnesota defined by the Canadian border on the north and Lake Superior angling up toward Thunder Bay on the south, would find it hard to believe that an airplane could simply vanish. The fact is that most of the Arrowhead is dense woods. The Boundary Waters Canoe Area alone accounts for close to a million acres of uninhabited property. The Superior National Forest accounts for even more acres as it stretches into Ontario. Except for a dwindling supply of loggers and folks in canoes, most of the area is home to moose, bear, and wolves. It is easy to become permanently lost in that immense country. I heard Milt Johnson and locals speculate that the plane got out over Lake Superior and went down and sank a few hundred feet to the bottom and all were claimed by the Big Gitchee Goomie.

Hovland, Minnesota is a small town on Lake Superior about twenty miles east and up the Big Water from Grand Marais. The Arrowhead Trail moves north out of Hovland. About five miles out of Hovland, the Jackson Lake Road intersects and goes east. Two or three miles up the Jackson Lake Road is a monument placed by the Carver Family that marks the spot where Chuck's plane went down. The plane or what was left of it and debris was found by a survey crew on May 24, 1983. None of the three occupants were located. Why the plane left North Fowl and headed due south or even southeast is not explained. Perhaps the plane was having some mechanical issues and Frenchy thought that maybe he could put it down on the Big Lake? Speculation that they had gone into Lake Superior proved to be wrong. The woods claimed them and kept them in nature's grip. It can be harsh and unforgiving in the Arrowhead.

Shortly after Earl lost his job as game warden, a new warden hit the scene. The "new broom sweeps clean" and the new warden was anxious to disassociate himself with anything connected to Earl. He gave Bruce a deadline to move his stuff out of the cabin and the cabin was sold and moved to a new location. Bruce was running out of time and was going to have to secure a new outpost. We went to the courthouse and looked around for some private land on Forlorn Lake. The Arrowhead is much like Alaska in that there is a shortage of private land. Most of the land is owned by the state or by the feds. We were finally able to locate a parcel across the lake, but with no road access. I told Bruce, "You do not want to mess with something without road access do you?" "Hell yes," was his reply. "No other cabins or neighbors to worry about, it sounds perfect." I was soon recruited to help Bruce get lumber and supplies across the lake. The cabin was built on a hill and that afforded a nice view, but made it tough to transport the lumber and plywood into position. There were no set-backs to worry about so the cabin went on the crest of the hill and all was well.

The property was owned by a courtly and good hearted gentleman from Duluth. He did not want to sell the property, as he did not want to establish a value for the county assessor. He was happy with his tax statement and did not see any reason to double or triple his property taxes. We were able to negotiate a 25-year lease with a renewal clause. It worked out well with old Lloyd for many years, but when his sons took over, things did not go as smoothly. We did eventually get a chance to purchase the property and bought around 120 acres. I ended up with 11 acres with lake frontage on two lakes.

We purchased the property in 1998 and shortly after we bought it, we were beset by the July 4, 1999 storm. The storm came through from the northwest and featured straight line winds of 100 mph. There was not much notice of the storm and it hit with the fury of a tiger. Some of Bruce's friends were at his cabin and cowered in fear under the kitchen table. As the storm developed it was not long until a large birch tree came crashing down on the cabin. It left a gaping hole in the roof. The friends emerged from under the table and exited the cabin to find a tangle of fallen trees and brush. The winds were of tornado force, but were straight line and did not feature the tornado-like twisting. Many towering spruce, birch, and balsam trees went over with a huge thud. Some of the trees were "topped" in that the tree broke off several yards below the top leaving a flat top rather than the typical cone top. Many of these trees would eventually die, leaving the landscape scattered with giant naked logs thrust up into the horizon. Almost twenty years after the blow-down, these dead soldiers still dot the horizon around my cabin. These lone logs projecting into the skyline remind me of the power of Mother Nature.

There are a lot of stories about the July 4 storm. Cary and Vanessa Johnson were camping in the Boundary Waters, and when the storm came up they took shelter under a low hanging cliff and waited things out. They emerged, shaken, but unhurt and proceeded to try and make their way out of the tangled mess. Other people we know were boating on Loon Lake and got off the lake when the storm came up and found shelter in a cabin. The amazing thing about the storm is that no one was killed. Most of the folks who camp in the Boundary Waters have a pretty good sense of the outdoors and determined in a hurry, that this was no simple squall and was nothing to play around with. There were no warning signals or sirens and the radio provided little advance notice of the impending storm. Most folks do not go up into the Gunflint area to listen to the radio, so a radio warning would not have been much help. From my own perspective, it strikes me that we are over-warned on developing weather problems. We have weather alerts, stand-byes, and ultimately warnings. If there is a summer shower in the offing, we get alerts, notices, and all sorts of "sky is falling" assessments. If I took shelter every time there was an alert, I would never get out of my house. Unless they are telling me to take shelter immediately, I pretty well ignore all the dire admonitions. I do what the folks in the Boundary Waters did on July 4th. I watch the sky and the wind and see what the birds are doing. If the birds are headed for shelter in the evergreen trees, you better watch out.

Before the July 4 storm, I was planning to build on a remote lake some distance removed from Forlorn Lake. Desperate Lake is a beautiful small lake surrounded by ledger rock and lofty pines. After the storm hit, most of those tall pines were flat on the ground or propped against another damaged pine. Our area was one of the hardest hit and up to 75 percent of the trees were on the ground. Later on, maps were published indicating the damage in the Arrowhead region and the maps confirmed what we could see with our own eyes. To build back on Desperate Lake would require days of effort to cut a trail back through the woods and clear out an area big enough to build on. Moreover, it involved a huge portage to get building materials and supplies back to that remote lake and that seemed like just too big a task. I had a decent lot on Forlorn Lake and

Getaway

it made more sense to build on Forlorn Lake or just forgo it. This would be my fourth and last cabin.

The good folks at Cook County had designated Forlorn Lake as an environmentally sensitive lake and put the building set-backs at 150 feet from the high water mark. This was a complicating factor as it eliminated nice building sites 75 feet back or so and required you to get far enough back from the water so that you could barely see it. I am not sure why Forlorn or Desperate Lake was any more environmentally sensitive than most other lakes in the area and why having your cabin out of sight or hearing range helped the environment. I guess I am as environmentally sensitive as most people, but if environmental requirements do not accord with common sense, then they need to be re-examined. The Politicians love to claim that conservatives are in favor of "dirty water, dirty air." I have never met anyone, who is sane, who favors dirty water and dirty air. Who in the world could support such a ridiculous cause? It was the Nixon Administration who passed the Clean Air and Water Act.

Bruce helped me locate a building site on Forlorn Lake and we proceeded to cut a trail back to the site. It took both of us, each working with a chain saw, two days to cut a trail 150 feet back to the construction point and to clear the area. One of us would make the initial cut and then the next cutter would further subdivide the logs so that they could be moved out of the way. Many of the spruce trees were better than three feet in diameter and this required the better part of an hour to cut an entry point through the log and then attempt to roll away the blockade. When we finished this rough trail, then we had to clear the building site. This was again a daunting task as fallen trees were everywhere. We started a fire and burned many of the branches and smaller trees as we cleared out the building site. To this day, my lot is dotted with huge brush piles that I have not been able to burn. Most of the time, one cannot safely burn in the summer time as it is too dry. The winters are a good time to burn, but the temperatures are cold and it is tough getting to the cabin. I have stayed in the cabin when it has been below zero and it has been very comfortable.

Cook County did not have building regulations or code, although they still required a land use permit as a revenue enhancing measure. They also required an outhouse permit and fee and did actually inspect the hole before granting the permit. That was the only thing on-site that was inspected. One dug down about 2-3 feet and banked the dirt on the edges of the hole. When you had about 2-3 feet of dirt piled around the hole, you were at around five feet in depth and good to go. The main thing is that you did not want to be hitting water as the point of the latrine requirement is that they did not want latrine waste finding its way into the ground water. It was a proud moment when I got my privy permit and was allowed to build my latrine on the approved site.

My building site does not have road access so all of the materials had to come across the water. As fate would have it, there was an old abandoned boat parked near the boat launch off the Gunflint Trail and we commandeered this unclaimed asset and filled the abandoned boat with lumber and towed it behind our boat. We also lashed two canoes together and loaded these with lumber and pulled them behind our boat. Most of the wide lumber such as 4' x 8' sheets of plywood had to be hauled on the wider canoes.

I ran into a local kid named Greg Lykins, who was the boyfriend of Sarah, a young woman who we had hired to take care of our son, Cameron. For those who are interested, I had a workers' compensation policy covering Sarah so I hoped it extended to cover Greg as well. I did not pay him a ton, but he did acquire a right to use the cabin and still uses it on a frequent basis. Greg is a big strong kid, but had limited construction experience. I had previously built a cabin or two and a few decks and a couple porches, so I at least knew the basics of building. After serving his apprenticeship under me, Greg is well regarded as a master builder.

Over the winter, I spent several evenings designing my cabin. I knew it could not be very big as every stick in the place had to be floated in and then portaged 150 feet over uneven and rocky turf. I decided on a 16' wide by 20' long structure. To get some extra space, I decided on a loft bedroom on one half of the cabin. In order to build the loft, I used 8 ft. wall studs on the loft end and put in my loft floor and then built a 2 ft. knee wall. The other half of the cabin called for 10 ft. stud walls. I built a beam over the loft by using three 2" x 10" rafters slightly over 10 feet in length and nailed them together in a sandwich. I built a pocket in the outside wall to support one end of the beam and a post with 2" x 4" struts supported the other end. I used 2" x 6" rafters for my roof on the loft side and they rested securely on the beam. On the other side of the cabin I used pre-made trusses with a 7 in 12 pitch. I somehow remembered enough of my high school geometry such that both sides, i.e. the beam side and the truss side matched perfectly and there was no roll to my roof. I covered the roof with tongue and groove 2" x 6"s. It made a very strong roof and also acted as a good insulator. The 2" x 6" roof boards are exposed on the inside of the cabin and make an attractive ceiling. Of even more importance to me, when I got the roof boards nailed down, my inside ceiling was also done.

Sometimes, even with a bad event, there can be a bright side, however dim it may seem. The blow-down left huge spruce and balsam trees scattered about. These logs made ideal posts for anchoring the cabin. Greg and I cut most of them in 3-4 foot lengths and I used them every 3-4 feet apart. They were in abundance so I used them without regard for the price. We located them on a rock if possible, or dug a shallow hole and put a large rock or two in the hole and rolled the post over to the area. If you build anything near the cities, the code requires a 42 inch footing to get below the frost line. It is a giant job to dig anything in Cook County as it is a giant rock pile. I would have had to use power diggers and it would have taken me a week to dig the holes and another week to fill them up with a pre-cast post or with my own cement. It would have been a back-breaking job for Greg and I. I wanted to build my cabin in as simple a fashion as possible, so I did not put in footings, but "let it float." So far after fifteen years it has not shifted an inch. The windows and doors still open and shut every spring without any trouble. Putting in footings was taking out rock and putting in cement so it did not seem to me like a real logical necessity.

I will have to admit that some of the spruce posts have started to rot so last summer we proceeded to replace a few of the dead soldiers. We used cedar or green treat this time. The cabin is still solid and level.

One thing that was somewhat troubling to me was that after the blow-down there was practically no harvesting of all that downed lumber. We tried contacting some loggers on prospects for logging our combined 120 acres, but we could not generate any interest. We did not have road access so the logs would have to be floated out on the lake or taken across the ice in the winter. We would have gladly given the logs away, but even free wood did not have any appeal.

The Boundary Waters Canoe Area was right in the heart of the storm and was strewn with fallen trees. The roads are very limited into the area and motorized devices are not allowed. That meant no skidders, loaders, or trucks to haul out cut up trees. Even more crucial, no chain saws were permitted to cut up the trees in the first place. There were some hearings on the issue and the forest service hemmed and hawed, but did not yield on the motorized ban and consequently millions of board feet of lumber rotted on the ground. In an interesting aside to that development: Hedstrom Lumber has operated a saw mill on the Gunflint Trail for over ninety years and also previously operated a mill at Silver Bay. A few months after the blow-down, Hedstrom announced that they were closing the Silver Bay facility. One of the reasons given was that they were not able to obtain enough logs.

I tend to be a conservative on both a personal and political level. By nature, conservatives are conservationists. We hate to see anything wasted. It bothered me to see good potential lumber just wasted. When I built my cabin, any extra lumber was carefully piled under the cabin for future use and any scrap pieces were set aside for the wood stove. There was no doubt that I would be relying on a wood stove for most of my heat. Greg located a propane range for me and connected it up and this serves us very well for cooking needs, but I certainly did not expect to haul in fuel to keep me warm. It does not make sense when you are sitting in the middle of thousands of board feet of lumber, rotting at your doorstep. I was willing to haul in twenty-pound propane tanks for the range and the gas grill, but that would be the extent of my fuel hauling.

At the end of the first summer, I had the building roughed in and it was closed up. During the second summer I added a 10' x 10' screen porch on the

Getaway

front and built a small deck. Greg and his father came up one day and we put up the floor joist for the porch and put down a sub-floor over the joists. The sub-floor consisted of 1" x 4"s that I obtained from a company in the western metro that offered free lumber in the form of packing crates that one knocked apart and removed the nails and hauled away. I used the wood for sub-flooring for the porch and later for the sauna and covered two of the cabin walls with the stuff. It was nice pine wood and looks great. I was originally just going to use it on the kitchen walls behind the cabinets, but I liked is so much that I used it on the kitchen wall and also on the gable end most of the way up. In the triangle part of the gable end, I put up particle board and painted it red. I probably got the particle board from the free wood place as well. The sheets were of various sizes but I figured that I could use them someplace in the cabin. I had enough to cover the gable end with no problem.

Phyllis and Cameron have not been huge fans of the cabin as it is not the most luxurious of spots. Phyllis does not appreciate the outhouse and the lack of a hair dryer is a problem. I should shop around and find a solar powered hair dryer. My niece visited the cabin during the second year and was somewhat impressed and sent me a solar powered light that I use on a regular basis. I plug it in faithfully every day and in the evening it affords me a dependable light source for reading and for trips to pee off my deck.

Despite her objections, Phyllis did join me to assist with necessary preparations for the arrival of the wood stove. I put down 3/4 inch plywood as a sub-floor throughout the cabin. Where the wood stove was going, I placed a 4' x 4' sheet of durock. I surrounded that with 2"x 2" cedar strips. I mixed up some tile setting mortar and Phyllis and Cameron proceeded to lay down the quarry tile. I selected a small red colored quarry tile that I had used on some other job and I had enough left over to complete my fire base. The tile turned out very nice and the base still looks great and the tiles have held like a rock. More importantly this gave me a solid fire-proof base to accommodate any reasonable choice of wood stove.

I located a small green Jotul stove in the classified section of the Pioneer Press (some folks still used the paper). The Finns knew about wood burning and saunas so I was anxious to see the Jotul. They had been offering this used Jotul at over $800 which was an outrageous sum, but I thought I may as well go and look at it and maybe they would come to their senses and offer it at a reasonable price.

I went to look at the stove on a Saturday morning and it was in nice shape and well-constructed with plenty of steel and cast iron. It was small and the box could not have been over 18 inches deep. The people offering the stove were a gay couple and I had a gay son, so that was no issue. One of them told me that they heated this two story house during the course of a cold Minnesota winter. At that point, the smell of BS was almost overwhelming, but I asked them what they wanted for this heat machine. They replied that they had looked further into the prices of used stoves and would sell it for $275. I offered them somewhat less and they took it and I threw it in the back of my Explorer and was on my way.

The Jotul was not too bad to carry in to the cabin as you could break some of it down. For example, the heat inserts were cast iron and removable. The door also came off. Greg and I managed to get it across the lake and got it hooked up with Class A piping through the roof, and we fired it up and waited for some signs that the cabin was warming. It did gradually warm, but it was a slow and cold journey. Moreover, the small box meant that all of the logs had to be very short and that meant more cutting. It soon became apparent that the Jotul looked good and was cute, but would have to yield to a more serviceable alternative.

David Munt used to rent from me and did various projects for me as the need arose. He was a good painter and a solid plumber. Moreover, he loved garage and estate sales. I told him to be on the look-out for a wood stove. He called me and told me he had located a barrel stove over nordeast that he could buy for $35.00. I told him to "grab it." It was a real gem. It had a long box and a good solid door. The feet were good and on top of the stove they had welded a nice level platform that would hold a kettle for heating water and a coffee or tea pot. Greg and I hauled it in and it was a heavy beast. We got it to the cabin and on the second installation we used 10-inch class A chimney from the stove pipe all the way up to the ceiling and through the roof and extended beyond the roof line. We took a lot of time with the installation, but I was convinced we had done it right and we should not experience any chimney fires. We got the flashing right so there were no leaks. The barrel stove achieved and exceeded all expectations. It had a long box so that it would accommodate a large log. It was the old fashioned radiant heat stove and the big barrel gave off a pile of heat. It used more wood than the new-fangled stoves with the after-burners and such, but the newer fuel-efficient stoves did result in more creosote build-up. More creosote means more danger of chimney fires. The old-fashioned burners actually burned cleaner than the newer airtight models. I was more concerned with safety than fuel efficiency. I had acres of wood that was rotting on the ground so I made up my mind to use it and avoid any worries over a cabin fire. Last summer we ran a wire brush through the chimney and it was practically clean.

The barrel stove worked great, but I soon learned not to over-load it or it would rubble as the fire roared and would give off so much heat, that you were soon opening windows and doors. One day, rather early in the year, I was on a rare trip with Phyllis and Cameron for an overnight at the cabin. We had hauled some cabinets into the cabin. Jon Johnson took them out of his cabin and they seemed decent for mine, on at least, a temporary basis. Jon told me where to find them at his place and we piled them on our boat trailer and headed for the cabin. We got to the landing and as it started to rain, we piled them in the boat and carted them across Forlorn Lake and then up to the cabin. Cameron later described this ordeal as the "worst day of his life." Cameron was probably around 10 or 11 and at that age he was not used to work, but he was fascinated with fires. That evening, Cameron asked to make and tend the fire so I assented as knowing about fires is a necessary life skill. I admonished Cameron to not over-load the stove. Phyllis told him the same thing. Shortly thereafter we headed for bed up in the loft bedroom. Phyllis and I normally like things cool, particularly during the evening. Phyllis always runs hotter than most people. The stove was rumbling and the hot air was collecting in the loft. Phyllis screamed at Cameron, but it was to no avail as we were stuck in the steam room. Cameron has always been inclined to do what he feels he should do. At that time, we only had a sky window in the loft so it was hard to quickly cool the place down.

The Jotul did not end up on the scrap heap as my nephew Erik came up with me to the cabin and we built a nice 8' x 8' sauna during one weekend and the Jotul has worked out well to heat a small sauna. The sauna serves as the bath house and heats up nicely and some hot water and soap gets one as clean as you could expect in the finest bath.

Erik is a single guy and operates a farm operation in western Minnesota. Erik is a shrewd businessman and operates the family farm, but most of his farming has been done on rented land. Farm land has enjoyed a terrific escalation in prices and so far has avoided the real estate depression that attacked the urban neighborhoods. The commodity markets have steadily risen propelled by dry summers, green fuel, and currency weakness. A rising commodity market has kept a floor under land prices. Even with good prices, Erik realized that it was hard to commit capital and service debt to cover land prices at close to $4,000 an acre. Erik has been doing well by renting. As I edit this work it is fair to note that commodity prices have come back down to earth and farmland prices may have softened a bit, but still remain at very high levels.

Erik was in the Minnesota National Guard for over twelve years and made staff sergeant. He was in the unit when the "Red Bull" was dispatched for thirteen months to Iraq. His unit was an artillery unit, but was re-trained to pull security. The Army soon learned that they could not send reservists or guards directly over to the area of operations (AO) without some sort of training or preparation. The experience level in the guard and reserve is just so diverse and varied that the high command could not assume that they could be sent directly to the AO and know what to do. In my experience, I met a lot of combat vets who served in the reserves, but that was not the norm. Erik trained in the States for five weeks before being sent to Kuwait and on to Bagdad.

Erik was a squad leader and his mission was to provide security to the captain who acted as liaison between the American military and the Iraqi police. Erik's mission carried him "outside the wire" just about every day. They had to vary their route on a daily basis in an effort to avoid ambush or the dreaded improvised explosive devices (IED). Erik learned a lot about leadership and directions during his tour in Iraq. When he first arrived in Bagdad, his squad had a single meeting before going on their mission. Erik found that confusion reigned with a lot of charges that, "You did not say that or tell me that." Erik solved that by simple repetition. His squad met after they returned from their mission and discussed the current day's operation and what was ahead for tomorrow. They returned in the evening for another planning session for the following day. Finally, on the day of the operation, they met again and reviewed the mission for the last time. Confusion died and soldiers lived. Repetition, one key to learning.

On one mission, soldiers came perilously close to dying. Erik was outside the wire when suddenly the truck ahead of him was hit by an IED. The first priority was to secure their perimeter and avoid any further damage. Obviously when a truck is hit and disabled, the squad or company is a prime target for further attack. Erik did a fast damage assessment and found that three of his buddies had been hurt in the explosion and one was gravely wounded. A second soldier was facing serious wounds and the third was only slightly hurt. All of the wounded soldiers were being feverishly attended to by fellow soldiers and a medic, but at least one of them required serious medical attention or he would likely perish. A life or death decision had to be made and made now. Do they call for a medivac and hope that a helicopter could make it to the area with no problem and land in a possible hot zone and return safely to the base, or do they drive like hell with the trucks and barrel back inside the wire as fast as possible? Erik and his squad elected to put pedal to metal and barrel ass back to post. This proved to be the right decision as all three of the wounded soldiers are still alive.

The most seriously wounded soldier was eventually sent back to the States or Germany and did not return to duty. The less seriously wounded soldier was laid up for a time but eventually returned to duty. The third or slightly wounded soldier returned to duty after a few days of rest. Erik is too modest to admit it, but he is probably responsible for saving that one soldier's life. I am sure that Erik would be the first to deny he was a hero, but he usually makes good decisions and he made another good one in this case.

Erik was pretty happy in that they went over with a battalion size group and they all came back. Before they left, they trained in a guard group from South Dakota who were taking their place. Shortly after Erik left, he learned that the Dakotans came under some serious fire and lost a couple men. Erik is still troubled by this tragedy as he wonders if there was something he should have told them or was there a lesson learned that he should have imparted. I am sure he told them everything he could; sometimes bad things happen even with the best of training.

Erik and I had a good time putting up the sauna. Erik is a farm kid so he can do just about anything, be it mechanical or carpentry. On the farm, one cannot always call in a tradesman as there may not be anyone to call, so you learn to do it yourself. I had roughed out a simple plan for the sauna as you need a plan to build any building including an outhouse. We built our framing walls one at a time and then joined them together at the corners. One of the walls called for ten footers so we would have a lean-to sloping type roof. The sauna was 8' by 8' in size and we used 10 ft. 2' x 4's on the roof and this afforded a decent overhang in the front and a small one in the back. We used rolled roofing for the roof so we had our roof shingled in an hour or so. We did use the 1" x 4" pine boards for the sub-floor and left a small gap so the water from the sauna would drain through. We got the walls and roof up and I looked at the sub-floor and said to Erik "I think we have our final floor installed." Erik looked it over and smiled "It looks like a winner."

We hooked up the Jotul in short order. I had some class A pipe for through the roof and we used black pipe part way up and we were good to go. I had some durock left over from the cabin so we used that to fire proof the wall behind the stove. We put in two non-opening windows so that there was natural light in the sauna. At the end of the second day, we were enjoying a sauna and a beer. It is hard to beat that. In many ways the building trades are more satisfying than the law. One spends a day or two on a project and then enjoys the fruits of their labor. One may spend days or years on a lawsuit and then fail to achieve a satisfactory result. I may spend hours reviewing a case and writing up a decision and often times neither side is happy with the result. For example, I may have awarded the petitioner some money, but they felt it was not enough. The insurance company probably believed I was too generous. One spends a couple days building a sauna and we have something that everyone is happy with for many years. I painted the plywood exterior with some stain so it would shed water until I got around to the siding job. Sometimes temporary fixes work just fine. Later on, I did put wood siding on the exterior walls of the sauna and this made it warmer and also made it look a lot nicer. I used the lumber that was left over from other jobs to side the sauna. I used three different lumbers on the outside of the sauna. It is fun to build cabins because you can do stuff like that. Everything does not have to match. One can be eclectic and enjoy it.

A dependable source of water was an early issue with the cabin. I have a lake full of water but that is 150 feet away and would require a pretty good generator and lots of hose and cords to get it near the cabin. The pump would have to be down by the water and I was hoping to establish a water source near the cabin. I got the idea of sinking a well with a sand point. The idea is to have

Getaway

a one-inch pipe with a point on the end that you sledge drive down and keep attaching sections of pipe as you go down until you eventually hit water. You attach a hand pump above ground and prime it and pump away until your bucket overflows. I knew that the point did not have to go all that far down as there is water all over the place and decent water should not be that deep.

    I went over to Fleet Farm and picked up my pipe and unions as well as a pounding post. I also bought a hand pump. This is pretty close to the same rig that my grandparents had on their rock farm in Willow River, MN. After the war when they got power, grandpa had rigged it up with an electrical motor so that we no longer had to hand pump, but it was the same principle.

    I got ahold of Erik and he was willing to come to the cabin and help me put in the well. Erik was familiar with hand pumps and local wells as his farm site still had the old pump and well located out in the grove behind his house. If you worked at it enough, sometimes you could still produce a trickle of water.

    We got to the boat landing and hauled the pipe across the lake and proceeded to find a location for the well. The books tell you that you should pick a site in a lower part of the property, as obviously there is less distance down to the water source. We moved down a hill away from the cabin and looked for a spot that seemed relatively free of surface rock.

    We were using 8 ft. sections of pipe so that we had to pound pipe from a chair or ladder. We put on our pipe pounder and started in with the 5 lb. maul. Almost immediately we hit rock. Our next thought was to dig a hole and get down below the surface rock and then pound away. We put down a foot or two, but there were rocks everywhere. We again tried the pipe pounder, but all we managed to do was tire ourselves out and damage the pipe. Erik had been through a war and survived, but he said, "I don't think this is going to work." Erik was more dejected than I was. The hole we dug had filled up with water and the water was fairly cold. I suggested it may serve as a beer cooler and all was not lost. Later, we had a cold beer and went fishing.

    I was still determined to get some sort of water source and concluded that rainwater was my next best source. I had a gutter across the front of the cabin and instead of allowing it to empty on the ground, I could divert it to a rain barrel. My home city of Eagan offered rain barrels for sale at a reasonable rate and it was hard plastic with a nice brass shut off toward the bottom of the barrel. The top featured a nice cover that was easily removable. I planned on feeding the water into the kitchen and it was not practical to use a pump, so I had to get my water source above the kitchen sink so that gravity would work for me. I would have to build a platform or stand. I built my platform about 7 feet in the air and attached it to the cabin. Thirty-five gallons is a lot of weight, so I located a native cut post that we did not use inside the cabin and used that to anchor the center and outside of the platform. It was pretty easy to run some downspout from the gutter to the rain barrel. Later on we ran a hose from the

Getaway

rain barrel and through the sidewall and under the sink and tied into a faucet. Presto and we had running water at the cabin. Skeptics thought we may not have any pressure, but there is plenty of pressure in the line. We put a splitter on the rain barrel with one line being the hose to the cabin and the other being a short section of dryer hose that was used to fill buckets for the sauna. It is interesting how sometimes we do not see the obvious. We had the spigot of the rain barrel pointed toward the kitchen and away from the deck and usually if you were filling a bucket you normally had to ascend a step ladder to turn on the faucet and direct the flow. Greg was going to the cabin early and I asked him to hook up the rain barrel for me and he gladly agreed. Greg turned the barrel around so that you could fill a bucket from the deck and no ladder was needed. He stepped back and looked at things anew and we made another improvement to the cabin.

Just to let you know, Greg makes mistakes as much as we do. I asked him to also connect up the hose to the kitchen faucet. I told him there was a faucet in the cabinet under the sink. For some reason, he did not use the single faucet under the sink, but got his hands on a regular kitchen faucet with hot and cold water feeds and a sprayer as well. He messed around with it, but did not get it connected. He told me about it over the phone and when he started to talk about the hot water line, I could not figure out what he was talking about. I asked him where he got the faucet and he replied, "Under the cabin." "I think you grabbed the wrong one," I responded. Also, he said that the hose we planned to use was no good as some animal was cutting his teeth on it when it was stored under the cabin. Greg said he had a hose we could have as well as a splitter. He was planning to bring a splitter, but had forgotten it.

About a week later, we went to the cabin and stopped at Greg's and located the hose and the splitter and moved on to the cabin. The single faucet was under the kitchen sink in plain sight. The other faucet was toast, but it didn't matter as we did not need a sprayer or a hot water line as all we had was rain water. We located the yellow hose with the teeth marks and found that we could cut out the bad part and still have plenty of hose to make our run to the cabin. We cut our hole through the cabin and had a tight fit so the mice could not get in to disturb us. The single faucet fit nicely in the sink and we clamped on the hose and we had running water. We still haul in drinking water as the water is very clear and soft, but you could not trust it for drinking as the roof may not be all that clean and is likely fouled by bird droppings.

When you undertake a building project by yourself it always takes much more time to do the job than originally estimated. I do have a tendency to underestimate what is required to complete a job as there always seem to be unforeseen circumstances. In two or three years, I had managed to rough the cabin in and build the front porch and a serviceable deck and sauna and get started on the inside, but still had piles of work to do.

Getaway

David, the kid across the street, was a young man who experienced some driving difficulties and needed legal representation. I thought he had been improperly charged. I suggested to his father, Paul Dutcher, that I could probably help him out and he could work off the fee by helping me out for a few days at my cabin. This seemed like a favorable arrangement for all concerned and David helped me out with a couple local projects. When we were ready to head north, David was having some health problems so Paul suggested he come along and help out and work off the debt. Paul is a skilled carpenter and his talents were a welcome addition.

The loft area was one of the first areas that needed a professional assessment. The loft floor was supported by three 4" x 4"s each 16 ft. in length that ran the width of the cabin. We cut some native posts to support the 4" x 4"s. I used 2" x 6" tongue and groove for the loft floor. The floor turned out to be a bit too bouncy for that big a span so we had to add a beam to the center of the loft floor. My supplier, David Munt, located a 14 ft. wooden beam that someone had tossed in a dumpster and he fished it out and asked me if I needed it for the cabin. I knew I would likely need a beam someplace up there and eagerly took the beam and prepared to haul it north. It was a weighty matter as it was a 5" x 13" fir beam so it carried a lot of weight. David M. is a big strong guy and it was going to be difficult for me to drag that fir post through the woods. I decided to cut it length wise with a skill saw and ended up with two 14 ft, beams each measuring 5" x 6.5". I used one of the beams to span the middle of the cabin and support the loft floor. Suddenly the loft floor lost its bounce. The beam extended a few feet beyond the loft floor and eventually was used to support my loft stairway. A couple years later, I painted the beam an off-white color and it looks very nice. The other beam was later used to straighten out an uneven portion of the cabin floor. Just about everything finds a use at a wilderness cabin.

One of the first things that Paul addressed was the stairway to the loft. I was using a ladder to get up and down and that was not a good long-range solution. We were able to use the extended loft support beam and anchor the top of the stairs to the beam. The cabin is quite compact so we did not have room for a big expansive and sprawling staircase. The stairs had to be somewhat modified from what was usually found in a full-sized home. We used cedar boards for the steps so it made for an attractive stairway. We went down by the waterfront and found a straight pole that made a fine handrail and located a couple sturdy posts to support the rail. We achieved a safe and very attractive stairway and it fit in with the wilderness motif. It is not easy to lay out a stairway when you have limited space requirements. I previously put one in at a cabin I finished off in Wisconsin, but it took me all day. Paul had the stairway built in a couple hours. He did point out to me that the limited space available required a possible bending of the rules in that the risers were maybe too high and the stairs possibly too narrow. We were operating in close quarters with a small cabin so you had to make allowances to put in something that fit. Had Paul been working on a project that had building inspectors, it may not have passed. I would still be using a ladder. If I fall down the stairs that is my own damn fault and I do not intend to sue anyone.

    I was not sure exactly how I was going to finish off the inside of the cabin but I had been accumulating various types of lumber. Paul had previously given me some cedar 1" x 6"s to "maybe use in the sauna" and I told him at the time that it looked too good for the sauna, it would probably be used inside the cabin. Sure enough, I nailed it vertically in the living room under the big windows. I installed the windows four feet off the floor to give me some sort of view of the water and also to discourage the bears. The big windows in the living room were a gift from a neighbor down the street who was replacing his windows. I hauled them up north before I started the cabin and stuck them in the woods near Bruce's cabin and covered them with plastic. The porch windows were also gratis from an old timer in southwest Minneapolis and I stored those under Bruce's shed until I built the porch and sized the openings to fit my inventory.

    I had some beautiful black walnut sticks that were new, but I bought at the Re-Use Center and Paul and I used that to complete the west wall overlooking the lake. I had piled the wood in the cabin to keep it dry and straight and it was nice to free up the room. We used the 1" x 4"s for trim on the big windows and when we ran short of those, Paul trimmed some of the cedar and it made nice window trim. Later on, we brought up 1" x 6" knotty pine with a groove that they call car siding and used that to complete the main floor.

    On our first trip, we also finished off the loft bedroom with knotty pine. I ran into a guy in south Minneapolis who had re-done his basement or attic and pulled out a bunch of knotty pine. It was all lying in a fairly big pile and a lot of the nails had not been removed. Some of the ends were cracked or worn and had to be trimmed, but most of it was in good shape. In the loft, we turned the boards around and used the flat and unfinished side as the face side. The wood had aged and gotten a bit dark, but had a beautiful grain and made a neat woody den. I had enough pine left that I used it later to finish off two sides of the sauna. On that project, I left the finished, or grooved, side exposed. The grooved side was already varnished so there was no urgency for me to re-stain it. Another advantage of used materials.

    The sauna did finish up very nice as it had the two sides finished with pine and the lakeside was redwood and the fourth side cedar. I really like the mixed woods that I used both inside and outside the cabin. The redwood was another treasure that someone was giving away. A guy out in the western suburbs was refinishing his house and pulling the redwood off. I originally thought it was cedar, but Paul enlightened me. The redwood was painted on one side and did have nails to pull, but the reverse side was clean and the nails came out without any problems. The homeowner was pulling off beautiful redwood and replacing it with plastic or metal and I had a hard time following that line of production, but it was not my decision. We finished the lakeside of the sauna with the raw redwood facing out and it was a nice touch. I tacked a pair of Phyllis' old skis on the redwood and I had the perfect north woods touch. The fourth side of the sauna was completed with cedar boards that I had left over from another job.

One thing that always amazes me is the huge inventory of used or practically new building materials that are available for the taking. The advent of Craigslist has made the inventory much more accessible. Also, just keeping your eyes opened reveals an even larger world just out there for the taking. David M. who located my beam and wood stove also found me a free toilet that I used in a rental. David happened to be going by a project or public housing area in Minneapolis and noticed a large supply of toilets piled outside the building. He stopped to investigate and found that the toilets were only a couple years old and were Kohler's which are probably the best. The existing toilets were energy efficient and used five liters a flush, but they were not efficient enough for some of the green bureau chiefs in Minneapolis so they were replacing all of them with toilets that used less than two liters a time. David thought there were at least 100 toilets being replaced. He asked the foreman, "What are you doing with those toilets?" The reply was not surprising, "Throwing them away." David asked if he could have a couple and the response was affirmative and he carted three of them away in his truck. My toilet was installed in a Minneapolis rental property so the Mill City got some of its own returned. We figured that the city spent at least $1,000 per stool on that project. By the time they pulled the "old" one out and paid to dispose of it and put a new one in, it had to cost at least a grand a poop. I wonder if anyone did the math and figured out what the pay back or return was on that operation. Water is still fairly cheap around here as we are surrounded by it. The new toilets are not full-proof as often they have to be double clutched to dispose of bigger projects.

The toilet "deal" is just one example of free items just waiting for a home. It is not unusual to find buildings that the owners want taken down and if you do it, you can keep the materials. When I was a kid, my old man bought a garage that the highway department wanted moved out of the way for a road and he bid a few bucks for it and I got to wreck it. One of my buddies came along and we proceeded to take the thing apart and most of the lumber was salvageable and the old man used it to build a new garage. I was around 15 at the time that project was done and my friend was 14. I was using an old pickup truck that Dad and I had fixed up and it had a shift on the floor. On the way to the job, I popped the clutch a bit and the universal joint came apart, but my friend, Dan, knew what he was doing and we repaired it on the road and were soon on our way to the job site.

If you know a couple remodeling contractors, those guys are always pulling old stuff out and replacing it with new. If you wanted to help pull things out and haul them away, there is lots of good lumber available. Just last summer we replaced Jon's old cabinets with a set that Paul pulled out of a kitchen he was working on. Cheap cabinets can often be obtained for free from kitchen remodelers, while one may have to pay to obtain better cabinets. The purchase is still a fraction of what you would pay for new materials and the old ones may be better than new.

I think if you wanted to spend a couple years accumulating your inventory, it is possible to acquire enough materials to get a start on a small home. If you do not have suitable storage space, you would have to rent a storage unit so that you had a dry storage spot.

There is a lot of stuff just lying around that you can use. I spotted a huge roll of Tyvek that had apparently fallen off a truck and I stopped and picked it up and later used it to wrap the cabin. The big windows in the cabin were spotted on my way home from court. A large coil of Romex was lying in the road for the taking. I used the wire to connect up a light in my shop. This is a very wealthy country and most folks have not had to salvage and skimp to provide for themselves, so we are just not accustomed to going that route, but there may be a time in the not too distant future when we may be forced to return to those early ways.

I stopped at an estate sale over in the West 7th area of St. Paul and started to look around. They had a lot of stuff in the yard and the garage was stuffed. The garage was a small one stall with a dirt floor. The house itself was a small two-bedroom frame house with tattered siding and in need of new roof. I usually keep a pair of field glasses in my truck just in case I need to look at a roof and do not want to get on a ladder. I like to bird watch and the glasses are also handy for spotting birds and wildlife. This roof was so obviously bad that all I needed was two eyes. The lot was an old 40 ft. wide parcel. I bought ten pounds of nails for a buck together with an old farm tool that I learned was a corn planter. The sale was conducted by an attractive young woman and I soon struck up a conversation with her. Her father had purchased the home in 2006 or 2007, at the height of the housing boom, for $120,000. She said it was worth $60,000 in the current market and I said, "That may be a stretch." She smiled and said her father had to be out next week. I said, "This is more like a foreclosure sale than an estate sale." She countered, "He bought most of this stuff at estate sales so I guess we are re-selling the estate items." The real estate market had gone off the deep end and there were endless stories of folks paying way too much and then having to bail out when the market corrected. All markets correct from excesses, but sometimes it just takes a little longer than folks expect.

I checked the garage again on the way out and found a nice splitting wedge that I picked up for a couple dollars. If you go to sales on the last day and toward afternoon, the prices do tumble from the opening offers. Another customer purchased a nice hatchet for $3.00. I already have two at the cabin that I bought at sales. They are great for chopping kindling wood.

I recently received a rental application from a fellow in his early 40's who had attended classes at a local art school. He worked part-time as a bus driver when he attended school. During his time at the art school, he managed to accumulate over $100,000 in student debt. He was able to do some computer consulting work and told me he made a couple hundred dollars a month doing consulting on a part-time basis. He was still driving a bus and was trying to figure out how to deal with a huge debt load. He was pretty well trapped in huge debt for the balance of his career. Some of the debt is on a variable rate so that when interest rates go up, he is going to be in a grim situation. He will be lucky to service the interest, much less make progress on principal. He lives in his brother's basement and that probably is not going to change. He had tried bankruptcy but found out the hard way that he could not discharge student loans in bankruptcy. Too many kids had gotten that idea and had run up a big tab and then flushed it when they graduated. Congress put an end to that caper.

I had a young person rent from me that had spent a year in college. He had run up between fifteen-twenty thousand in debt, but at least he found out he was wasting his time and reasoned that he did not need to run up a $100,000 bill in order to drink some beer and waste his time. He was behind in his payments, but at least he had a chance of getting out from under his burden.

If I had it to do all over again, I do question whether or not I would bother with college or law school. It has gotten way too expensive and I could not see going into hock for thousands of dollars just to enter an overcrowded field. I think I would gravitate into one of the building trades and it would probably be carpentry. I would go the service route in the first place and use my education benefits to go to a trade school. If I had anything left over, I could give college a whirl, but not as my first choice. For many folks, college is a poor choice. A degree in art appreciation or political indoctrination is nice, but if you cannot make a living with the degree, then I would much rather opt to swing a hammer. I have told Phyllis of this and she gets upset and says, "I never would have married you if you did not have a college background." That would be my loss no doubt. Good looks can only carry you so far.

Paul loves to be in the outdoors and is happiest fishing or just tramping through the woods. He likes to get up at dawn and be on the water at sunrise. This is not my idea of fun, and I usually sleep in each morning until Paul gets off the water. He usually catches some fish and has some fun. I have a 14 ft. elderly Alumacraft scow and a small motor, so it is not fancy, but the seats are comfy and it serves us well.

Paul also likes to have a beer and cigar once in a while, so between fishing, an occasional beer and smoke, the cabin is hard to beat. The next time we were ready to go back to the cabin with David, Paul again volunteered to help out. David was trying to pay down his debt, but was still having some lingering health issues, so Paul again came along to balance out the work load. I think he was also getting hooked on the place. The next time up we installed two windows on the gable end of the loft. I had a sky window in the loft that opened, but it was not sufficient to cool the loft on a hot day or when Cameron decided to build a fire. I concluded that I needed more ventilation and also more light in the loft. I splurged and bought two new Marvin's for the loft.

By the afternoon we were ready to put in the gable windows. Greg and I had put in the other windows and none of them leak so we must have done something right. These windows were different in that we were up in the air and were working off scaffolding rather than on the ground. We cut out two window openings and built two rough openings to accommodate the windows. I worked from inside the cabin and managed to hold the windows from the inside while Paul leveled the windows and secured them in place by nailing in the window flashing.

I had decided to use half log pine siding on the exterior. I used the thick, 2" stuff on the front of the cabin and it was nice, but it was also heavy and I had to haul every stick across the water. I elected to go with the 1" on the two gable ends. On the back of the cabin, I put up a 3/4" plywood with a rough cedar-like face. I threw that on myself and it went on in a short time. I had taken the 1" half logs across the water and Greg and I had started putting them on the cabin, but had only gotten up a few feet. We tacked them on with maze nails as they are galvanized or aluminum nails and have great gripping strength, but were pretty easy to drive and most important would not split the wood. Paul told me about them and advised, "If you bend them, do not try and pull them out, just use your hammer and break them off." That made life easier as it can get hard to pull out bent nails.

Our little crew of three continued with the siding on the gable ends of the cabin. We started out working off ladders and as we got up toward the roof line, we shifted to scaffold. We had ladder jacks and were able to fashion a decent scaffold with the jacks. I was not real comfortable working up in the air and was glad that Paul and David were on hand to do the higher work. I did most of the cutting on the ground and managed to keep the two of them stocked with wood. David and Paul would take the siding and start at each end and slowly pound their way back to the middle of the board.

David quit going to the cabin as health issues persisted that made it difficult for him to function in a wilderness setting. Paul continued with the program. One of the most essential items in any cabin is the deck. I am on my fourth cabin and on each one I have built a deck. A deck provides a place for you to park your grill and cook your food while you look at the lake. Our sauna is built adjacent to the deck so that one can go barefoot out to the sauna and back. The deck also serves as a great spot to take a pee in the middle of the night. I usually get up once at night whether or not I am home or away. It is nice not to have to tromp out to the outhouse when all is dark.

I originally built a 10' x 10' deck along the front of the cabin. I added the 8' x 8' sauna and built that adjacent to the deck. I soon realized that the deck was too small and added 6 ft. going toward the water. I built the 6 ft. along my original deck, but also added 6 ft. on the lake side of the sauna. My deck addition then became 6' x 18' (10 ft. plus 8 ft. for the sauna). A couple of my reserve pals came up with me and we built the addition. They were fairly skilled and it only took us 3-4 hours to build the addition. I cut some native posts and we used those to anchor a railing around the deck. My reserve friends seemed to have a good time at the cabin, but I read things wrong and they did not. It was too tough and too primitive. I found out about it through another Army friend. So much for Army Strong. Actually I have slowly learned that this rough and primitive cabin is not for everyone. I love the place so it was hard for me to believe that others would not share my view, but we are not quite as hardy as we used to be. Modern day campers are looking for golf and tennis and a hot shower at the end of the day. The Army buddies are still my friends; I just do not ask them to return to the cabin.

Decks are never big enough and ours was still on the small side. Greg suggested we extend the deck across the front of the porch. This would entail a 6' x 10' addition. Since Greg came up with the idea to expand the deck, I asked him to cut us up a couple of posts about 4 ft. in length to anchor the new addition. The long side of the deck was anchored to the cabin and the existing deck served as support for the inside short side of the deck.

Greg had cut a couple of birch logs and each was about 24" in diameter so it was a formidable foundation for the deck expansion. We found some large rocks with a flat side so the deck was going to be very stable. Paul and I hauled the materials to the cabin and we used green treat for the supporting structure and we continued with cedar for the decking. I had some 4" x 4" redwood posts that I had acquired along the way and I had hauled them up to the cabin during an earlier run so we fished them out and put them in to serve as the support for a railing. Someone had painted the posts a light blue color, but it was fading away. I could bring my belt sander to the cabin and fire up the generator and buzz off the color, but for some reason, I am content to let the snow and rain take care of the blues.

The new section of deck is nice as it accommodates two comfortable chairs and a decent beer table. We added a lower rail that serves as a foot rest. Later that night, after we had finished the deck, we were sitting out on the new part and enjoying an adult beverage and suddenly an object streaked out of the northern sky. I said to Paul, "Hey did you see that?" "Yes it was a shooting

Getaway   135

star." How often do you see that sitting around your suburban dwelling? I have also been to the cabin when the Northern Lights or the Aurora Borealis are in full bloom. I have come out on the deck at night and been treated to the most awesome sight. Stars on top of stars just sitting out there in the northwestern sky. In the movies or on TV one has seen gold dust poured from a bag and marveled at how it glistens and shines. The Northern Lights are real life gold dust only poured from the hands of Mother Nature. I went in the cabin and made my way up to my loft bedroom and turned on my back and looked up through the sky window and caught the second act of the northern lights before I drifted off to sleep.

    One of the recent additions to the cabin has been the horseshoe pit. I like to pitch a few shoes once in a while and Paul and I have made the horseshoe tournament a part of every trip. We try not to let building cabins and other projects get in the way. We did not have enough flat space to build a regulation, 40-foot course, but we are a bit over 32 feet and that distance seems to serve us well. It is right adjacent to the last edition of the deck so there is a comfortable viewing stand for spectators. So far attendance has been down. Matches have been very close and competitive so I look for attendance to pick up.

    Phyllis and I were on a recent vacation and we played some golf and I enjoyed it after a 42-year hiatus. I got the bright idea to rig up a hole or two at the cabin. The cabin is on rocky ground and full of underbrush. It took us a couple hours to grub out an area for the first green. Paul located a steel rod and we pounded that down a foot or two and encased it with a 6 foot section of white PVC. We had hole number one "green". One of the horseshoe pits is tee number one. I plan on fashioning green number 2 another 40 feet removed from hole number 1 and further down toward the lake. I can use the same tee. I am working toward my own 18 hole course known as Forlorn Hills. I may call it God Forsaken Brush as that sums up my game.

    Winter is a completely different experience at the cabin. The weather is always variable and hard to predict, but in the winter, it is even more difficult as a Canadian front can blow across the border without a lot of warning. Greg has been at the cabin during periods when it reached -30 below and has found that the cabin stays nice and warm. It does take time to warm up the wood inside the cabin, but once that is done, it stays warm for a long time. We insulated the floor and the walls of the cabin so it was built to stay warm. When I framed it we started with the floor joists and we used 2" x 12" each 16 ft. in length. On the bottom inside of the joists, I fastened 1" x 2" wood strips. I then cut 1/4" plywood in panels 14 1/2" wide by 8' lengths or less and secured the panels to the strips with small screws. The insulation then was laid on top of the plywood. This served to make for a warm floor and the floor was also very tight and served to keep out vermin and small animals. The walls were insulated in a regular fashion and the ceiling is open and not covered. The ceiling does consist of 2" x 6" boards (1.5 inches thick). The roof has felt paper and shingles, but even more important, during the winter, the roof is covered by a large blanket of snow. Snow is a great insulator, just ask any bear.

The winter of 2011-2012 was an unusual winter in that it was very warm. We decided it was opportune to take advantage of the warm weather with a trip to the cabin. There is always plenty of snow in the Arrowhead, so lack of snow was not a problem on the Gunflint Trail. My nephew, Erik, has an ATV so he elected to bring it along and use it to run back and forth from the Gunflint Trail to the cabin. I did not think we needed any vehicles, but I had no objection if Erik wanted to bring it along. My two grandchildren, then from Florida, Matt and Bill made the plane trip from Florida to join our excursion. We checked out the local Goodwill store and found a nice coat and pair of ski pants for Bill. I have many winter coats as well as ski pants so it was no problem finding gear for Matt. My oldest son Kyle filled out our little squad.

Matt and Bill seem to have developed an interest in the outdoors as they have been going on canoe trips in the Gunflint for the last few years. They had been going out of Camp Menogyn on Hungry Jack Lake. My son, Lars, and his kids play hockey and lacrosse so that does not leave a lot of time for canoe trips. Evan did get in one trip to Menogyn and was on one of our trips to Lake of the Woods, so he has drifted away from the team sports and more to outdoor pursuits.

We rode up in Erik's truck and parked at the boat landing and unloaded the ATV and took it out on the bay for a trial. The lake was blanketed by a foot of slush and snow so it made for a sloppy ride. Erik quickly realized that the ATV was not going to be of any use on this trip and we reloaded it on the truck. We moved down the trail and parked in an area that was closer to the cabin via foot travel. We had a couple plastic sleds so we put on back packs and filled up the sleds and started across the water. The cabin was less than a mile from the parking area, but walking in slush and snow made for a tiring trip. We instinctively spread out as we traveled across the frozen lake so there was no need for me to spread us out. I carried a section of rope in case there was a problem.

We were not able to get everything in one trip so Bill and Matt "volunteered" to go back and pick up the final items. We got a fire going and it did take about two hours to warm the cabin, but once it was warm, it stayed comfy during the rest of the trip. Matt slept out on the unheated porch and claimed to have a comfortable night. He spent the night in my Army sleeping bag and that thing is rated to -20 below and it was not close to that so I believe he did have a comfortable night. Those of us in the cabin were fine. I got up to take my nightly whiz and threw a log in the barrel stove so we stayed warm.

The following day, Erik was up early and had coffee ready and cakes on the grill. The propane range works without an equal. Following breakfast and necessary cleanup, we grabbed my ice auger and some fishing line and headed down to the water. Although the air temperature was in the 40's, we discovered that there was still 18" of ice. The snow on top of the ice served to insulate the ice. Once the snow was finally gone, then the ice would melt in a matter of days.

Cutting holes in the ice by hand is slow work and good for the arm strength. Our forebearers did so much work by hand, that it is no wonder they had strong arms. Wood was cut with a hand saw as was ice to keep the ice box cold during hot summer days. Nowadays, one goes to my cabin or a health club if you wish to maintain a degree of power.

It took about a half hour to sink a hole and that was with a rotating schedule of auger turners. It is very hard work and it was not long before we had shed our coats and were out on the ice in either a sweatshirt or even short sleeves. One of us brought a football down to the lakefront and we had some touch football on slushy ice. We had the first annual Slush Bowl.

We have a lot of deadwood everywhere on my property so we harvested some nice dry wood and built a fire on the ice. Football and fires, what a day. We filled our water buckets toward late afternoon and hauled some water back to the cabin.

It is gratifying to see Matt and Bill develop an interest in the outdoors and the cabin. Matt is not interested in team or organized sports and prefers outdoor activities such as canoeing or climbing. Bill likes to play lacrosse, but also appreciates the outdoors and went on his first canoe trip out of Camp Manogyn a few summers back at the age of 12.

Many of the modern day kids are losing interest in the outdoors. The DNR reports that hunting and fishing license revenue has been on the decline for the past several years. The older sportsmen have been dying off and the kids are not following suit. The emergence of women in the blinds and boats has helped to stem the tide. My Son, Lars, is a terrific father and coaches his boys in hockey, football, and baseball. Hockey has emerged as a year around pursuit and it does not allow much extra time for fishing or hunting. Some kids are so occupied with video games and social media that they would not dare venture away from the cell phone service area.

My cabin is definitely a "throwback" in that it is not modern and reminds me of the rough cabins that folks would enjoy when I was young. That has all changed as the modern cabin is fully modern and "wired" for whatever gadget or device one could use. What most folks have done is move Edina or Eagan north and seek to enjoy the same weekend in the north that they could experience at home in Eagan. My cabin provides a stark contrast to my home in Eagan. It is not modern, but it is a true change of pace and a getaway and that is what I cherish. I find that as soon as I get close to the cabin my every day cares and concerns seem to slip away.

The Gunflint Trail continues to yield a never ending supply of stories and lore. Recently I encountered Ryan, a long time hunter and area guide. He knew exactly where my cabin is located and had canoed past it. He related that as a youth he spent a lot of time in the spring netting suckers. I knew they were present in some of the local lakes because I had seen them. He would net the rough fish by the barrel full and gave them to the Sucker Creek Resort, usually in exchange for a case of beer. They went in the Sucker Creek freezer only to be sold later as walleye sandwiches. They were deep fried and no one ever knew the difference. The profit margins on that menu *entree* were very good. I was very familiar with the Sucker Creek Resort as Bruce and I had been in the bar and BS'd with the owner. I never had the "walleye" sandwich, but it looked good.

Chapter 6
Family Times

In any chronicle, the family background has to enter into the story. This could probably merit a book in its own right, but I choose not to go in that direction. I had a brother, Craig, who was nine years older than me and a sister, Gail, who was over six years younger. I never did like the idea of a family so spaced out in age and swore I would never make that mistake, and with one exception I did keep that promise. I called this chapter family times and not family fun as growing up there was not much in the way of fun. My father was scrambling to make a living and we had pretty much a paycheck to paycheck living. He did work hard, but was usually preoccupied with a project. When he did interact with me he was usually negative and frequently mean. We lived in a basement for nine years and finally finished the upstairs and the old man then sold the house as soon as it was completed. We lived in a one room basement for nine years and then never enjoyed the product of much suffering and hard work. During our time in the pit, we never took a vacation and much of my free time was dominated by jobs and building the upstairs. I grew up poor and that is why I do still have a propensity to watch the bucks. I do not want to end up back in the basement.

We lived on Lake Josephine in rural Ramsey County, and the water was essential for us during the first 2-3 years. We had no running water and used the lake water for bathing and toilet use. We got our drinking water from one of the neighbors, the Boehmer's. My brother was normally responsible for hauling water back and forth from the lake. In the winter, that involved chopping a hole in the ice so the ice cold water could be drawn. One day there had been a fairly deep snow and Craig moved down to the water to fill a couple buckets and could not find the previous hole and fell in. He came back soaking wet and the old man had a good laugh at my brother's expense. A few days later, Craig was not available so dad went down to fetch some water. You guessed it, in he went. About that same time Herman Boehmer showed up and announced, "A little early for a swim Milt. You might be rushing the season." Craig enjoyed that story.

The whole concept of family fun was hard for me to grasp. I recall when I was working as a teamster and one day we were on a break and one of the teamsters was talking about his kid. Fred Libby piped up that, "If you did not have that kid, you could dress a little better. In fact, you could have some nice suits in your closet." The teamster replied, "I have more fun with my kid than I would have with a whole closet full of suits." I was stunned by the answer. First of all, why would a teamster need a suit? Way beyond that question, how do you have fun with your kid?? This was a totally unknown concept to me and one that had never entered my mind. At the time, Connie was pregnant and the idea of having fun with a kid was a completely foreign thought. It was hard to shake off the way you were raised.

My wife, Connie, and I had married when we were around age 21 and had not had a lot of life experience. Connie had lost her mother when she was a young teen and had endured a callous stepmother and a stern father and was not schooled in the best way to start a family of her own. I grew up in an unloving home as well. My mother grew up on a rock farm in northern Minnesota and came away with the view that boys can take care of themselves. She harbored fantasies of having a daughter and providing to her many of the things she could not attain. She was able to live out that fantasy through Gail, my younger sister. My older brother and I were left to our own devices. My mother was annoyed if I asked her for anything, but her usual response toward me was indifference.

A quick story on the parents will illustrate my point. When I graduated from high school, my high school chum, Dennis Hoppe and me, got the bright idea to hitch-hike to California and back. We ultimately made it out and back and had quite an experience. One person we met was a guy who had served as Gene Autry's bodyguard. He related that "The Cowboy" was quite a drinker and he had spent many a night as Gene's drink runner. Dennis piped up that a few years earlier he had seen Gene Autry at the St. Paul Auditorium in an appearance and the show featured Autry and his wonder horse, Champion. Gene had managed to have a drink or two before he and Champion emerged for their portion of the evening. Autry was so drunk he fell off his horse. The bodyguard replied, "That sure as hell does not surprise me."

When we started our trip, Dennis' parents took us out to Shakopee so that we could get out of the metro area and get started. They hung around in their car located down the road for quite some time and came back later and asked, "Do you still want to do this?" We were not ready to throw in the towel and insisted we would continue. Shortly afterward we landed our first ride. That first day took us all the way through Iowa and we reached Omaha as it was getting dark. We were dropped off in a busy intersection and probably should have begun looking for a place to stay, but were still looking for a ride. We soon encountered a young black person about our age and he asked us what we were about and we advised that we were heading for California, but needed a place to spend the night. He lived at Boys Town and said, "Help me get a ride to Boys Town and maybe you can stay there tonight." We asked how we could help and he just said it is hard for a black kid to thumb a ride in Omaha so maybe he could just stand aside and one of us could thumb a ride.

I thumbed a ride in a few minutes and Dennis and our new friend jumped in the car. The driver said, "Who is the stranger in the back seat with you guys?" I responded that we were just going up to Boy's Town and the driver was okay with that answer and away we went. We got dropped off at the main gate to Boys Town and it was almost dark as we headed to our friend's cottage. The boys lived in cottages or houses and each house had a supervisor or house boss. The boys checked with the powers that be and they were told that we could not stay and had to leave. That did not strike me as too hospitable for an organization whose mission was to take in stray boys. I sure felt like a stray at that point.

The boys were undaunted by the denial and grabbed a couple mattresses and took them downstairs to the basement and placed them on the floor and the ringleader advised, "You can sleep here tonight and no one will bother you. Just be out before 7:00 a.m. tomorrow and everything will be fine." They assumed we were hungry and located some crackers and a couple candy bars to get some food in us and that kept us running till morning. We got up the next day and left early before any of the supervisors showed up.

I still have a special place in my soul for Boy's Town. I have contributed to their cause for many years. We did make it all the way to California and back and survived a few harrowing experiences, but made it. One experience occurred when we were in Arizona and traveling on the road to Flagstaff. We needed to get up the mountain to my uncle's place in Yarnell, AZ. It was just starting to get dark and we were hoping to catch a ride up the big hill. A highway patrolman spotted us and asked where we were going and when we told him, he replied that we should not be hitch-hiking. We told him that was fine, but it looked like we had a long hike up the mountain. With that, he told us to "get in." His partner threw our duffel bags in the trunk and Dennis and I climbed in the back seat. As we made our way to Yarnell we zig-zagged or switch-backed up the Mountain. We were about half way up when I spotted an oncoming bus that had swung out to pass a car and was in our lane of traffic. I screamed, "What the hell is that bus doing?" Fortunately, we were by a bend in the road that had a wide out and the patrol car pulled off into the wide out. The patrolman quickly turned around and pursued the bus at high speeds down the mountain. The bus driver got a well-deserved ticket and we experienced our own chase scene. Eventually we got to our destination at my uncle's place and had another story to tell.

My Uncle Grant was a real character. He ran a small grocery store and bar. Grant concentrated on the bar and made it a point to sample some of the wares. Grant loved to BS with the customers, but during the day things were slow so Dennis and I became his new sounding board. He put us to work as soon as we got in the door. I had worked at a grocery store and Dennis' parents had run a small convenience store so we knew the business and we were soon filling the beer cooler and helping out on stocking shelves. Grant had some dirt he wanted moved and quickly showed us to the shovels and wheelbarrow. Grant kept telling us, "That's how I got my start." He figured we were dying to run a bar in a town of a couple hundred lost souls. We had a memorable visit with Grant, but it was soon time to head back to Minnesota.

When we got back from our trip we made our first stop at Dennis' house. Mrs. Hoppe saw Dennis and ran to him and threw her arms around him and was truly overjoyed. She then looked at me and said, "Hi Ron, how are you?" She had tears in her eyes and was in ecstasy. We soon took our leave and Dennis grabbed his car and took me home. It was a nice August Sunday afternoon. We parked and walked in the front door and found my mother reading the Sunday paper. She looked up and said, "Oh hi. Where have you been? Hi Dennis," and went back to her paper. That was my welcome home. She was consistent. I could not imagine any of my kids hitch-hiking even to Minneapolis, but times were much different. My dad had some reservations over the wisdom of this adventure, but Mother did not care as it was not on her dime.

Connie and I got married during my junior year at the University of Minnesota and it was not long before we had our first child, our daughter, Faye. We saved money over the summer and I worked during the school year and we managed to pay tuition, rent, and food bills and get through my senior year and on to graduation. Connie's father paid the hospital bill when Faye was born and that was a huge help. The bill was under a thousand bucks, but that was a lot of money in 1962. I am sure we could have qualified for food stamps, but we never gave it a thought to apply. My parents never offered to help with tuition payments or otherwise assist us with any financial help. It was just as well as I was able to work my way through on my own. I made good money working as a teamster over the summer and caught on as a part-time janitor during the school year.

As a janitor, I ended up working at Lake Owasso School in Roseville and that was the same school I had attended for my first six years. The old building was a two story brick building located on the shores of Lake Owasso. The playground was an asphalt slab. There was no kindergarten so I started in the first grade. The Catholics had a kindergarten at St. Rose of Lima church and school, but my parents were not able to muster the resources to send me. They made some excuse about, "They did not want me becoming a Catholic." It is difficult to imagine a 5- year-old becoming converted to Catholicism. We lived in the country and I had very little association with other kids and I do think that kindergarten is important. For all I know, the book entitled, "All I needed to know, I learned in Kindergarten" may be true, but it does not apply to me.

In first grade, I was in a combined room with the second graders. The third and fourth graders were combined and grades 5-8 were also in one room. Miss O'Keefe was the principal and also taught the top four grades. She had a reputation as being a tough old task-mistress who did not back down from anyone. If you stepped out of line the teachers had no compunction against using corporal punishment. There were no big disciplinary problems and there was no school nurse available to dispense drugs.

When I was in second or third grade, Miss O'Keefe retired and she was replaced by a male teacher named Bob Ramstad. Mr. Ramstad taught grades 5-8 and became the principal. One day, a couple kids got into a scrape out on the playground. One of the kids was named David Ruthenbeck and his father was our Lutheran Minister. The other kid involved (I cannot recall his name so we will call him Tom) was older than David and also had a brother in school as did David. Mr. Ramstad came out on the play-ground to break up the fight and admonished Tom for his conduct as he was older and should have known better. Tom had been held back a year or two and was probably close to 15. Tom made the mistake of taking a swing at Mr. Ramstad and Mr. Ramstad countered and put Tom flat on his back. Mr. Ramstad then told Tom to leave and go home and Tom walked down the road and hurled insults as he went. Bob Ramstad was a World War II vet who undoubtedly used his GI Bill to get an education. He had been in combat, so a 15-year-old was not something for him to worry about. He used to say he could make more money driving a truck, but he liked teaching. I was fortunate to have him as my teacher for 5th and 6th grades.

One aspect of country schools that was unique is that they had a graduation ceremony from 8th grade. There were still a lot of farm kids in the area and for many of those kids, 8th grade was probably the end of the formal education road. Having a graduation ceremony from 8th grade made some sense. By the time I got to 3rd or 4th grade, the 8th grade graduation ceremony was history, in fact so were the 8th graders as they had been sent elsewhere as the baby boom generation was slowly taking over the old country school. The little red school house is now much maligned, but having older kids in the room served as role models and also I frequently listened in on their lessons to get a preview of what was ahead of me. When I was older, I got a review of what we had covered by paying attention to the lessons of my juniors. By the time I was in third grade the students had bus service. I walked for the first two years. A mile back and forth each way and always up hill. I did walk about half way to school on Lexington Avenue and in those days Lexington Avenue was also serving as U.S. Highway 10. Sending a kid out the door to hike that road at age 6 in this time frame would certainly qualify as child abuse or some sort of endangerment. I never felt that way and still do not. I was smart enough to figure out how to walk down the highway without getting run over. By the time I was in 6th grade Lake Owasso School had expanded across the street into a new building.

As a janitor, it was somewhat surprising to return to the school I had started out at as a first grader. I was now a "custodian" and by all appearances I had not made a lot of progress. I was planning on going to law school in a year and I had hopes of moving on. The old two story school building housed only first and second graders. The new school across the road took care of the balance of the grades through the sixth. The school now had three full-time janitors and a full-time principal, who did not teach or monitor 15-year-old students out on the playground.

My job as a custodian was to sweep out the classrooms after the kids departed for the day and empty the trash and clean the bathrooms. They were also using a local church for classrooms and I frequently went up there to do the same routine. I routinely drove to the church and would clean the classrooms myself and head back to the school. The church had two young attractive women teachers that were about my age. One of the women was single and did take an interest in me. I could have had a relationship with her, but I did not have time for any distractions and ignored her romantic suggestions. I also went across the street to my old school and cleaned up that place and finished up at the newer building. A high school kid named, Walter (Butch) Parsons, came in and helped out. Butch was on the high school wrestling team and sometimes was busy with meets or other activities, but he did show up most of the time and was a good worker. I was contacted by Butch not too long ago and discovered he was a successful orthodontist in Maplewood. We had a great time discussing our janitorial careers. Walter went on to serve on the Roseville School Board.

Not too long after we started as janitors, Butch and I were sent to the principal's office. We had no idea what the hell he wanted. He told us the janitor boss, Don, was not happy with us and we had to work faster. I do not know why Don could not have told us that, but for some reason he passed the buck. Don probably wanted to can us, but the principal has sense enough to talk to us first. Neither Butch nor I wanted to get bounced from our prestigious positions so we did the sensible thing and started working faster. We practically ran through the three buildings, but we got them all cleaned up and were out the door on time. We sometimes wondered what those other three full-time guys were doing. During school breaks we took up the old wax from the floor and re-waxed and polished the floors. I learned how to operate a floor polisher with one hand. It looks difficult as the polisher spins rapidly in a circular manner and seems to want to rapidly gyrate back and forth. Once you get the hang of it, it takes very little pressure to hold the polisher on course and it practically steers itself. I could easily manage a cigarette in one hand and the polisher in the other. Years later, I had an injured worker testify how tough it was to operate a floor polisher and I knew that this guy was puffing his testimony.

Not too long ago I went by the old school on the shores of Lake Owasso and found that it had been replaced by an elder care facility. At my stage in life, I could return to my original venue and be right at home. The site of the "new" school had been sold to a cable company and that building was later demolished and a park graces the site of the "New Lake Owasso School." Thinking back on those structures, I am sure they were full of asbestos. The furnace piping in the old school was certainly wrapped in asbestos as I can remember the white-wrapped heating pipes in the furnace room and kitchen. The tile on the floor was likely made of asbestos as well. When the average person hears of asbestos it is almost like one has unleashed a mad dog. It is not quite that bad. It is likely no problem unless it is disturbed. If one starts ripping out pipes or taking up old tiles, then a lot of dust is going to be raised and therein lays the problem. I am practically positive that every school I attended was probably full of asbestos. I don't seem to have any lung problems and most people my age are not aware of lung issues unless they smoked. I always liked to smoke, but have generally avoided it as it never agreed with me on an extended basis. I do know of two friends of mine who have encountered lung issues and neither one smoked. Those could have been asbestos related problems, but at this point it is nearly impossible to prove as most of the old schools have been demolished, maybe because of asbestos issues.

In our modern "risk-free environment" if there is even the faintest chance of some sort of exposure to asbestos, then the tile has got to get peeled off the floor and the heating and plumbing pipes have to come out. That means if you are going to salvage an old building, then the folks with the white space suits have to come in and clean up the joint. The building is going to be out of commission for a long time and it's going to be very expensive to employ the astronauts. It is usually cheaper and supposedly safer to simply tear the place down. No more little red school house.

I was talking to Dave Munt recently about the asbestos things and he related how the workers always make a big deal out of the job by entering the subject building in full uniform like it was the stricken World Trade Center. When they get on the job and the rest of the folks clear the building, things are often different. Dave said he has been on jobs and seen the Astronauts sitting around on breaks with masks off and puffing on a Lucky. It is like anything else, if you do something enough times, a certain routine usually unfolds.

Later on when I was in the Army, was the first time in my life that I experienced family fun. It did turn out to be fun. We went on a lot of trips and saw quite a bit of the world. I actually had some evenings at home with the family. This was unique as when I was city attorney, many of my evenings were spent at council or planning meetings or endless other gatherings or events. I am glad we had time together as it was long overdue.

After I finished my active duty with the Army, I was offered a job in Oregon as a teacher at a community college, but an uncertain relationship caused me to pass on that job. Connie and I did separate and I took up residence in the basement of a friend's place that lived not too far from the kids. I ended up back in the basement after all.

I needed a steady paycheck and that motivated me going to work for the State as an Unemployment Referee. I conducted hearings on unemployment cases and issued written findings and conclusions. This was high volume litigation and most of the cases were *pro se* in that neither the employee nor the employer had counsel. It was a fun job and although the pay was low, the work was interesting and my colleagues were enjoyable people.

The agency I worked for was called The Department of Employment Services. I knew a little about the agency as I had worked for them for a year as a full-time employment interviewer when I was in law school. My job as an interviewer was trying to get unemployed people back to work. It was interesting work, but difficult. In those days, people drawing unemployment compensation were required to register for work with the employment service. Lots of those people were seasonally unemployed such as construction workers and those folks were going back to work in the spring and were spending their winters ice fishing and drinking beer and were not too interested in obtaining employment at a job paying less than their unemployment. When I did find someone who wanted to go to work, I had trouble helping them as I only had a limited supply of jobs. Lots of the unemployed relied on head hunters or private employment agencies to find work. To my 22-year-old shock, I learned that private enterprise may have been more efficient than a government agency. I was wasting a lot of time talking to folks that were not excited about working as they were required to talk to me and consequently I was not devoting enough time helping those that actually wanted a job.

When I was an employment interviewer, I think the agency was called the Department of Economic Security. The agency changes its name on a continuous basis and has been called the Department of Jobs and Training, Department of Economic Opportunity, and a million other things. If you call it "The Unemployment Office" everyone will understand what you are talking about.

When I was an unemployment referee, we heard most of the cases in Minneapolis and St Paul, but we also heard cases all over the state. We heard them in a spare room at the local unemployment office. We taped all of the hearings and most of the time we did all the questioning of witnesses. Only occasionally was someone represented by counsel. We gave a short canned spiel at the start of the hearing and then placed the witnesses under oath and proceeded to question them. I learned early on that you could not simply ask someone, "What happened?" You would soon find out where the witness was born and how they met their wife, but you would not find out why they got canned or quit their job. I had a pretty standard routine I followed and I asked specific questions and held the witness to the question asked and managed to get a hearing done in less than the allotted time. We usually had 10-12 hearings set per day so each one took less than an hour. It was a high volume operation and the only practical way to keep up was to try and write them up the same day as you heard the case. If, following the hearing, I had five or ten minutes to spare before my next hearing, I would quickly dictate the decision and go on to the next hearing. If you followed that pattern, you managed to keep up with your decisions and not fall behind. There were times you did not have any time between hearings, so then you were forced to rely on your notes or listen to the tape and write up the decision at a later time. You did not want to get too many of those cases as it was so much quicker to write up the decision immediately after you heard the evidence. Some folks may criticize me for not taking a lot of time to think matters over and check the law and draft "The Great American Legal Opinion" in beautiful legal prose. It sounds wonderful, but usually I was in the best position to write a decision when the facts were fresh in my mind. I did not have to scratch my head and remember what witness Jones had just stated. I knew what was stated as I just heard it. Most of the cases involved fact questions so there was no need to check the law and write a lengthy memorandum. The law was fairly settled and not that complicated, so in most cases you did not have to devote a bunch of time to research.

 I liked the job, but I was not interested in putting in a lot of time over my paid 40 hours a week and that is another reason I wrote them up right away. When I started the position, I was only paid around $16,000 a year and that meant there were lots of folks in the building making a lot more than me, so there was not much incentive to donate time to the organization. Fortunately, I was in the Army Reserve and making extra money and I also did some private law cases to keep the wolf from the door.

 We did go out of town to hear cases once per month. One week I was assigned to northern Minnesota in the middle of January. It is always cold in January in Minnesota, but northern Minnesota is in a class by itself. On this trip, I went to East Grand Forks, Crookston, and Bemidji. In Crookston we always stayed at the hotel that had a bowling alley built into or adjacent to the hotel. This was the only hotel/bowling alley I had ever heard about. If you got bored at night, you could go down and roll an alley or sit down and watch the beer leagues play. If you were lucky, there was a women's league going and you could admire the local lady rollers. I always seemed to land in Crookston when the Legionnaires or the VFW was bowling.

 On the trip in question, I finished up at Crookston and drove on to Bemidji. It was January and per usual it was colder than a well digger's nut. We usually stayed at the Bemidji Holiday Inn near the airport. Connie and I had separated and I was living in the pit and it was kind of nice to travel because I got all my meals paid and did not have to rely on my own pathetic attempts at meal making or locate a cheap greasy spoon.

My hearings in Bemidji seemed to go well even though most of the people kept their coats on as it was so cold. All of the folks did not keep their coats or tops on. Toward the end of the morning, one of the claimants came in for his hearing and brought his girlfriend. She was in her 20's and very attractive and had a baby with her. We barely got into the hearing and she had her top off and was nursing the baby. It was a little disconcerting, but I did not say anything, but did remain very attentive during the course of the hearing.

I always swam and did a sauna when I was on the road and in those days I was usually jogging. I liked to jog when I traveled as it passed the time and eased tension and gave me a chance to explore the local area. On this trip, it was too damn cold to jog, so I swam and did a sauna. The sauna in Bemidji was tame and not near as interesting as the European variety. Years later, I went on a trip to Germany and found out the saunas in Deutschland are coed and suitless. I had been alerted to this phenomenon so I entered the sauna with simply a towel around me and then sat on my towel. I was surprised that the women did not seem at all concerned about being naked. It did strike me that U.S. women would not be as non-plussed about displaying their bodies. On this particular evening in Monschau, Germany the women were young and shapely. They appealed to these older eyes.

Undoubtedly, the best thing that came out of my time at the Employment Service was that I met Phyllis. Phyllis was also employed as a referee. She had been there about a year when I started.

When I first met Phyllis, I was seeing someone else and was not romantically interested in her. I did notice that she wore her skirts rather long, but she did have well-turned ankles. Phyllis was warm and friendly and occasionally I would stop in her office and ask her a question or two. Shortly after I started, the office had a Christmas party and Phyllis asked her local boyfriend, David, to accompany her and I went by myself. I got to know a couple of single women in the office, but nothing materialized. Christmas can be tough under any circumstances but when you are recently separated it is even more grim. I had the boys over on Christmas Eve and we ended up going to Kentucky Fried Chicken for Christmas Eve dinner. We always had lutefisk on Christmas Eve when I was growing up and many folks would tell me that they would prefer COL Saunders over dried cod.

The referees were a congeal group and usually went out to lunch together. Phyllis and others in the office spoke frequently of the bowling tournament that the office usually attended. It was for all state employees, but the office had successfully hijacked it and turned it into an office party. The party was usually in the spring. It was held at Minnehaha Lanes in St. Paul. I was never much of a bowler, but felt compelled to show up for this much ballyhooed event. It was a mixed double event and I was paired off with one of the single women I had met at the Christmas party. I never paid much attention to that stuff, but the pairings were probably done by the single women in the office. I had a good time bowling and after bowling we had some food and a band turned up and we did some dancing. I danced with several women and then noticed that Phyllis was available. I sensed that she wanted me to ask her to dance so I did so. I spent the rest of the night dancing with Phyllis. She was always great to talk with so I had no problem in making conversation. I did make two other observations. I could tell she had a lithe body. She moved very well and her body was supple and alive. I also liked the way she smelled. It sounds rather primeval, but I found her scent to be very compelling. To this day, I love her scent and I find it sensual and inviting. Phyllis has told me that I was the only man she met that complimented her on her scent and I told her I had never said it to another woman.

The bowling party started to break up and Phyllis and I ended up in the parking lot with some of our colleagues. Some interesting couples appeared. Phyllis and I were hitting it off well and we decided to go to the Embers on University Avenue for coffee. We had a nice evening and I found out she was going on a trip out west with her boyfriend. This was her boyfriend from Michigan named Bill. She had worked for three years in Michigan in the legal service community serving as a lawyer for migrant workers. Phyllis and Bill had planned this trip for some time. She said she would send me a postcard and talk to me when she got back. True to her word, I soon got a card and I was out of town on a road trip when she got back. I asked her if she could pick up my paycheck and I could make arrangements to get it from her. She was amenable to that and said she could drop it off on her way to St. Cloud on Friday evening. Phyllis stopped by and I was on the couch watching the Twins play baseball. Baseball has always been one of my chief hobbies and I was delighted to learn that Phyllis liked baseball and in fact her father had been a professional ball player. He had played in Puerto Rico and in the low minors.

Phyllis and I stopped over to one of the local watering holes and had a drink and made arrangements to get together sometime when she got back from her current road trip. We did indeed get together and three years later we got married. It was truly a fortunate turn of events that I met Phyllis. She is always ready with sensible advice and puts up with my quirky ways. She liked my three boys and they also took to her. I had the boys every other weekend and also saw them one night during the week. My daughter was older and pretty well made up her own mind whether or not she wanted to see me or not. My daughter, Faye, has grown closer to Phyllis as they have both aged.

Phyllis ended up transferring to the Office of Administrative Hearings and became an Administrative Law Judge. I got back into workers' comp and a couple of years later was appointed a compensation judge by Commissioner Harry Peterson. At the same time, my friend from the Army Reserves, Mick Hanson, was also appointed a judge. Harry Peterson figured out that most of the cases settled the day of trial and it would make sense to bring the parties together at an earlier time and resolve the case and clear the deck for the disputes that could not settle. Mick Hanson was the judge that really got the settlement judge program off the ground.

Frankly, I was surprised when I was appointed, but I did not doubt that I was qualified. I had a lot of good solid experience and was confident I would make a good judge. At least one of the other applicants for the position did not share my view. One of the disgruntled applicants challenged the appointments in Federal Court because he claimed he was more qualified. Morton had been an ALJ but had been forced to retire because he reached mandatory retirement at age 65. Soon thereafter, the law was changed and compulsory retirement was extended to age 70. Morton was in the window between age 65 and 70 and was passed over and brought suit for age discrimination in Federal Court. He probably would have based his claim on a veteran's preference angle, but Mick and I were both vets so that claim went out the window. He could hardly claim that he was ill treated as a vet when the state had just hired two vets.

I had known Morton when he was with the department and we got along well. John Keeler told me a story about Morton that when he started with the department, Dan Gallagher asked him what was the name of the new guy? Keeler responded, "Millard." Gallagher called him Millard for the next few weeks before someone finally told him the new guy's name was Morton.

Morton's claim eventually came on for hearing in Federal Court before Judge Bob Renner. The defendants, the State of Minnesota, and The Department of Labor and Industry were represented by the attorney general's staff. The staff attorney general interviewed me a couple times before the trial and called me as a witness. I had a lot of trial experience and Mick had trial experience and also a background in doing settlement conferences. The department took the position that they were looking for varied experience and both Mick and I offered decent backgrounds so there was a reasonable basis for the department's position and the judge should not second-guess the department. The department stressed that they wanted to go "in a new direction" and that myself and Hanson were better prepared to get them there. I hoped I was not leading the department over a cliff, but perhaps there was a new direction out there someplace. This made sense to Judge Renner as the courts do not have time to make all of the hiring decisions on behalf of the state. Mick would later remark that, "Erickson and I are the only compensation judges who have been federally certified." I guess on a personal level, I could not imagine me retiring and then later deciding to come back and run someone else off the bench. I was somewhat surprised that my friend, Jim Otto, had testified on behalf of Morton. He and Morton lived in Edina and had car-pooled together so I guess that forged some sort of bond. Edina-ites apparently stick together.

After I had been a judge for about two years, the legislature made a change and transferred all of the compensation judges to the Office of Administrative Hearings. The theory behind the move was that the judges were too close to the Department of Labor and Industry and were too liberal as a result. Historically most of the judges had come through the ranks at L and I and were not from outside the department. The transfer to OAH did open up the judicial appointment process and also lead to a judicial training program and resulted in a more professional bench.

As a result of the transfer, Phyllis and I landed back in the same office. She was eventually appointed to the Public Utility Commission and served two terms with distinction. Phyllis is exceedingly talented and can do anything she puts her mind to.

When Phyllis and I got married, I was already blessed with four children and had decided that I had done enough to increase the population and perhaps I should stand down. My kids still demanded a lot of my time, attention, and resources. I was concerned about how I was going to get four kids through college and had little if any savings. One thing that Connie and I did agree upon was that it was important for the kids to get some sort of post high school training and we had to find some sort of fund source to achieve that goal. We had a small cabin on Lake Mille Lacs that we had put together before I went in the Army and we agreed to put that in a trust with her brother, Jeff, and my sister, Gail, as co-trustees and the money was to be used to further the education of the children. We rented the cabin for a few years and when lake property boomed in the late 70's we sold the property. The lot had 100 feet of sandy beach that I bought for around $1,400.00 back in the early 70's and we added a used mobile home and had an instant cabin. Al Flynn owned a cabin up near mine and did not believe me when I told him what I had got for my cabin. I built my first deck at this cabin and nine or ten were to follow. Jennifer Patterson showed me a cartoon with a house surrounded by decks all over the place and the caption showed a forlorn wife and said: "I kind of blame myself because I got him that book on how to build your own deck."

Phyllis had not been previously married and we never talked about having any more children before we got married. Phyllis probably realized that after four children, I was not exactly ready to start another family. One thing that makes the human species somewhat unique is that we do possess a facility to change our mind, even though it may mean tossing aside deeply held convictions. When I first divorced, it seemed to me that I would never again marry. That idea gradually melted away after I met Phyllis. I made a decision many years ago that I did not wish to have any more children and it seemed prudent for me to take steps to achieve that goal. After having four children, it seemed like the prior methods of birth control seemed to be unreliable.

I was around 30 years of age and was looking for a family planning expert and settled upon Winston Ehlman, a special assistant attorney general who was representing the special comp fund. Winston was an interesting sort who talked a lot about his divorce and also about his vasectomy. Winston was an assistant attorney general who had done a lot of condemnation work and must have crossed his supervisors as he was dispatched to Labor & Industry to defend the Special Compensation Fund. This was back in the 60's and being sent to the fund was like being sent to a gulag. My friend, Dale Gruis, used to describe Ehlman as a "prominent St. Paul divorce attorney." Winston did tend to dwell on certain subjects. Winston was a WWII vet who had served as a grunt in the Canadian Army.

Winston related that after some searching, he had located a general practitioner located in Lost Jewels, Minnesota who performed the relatively simple vasectomy surgery in his office, as an outpatient surgery. "He gets the $100 up front and does require a note from your old lady." I looked rather perplexed and he said, "He requires a note signed off by your wife authorizing the procedure." I thought he was dragging my mother into this thing. If I had to get her permission for anything, this thing was not going to go too far. Ehlman told me that he had consulted with several doctors and they all wanted to "throw me in the hospital for 2-3 days and make a big f—cking deal out of it." He assured me that, "Your sex life is just as good and maybe better after the operation because you are no longer worried about having any more children." Who needs consulting doctors when you have Ehlman?

Winston did look with derision upon the modern day male who roamed about the land scattering his male seed much like a current version of Johnny Appleseed. The modern Johnny scattered his seed and did not seem to care where the trees popped up. Johnny Appleseed at least planted his seed with some care and took precautions to locate a safe and fertile spot. Winston advised me that because I had a job and a modicum of property that if I were to spread my seed upon the populace and achieve a germination, that the local DA will "sniff you out and jump on your poor little apples with both feet. Son, you are nailed to the earth as a career lawyer and should you spread your seed, you will be hunted down like a mad dog." Winston was a strong advocate of family planning.

I contacted Dr. Know Moore in Lost Jewels, and he soon sent me a form to sign together with an explanation advising that the procedure was irreversible. At least he made it clear that once the faucet was turned off, it was not likely that someone else could get it running again. Connie was very reluctant to sign off on such a proposal but after a time, she did agree. I thought about just signing the damn form and taking it with me, but that did not seem like the route to

Family Times

go.

I contacted Dr. Moore's office and arranged for an afternoon appointment. It was a crisp November day as I headed west on Highway 212. I soon located his office on Main Street and shuffled in with my hands in my pockets and pulled out a hundred dollars and my permission slip. I was soon looking very vulnerable in a hospital gown and paper slippers. At that point I encountered Dr. Moore and he directed me to a prone position on top of his cutting board. He explained that he would be making a rather small incision in my scrotum and then would be snipping the two vas deferens tubes that carried the live sperm from the testicles to join with seminal fluid and be discharged during intercourse. Without active sperm, I would be shooting blanks. I asked, "Are you using an anesthetic?" He assured me he was going to numb it first and I breathed a sigh of relief. Before I could change my mind, he injected my scrotum with a Novocain-like ingredient.

I watched Dr. Moore make the initial incision to that little sack but soon weakened and turned my head to the side. There was no pain, but there was a pulling sensation that reminded me of getting a tooth pulled except my mouth and gums were fine. The good doctor was tugging on some stitches. I asked him how many of these he had done and he said, "About a thousand." Good business, I thought, and did the math and that was a hundred grand in the old bank account. It was all cash and he did not fill out any insurance forms as most of the insurance companies did not cover the procedure. They preferred to cover maternity costs as they seemed to think that was a good way to save money.

Dr. Moore asked me if I had someone to drive me home and I lied and responded with a "yes." His instruction sheet had advised me to have a chauffeur for the return voyage. My medical consultant, Dr. Ehlman had told me that he drove himself home after the procedure, so I concluded that I could do the same thing. The doctor was a little late with the question as he was already shutting me down. If I had told the truth and said I was on my own, he would have patted me on the head and told me to "be careful" and send me on my way. I was being careful and that was why I had come to Lost Jewels. Dr. Moore's parting advice was to ice down the family jewels and stay off your feet. I figured to ice down a brandy and hoped that would help matters.

I drove myself back to Coon Rapids and returned to my office as city attorney. All went fine, but that evening I awoke at 2:00 a.m. with great pain and goodness gracious "great balls of fire." I located the freezer and grabbed all the ice I could carry and applied it liberally to my screaming balls. My main concern was that the stiches would break. There was blood in the area and a sharp pulling sensation. After a couple hours, I fell back to sleep and slept in the following morning. I hit the floor the next morning like I was walking on egg shells or my nuts. I went in the office late in the morning as I did start to feel half way decent.

My Scandinavian background dictated that I say nothing about this little adventure as the subject dealt with the swimsuit area of the body or sex and that topic is off limits with my tribe. Sexual relations were allowed and sometimes encouraged by the Scandinavians, but do not talk about it or even mention the word "intercourse" because then the whole subject becomes disgusting. I realize that to most rational beings, this makes no sense whatever, but this was the way it was and no exceptions were allowed.

I recall my mother telling my Aunt Hazel that "her kids knew all about sex" although she or my father had never mentioned the subject. If they did mention it they would spell it out s-e-x. Aunt Hazel had told my mother that she had dutifully supplied my two cousins, Gary and Dean, with some books on the subject. My mother's response was attempting to paper over with ignorance her own indifference in dealing with my education. My education had gaps that would easily accommodate a deuce and a half so my sex education was not exactly standing out there by its lonesome with no clothes. Perhaps she believed that I had gleaned the facts of life from the pimply-faced kids on the playground, but there were no subjects whatsoever that I knew "all about."

Meanwhile, back in City Hall, I quietly resumed work and following my stoic heritage I did not broach the subject of infertility with my coworkers. This was a subject best left to silence. I did submit a bill for Dr. Moore's services to our group insurance carrier and thought it might be quietly paid. The charges were denied and the mayor's friend George turned up at City Hall and proclaimed for all to hear that, "Vasectomies are not covered, it's discretionary surgery. I had my vasectomy when I was stationed in Japan." George seemed rather proud of his decision and assumed I was out of the same mold. Word traveled around City Hall and soon my surgery was a favorite topic at coffee breaks. George went on to be elected Mayor of Coon Rapids and continued in the insurance business. He told me one day he was going to be Mayor of Coon Rapids some day, and sure enough he was true to his word.

Phyllis eventually wanted a child of her own and I had never given much of any thought to the subject. One of our friends had gotten re-hooked up and I did talk to him about it. Vern told me that he went to some quack and the quack doctor threw him in the hospital and cut him open and only hooked up one side. There are two vas deferens tubes and you should have both hoses running as it gives you twice the chance to impregnate your mate. Why anyone would do only half the job did not make sense. A half-assed doctor, in my opinion. Vern had enough of Dr. Quack and did not go back for another round but went on to see Dr. Ercole at the University Hospital. Dr. Ercole fixed him up without a lot of unnecessary cutting and soon Vern was a father again.

I made an appointment to see Dr. Ercole at the hospital. He talked to me and told me that my wife would appreciate me for the ordeal that I was volun-

Family Times

tarily submitting myself to and that it would enhance our marriage. Further, I was an experienced parent and would likely do a better job this time. He did not mean that I had crapped out the first time around. My kids would agree with him that there was room for improvement. Dr. Ercole then examined me and he checked my scrotum and checked the posts or vas deferens tubes coming from my balls to find out if Dr. Moore had left a long enough tube so that he would be able to splice the two ends back together again. He said it felt good, but then he corrected and said that the tubes seemed to be of sufficient length to allow him to reconnect my plumbing. I liked Ercole and he seemed to be optimistic. Once again, this was discretionary surgery and I would have to pay the bill. At this time, a reconnect was much more than the $100 disconnect fee I had paid to Dr. Know Moore. "We" decided to go ahead with it and let Dr. Ercole "putz with my nuts."

Once again, the routine was that I had to bring someone along to drive me home. This time, I did not lie and Phyllis drove me over to University Hospital. Not a storefront operation on the second go around. I did not need a consent form from Phyllis or my mother for the reconnection surgery. Apparently the theory was that this was a type of reconstruction surgery. He was just putting things back in place. Phyllis gave me a nice send off before they wheeled me off to suffer my fate. I was in the pre-operating room when Dr. Ercole came in to talk with me. As we were discussing the operation, Dr. Ercole got to work and shaved my scrotum. I was kind of surprised that he did that job, but it gave us a chance to talk and I actually almost relaxed. It was kind of like talking with your barber. The surgery went fairly fast but I forgot to askCed-how many of these he had done. He finished in about an hour or so and then cautioned me not to have intercourse for a couple weeks and I was to return in a month with a sperm sample. Phyllis drove us home and this time I did follow orders and iced things down. I did ignore one piece of advice as Phyllis and I made love that afternoon. I thought as long as we were having a kid, we might just as well get on with it. Everything held up fine as Dr. Ercole did good work.

Phyllis got pregnant at age 43 and Cameron was born when she turned 44. Cameron is a bright and engaging young man and has kept both of us young and involved. He recently graduated from DePaul University in Chicago. He spent a year studying at a yeshiva in Israel and has recently returned home.

I cannot complete the family picture without talking about my late and beloved son, Kurt. Kurt was a brilliant kid and very funny. Kyle was the oldest son and Lars the youngest and Kurt was the middle child. Kurt was probably the hardest working of the kids. He worked at McDonalds when he was 15 and pretty soon he was closing the place down at night. After running the place they gave him a nickel an hour raise and he left and went to Perkins. He soon moved up to wait on tables. Kurt started college, but did not care for it and transferred to a business school. He finished an 18-month course and caught on with Northwest Airlines as a flight attendant. He was well suited for the job as he was personable and very verbal. Other attendants always liked to work with him as he was so witty and smart. He was short, but powerfully built and very fast. His two brothers were much bigger but backed off when Kurt was mad.

Unfortunately, Kurt is no longer with us. Everyone in the family still misses him very desperately even though he has been gone over eight years. He was a wonderful uncle to my grandchildren. My grandson, Griffin, had some developmental issues and there was some lamenting over his progress and Kurt remarked, "I will take a hundred like him." Kurt was right as Griffin is very bright and these days we swap history books back and forth.

When Kurt departed I received such a gracious and heartfelt response from the workers' compensation community that I was stunned, yet so grateful. It was a marvelous outpouring of support and love and I shall always treasure the response. The reason for the response was raw and harsh, but the support did help.

When a dire family event occurs there is always self-examination and recrimination. The survivors feel guilty and ask what could I have done to avert this tragedy? There is always more to be done and one cannot escape the nagging thought of failure to exercise due diligence. You are stuck with what you have done and also what you failed to accomplish. Often, failure, like regret, seems to be most assertive. One gradually moves away from that lonely road because it leads to a dead end. There are others who took another turn a few miles back and they may run out of gas or experience road hazards. There is still a destination ahead of you and help may be needed so you better turn around and move down a different road. There are bumps ahead and dangerous turns, but that is the only road to travel.

I have no doubt that I was not the best prepared person to parent anyone. This is a trade that is passed down from family to family. Some families are more skilled and are able to impart their trade secrets from generation to generation. I think I was in the correspondence course and did not get all of the course work. I had some make up work to do and should have been more diligent in seeking its completion.

Fortunately, all of the children are and were successful so we must have learned on the fly and done something right. Faye has a master's degree in audiology and is a devoted mother. Kyle is a special education teacher and has his son, Griffin, and a step-daughter, Ellen. Lars is a lawyer and has three boys. Lars did some comp work on behalf of intervenors, but has moved on and does mostly construction law. Faye has been a single mom for the past few months and has done a great job under difficult conditions. Cameron is learning the Torah and hopefully preparing for life. He recently returned and secured a position working on a political campaign. He is looking for a permanent job. Kyle and Lars are the best fathers that I have ever known.

Family Times

From left, Kyle, Kurt, Faye, and Lars

Ron's cabin from the inside. The loft is in the background.

Ron's wilderness cabin. The sauna is in the right foreground.

Forlorn Lake as seen from cabin.

Family Times

On the ship to Sweden. From left, Lars, Kurt, Kyle, and Faye.

Ron and cousin, Marcia, in front of his boyhood home on Lake Josephine circa 1946/47.

Phyllis on patrol at Golan Heights 2016.

Cameron and Ron in front of Western Wall, Jerusalem 2016.

Phyllis is smoking hot in New Zealand in 2012.

Ron and Cameron

Family Times

Cameron, Phyllis, and Ron in Berlin during the summer of 2012.

BG Nitzan Nuriel (Reserve force) with Ron at Tel Aviv 2016.

Chapter 7
Inconsistencies

The backbone of our industry has always been the back injury. As a judge, I was frequently looking at another back case to try. I wish I had kept track of the number of back cases I have tried. It certainly numbers in the hundreds. Our cases for hearing were assigned for trial several months before the trial date, but we frequently did not get a chance to review the file until shortly before game time. Files for hearings on any given week did not hit my office until the prior Friday afternoon. We usually had pre-trial conferences on Monday so most of the time I did not review the file until the morning of the trial. Normally, my file review was rather perfunctory; I read my pre-trial notes. The pre-trial conference was held 6-8 weeks prior to the trial and was normally held without the employee being present and involved only the attorneys and the judge. We found out what the claims were, what issues were involved, what defenses were asserted, and the names of the witnesses involved. In rare cases, there was correspondence in the file indicating that the attorney for the insurance company intended to introduce surveillance movies of the petitioner. (petitioner, a/k/a plaintiff or injured employee) I usually perked up a bit when I saw that movies were involved as that often stimulated an otherwise boring case

Movies are frequently very effective from the standpoint of the insurance company. Most experienced petitioner's counsel made it a practice to always warn their clients that Oliver Stone may be around the corner, so be careful (it is true that some injured employees may be given to hyperbole). Movies are certainly the exception and not the rule. It is not cheap to hire an investigator to run around in a van for several days and take pictures of an injured worker. The insurance companies do not usually authorize films unless they get a tip or stumble across some information indicating that Mr. or Ms. Employee is a faker. Usually ex-lovers or former boy/girl friends are one of the biggest sources of tips. Hell hath no fury like an ex-lover scorned. Some of us may know that to be true.

I left the bench before the social media such as Facebook hit the scene. People put the weirdest things on Facebook and sometimes on email. I am

Inconsistencies

164

sure some enterprising comp judge could compose a book writing about cases washed down the drain with stupid Facebook activities.

It was fairly early in my judicial career when I drew another back case and one of the main witnesses for the employee was a chiropractor. The employee was previously working as a carpenter and claimed a low back injury. He claimed to have a very low level of capability at the present time. He could certainly not work as a carpenter. The pain prevented him from working at even light employment.

The testimony of the chiropractor confirmed that the employee was certainly disabled and could not possibly work as a carpenter. He could not even do light work. He continued with a complicated diagnosis and a poor prognosis.

The insurance company introduced movies of the employee working as a carpenter on a piece of real estate OWNED by the chiropractor. The Crooked Chiro had hired the employee to re-habilitate a rental unit that he owned. The movies showed the employee manhandling tools and equipment like The Terminator. He was busy lifting sheetrock and two by fours and sawing, cutting, and hammering. It looked to me like he was working as a carpenter. Sheetrock or gypsum board is very heavy and hard to handle because of its bulk. A standard 4 x 8 ft. sheet has to weigh close to 60-70 pounds. It was apparent to me that both the employee and the chiropractor had committed perjury. Perjury is lying under oath in a court proceeding. I had practiced as a criminal prosecutor and also done considerable criminal practice when I was in the Army (JAG) so I felt I had a duty to contact the county attorney. I secured an extra copy of the video tape and sent the tape and a letter over to the Hennepin County Attorney's Office and told them that there was a double dose of perjury in this case and they should look into it.

Months after my letter to the county attorney, an investigator showed up in my office and asked, "Are you still interested in pursuing this?" I replied, "I am not pursuing anything right now, but I thought the county attorney should be interested in two crimes committed less than a block from his office" (we were in a slum-like office a half a block from the county attorney's digs). I asked Sam Spade if he had read the transcript of the trial or looked at the film. His halting reply told me that he had not reviewed the case, although he replied in the affirmative. I was tempted to put his ass under oath, but I did not want him investigating me. It was apparent to me that he was not investigating the case, but was investigating me. He was sent over by the DA to find out if I was going to raise a fuss if they did not pursue the employee and the Good Chiro. Being an experienced investigator, if not a diligent one, he concluded correctly that I was not going to the papers if the county attorney gave the perjury case, that I handed to him on a dusty platter, the deep six.

I concluded that this was probably the end of my "Liar, Double Liar" case, but that was not to be. Months later, I read that the employee had appealed my

Inconsistencies

flat denial of his claim and secured a new trial on appeal (that was before the legislature changed the scope of review and adopted the substantial evidence rule, which limited appellate review). The Workers' Compensation Court of Appeals (WCCA) was the court that reviewed our decisions and in those days they could do just about anything they wanted on appeal and political considerations were sometimes the most important criteria or issue on appeal. The members of the WCCA were appointed by the governor for six year terms. When I started out there were three members, but it was later expanded to five judges. It was and is a nice job and they all have law clerks to do a lot of the heavy lifting so it is a job that one would like to retain. My crooked carpenter case was brought by a politically influential lawyer who someone concluded may be able to help out with a reappointment, and that case merited a closer look. After miraculously securing a new trial, the Liar Employee got his case heard by one of my more generous colleagues, Judge Claus, and presto-chango he ended up with some money. The employee should have been spending his time in jail, but ended up being rewarded for his clandestine carpentry. That case would likely not have been overturned under the current more restricted scope of appellate review.

One other movie case that comes to mind is the case of the Prevaricating Preacher. This was another back claim and the preacher was actually a part-time reverend and had sustained a claimed back injury while working his day job. He claimed that his back problem was so severe that "he could not even lift a pencil." The Right Reverend was indeed claiming a serious debilitating claim that prevented him from doing any substantial employment. He did continue with his part-time Sunday morning gig. The cleric's counsel was particularly aggravating and that made for a difficult trial. At one point in the testimony, the witness was trying to illustrate a unit of measurement or dimension. To help the witness and move the trial along, I suggested that he meant about 30 inches or about the same height as the counsel table. Counsel for the employee refused to stipulate to that dimension and said he did not know the height of the counsel table so could not stipulate. I told him, "Most tables are about 30 inches in height and this one looks about 30 inches to me." He still persisted in his refusal. I took a recess and secured a tape or yardstick and measured the table in front of counsel and announced on the record that it was 30 inches in height. Counsel then announced that he had no problem with my declaration of dimensions and I replied, "You objected to my estimate so you gave me little choice but to measure the table." Obviously the height of the counsel table was not the issue in the case, and I still wonder how or why the lawyer would risk making the decision maker aggravated over a trivial matter. I guess they did not teach the counselor common sense wherever he went to law school. Another thing the counselor did that was most aggravating was he could not formulate a question. In trying to elicit testimony from his own medical witness, he would read large passages from the defendant's medical witness report and then attempt to ask his witness whether or not he agreed with that long epistle. It made for a painful trial and needlessly prolonged the agony. After putting up with it for too long, the defense counsel objected, "Counsel is testifying and also leading." The objection was right on and I sustained it. Petitioner's counsel went into a whine, "How am I going to examine my witness?" I replied, "I suggest you ask him some questions. I can read the report and you do not have to read it for me. You are supposed to be questioning your witness. I am sure he did not come down here for you to read to him."

After struggling through a day of trial with Perry Mason, it was late so we had to reschedule the defense case. Most cases are easily concluded within a day, but I was wasting a lot of time measuring tables and trying to enlighten counsel on how to ask a question. We went late into the day just to finish up with the employee's case.

We returned for day two of the trial and the defense counsel announced that they would be showing surveillance movies. The general rule on movies was that the lawyer with the movies (usually the defense counsel) had to advise the attorney for the employee that he had movies and give the plaintiff counsel an opportunity to see the film prior to the hearing. This is subject to a litany of exceptions that is not germane to this case. In this case, the crack petitioner's lawyer had not bothered to watch the movies although he had been advised of their existence.

The movies showed the employee pumping gas, driving his vehicle, and moving his head and neck around. The most damaging film was the employee leaning into his vehicle trunk and lifting out a television set. Now this was before plasma or thin screen televisions. This was the older and heavier version of television. The 27-inch screen was housed in a sizeable chassis. Remember, the preacher had already testified, "he could not lift a pencil." Another thing that was different is that the reverend was not wearing a neck brace, but he did wear one at the trial in front of me.

The reverend lost his case in front of me. He appealed and this time he lost on appeal. Later on the case did come back to me and when the case came on for pre-trial, the employee's slick counsel announced that he had failed to file an affidavit of removal against me and asked me to voluntarily remove myself. I responded, "I think I can be fair to your client so I do not see any reason to remove myself." It probably seems surprising to most folks that I said that, but I did mean it. The employee had exaggerated his condition, but he was stuck with that problem no matter what judge was assigned to the case. The prior decision was the "law of the case." It was evident that I did not like the reverend's lawyer and I did consider him to be in the wrong line of business. On the other hand, it is not fair to the employee to punish him for having a boorish counsel. I did make an effort not to consider the lawyer in reaching a decision. I remember Judge Barker telling me early on that, "He could not worry about who the lawyer was or how much sway he had. I have enough to worry about with the employee and trying to figure out the merits or problems with his case." Judge Barker gave me some good advice and I tried to take it to heart. The judge seldom met a claim that he did not like, but he was spot-on in his analysis of the impact of counsel in your role as a decision maker.

I did hear the preacher's plea once more and on Judgment Day I did have to turn him down for the second time. I do not believe they appealed a second time, but that was probably the preacher's decision to end his pilgrimage through the dark passages of the compensation system.

One of the more bizarre cases involving surveillance film dealt with a tape that was taken at a New Year's Eve party held at a legion club located in southern Minnesota. The employee lived in a small town located down near Rochester, MN. The employee was kicking up his heels on New Year's Eve and was certainly having a wilder time than most of my New Year's Eve parties. He was shown dancing with his girlfriend. If it was an ordinary shuffle, he may have been okay, but he was doing the Charleston and he was moving. The Charleston was a favorite of my mother during the roaring 20's, but somehow it seemed to involve too much in the way of movement for my old man. It takes some effort and decent coordination. I suspect it was the employees ex-wife that arranged to have that incriminating tape fired off to the insurance company. He should have paid his support or alimony on time.

The problem was that the employee was receiving money through a prior award finding permanent total disability. He had previously entered into a settlement with the insurance company and was getting a weekly check. The insurance company did not think he was disabled at all and wanted to set aside the prior settlement. My job was to make findings as to his condition and recommend to the W.C. Court of Appeals as to whether or not they should set aside the settlement. It would seem to most people that they could just stop making payments and leave the fast dancer to his own devices. The workers' comp system does not work that easily. Once the insurance company had bought the farm or agreed to make payment, then they were on the hook and could not stop payments until there was a hearing and a finding that they can stop making payments. The case was assigned to me to hear evidence and make findings and a recommendation to the Court of Appeals on how they should proceed. One would think that the Court of Appeals could do their own hearing, but no one up there seemed to be up to the task so they bucked it down to me.

When the employee entered the courtroom for the first day of trial, he displayed one of the more bizarre gaits that I have ever observed. His walk was something of a shuffle and he held his arms in front of him as if making an awkward salute with his right hand while supporting his right arm with his left arm. At the break, I checked his medical records to determine if there was some neurological or muscular basis for holding his arms in such a *faux salute*.

If he had an injury to the upper back, that could manifest itself in arm problems, but he was claiming a low back injury. He was moving a lot slower and with much more effort than he had shown on New Year's Eve. His explanation for his newfound New Year's Eve vigor was alcohol. It had masked his pain, and he was able to perform at a high level. I should have found out what he was drinking and had the same thing. My knees are constantly hurting from years of jogging.

Our local Arthur Murray claimed that this New Year's Eve event was a one-time isolated incident and most of the time he just sat around and suffered through his pain and further he had mended his ways and no longer drank. After the first day of trial, the insurance company did not finish their case so we set it for another day of trial about two months down the road when I had an open date.

The Employee lived in a nice old home located across the street from a landmark hotel. In his backyard he had a nice deck with a hot tub. A fairly high privacy fence blocked his yard. The insurance company located a prominent roost, either in a neighbor's home or rented a room at the hotel. Soon the movies were rolling. Every afternoon was party time on the deck. The employee did not have any trouble moving tables and chairs and displayed no evidence of the bizarre gait that he had adopted for courtroom purposes. To further torpedo his tenuous claim, it was evident he was drinking. Remember, he told me during the first day of trial that he had stopped drinking. He lied.

The employee was caught on tape on more than one occasion drinking cans of beer. My areas of expertise are limited, but I do have some experience drinking beer. It is difficult to spend three plus years in the Army without popping a round or two of brew. I described the employee's drinking as follows: the can opened like a beer, it poured like a beer and he drank it like a beer. It was a beer and not a duck.

We finished up the second day of trial after watching back yard films taken between the first and second day of trial. I recommended that the employee go back to work. He was spending his free time getting a good start toward alcoholism and I may have saved him from his own demise by getting him out the door and doing something productive. This was Erickson's Rehab Program and I sincerely hope he benefited from it.

Most of the surveillance films are taken from public property or streets. On occasion the movies are taken from adjoining private property. The objecting counsel will suggest that the filmmaker trespassed or violated property rights and the movies should not be shown. I had that occur in a case where the employee spent almost every weekend at a cabin retreat some 3 to 4 hours north of the Twin Cities. The employee had a back injury and had a fairly easy

Inconsistencies

office type job. She claimed constant pain and difficulty sitting. She somehow was able to sit in her car for 6 to 8 hours every weekend without a great deal of problems. The investigator managed to locate her northern redoubt and tramped across an adjoining farm and took some pictures of the employee. The employee's counsel contended that the pictures should not be shown because they were obtained through some sort of illegal means. Essentially it was a criminal case type of argument. Counsel was contending that the pictures were "the fruit of the poisonous tree." It should be clear by now that I was occasionally dealing with criminals, but this was a civil case. Constitutional provisions limiting searches apply to state or governmental action and are not a limitation on private parties. The investigator denied going on the employee's property and there was no evidence to the contrary. If there was any trespass it was up to Mr. Farmer to bring an action in trespass because he was the property owner. A stranger to the property lacked what the law calls "standing" to enforce someone else's private property claims.

The employee liked to garden and they had lots of film of her bending and stooping over her garden. She was shown moving a wheelbarrow around to transport tools and plants. She moved well and I did not see any grimacing or grabbing her back to indicate any pain. She denied going to her cabin on a regular basis and stated in her pre-hearing deposition that she had not headed north on specific weekends. The defense counsel did a good job and obtained her cancelled checks through discovery and produced several checks she had written on the weekends in question at the local Red Owl in Hackensack.

The employee was lying on a number of material points and I had difficulty accepting any of her testimony as being truthful. I denied her claim in all respects, as it was clear to me that she was a complete faker.

The employee appealed to the Workers' Compensation Court of Appeals and what I found and concluded following two days of trial, was set aside and she was awarded benefits. It was one of those political decisions I mentioned earlier and it was issued before the substantial evidence rule was adopted. I tried not to get upset when those things happened although it was most disconcerting when out and out liars were rewarded.

Years earlier I had been a city prosecutor for several years and occasionally we would lose a drunk driving case because the officer had failed to properly advise the accused or perhaps there was a problem with the alcohol test (yes, on occasion the prosecutor also made mistakes). I used to tell the officer involved that mistakes are made and drunks will walk out the door, scot free, but sometimes, "you just have to shake your head and walk away from it. If you dwell on all that stuff, you will drive yourself crazy." The more "fortunate" aspect of prosecuting drunk drivers was that if you did not get a conviction, fear not, the drinker would be back for another trip to the courthouse. Typically, the drunk driver was a regular customer. They were drinking every night.

Inconsistencies

One of the witnesses at the Master Gardner's trial was Jim Dupre, my next door neighbor when I was in high school and growing up in Shoreview. I used to babysit his boys. After the trial, I happened to run into Jim in St. Paul and he mentioned that the folks in his office realized the employee was a faker and were quite upset that she had gotten paid. Decisions do have consequences. Jim was mystified that this total faker and liar could get money out of the court system. I told Jim, I was not smart enough to explain the intricacies of the court system, but I did what I believed the evidence warranted and was still just as mystified as he was, so try not to feel bad about it.

At times clandestine movie making will result in some embarrassing moments for the litigants. We had a case involving an employee who was filmed meeting his girlfriend in a parked car. They would embrace and he was observed petting her breasts. They were parked on a public street so there was no privacy issue. Fortunately for the employee, his wife did not show up at the trial.

Not too long before I left the bench we had a case dealing with outdoor sport. Minnesota is a great outdoor playground, particularly in the summer and sometimes employees will become involved in play activities that seem to be in conflict with their medical limitations. I have had cases dealing with golfers and ball players, but in this case it was a water activity. We got into the trial and the employee was a fairly tall young woman in her late 20's. She was attractive and I have never been known to dislike an appealing female. She had a fairly ordinary factory job and a typical low back injury. She had been out of work for a time and did not seem to be in a rush to return. Shortly before the Labor Day weekend, she had seen her doctor and had been advised to continue to "take it easy and avoid bending, lifting or pulling." He did not advise her to avoid jet skiing, but I strongly suspect he was not recommending it.

The insurance company got wind of the fact that the employee would likely be spending the weekend at a local cabin. They were prepared and hired a surveillance expert and he obtained some incriminating footage. The employee was filmed operating a jet ski and her male companion was on a large inner tube being towed behind the watercraft. She made it a point to guide her companion back over her wake, causing bouncing to her and her companion alike. She dismounted from the machine with ease and pulled the tow rope and tube through the water without apparent pain or discomfort. She was shapely and attractive in her swimsuit and my older eyes did not stray from the video. Sometimes movies make me sleepy, but in this case I stayed awake without a problem. I kept wondering to myself if she was going to ride that inner tube. Sure as pop, within a few frames, she was on top of that tube and was towed around the lake. She caught her own wake and took the bouncing without apparent problems.

The petitioner's counsel argued that the films represented only 15-30

Inconsistencies

minutes of the employee's weekend and were not really representative of her condition. In other words, "It was an isolated incident." It might have been isolated, but it was very compelling footage. The employee, to her credit, did not offer a lot of lame excuses or out and out lies to explain her activity. She owned up to what she had done and did not deny that jet skiing was not recommended by her physician.

I realized when the trial was concluded, that I was going to have a most difficult time awarding this pleasant and nice appearing, young woman any continuing benefits. Good looks or not, it was evident to me that this young person had to get back to work. I tubed her quest for benefits and the Court of Appeals later agreed with me on appeal.

We currently live in the social media era where we all have to let our peers know exactly what we are doing on a minute-by-minute basis. I am old fashioned and do not want people to know what the hell I am doing. I am so slow on all the gadgets I would get nothing else done if I was keeping a running account of my limited activities. I would hate to have to tell the world that my life is quite mundane. When my youngest Son, Cameron, was in his last year at DePaul U, he was constantly on Facebook telling the world of his every move. I told him that it just is not a good idea to let the universe know of your whereabouts on a 24-hour basis. Cameron was active with the Jewish community on campus and was President of the Students Supporting Israel. Cameron did receive an award from the American Israel Political Action Committee (AIPAC) as the activist of the year. He was always an activist around the house so that award was no surprise to me. There was more and more anti-Semitism around and I did not like the idea of him reporting his situs on a minute-by-minute basis.

I am confident that some of the judges could tell a story or two about a petitioner who posted something on Facebook that was contrary to their medical restrictions. I do not twitter, but can foresee that *tweeting* could result in some problems for a petitioner. Electronic mail or email generally seems more private than some of the other mediums, but emails are forwarded all over the place. People who are pictured doing active or outdoor things are a favorite attachment. The experienced comp attorneys are probably telling most petitioners to take down their Facebook sites and avoid Twitter. It is pretty hard to prevail on a younger claimant to forget about email, but that would be the safest course. Email can be risky, just ask Hillary Clinton. Just about everything that young people do is a social media event. It certainly poses challenges for the petitioner's bar.

In my branch of the judicial calling we had numerous deadlines hanging over our heads. By statute we had to have our decisions issued within sixty days from the time the record closed. Usually it closed at the conclusion of the trial. If the decision could not be issued in sixty days, then the judge had to go

Inconsistencies

to the Chief ALJ or his assistant and ask for an extension of time. Most times I got my decisions out pretty fast as there is no real choice in the matter. For one thing, my recollection of what happened during the trial was going to be greatest during the days immediately following the trial as opposed to sixty days later. My job got tough when I drew a string of four, five, or even six cases in a row that did not settle and the records closed and the decisions all came due at about the same time.

Workers' Compensation cases often rise or fall on the strength of the medical evidence. Injured workers obviously require more medical attention than most of us and as a result, they acquire a vast and lengthy medical record. Usually most of the medical history is introduced as an exhibit at the trial. If the petitioner omits any of the medical records, the defense counsel is sure to offer the missing documents as well as their own medical reports usually consisting of a medical examination conducted by a doctor of his choosing, called an independent medical examination (IME) or sometimes an adverse exam. It used to be referred to as an adverse medical exam, but in the hope that it would be given more weight, they changed the name to an independent medical examination. Our cases frequently involve back or extremity injuries so you tend to see the same small group of orthopedic physicians on a recurring basis. If the defense counsel gets a favorable report from Dr. Knowitall, then the tendency is to send the next employee back to the same doctor and hope for the same result. As long as the results are good, it turns out to be a lucrative business for the examining physician. The price tag for an independent examination and report can easily fetch two grand (this was over ten years ago. Tell your kids to grow up to do IME's) When the examining doctor is knocking that kind of money down for a 20 minute examination, one has to wonder; how independent can the examination be? Obviously, the doctor wants to keep that business coming and if one gets "too independent" then the exams may go elsewhere.

Occasionally something will come along that will upset the smooth relationship between defense counsel and the examining doctor. Our good friend, Dr. Knowitall became entangled in a messy and conflicted divorce. Mrs. Knowitall was apparently attempting to show how wealthy the old SOB had become by doing defense examinations. The Good Doctor was making a very healthy living by doing insurance examinations. He hardly practiced medicine, but did practice IME's. It was a great deal for the doctor because he did not have to listen to his own patients moan and groan and complain and then proceed to do something to fix their problems. The patients he saw did plenty of moaning and groaning, but he examined them and kicked them out the door and sent them back to their own physicians without having to fix a thing. There was no malpractice to worry about because he did not practice. The doctor managed to fashion a very good living and among other things he had acquired an extensive and expensive wine collection. Expensive wines are beyond my means as I

Inconsistencies

frequently pop the Three Buck Chuck found at Trader Joe's. The Good Doctor was drinking the good stuff and it was all compliments of the insurance companies.

As these things frequently turn out, the divorce deposition testimony of Dr. Knowitall somehow leaked out and became public information. I have a sneaking suspicion that his ex-wife may have spilled the beans, but that is only a guess, but probably a good one. The petitioner's attorneys began to offer part of the divorce deposition in an effort to undercut the greedy doctor. Dave Cody was in front of me and was explaining why the deposition testimony should be received. I asked him, "Do you want to show that the Good Doctor is cleaning up?" He responded, "Why no judge, we want to show how most or the majority of his income is from independent medical examinations and not medical practice. The Good Doctor is no longer a medical practitioner but merely a hired gun." I said, "It looks to me like you want to show that Dr. Knowitall is cleaning up." Dave countered, "Yes, I guess he is cleaning up." He was cleaning up in the sense that he was making a good living for very little effort as IME's seldom take more than a half an hour for the actual examination and he did not have to deal with patients. I have had many workers testify that, "I was in and out of that exam room in ten minutes or less." Most petitioner's lawyers tell their clients to time the examination. The IME physician should have reviewed the pertinent medical and other records in advance of the examination so normally the actual physical examination probably should be the shortest part of the process. Dave Cody's father was an attorney in St. Paul and I had known him when I was just starting out.

These are just some of the factors that any judge has to consider in reaching a decision. The petitioner may well have been sent to a physician primarily for an opinion as opposed to treatment. There are doctors who generally favor the injured employee and the knowledgeable counsel will steer an injured employee over to Dr. Heartwarm for a favorable opinion relating to his client. This does not come cheap and the lawyer may be on the hook for the exam and report fee so that he has to have a pretty good view of his case or he stands to be out some money. So that is the way it is. There are plaintiff doctors and there are defense doctors. This rule is subject to all kinds of exceptions as the defense doctor may well come out strong for an injured worker when the worker is his patient. Years ago, some doctors took the pristine and so-called high minded view that they would not get involved in any litigation and would not cooperate with petitioner's lawyers in providing medical information and opinions to counsel. While that may sound noble in that they are "remaining above the fray," it makes little practical sense. The injured worker is the one who needs money to pay a mortgage and put food on the table and even pay the doctor's bill. Left with no job income and no workers' comp benefits, then no one gets paid. The treating doctor has a duty to his patients to provide copies of his medical records and if asked for an opinion, render a fair and honest statement of his medical conclusion. If he is giving opinions, a fair charge for his opinions is probably in order. Lawyers charge for their opinions, so it is probably fair that doctors do the same thing.

What does a judge do in the face of dueling experts? I usually looked pretty carefully at what the treating doctor put in his examination notes. This may differ from what he puts down in a letter to the employee's counsel. For example, if one is dealing with a back injury and the employee is seen on numerous occasions by the treating doctor and they have carefully noted the examination findings in the office notes, one would look to see if there is consistency in the examination findings. If the physician is recording back range of motion in their notes, is the extension of the back usually 10 degrees and the flexion of the back around 45 degrees? Normal extension is probably 20 degrees and flexion would be 90 degrees. If the extension is 20 degrees on some occasions and 10 degrees on other occasions and if flexion is 90 degrees one day and on the next examination only 45 degrees, there is inconsistency shown and it should be explained. Perhaps on one day, the employee was experiencing severe back spasms and could hardly move. Check the medical records further to see if there is an explanation for the inconsistent performance. A diligent petitioner's attorney will deal with it on direct and seek to explain to the judge exactly why there are some inconsistent performances. Perhaps the employee had been active in physical rehabilitation and usually felt quite good following a session and did unusually well on examination finding in the doctor's office the next day. If he showed up the following day with very limited range of motion, perhaps he had pushed too hard the day before in rehabilitation and consequently his out of the ordinary examination findings can be explained by that scenario. The discerning judge is looking for consistent performance, and if that is not the case then looks for some reasonable explanation for the inconsistency.

Any examining physician in evaluating a back case will always use the straight leg test and look to see if it is consistent in different positions. Typically, the doctor will ask the patient to lie on their back and move their legs bilaterally or one leg at a time up to 90 degrees and record how far up they go. Normal range would likely be to 90 degrees. Active range of motion would be the range of motion that the employee generates without any assistance from the doctor. Passive range of motion would be the range of motion that the employee can achieve with some assistance provided by the doctor in lifting the patient's leg. With passive range of motion, the doctor relies on the employee to advise when the point of pain is reached and the doctor should release. Let us assume that the doctor goes to 45 degrees with each leg and stops because the patient advises that there is pain and the doctor should stop.

To check for inconsistencies, the examining doctor will seat the employee at the edge of the examining table with the legs dangling over the edge and check range of motion, active and passive. Let us assume that the doctor passively moves the patient's leg in extension out to 90 degrees without pain. Think about this, it is exactly the same movement of the legs, whether one is lying on one's back or in a sitting position. In both cases, the object is to move the legs to 90 degrees. If the worker goes to only 45 degrees while in a prone position, but goes to 90 degrees in a sitting position, there has been inconsistency shown.

I am not saying that an inconsistent straight leg raising test is going to torpedo an otherwise valid claim, however if there are other inconsistencies shown in the case, then it may be a doubtful claim or one that will have to be denied. For example, one may be asserting a back claim, but have no mention of back problems in the medical records during the first month following the accident. Perhaps the employee was being treated for an arm injury. The employee could offer that he mentioned back pain consistently, but the medical providers were concentrating on his arm and failed to note his complaints. This may be true, but if other inconsistencies begin to surface, then it may be a questionable claim.

If I had to point to one thing I normally checked very carefully, it was the range of motion physical examination findings that were recorded by a diligent treating or examining doctor. If the range of motion examination is made fairly regularly and the findings seem consistent, one is looking at a pretty good claim. If the findings are all over the map and no explanation is discovered, then perhaps the petitioner may have a burden of proof problem. One needs to review the entire record with time and care. I always read every record, front to back and did not take short cuts. I do not know how one can do the job without that degree of diligence. I recall talking with one of the judges and she remarked that she was having trouble reaching a decision and found it necessary to read the entire record before making a decision. That should be job number one in all cases we decide.

Chapter 8
Death in St. Paul

Death claims in workers' compensation frequently present an intriguing area of litigation. The magic words in the statute are the injury (death is an injury under the law) must "arise out of and in the course of employment." The injured worker must show a connection between the work activity and the resulting injury. If worker Jones sustains a heart attack at home while having a beer on his deck, it will be most difficult to prove a connection to his employment. If worker Jones is on his employer's property and in walking up a flight of stairs to deliver a five-page report to his boss and sustains a heart attack, Jones is at least "in the course of employment" as it is on the employer's premises and during his normal hours of work. The difficulty with the claim is, did the injury "arise out of" his employment activity? In other words, is there a connection between the injury (death) and his employment? Simply being at work is not enough. Jones may well find a cardiac specialist who will conclude that the act of ascending the steps put enough strain on his heart so that it created an oxygen deficiency and the result was that Jones had a cardiac event with infarct and died. Mr. Jone's employer will have no problem in finding a cardiac specialist who will conclude that there was no connection whatever between the employment activity and the resulting death and in fact, the injury could have occurred anywhere and it just happened to occur at work. Now if the facts change slightly and Mr. Jones is carrying a 100 lb. bag of fertilizer to give to his boss, then Jone's case becomes much stronger. Like any case, the result has a lot to do with the facts.

Raymond Gibberd was an English gentleman who had come over to Minnesota with his family to work on computers for the Control Data Corporation (CDC). World War II provided much of the impetus for computer development as the US and British Armies were both in need of some way to manage large amounts of growing data. During the Polish invasion, the Polish Army acquired a German machine called the ENIGMA and passed it on to the Brits. The German U Boat fleet used ENIGMA encoded messages to communicate with their naval headquarters and provided information on location, fuel status, and other logistical details. The British worked off the ENIGMA and began to develop their own machines for managing data and code-breaking. This information was passed on to the Americans shortly before our entry into the world fray.

One of the Naval personnel who worked on code-breaking and submarine location was LT Commander William C. Norris, with the Communications Supplementary Activity in Washington. Following the war, the Navy wished to keep this valuable activity going and provided civilian contracts as an inducement for the continuation of computer work. The result was Engineering Research Associates of St. Paul formed in 1946 and Control Data Corporation was to follow with civilian, Bill Norris, as its longtime leader.

Control Data Corporation had prospered after the war and soon had plants located at various locations around the Twin Cities. Mr. Gibberd and his wife and two daughters came to Minnesota on Raymond's work visa in March of 1985 and commenced work at the CDC plant in Minnetonka. He was later transferred to the Control Data plant in St. Paul located on Dale Street and near interstate freeway number 94. The Control Data plant on Dale Street was known as the World Distribution Center (WDC). Mr. Gibberd was recruited from his native country to come here and work on information retrieval. A skill that most of us have needed a time or two.

August 26, 1985 was a clear, sunny summer day in Minnesota and Raymond Gibberd arose early and had breakfast and kissed his wife goodbye and headed for work. His two young daughters were still in bed. He called home around 4:30 to talk to his oldest daughter, Anna, who had just started school. She did not have time to talk to her father as she was busy playing with friends. Raymond did call Anna back around 7:30 p.m. and advise her that he was going down to Wendy's to get a bite to eat. He signed out on the company log at 8:05 p.m. and walked the few short blocks to Wendy's located on Dale Street and University Avenue. It turned out to be his last sign out.

Mr. Gibberd did not return to work because he was shot in cold blood on Dale Street some 3-4 blocks removed from the World Distribution Center. His killer was never apprehended and to this day there remains no apparent motive for this execution-style murder. Mr. Gibberd was survived by his wife and two small children. His wife, Elizabeth or Betty, brought a workers' compensation case on behalf of herself and two minor daughters. Mrs. Gibberd was the petitioner in this case because she was the person seeking payment of compensation benefits.

The first witness called by the petitioner was the young daughter, Anna. The lawyers stipulated that if she were called she would testify that her father called her around 7:30 p.m. and told her he was going to Wendy's to get a bite to eat. The daughter was a young child and her testimony dealt with the last words she had with her father. It would have been a difficult and likely tear-filled testimony. Often, lawyers will call young witnesses to engender sympathy for their cause, but it is hard on the witness and sometimes not worth the price. If it was a jury case, the petitioner maybe would have called young Anna.

The parties stipulated as to Anna's expected testimony. They did not stipulate that the testimony was admissible. The attorney for Control Data objected to the testimony as hearsay. On the face of it, it looked like hearsay, because the witness was testifying to an out of court statement made by someone who was not available for cross-examination. Mr. Gibberd had allegedly made the statement "I am going to Wendy's to get a bite to eat." Mr. Gibberd was certainly not available for cross-examination as he was dead. One exception to the hearsay rule is the so-called dying declaration. The basis for this exception is that people are likely to tell the truth when they are facing the Grim Reaper and such statements made when death is imminent have a strong likelihood of being true and should be received. Mr. Gallegos, counsel for Control Data, pointed out that Mr. Gibberd certainly did not know he was going to die when he announced his dinner plans so therefore the exception does not apply and the statement should be excluded. I told the parties I would take the matter under advisement and tell them of my ruling before the trial was over. Most of the time I did not have the luxury of time, but this was going to be a two-day trial and I could sleep on it if necessary. I so often found that in dealing with trial problems or even life's every day difficulties, that a good night's sleep brings clarity to an issue. I seldom have any problems sleeping at night, and frequently, the next morning brings clarity to issues that seemed complicated only eight hours earlier. I was probably going to receive the statement, but would advise the parties later.

The first "live" witness called by the petitioner was the surviving spouse, Elizabeth Gibberd. Mrs. Gibberd was a nice appearing, soft spoken, and intelligent witness. She was "likeable" and that is a great asset in any case. Sometimes we get the idea that likeability is only important with jury cases and judges are such a hard-hearted lot that we can set aside all of the personal elements and make decisions only on the cold hard facts of the case. That is not true. Judges are people too and it is very important to have witnesses come off as likeable. They are much more likely to be accepted by the fact finder. Mrs. Gibberd was certainly going to be an asset to her case, but that did not mean I was going to decide in her favor. She was originally an Irish citizen and was currently 35 years of age. I always liked the Irish. They have a great spirit and a wonderful sense of humor. I have a dear colleague on the bench named Dan Gallagher who has a dry sense of humor that often characterizes the Irish wit.

The Gibberd's were originally planning to stay in the USA as they wanted to raise their children in this country. Mr. Gibberd had received his green card to work in this country, but Mrs. Gibberd was here on a visitor's or guest visa. After Raymond's demise, she was told by those hard-hearts at INA that she was going to have to leave. Mr. Gibberd had previously worked for IBM in Boulder, Colorado and later was shipped back to England and before he reached the English Channel, he spoke with Control Data Corporation and found out they had a need for someone in his area of computer expertise. They spent a year back in England and then in March of 1985 he returned to the States to work for Control Data.

Apparently, the Gibberd's had discussed the availability of handguns in the States and viewed that as the only negative point about coming to the US. It obviously did not deter them so probably that topic was only briefly discussed. Betty Gibberd mentioned that the English police were not even armed. Much has changed since this trial took place as the Bobbies are now armed and we have lots of laws on the books regulating or prohibiting hand guns and they do not seem to have accomplished much of anything.

Apparently, when Raymond left IBM in Colorado, they gave him a statue of a cowboy but had to take pains to find an unarmed cowboy. A cowboy without a gun sounds like an oxymoron. They probably had to take the cigarettes away from the poor cowboy as well.

The Gibberd's were also concerned about the Minnesota weather as friends had commented, "You must be mad to go there because of the snow and everything." Some of their friends were on the mark, as after a tough Minnesota winter, I feel like I just survived six months in a gulag. They were sent a Twin Cities guide and they looked that over and concluded it only snows for six months a year and there is some sunshine on special occasions. The guides usually do not feature January blizzards and sub-zero cold.

Ray was originally scheduled to work at the CDC Plant in Minnetonka, MN and the offer letter stated he would be in the nice suburban location. Ray worked long hours and sometimes worked into the wee hours of the morning. He often worked outside of the normal 9-5 as he was able to use the computer or get more efficient computer time during non-peak times. Mrs. Gibberd testified that the computer worked faster when there were not as many users making demands on the machine. Mrs. Gibberd was certainly getting into the area of hearsay or foundation problems as she was relaying what her husband had told her about computer use. There was no objection voiced by the lawyer for CDC and it was not my job to object.

On one occasion when a defense witness happened to be a mentally challenged adult and the petitioner's counsel asked him a question that assumed a result such as the classic "when did you stop beating your wife" question, then I did intervene and stopped that one from the bench. Many times counsel does not wish to object for strategic reasons and I did not like to second-guess their strategy.

Counsel for Mrs. Gibberd then asked, "Would you say it was for the benefit of Control Data, that he worked those hours?" This was objected to as a conclusion and I sustained it. Lay witnesses such as Mrs. Gibberd are supposed to testify to facts and not opinions and there are many reasons people work long hours and unless she had some special insight, she was not qualified to express an opinion. I knew from my own experience that people worked long hours for a variety of reasons. I knew lawyers that put in miles of hours because they loved what they were doing or other lawyers that simply did not like to spend time with their spouse. There is always something pressing in the law so it can be a great avoidance mechanism. Further, I was not sure Mrs. Gibberd was in a position to know what benefitted Control Data Corporation. That was outside the scope of her knowledge and a conclusion.

Not long after arriving in Minnesota, Raymond began working in St. Paul at the World Distribution Center (WDC) located on North Dale Street. In his application for alien employment, it stated he would be working at the North Dale Street Plant. This seems to be at variance with the employment letter he got from CDC as that put his place of work in suburban Minnetonka. It seemed to me that this was informative information and not some sort of guarantee as to place of employment. There was no record of Mr. Gibberd complaining or objecting to the WDC as his place of employment. He apparently went to work there without objecting to the location.

When the Gibberd's arrived from England there was a group of CDC co-workers who served as an informal welcome committee. The petitioner's counsel asked if, "any warning had been passed on to you or Ray that the Dale plant was in an unsafe area of town?" A hearsay objection was made and I overruled and allowed her to testify that no warning was made. We did not know who these coworkers were and what if any authority they possessed to speak for the employer. There was no testimony that they were management. The testimony was probably irrelevant, but I did not get that objection, so I overruled the hearsay objection. She was then asked, "Were you aware that this was an unsafe area of St. Paul?" This was objected to as leading and lacking in foundation. It was leading and she testified she had not been warned and did not possess any special knowledge of the area so she was certainly lacking in foundation. She was from England and not from St. Paul. That was like asking me if it was safe in Buckingham Palace. I don't know, but guess it would depend on whether or not Patricia Bowles was around or not.

On the morning of August 26, 1985, Mr. Gibberd left for work around 7:00 a.m. She gave him a $10 bill and it was apparent he was not a high roller, but counsel asked if he usually carried a lot of money. He did not. He called home around 4:00 p.m. and advised he would not be home for dinner. He also talked to his daughter Anna.

Mr. Gibberd called back later between 7:00 and 7:30 p.m. and talked to Anna about her first day of school. I have had several of those conversations myself over the years and I always sincerely wanted to know what happened on the first day of school with each of my children, but somehow nothing ever occurred. I am sure that somehow nothing happened in this conversation either, but for some reason I got another hearsay objection. I hemmed and hawed around and ended up over-ruling the objection because the only relevant point was the time of the conversation and there was no objection to that testimony.

Mrs. Gibberd then testified that Ray told her, "That reminds me, I'm starving. I'm going out to have a bite to eat." The CDC counsel again objected on hearsay and I told them I would rule on the phone statements later as they all have the same objections. I am not sure why I was waiting as the case was not going to turn on Mr. Gibberd's phone conversations with his wife or his 6-year-old daughter. Usually the safe course for a judge to follow is to let the evidence be admitted as a civil case is almost never tipped over if the judge lets something in that should not have been allowed. This is particularly true if the judge finds in favor of the objecting party. In other words, if the defense is going to win, then let the plaintiff put in the kitchen sink and then they cannot appeal and get you overturned on an evidentiary ruling. On the other hand, if the evidence is excluded and the offering party loses, they will argue on appeal that the judge excluded evidence that would have turned the tide in their direction. I had no idea how this case was going to turn out. I knew this case was a tough one for Mrs. Gibberd to establish and that is why it was being tried, so maybe I was more inclined to allow the petitioner some leeway so I could find out where they were headed.

When I was in the Army, Judge Snyder, when he had made up his mind to convict, would go back and change all his rulings in favor of the government and rule for the accused. Sometimes the accused would take heart at his new found success. However, it was apparent that he was going down. I knew it was goodbye old buddy, so I never took heart at my new-found courtroom brilliance.

Mr. Gibberd usually went to eat at Wendy's because he liked the salad bar. He frequently went to eat with two colleagues, Dennis Piper and Wayne Hoff. Mrs. Gibberd did not hear of any employer objections to his going out to eat.

Mrs. Gibberd was then asked the next time she had any word of her husband. At about 11:00 o'clock that night the police came to the door and asked, "Mrs. Gibberd?" She responded, "Yes" and they continued, "Raymond Paul Gibberd?" She again responded, "Yes." The poor cops did not know the details and called the station and were given a report of a robbery. Mrs. Gibberd told them it could not have been a robbery as he only had $10 and he would have surrendered that amount with no resistance. He was not about to fight over a few bucks. The police then recalled the station and tried to find out more details on the reason for the shooting. It was then reported to be a random shooting.

I cannot think of a worse job for a policeman than going out to a dark house at 11:00 at night and telling a nice young woman that she has lost her husband in a random shooting. The police had done the same thing when I was at Coon Rapids and always sent two people. One of the two was usually a sergeant or above. The sergeants had done it before and usually knew what to say. The military always sends two people as well. One is normally a chaplain. During WWII, when there were so many casualties the military sent a telegram, but because the public thought it cruel and heartless, they eventually changed to a personal visit. During the Vietnam period, word eventually got around that if a military vehicle pulled up and two officers got out, they were not going to tell you that your son just made corporal.

Mrs. Gibberd testified that Ray had no enemies, had not been threatened and had never been in trouble with the law. He did not take drugs and did not own a weapon. He usually wore a Control Data name tag on his top left hand pocket. She knew that because he frequently forgot to take it off and often wore it in the grocery store and other public places. I could relate to that as the judges had badges or name tags that also served to open doors and I practically wore mine to bed. Guys do not have a purse that they can tuck it in when they go off premises. In all likelihood even with a purse, I would still wear that damn thing all over the place as I just do not give that stuff a lot of thought.

Ray would not have been in an area where he thought it could be dangerous. She testified that he was not a risk taker. This testimony was a bit conflicted as they seemed to contend it was a dangerous neighborhood and the employer put the plant in a dangerous area, but if it was dangerous, Ray would have avoided it.

The direct testimony of Mrs. Gibberd was concluded and counsel turned it over to Mr. Gallegos, the attorney for CDC, for cross-examination. Cross-examination is a bit like a loaded gun. It can be lifesaving, but you can also shoot yourself in the foot if you are not careful.

The defense counsel asked Mrs. Gibberd if her husband had been working long hours since he came to Minnesota. The reply was that he had worked late at least three days per week during May of 1985, but she was unsure how many days he worked late in June of 1985. Upon further inquiry she responded that in a typical June week he worked late 2-3 days a week. Mr. Gibberd frequently would go home and have dinner with the family only to return to work and not return home until 11:00 p.m.

When Mr. Gibberd worked late, he ate frequently at Wendy's, located a short distance from the plant. He would typically return to work after eating at Wendy's. Mrs. Gibberd correctly pointed out that there was no point in going to Wendy's to eat and then turning around and heading for home. Counsel asked if he was wearing his badge outside and she replied that he had it on his person, but she had to admit that she did not know whether or not he was wearing it outside.

I did not usually get involved with a lot of questions of the witnesses that appeared before me, but sometimes if there was an area of concern, I made some inquiry. Some judges have an overpowering urge to ask a bunch of questions in an effort to show everyone how smart they are, but frequently it only shows they are grandstanding or not very savvy. I usually interjected only if I believed the counsel may have missed something or there was an area that needed further inquiry. I have had counsel object to my questions, but not too frequently. I got a foundation objection one day and sustained the objection and then proceeded to lay further foundation for my questions. I don't take offense to those types of things and would not punish a client for any perceived transgression committed by counsel. Some of the district court judges I have encountered think they are the next thing to Deity and it is hard to say how some of those bastards would react.

 I asked Mrs. Gibberd if either she or her husband had been involved in any automobile or other accidents since they had been here. I also inquired as to whether anyone in the family had been involved in any assaults or fisticuffs since arriving in the USA. She responded in the negative. I asked if her husband used alcohol and she said he did. Counsel for Mrs. Gibberd asked her to describe her husband's use of alcohol and he was described as a social drinker who maybe had a beer in the evening. He did not use drugs.

 I guess the motivation behind my questions was that I wanted to determine or rule out any possible enemies that Mr. Gibberd may have engendered by being involved in an assault or an automobile accident that could have sparked some ill-will. I asked about the alcohol use to rule out in my mind the possibility that Mr. Gibberd may have been headed for a bar during the fateful night. He was not a drinker or a fighter so it began to appear that we could rule out a personal problem contributing to his demise. Most of the time, I ask counsel if they have any questions based on my questions and I forgot to do so in this case, but Ms. Bjorklund, the lawyer for the petitioner, stepped in anyway and did an effective follow up on my questions on the use of alcohol. I was glad that she was not hesitant about following up on my questions.

 Ms. Bjorklund next called as a witness I will call Mr. Dennis Piper, a coworker at CDC. Mr. Piper worked at the World Distribution Center and saw Mr. Gibberd on a daily basis. Mr. Piper was a hardware/software engineer and he was familiar with Ray's work. IBM had a program in effect for many years to access information from broken computers and thereby make it easier to fix the computer and avoid future problems. Control Data had been trying to develop the same program without much success so that is why they hired Raymond. Mr. Gibberd had the experience with IBM and the know-how so it made sense for CDC to try to leverage some of that experience to their benefit. I doubt if he possessed any so-called trade secrets, but he did have valuable work experience and people trade on their work experience every day of the week.

 Mr. Piper did not receive any special warning when he went to work at the

Death in St. Paul

WDC on Dale Street. He frequently worked at night and often would be there in the evening with Ray. Ray was working on a project that required him to modify the software or program that he was using and shut the machine down and re-start the computer and see if the program ran or crashed. I guess in terms of modern day computers he was working on retrieval of information. I am no computer genius, but this trial was in the day before personal computers and cell phones and all the rest of the modern day nuisances. From a technical standpoint, I had very little background to decipher any of the technical stuff they were talking about. It really did not matter as he was not killed by a computer.

Mr. Piper wore a pictured identification badge as did Ray and other CDC employees. I asked if it was about the size of a driver's license and Mr. Piper replied in the affirmative. Mr. Piper produced a badge and I described it for the record as about the size of a driver's license with the words Control Data Corporation on the badge and also the CDC logo. The badge itself was not offered in evidence as I gave a good description of the item and putting the badge itself in would have just been redundant.

Some folks put all sorts of things in evidence when there is no special need for it. I can understand when it is important in a jury trial to put into evidence items that the jury can see and hold. They call it demonstrative evidence in the jury trial trade. In most cases with a court trial the judge can frequently figure out what you are describing by testimony or a picture and an elaborate and expensive exhibit is not needed. For example, if you are talking about a certain tool used in a trade, you can show the item you are talking about to the judge and have the judge fondle it, but in most circumstances there is not much need to put the item itself into evidence. I had a case one time involving a brick layer and one of the tools he was talking about was a brick layers' trowel. The trowel used by professional brick layers was much heavier than the flimsy tool that a weekend brick layer would pick up at Home Depot. The pointy metal part of the tool featured heavy gauge steel at least 1/8 inch thick. The handle was steel covered by a wood overlay. The tool had to be heavy duty as professional brick-layers would hold a brick in their hand and crack the brick with a trowel to break it. One could not do that with a cheap trowel. The attorney representing the brick layer was describing the work done by a brick layer and it was hard work. He then got into describing the tools used in the trade. He produced a trowel and described it and then offered it into evidence. It was received without objection. After the case was concluded, the exhibit remained in my office for several months. No one bothered to retrieve it or ask for it back. I finally took it home and parked it in my shop. I used it on several occasions when I was doing some cement work on various jobs. I just used it a month or two ago. If the litigants want it back, I stand ready to return it to the rightful owner.

Mr. Piper testified that with CDC he worked all sorts of different hours. He worked during the day and sometimes at night. He said that part of his job description specified that he was on 24-hour call with Control Data and available 365 days a year to go anywhere they tell him to go. It sounded to me a lot like my job description with the Army. Actually I never saw my job description but I did realize that I was on call seven days a week and twenty-four hours a day. That was the case with almost all officers. When I was in Germany, on occasion, I would get a knock on my door at some odd hour and a MP would ask if I could counsel some poor guy that had messed up in a bad way and they wanted to send him to pre-trial confinement. Army Europe had a rule that one could not go into pre-trial confinement unless he had seen a JAG first. In those cases, I did not spend a lot of time with the accused, but I did advise him that he was going to the slammer and another lawyer would be appointed his lawyer, but in the meantime he must shut up and do not discuss his case with any of the jail personnel and to be careful about saying anything to any other inmates. Occasionally a colleague from the jail will rat someone else out so that they can get a break on their sentence or some other special treatment. Watch what you say because those jail house walls have ears.

    Mr. Piper had been out to eat in the evening with Ray on several occasions. They had gone to Sweeney's, a bar and grill south on Dale Street some four blocks from the World Distribution Center or north on Dale to Wendy's. There was a cafeteria on premises, but it closed at 3:00 p.m. Apparently, CDC personnel made a daily work report to management and that usually required some sort of summary of what you worked on and if you went out to eat and returned, that information was usually included in your report. There was no company prohibition against going off premises to eat.

    There were vending machines on premises, but they stocked candy and potato chips and not the usual dinner fare. One needed change for the machines and sometimes the change machine did not work. It was not a healthy choice to use the vending machines, but sometimes it was a healthier choice than leaving the premises.

    Mr. Piper was working during Ray's last night and was in his regular "cube" located some twenty feet away. He described the distance separating them as "about the length of this courtroom." Being the ever vigilant judge, I described the courtroom as being about, "Twenty feet long." I usually ask the attorneys if they agree with my measurement, but I skipped that technicality this time and kept my foot on the gas. I took the silence of counsel as their assent. My experience as a builder came in handy when it came to describing distances or measurements and I was usually pretty accurate. The ultimate decision could be off, but the measurements were correct.

    It is important for a trial judge to make a good record so that a reviewing court can determine what is being done during the trial. I recalled a workers' comp case I tried years ago up in Detroit Lakes and I was representing a local

Death in St. Paul

rube claiming to be disabled from bilateral carpal tunnel. We tried it in the summer and the employee came in wearing a short sleeve shirt. He was tanned and well-muscled and the defense attorney, Carl Knudson, described the man's arms for the record as tanned and well-muscled. I disputed the description, but in all honesty, it was not too far off the mark. I should have told the guy to wear a long sleeved shirt. The judge, I think it was Joe Murray, ended up cutting the guy off from weekly benefits. The guy did turn out to be a jerk as he did not want to pay the doctor for coming in to testify when I had sent him a letter before the trial telling him he had to pay the doctor's bill and we could recover it if he won. He claimed that was a news flash. I think he found another lawyer.

Mr. Piper had just returned from a business trip to England where he had taught a course for Control Data in London. He asked Ray about a particular destination in London and though it may have been near Trafalgar Square. I had been to London a couple times when I was in the Army and a couple times thereafter so I was familiar with the point of their discussion. My first time in London, I had the good fortune to see Jimmy Stewart play Elwood P. Dowd, the eccentric professor in the wonderful production of "Harvey." We caught a matinee and sat four rows back, center stage. This experience was one of my favorite times, whether in or out of the Army.

Mr. Piper had his "London conversation" with Ray at around 7:35. I wondered how he could be so accurate with the time, but some people are very precise about time. Phyllis is like that, she always knows precisely what time we left the house and what time we arrived. She is generally correct on time as well as all other subjects.

Mr. Piper and Ray talked for a while and then Ray said, "Well, I've got to be getting back to work." Mr. Piper relayed that he recalled what was said because Ray had a charming English accent and he always admired a British accent. I could relate to that as I was somewhat taken by the accent as well as some of the expressions or figures of speech. I kind of liked the working class or cockney form of speech. We were camped on the coast of France one time and I ran into a butcher and his family from London and we had a wonderful time. When we left, he gave me his card and a beer and toasted me with a, "To Sir Ronald." So I was knighted.

Mr. Piper worked till around 10:20 and then headed home. He was hoping his wife was not upset with him for working late. I could relate to that. Any lawyer could. He had no idea what had befallen Mr. Gibberd until he arrived at work the next day.

Mr. Piper arrived for work at ten to eight the next morning and received the bad news about Mr. Gibberd. They checked the computer and found that Ray's processes were still running. Mr. Piper said, "We better capture this program." This showed good sense as one never knows what might be important when someone departs under unusual circumstances. Ray had been working on a production process and a personal user process. Ray would not have left the processes running if he did not intend to come back to the computer. This was a security issue and they did not leave the system open for any extended periods because there was a chance that someone could enter the system and do damage or swipe information. Security was a concern even in those days. I asked him what a process was and he said it is whatever you are doing or working on with the computer. If I was checking a girlie site, it was a process. A very secret process. When he got in the next morning the machine was in a running mode, but not working on any special process. It was in an idle mode. Like a car in park with the engine running. The computer he had been working on was not a Control Data made product. For some reason, they were not eating their own cooking at CDC. When one got done with the computer, it was customary to log off and if it had been done, it would show up on the hard-drive. There was no log off on Ray's session.

I asked him if there was any way he could tell when the "machine went into idle?" They were able to tell when he started the process but not when the machine went into idle. He started the process late in the afternoon after 4:00 p.m..

After they checked Mr. Gibberd's computer entries, they went to Ray's cubicle and observed that his briefcase was open and his light was on and papers and books were spread out all over his desk. It sounded like my desk. He saw a gold pen on the desk. Mr. Piper said the desk and office looked like he had just departed for a short time, such as when one goes to the rest room. They put a tape across the cubicle so that others would stay out.

The building or company maintained a sign-in and out log and Ray signed out at 8:05 p.m. CDC had admitted in their pre-trial statement that Mr. Gibberd had gone to Wendy's to eat, but apparently at this point they were backing water and not prepared to admit that Ray had gone to Wendy's. The petitioner offered the pre-trial statement and I asked counsel if it was offered as some sort of "judicial admission." She laughed and questioned if it was a judicial admission. That was funny as obviously I had not made any admissions so it was not a judicial admission. I corrected and called it an in-court admission as it was submitted to the court. I thought it had some probative value so I received the pre-trial statement. Ms. Bjorklund was claiming penalties for a wrongful denial of claim and the exhibit was offered, mainly on the penalty issue.

Ms. Bjorklund then went into a line of questioning with Mr. Piper regarding personal safety in the area. Mr. Piper had done a lot of traveling for CDC, including places such as Vietnam, West Africa, and North Korea. "Those places were occupied by the Russians and Libyans and you learn to watch your back." I am not sure the Libyans and Russians were in Vietnam, but several of my friends told me that it was not a very safe place as people were shooting at them.

Mr. Piper related that he saw youths in the parking lot on a summer night around 10:00 p.m. and he felt like a potential target. Mr. Piper probably had some valid concerns about personal safety in the area where he worked, but there was no indication or testimony that he brought those concerns to the attention of CDC management prior to the demise of Mr. Gibberd. Attorney Gallegos objected to the testimony as irrelevant, but I allowed it to come in anyway. Again, the safe course was to let it in.

Mr. Piper was asked why CDC built in that slum and he admitted it was conjecture, but someone told him that the company wanted to create jobs in "blighted areas or whatever." Apparently, CDC had become more interested in urban renewal than in making computers. It is sometimes dangerous for a company's long term health when they get too far removed from their original mission. Apparently, before CDC started their reclamation project there was a sleazy bar in the area and it was crime infested. I missed that old place. The bar had gone away, but Piper claimed the area was not safe and Ray was a bit naïve and was not conditioned to watch his back.

Mr. Piper and some of his coworkers wrote a letter to CDC management the day after Mr. Gibberd's demise and asked to be moved out of the area. Management responded to the grievance and advised that they could not move as it was a fairly new facility. As a practical matter, they probably did not have the funds to pack up everyone and move to a new location. Moreover, where is a crime free location? Such a place is hard to find in this day and age. Management did advise them that after normal hours they could park in the visitor spots located next to the building. The lighting was better and they could request a security guard to accompany them to their car. Mr. Piper did not believe the security guards could protect him as most of them were overweight and unarmed. That seems like a job requirement with security people.

Generally, after-the-fact action is not admissible. For example, if there was no railing going down a stairs and someone falls and sues the building owner, the plaintiff cannot testify that they put a new railing in a week later. The reason for that rule is that if subsequent measures were admissible, then the property owner would not put in a new railing and someone else would fall. Society normally wants people to fix problems and the law does not want to get in the way of remedial action or repairs. The law does get in the way of just about everything else so it is surprising to see such reluctance. Much of Mr. Piper's testimony related to remedial action or after the fact happenings. I did not get an objection related to remedial action so I let it all in. The testimony on the parking lot was interesting, but this was not a parking lot case. If Mr. Gibberd had been killed in the parking lot, we would have a far different case and CDC may well have paid it. The employer can control what happens on their property and has some responsibility to do so, but can they control what happens out on the street? Are they responsible for what happens off the premises?

This is the million-dollar question that I was going to have to answer.

Mr. Piper was asked about Mr. Gibberd's business reputation and responded that he was well respected by his work colleagues and did not have an abrasive or aggressive personality. On the Friday before, his death, Mr. Piper and Ray were joined by Mike and Wayne at Sweeney's Bar, near the office, and Ray kept busy reading while the three colleagues engaged in a heated discussion over a project they were working on. Ray had chuckled about it and finally said, "Well, if you three are finished with your palace rebellion, maybe we can press on and enjoy a pint of beer." Ray knew what was important.

Mr. Gallegos moved to sequester the witnesses prior to his cross-examination of Mr. Piper. In moving to sequester, he was asking that the other witnesses be excluded from the courtroom so that they did not have a chance to know what the cross-examination was going to cover and thereby prepare for their own testimony. The parties to the case cannot be sequestered as they have a right to be present, but there was one future witness named Wayne Hoff, who was present at the beer fest at Sweeney's, so I asked Mr. Hoff to wait outside the courtroom until he was called.

In response to cross-examination, Mr. Piper related that his job title was Senior Technical Support Engineer. His job was to solve technical problems with CDC computers. This was done over the phone or in person. He also worked on the computers in the building when they had problems.

He testified that Ray's job was to develop a program to retain data in CDC machines. Ray's job was different in that he did not have to talk to customers in the field. Mr. Piper had testified that he was on duty 24 hours a day and Mr. Gallegos asked him about his job description and Piper had not read it in a while, but thought it said available 24 hours a day and go anywhere in the world as assigned by CDC. His job was sounding more and more like the special-forces. He advised that others who had read his job description asked if there was anything you do not do? His response was, "windows." A little humor often slips into the courtroom. Mr. Piper had never read Ray's job description.

Having an employee available to the employer 24 hours a day may sound good to an employer, but if the employee gets hurt, it makes it hard for the employer to argue that the employee was not at work as he was theoretically always working. The petitioner's attorney was probably wishing at that point that her client had been graced with Mr. Piper's job description. I would like to read Mr. Pipers job description. I had my doubts as to whether his job description would confirm he was a 24-7 employee. In any event, we were wasting too much time on Mr. Piper's job description, as it seemed to be hijacking the trial.

They served lunch on the premises from 11:00 a.m. to 1:00 p.m. The lunch room and work space was all part of the World Distribution Center. Mr. Piper had gone out to eat with Ray in the evening on two occasions and thought they went to Sweeney's. Mr. Piper was asked the procedure governing the sign-in and sign-out log. The guard did not sign people out, the employee filled in the name and sign-out time. He said he knew there were inaccuracies in the log, and Mr. Gallegos interrupted and asked how he knew there were inaccuracies in the log. He testified that on Ray's last night he noticed that the person who signed out ahead of him had used the wrong clock time. Mr. Piper was asked, "So your testimony is at least on one occasion you saw an inaccuracy?" "Yes." (Q) "Okay you can't testify as a matter of fact that there are more inaccuracies, can you? (A) "No, I couldn't testify to anything like that." This was a good lesson in how cross-examination can bring out the truth. The witness testified with a flat statement that there are inaccuracies in the log. The facts were that he knew of only one inaccuracy in the log. The truth is that he does not know if there are inaccuracies in the log or not. I did not know at this point whether or not the log would play a significant role in the case, but at least if it did, it may even be accurate.

Mr. Gallegos then reminded the witness that he testified that management was aware that they would go out for meals. Dennis replied in the affirmative. Mr. Gallegos then followed up, "Who in management was aware?" He named two managers and said he was sure they knew we went out to eat and came back. Mr. Piper then said that Ray was a consultant and not paid overtime and it was evident that he did not know whether Ray had a reporting requirement for eating off premises or not.

Mr. Piper was a witness who was obviously trying to help the petitioner's case, but much of what he testified to was company rumor or things that he took for granted and that is not often a good basis for courtroom testimony. For example, the word around the plant may have been that the sign-out log was inaccurate, and he so testified, but the fact was, he had only a flimsy basis for concluding whether or not the log was accurate or not.

Mr. Piper was then asked about the vending machines. He had previously stated they were frequently empty. He conceded on cross-examination that he did not monitor the machines. He said take out was available, but they needed to take a break. He preferred to leave the building for his breaks, but that was a matter of preference.

Mr. Piper had testified on direct that in certain areas, as a white man, he had concerns. He had described it as a "gut feeling" based on his experience of being in many areas where he did not feel comfortable. He was unable to relate any specific bad or negative experience that gave rise to his "gut feeling."
He had this same feeling when describing the area around and near the WDC facility. It was like other bad areas he had visited and then reeled off names such as Watts or the Combat Zone in Boston. He then backtracked and said the immediate area was not a ghetto, but there were people who were out of work that would make him a target. Mr. Gallegos was persistent and asked, "Do you

have any facts to say how many people are out of work in that area?" Answer: "No." Mr. Piper then continued with his uncomfortable theory. He was asked again if this was a black area. He said, "Not necessarily black, it's just I—I—smell trouble there." He was asked for a specific incident, but instead talked about bag ladies and people with torn trench coats. I was not convinced we had a Watts or Combat Zone on our hands.

Mr. Piper was asked about Sweeney's Pub to the south on Dale Street and he described it as a more law school or professional crowd. Wendy's was about the same distance from the WDC only located to the north. Dennis then backed water and said that Wendy's was closer. It was probably two blocks from the WDC. He was then shown a map of the area and seemed to confirm his answer at two blocks. It looked longer than two blocks to me.

Other than Mr. Gibberd, Dennis was not personally aware of anyone being assaulted during the prior five years, either on or about the CDC premises. Then, without being asked a question, Mr. Piper related that he was in Sweeney's one evening and the police came in and relayed that some women had been slashed in the vicinity of the bar and the WDC. He claimed to have seen some news reports of assaults in the area. He was never assaulted and other than Mr. Gibberd, he had never heard of a CDC employee being subjected to an assault while in the vicinity of the World Distribution Center. Mr. Piper had the habit of answering a question and then following up with some sort of spontaneous remark. He should have been stopped as there was no question before him, but he was allowed to ramble on. Mr. Gallegos probably should have stopped him, but for the most part, none of the rambling seemed to hurt him. I found it a bit aggravating and was becoming more and more convinced that Mr. Piper had little to lend in the way of facts that would help me resolve this case.

Mr. Piper was asked by Ms. Bjorkland about the University Avenue neighborhood (Wendy's was on University Avenue) and he said it was a seedy neighborhood, but he was not much aware of it, but had heard others talk about it. He was devoid of personal knowledge on the subject. He was again unable to relate any specific complaints he had made to management about the safety of the area, until after Mr. Gibbert's demise.

The lawyers were finally concluded with Mr. Piper and I followed up with a couple of questions. What was the primary function of the World Distribution Center? It was primarily a parts center, but as CDC needed the space, they placed other employees such as Piper and Mr. Gibberd in the same facility. The official address was 304 or 308 North Dale Street. I asked how many employees at the facility? "There's a lot. There's got to be several hundred."

The Building was located a few hundred feet south of Interstate 94. A large parking lot was adjacent to the building and between the building and the parking lot the WDC complex occupied practically two square city blocks. Wendy's was located North on Dale Street and across 94 and about a quarter mile from the WDC. The most likely and common walking route to Wendy's would be north on Dale St. and across I-94 and then 3-4 short blocks to Wendy's at University Avenue. Sweeney's was 3 or 4 blocks away from the WDC going south on Dale Street. Piper testified that if he went to Sweeney's or Wendy's that he always drove. It was a European thing to walk, but he was a lazy American like the rest of us and always drove. Mr. Gibberd's immediate supervisor was located in a remote location and not in the WDC facility.

Mr. Piper had testified to other crimes that had taken place in the vicinity of the WDC facility and I wanted to find out when they occurred. The petitioner was trying to show this was a bad neighborhood and the frequency and type of crimes would certainly bear on that issue. Mr. Piper spoke of a theft in the building and someone stealing hub caps in the parking lot. The assault near Sweeney's was more serious, but we did not have a date. The witness was talking about two minor crimes and a possible more serious event in a five-year period. This would have been an exceedingly slow night in Watts.

Mr. Piper's testimony was rather inconclusive. He was trying to show that the WDC facility was in a crime-infested area and was an improper venue for professional workers to be employed. I grew up in the St. Paul area and any attempt to portray the neighborhood around the WDC facility as some sort of Watts or Bowery was pure hyperbole. One had to maintain a certain level of consciousness in any metropolitan area and the WDC neighborhood was no exception. The broader question was, is the employer obligated to choose a crime-free location for their business premises? Is there such a place? My workers' comp case was raising all sorts of social and economic issues. My own experiences spill into the case, as they must. The last thing we want from a judge is someone without a wide range of life experiences, because it is through life experiences that one gains knowledge and hopefully some degree of wisdom. I hoped I had acquired enough experience and maybe a little wisdom to decide this case properly. This is a decision that I spent a lot of time mulling around during my evening jog. My nightly run was always a good time to tackle issues or problems that were troubling me.

The petitioner next called Sergeant Dale Hartman of the St. Paul Police Department. SGT Hartman was a 16-year veteran of the force who had recently been promoted to homicide investigator or detective. SGT Hartman had come up through the ranks, starting as a patrolman and eventually becoming a supervisor and branched out into investigations starting with petty thefts and proceeding to auto thefts. He had learned how to investigate and handle crime scenes. Officer Hartman had attended some training sessions on crime scenes and investigations, but mostly had learned on the job. He did not have a college background, but that did not make the least difference with me. He had handled over twenty homicide scenes, plus he had years of experience on the streets. He could testify as an expert in my courtroom.

It was surprising and somewhat gratifying to learn how much time the St. Paul Department had devoted to this case. They had spent a total of 1500 hours on the case and this included eleven homicide investigators, three narc investigators, and four special investigative unit (SIU) people. Detective Hartman had spent 600 hours on the case in 1985 and 150 hours in 1986. It was still considered an open case. As I conclude this story (some 31 years later), the case is still considered an open case by the St. Paul PD and I could not access the case record. There is no statute of limitations on murder and that is likely the reason the file is still considered open and ongoing.

SGT Hartman then revealed that the Gibberd case had a companion case called the Russell Sherer case. Mr. Sherer had been assaulted in a similar manner and it occurred within an hour of the Gibberd shooting and only about a mile away. That case was being handled by SGT Whitman. The "team" found that the assailant had been described as possibly the same person and the manner of the assault was similar and the time and distance also matched. At least one theory was that it was same assailant attacking two different victims.

The police artist, a Mr. Johnson had prepared a map of the area where Mr. Gibberd was shot and SGT Hartman and his colleagues had used it in their investigation. He did not know if it was to scale, but it was a reasonable depiction of the area. We did not need a scaled map as this was not a boundary dispute. We just needed something to acquaint us with the immediate area around the crime scene. SGT Hartman described the map as a "Xeroxed copy." In those days the copy machine was usually referred to as the Xerox machine. Xerox led the way in the copy field for many years, but now had morphed into a consulting or idea company. I believe they still make copy machines at this juncture, but it is not the majority of their business.

Maps are useful tools both inside the courtroom and in your home or car. One can spend several minutes trying to describe a place or destination, but a minute or two looking at a map and everyone knows what you are talking about. Some of the prima-donnas in district court may be inclined to force the parties to produce a scale drawing, but that was a pointless requirement that only adds to the cost and travail of litigation (a copy of the police map is included herein as Appendix Exhibit No. 2).

Mr. Gibberd was shot near the northeast corner of Fuller and Dale Streets. A black circle with a white cross, illustrated rather ominously where the victim was found. The words "victim shot" appears next to the circle. There were nine numbers circled on the map and they indicate the nine witnesses that were located and identified. The witnesses were accompanied by dots and arrows which indicated the direction they were traveling.

Fuller Street is located two short blocks south of University Avenue. Fuller runs east and west, the same direction as University Avenue and Dale Street runs north and south. SGT Hartman testified that Mr. Gibberd was first observed by witness numbers 1 and 2 when the witnesses were crossing a parking lot shared by Wendy's with a small shopping mall, and walking in a southwesterly direction back toward Dale Street.

The same witnesses (number 1 and 2) who observed Mr. Gibberd walking south on the sidewalk also observed a black male also walking south on the sidewalk near the driveway and also on the east side of Dale Street. Witness number 1 had crossed the north bound lane of Dale Street and was in the narrow center median when the first shot rang out. Witness number 2 had already crossed Dale Street. The map marked an x with a circle and the note, "1st shot." Witness number 1 remained in the median and watched the assailant walk from the shooting scene across Dale and west on Fuller.

SGT Hartman had interviewed all of the witnesses who were indicated as numbers on the map and witness number 1 who was observing from the center median, told SGT Hartman that he observed the assailant bending over the victim and fire a second shot into the head of the helpless man. He then calmly left the area. I got a hearsay objection to the officer's testimony as he was clearly testifying to something told to him by someone else. It was not really a statement but a description of what the witness saw or observed. Traditional hearsay is relaying what someone else said. The officer was relaying an observation. The testimony was certainly not offered to prove the truth of the statement alleged as there was no statement, so I allowed the testimony on that basis. The case was certainly not going to turn on how many times the decedent was shot so it made sense to allow the testimony. I did not expect to force the petitioner's attorney to run all over town and subpoena nine or ten people just to bring in testimony that did not have a great deal of relevance in the first place. This was not a criminal case, and I could not see any need to make the case more difficult than it already was.

SGT Hartman was asked the cause of death and he was allowed to testify citing the coroner's report that Mr. Gibberd was shot twice and the first round severed the spinal cord and the second round went into the brain. Either shot could have been fatal. There was no objection by defense counsel.

The criminal investigators tried to re-trace or establish where Mr. Gibberd had been that evening. They screened all of the business establishments within a block of Dale and University to determine whether or not Mr. Gibberd or any suspects had been present in the establishments. The police had pictures of Mr. Gibberd and also men whose names had surfaced in the course of the investigation. The people who seemed to float to the top were generically called "investigative leads," although we lay people may refer to them as suspects. Investigative leads (IL's) in this case were more accurate as the police were desperately searching for any information they could gather just hoping that something would turn up a lead. The pictures of the IL's together with Mr. Gibberd's photos were shown to local employees or workers in an effort to unearth information from someone who could shed more light on this tragic event. This is just plain old gum-shoe police work and it is time consuming and sometimes tedious. The method may be old, but it often yields results even in this current high tech age where everyone has a computer and a phone. In this case, the yield for much effort was not great. In this day and age with nine people around, there would have been at least six cell phones out and someone would have taken a picture. I am so slow with my phone that the ambulance would have arrived before I was prepared to take a picture. Hi-tech in my day was a transistor radio.

The police did an investigation of Mr. Gibberd in an effort to ascertain his patterns and habits. Most of us are creatures of habit and often something in our past will explain or determine what happened on a particular date or time. Mr. Gibberd was in the habit of working late and sometimes would work all night. He usually phoned home and relayed his plans to his family. He phoned home on the night in question and relayed that he was going to Wendy's to eat and then return to work. It was not uncommon for him to go out and eat and return to work. The police were not able to substantiate that he had gone to Wendy's or to a nearby Clark submarine shop. Despite considerable effort, they were unable to find anyone who could put Mr. Gibberd inside Wendy's or any other restaurant on that August evening.

It was strange that with all of the workers at Wendy's that no one recalled seeing Mr. Gibberd. Was it a case where they were afraid to step up and say something for fear of reprisals or was it a busy evening and the faces at the restaurant all seemed to run together? If the restaurant had been busy, then it would not be surprising that no one could recall the victim. On the other hand, it was after 8:00 p.m. and that was after peak dinner-time hours. One would think, that a customer with a British accent and wearing a tweed jacket would have been remembered during a slack time.

I do not always engage the fast food people in conversation when I eat in their establishments, but sometimes I do and when I do, the server is more likely to recall my presence. I recall one day stopping at a McDonalds in Lakeville as I was on my way down to southern Minnesota to hear a case. The timing coincided with the event when Sir Ronald had been sued for serving hot coffee and not warning the customers that they could get burned. It seemed to be an obvious thing, a little like warning pool patrons that they could get wet or be careful, you may drown. I told the McDonald's waiter that I wanted a coffee and I was prepared to take my chances on it being hot. He picked up on what I was saying and when he returned the coffee, he pretended to have some documents for me to sign, prior to dealing with this very hazards product. We had a good laugh and chances are good he might even recognize my likeness for a week or two.

The lawyers have taken over the writing of directions for most consumer products and the information or instructions have become less and less helpful. For example, if one buys a tool such as a power saw, the warnings are endless. If you read them, you would be scared to death to use the product. I usually skip all of that and dismiss it as the "lawyer stuff" and try and find the instructions. I generally rip out the Spanish or French instructions and cast them aside as it makes for less paper to worry about. The instructions are often times not helpful as they are often written by someone who does not speak English as a first language.

Recently I bought a battery-powered stud finder at Target and got back to the work site and discovered that the battery was not included (one may ask: why in the world a specimen like me would need a stud finder?). They did disclose the MIA battery, however only in very fine print on the package. The product was overpriced and contained no battery to boot. When I looked at the instructions, they were all in pictures and small, hard to read pictures at that. The lawyers must have concluded that it is best not to say anything and put up lousy pictures and if something goes wrong they cannot be blamed for giving you faulty instructions. They likely do not have a duty to provide instructions on how to use the product, so if they say nothing, they cannot be faulted. With the law, it is often better to do less and if you do nothing you probably have the least liability. For example, in the absence of some special ordinance, if you do not shovel the snow from your walk and leave it sit, you are probably less likely to be legally responsible if someone falls, than you would be if you shoveled it. If you shovel it, you have undertaken a duty and if a slippery spot then develops, you may be responsible because you tried to make things safer and failed. The law punishes failure; it does not reward "nice tries." You failed so you lose. In the case of the stud finder or other products, even if the manufacturer does not have a duty to provide instructions, if they undertake it and screw up, then they can be held accountable. They decided to just use pictures and then they could not be accused of saying something wrong. Certain aspects of the law can be aggravating.

SGT Hartman had an investigator with the department leave the WDC or CDC premises at Mr. Gibberd's sign out time of 8:05 and walk the same route as they believed Mr. Gibberd had traveled. Mr. Walker was instructed to walk as he would travel if he were going to eat and was not trying to catch a bus, but did not have all evening to spend on eating. They found it to be a ten-minute round trip from the WDC down to Wendy's and return.

The autopsy report had been received into evidence and it was performed by the Ramsey County Medical Examiner. The autopsy report found the victim's stomach contained 10-11 ounces of poorly digested vegetables and meat. This indicated he had recently ingested a meal. The examiner also screened Mr. Gibberd for alcohol and drugs. They screened his blood, urine, and serum levels for evidence of drugs or alcohol and all tests were negative. This was also consistent with the assumption that he had gone to Wendy's as they do not serve alcohol.

The officer was asked about the report and whether it was something he relied upon in determining that the decedent had gone to Wendy's for supper. It was objected to but I over-ruled as it seemed fair to ask the basis or what the expert investigator relied upon in drawing his opinion that Mr. Gibberd had dined at Wendy's. I was wondering to myself why the defense counsel was objecting because Wendy's was off the employer's premises and certainly CDC wanted the employee off premises for his dinner. If he was on the employer's property when he met his demise, then there were not too many circumstances to deny him coverage.

The officer was asked what the decedent was wearing when he died. He was wearing casual shoes, dress slacks, shirt and tie, and a tweed jacket. A Control Data Badge was found and his wallet contained $8.00. I got the impression the CDC Badge was found in a pocket and he had not been wearing it. The Supreme Court in its later opinion mentioned the CDC Badge as a possible element linking Mr. Gibberd with Control Data, but I did not conclude that he was wearing the badge at the time of the shooting. It is unclear if the shooter even saw the badge as he approached his victim from behind. The tweed jacket he was wearing was very English. I pictured the tweed jackets that my college professors had worn back in the 50's and 60's. I loved the tweed look and all it took was a pipe to complete the outfit. I started smoking a pipe in law school as did many of my classmates. The pipe would raise hell with your tongue for the first few days or weeks until you got used to it and then it would be fine. I liked the pipe because you did not really smoke all that much. Most of the time was spent filling, packing, and lighting the contraption. It was hard to keep it going so you needed a lighter to do that. I had one of the nice Zippo metal lighters that were popular in the 50's. The lighters must have been an issue item in the military as most of the ex-servicemen seemed to have a Zippo. When I was in the Army they still issued cigarettes with C Rations and they also included water-proof matches. It seemed to me that the Army would not give me cigarettes unless they wanted me to use them. The Zippo had a metal case with a hinged metal cover. If you practiced for a time, you could learn how to open the thing with one hand. That was functional for pipe smokers as you could hold the pipe with one hand and open and light it with the other. I suppose there was someone around who could open and light the Zippo all with one motion, but I was not that gifted.

The police had conducted an intensive background investigation on Mr. Gibberd and found nothing in his background that stood out and nothing of a suspicious nature. They found no evidence to indicate that the attack was personal to him. What they were looking for was perhaps a girlfriend or a drug habit or maybe a gambling addiction. Any one of these types of personal issues could have provoked an attack. For example, a jealous boyfriend or the holder of an unpaid gambling debt may have sought out some sort of retribution from the decedent. There was no evidence whatever found to justify this sort of twisted revenge. The tragic death had no motive that could be found.

Any first year law student knows that to convict someone of a crime, the state does not have to establish a motive for the crime. The motive may only be known to the perpetrator and the criminal prosecutor need only establish that the accused had the requisite criminal intent. On the other hand, the motive is important for the police investigator, because it often leads to the discovery of the perp. Jealousy, money, sex, and drugs are what frequently drive the train in the criminal world and if the police are able to ascertain the motive for the crime, that frequently provides a path to solving the crime. In this case, there was no apparent motive and few pathways to follow. Juries also like to know the motive for a killing as the motive frequently points to the killer.

The petitioner offered the map of the crime scene that had been prepared by the criminal investigators. The defendant objected that it was not to scale, but I asked the witness if he had walked the terrain depicted on the map or drawing. I also asked if the drawing seemed to accurately reflect the terrain as he had observed it during his time on the ground. I over-ruled the objection to the exhibit and received the drawing or map in evidence.

I asked SGT Hartman what the term "UI" meant on the drawing. It meant unidentified and the drawing showed an unidentified female and unidentified motorist. These were additional witnesses that the police were seeking out. The unidentified female was very close to the area where the shooting occurred and the UI motorist was across the street from the crime scene. The police were looking for both parties, but without much luck.

On cross-examination, Mr. Gallegos asked SGT Hartman about the area where witnesses 1 and 2 first saw the victim. He was seen in a driveway at the southwest corner of the Wendy's lot and this driveway also serviced a small mall called the Uni-Dale Mall. The Uni-Dale Mall housed a number of small businesses that catered to a less than affluent clientele. These included a Goodwill, or second-hand store, a liquor store, appliance rental store, a small grocery store, and some sort of restaurant. Upon further questioning the officer recalled an insurance agency, dry cleaners, and some sort of social service agency. For some reason, the local bail bondsman had not set up shop in the Uni-Dale Mall. Where was the pawn shop when we needed one?

SGT Hartman was asked if robbery was considered a possible motive for the attack. He responded that robbery could well have been a motive for the attack. The police follow several scenarios that they construct in trying to solve a crime and then check the facts against the scenario to see if they fit or make sense. Robbery was one of the scenarios that the police were working on. Robbery was not the highest scenario that the police were working on, but the officer did not wish to comment on the highest scenario. He was asked by Mr. Gallegos if we could eliminate (as a scenario) that his employment had anything to do with his killing. He responded in a halting, "I, yes, yes." Q. "That's completely out of the reasons here?" (sic) A. "That's correct."

That last bit of testimony was very telling. The police had spent hundreds and maybe thousands of hours investigating this crime and had not found any basis or even a scenario connecting the crime to the victim's employment. This was tough testimony for the petitioner to handle. For the petitioner to prevail there has to be some connection between the death and the work activity. At a minimum there better be some connection between the death and the place of work. For example, long time Worker Joe has a heart attack while playing cards in the break room at work. The work may not have had a thing to do with his death, but at least you could put old Joe at his place of employment and maybe even at his most favorite place of employment. In this case, clearly Mr. Gibberd was not at his place of employment at the time of death and we, like the police, were still looking for some connection between his death and his employment activity.

There was more testimony to follow and more argument to hear so I reminded myself not to make any decisions at this juncture. Most of the time I did not make a decision on a case until I start writing the decision. At that time, I go through all of the evidence and then start the, often painful, process of putting facts down on paper. The judge has to make findings of fact. Put another way, the judge has to tell what happened and the scenario has to be supported by facts in the record. It may sound easy, but if the question is whether Worker Joe slipped and fell on May 21 at 10:00 a.m. on the south stairway at work, you may be faced with 3 or 4 different versions as to what happened. Joe may not have related the same story to his doctor. A coworker who offices adjacent to the stairway may not have heard any fall or commotion. Joe may not have reported the fall to his employer until two or three days later. Joe may have told a coworker he hurt himself slopping hogs in his back yard. Hence, the infamous hog-slopping defense. It is up to the judge to sort through this morass of testimony and make a finding supported by credible evidence that Joe fell at work or Joe did not fall at work. Not always an easy task.

I had at least two or three cases featuring the hog-slopping defense. These were not cases in an urban setting, but cases heard out in rural or farm areas. They involved folks that worked at a local factory, but had a few acres and did some part-time farming. The petitioner was usually a rural gentleman with a straw hat and a midwestern twang in his voice like "Country" Jerry Kill. The argument was usually that "Ma" or "Junior" took care of the hogs and he did not get involved in any "hog slopping."

I suspect that some of the attorneys involved in the system were of a view that I walked into the courtroom and had already decided the case. Nothing could be further from the truth. I realize this sounds self-serving, but for one thing, when I walked in the courtroom, I do not know very much about the case. I may have pre-tried the case, but that was months earlier. I never did spend a lot of time getting ready for a trial, because the case may settle and in any event, I did not have a lot of spare time. I was usually a pretty quick study and could get ready for the trial by having another short pre-trial before the case started and also I would listen carefully to the opening statements. I have had many cases where at the end of the day I thought I might rule in a particular fashion, but when I read the medical records and reviewed my trial notes, I changed my mind. I usually went through the record and started determining the facts and that usually led me to the decision.

The petitioner resumed direct examination and this revealed that the St. Paul Police Department, like all police units, keep statistics on all crimes committed within the city. We were most interested in those numbers dealing with homicide or the unlawful taking of life by another. The police department had cut the city up into geographical areas or grids and kept track of crimes occurring within each grid. Each of the approximately 200 city grids measured a half-mile on each side. The grid map was a useful planning tool, as the department could determine where more police presence was needed. The area where the Gibberd Murder occurred was in grid number 109. The WDC was also located in grid number 109. For comparison purposes the police department put eight grids into one package and called it the Summit-University area. This was an area running two miles or four grids east and west and one mile or two grids going north and south. The north boundary was University Avenue running east and west. The south boundary was Summit Avenue. Lexington Avenue ran one mile north and south and bordered the west, and Rice Street with some variation, bordered the eastern one mile. The petitioner asked SGT Hartman if the Summit-University area was a high crime area. Objection was made to foundation, and relevance and no probative value to his opinion. I over-ruled and let the officer testify that the Summit-University area was a high crime area. I have included a map showing the grids as Appendix Exhibit No. 3. The area highlighted on the exhibit and containing therein the eight grids is the Summit-University area. A dot within grid 109 shows the approximate location of the Gibberd killing.

There was no doubt that a significant number of the homicides occurring in the city were in the Summit-University area, but this was a big area and fairly densely populated. City-wide for 1984 there were fifteen homicides and seven in the Summit-University area. That eight-grid area was accounting for a third to 46 percent of the homicides. Given the size of the area, some of the crimes were committed a mile from where Mr. Gibberd went down and was that a valid comparison? A mile can make a dramatic change in any urban neighborhood. A mile in New York City can seem like a 100 miles in another part of the country. It was certainly true that there were crimes committed in this area, but the subject crime was unique in that it did not seem gang-related and had no apparent motive. Also it occurred in broad daylight, and it was not clear as to the timing of the other homicides as to whether they were in the dark of night or in the early evening when this crime went down. It was hard to make comparisons.

Testimony was also offered with respect to the other violent crimes committed in the Summit-University area during 1984. The area accounted for 21 percent of the rapes, 19 percent of the robberies, and 16 percent of the aggravated assaults. In 1985 the number of murders in the Summit-University area dropped to five from seven, but the overall city homicide rate stayed at fifteen.

The officer was asked on cross-examination the size of the Summit-University quadrant. He did get confused and testify it was two miles by two miles, whereas it was two miles east and west and one mile north and south. The case did not turn on the size of the quadrant. The quadrant was predominately single-family homes, with multi-family and commercial uses scattered throughout. It was considered densely populated. The officer was asked if he would expect more crime in the area because there were more people and he responded with an obvious "yes."

SGT Hartman was asked about crimes in 1984 in grid 108, which was the grid across the street from the crime scene. There was one homicide in that grid during 1984. That death was arson related as a small child got caught in the middle of a domestic dispute. None of the homicides in St. Paul in 1984 involved inter-racial killing. The following year in 1985 there were no homicides in grid 108.

Mr. Gibberd was killed in grid number 109. The WDC is located in grid 109, but across Interstate 94 and further south from the crime scene. In 1985 there were two homicides in grid 109 and one involved Mr. Gibberd. The other homicide involved a white "John" who was stabbed to death by a prostitute. The precise location of this other homicide within the grid was not presented. These two killings in the same grid were the only black on white homicides in the Summit-University area during 1984/85. It was interesting, in that the eight grids that border grid number 109, there was only one other homicide during 1985. On the other hand, during 1984, in the same eight grids bordering grid 109 there were seven homicides. At least based on the surrounding neighborhoods, grid number 109 did not seem to be going downhill, but maybe even improving.

It was difficult to discern much of any pattern to all of the crime statistics. For example, grid 128 located across the street from the crime scene and south of Marshall Avenue, accounted for four homicides in 1984, whereas in 1985 there was one. Once again, it could be argued that at least the area around the crime scene was not going downhill, but maybe even turning the other way.

Death in St. Paul

The problem with statistics is that there are so many numbers jumping around that they can be interpreted in many different ways. I was not going to be able to rely on numbers or statistics to figure this case out.

SGT Hartman did establish that it was not uncommon for Mr. Gibberd to walk north on Dale from the WDC, but he did not do it on a daily basis. This information was gathered by conversations with Mrs. Gibberd and other Control Data personnel. Counsel asked the witness if 60 percent of the information came from Mrs. Gibberd or was it 50 percent or what was the percentage? I mentioned that he only had one conclusion. Counsel for the petitioner objected on relevance. He only had one conclusion and I thought it was impossible for the witness to break down the testimony in such a way as to attribute his conclusions on a percentage basis to any part of the evidence. There was no company rule providing that Mr. Gibberd had to be chained to his desk for eight hours per day. He was free to leave the building and get a bite to eat and if he did not wish to drive, he was free to walk down the street and get something at Wendy's or another local eating establishment. He was also allowed to remain in the building and have a sandwich brought from home or something from the claimed erratic vending machines. It seemed to me that it was already clear that the eating options rested with Mr. Gibberd. He was obviously a well-paid researcher and CDC was prepared to give him some leeway when it came to working hours or conditions of employment.

The Police did check Mr. Gibberd's sign-in and out sheets for the day of the crime, but for some reason did not get back to check on the prior sheets. The prior sheets were not available when they stopped at CDC to check them and they did not get back for a follow-up. That was probably not a critical piece of evidence as Mr. Gibberd did not seem to follow a pattern with his mealtimes.

I thought of my own lunch habits and how they related to Mr. Gibberd's. I was on so-called flex-time and started at 8:30 and worked till 5:00. I suppose there were times when I arrived after 8:30 but I was usually there by that time. We had a long-standing tradition of going to coffee at 8:30 so I usually tried not to miss that morning event. Throughout my last years on the bench I usually joined a few of my friends such as Bernie Dinner, Jim Otto, and Paul Reike for the morning ritual. I am sure we were referred to as the old farts. When Dinner and Otto were forced out by the age 70 mandatory retirement rule, then the group expanded to Rolf Hagen, Dan Kelly, and Gary Mesna. It was a fun group and occasionally we talked shop if someone had an unusual or special event transpiring.

As far as lunch was concerned, I was so busy with work and personal events that I usually had something to eat at my desk and used the time to make a phone call or two or sometimes to run an errand. I remained in the reserves until 1994 so I frequently had something to read or someone to call on reserve business. I was so busy, I did not have a lot of time to waste. Maybe that was a mistake as perhaps I would have been better off to leave the premises at noon and get away and relax. One problem that I frequently encountered is if it got close to noon and if there was not much testimony left to hear, then the parties usually wanted to work through lunch and finish and avoid coming back for just an hour or two of testimony. I usually tried to accommodate counsel, but sometimes I did have plans for lunch and had to take a break. It was evident, that my meal plans boiled down to my own personal decision. It looked to me like Mr. Gibberd's lunch time decisions were much like mine. It was his own individual decision.

SGT Hartman obtained photos of Mr. Gibberd and checked with the local establishments to see if they recalled seeing Mr. Gibberd. They located one worker who thought it might be Mr. Gibberd and he said, "Yes, he was here." Subsequent investigation revealed it was probably a look alike. That struck me as an unlikely possibility, but the police drew a blind alley on trying to unequivocally determine Mr. Gibberd's destination on the evening of the murder.

The companion case to Mr. Gibberd's case was the Sherer case. Mr. Sherer was a William Mitchell Law Student who was also shot on the same evening as Mr. Gibberd. He was shot in the vicinity of Summit Avenue near William Mitchell Law School. He was also allegedly shot by a black man and like the Gibberd shooting, there was no apparent motive for the crime. It turned out that Russell Sherer was also employed in the computer industry and had been wearing a sport coat, tie, dress pants, and dress shoes. He had been dressed much like Mr. Gibberd.

The police did rule out any narcotics connection in the Gibberd murder. There was no evidence that Mr. Gibberd had been drinking on the night of the crime. They were able to narrow the search for the killer down to a few suspects, but were not able to narrow it down to one person. They did conclude that the assailant was likely from the Twin Cities area and most likely from St. Paul. There was no indication that this was a personal crime or that the assailant targeted Mr. Gibberd for robbery or an assault because he knew him and wanted to rob him. It still appeared to be a random crime rather than a targeted or personal assault. There was no indication that the assailant knew Mr. Gibberd.

I asked the officer if Mr. Gibberd was wearing his Control Data identification badge at the time of the crime. Officer Hartman said that he was. I should have followed up with SGT Hartman to determine the basis for his conclusion. The earlier testimony did not mention his badge being worn. I did not get the impression that SGT Hartman was on the crime scene during the night of the murder. The CDC Badge featured a picture of Mr. Gibberd and the words "Control Data Corporation" on the top of the badge. We did not know whether or not the badge with the CDC identification was of any importance to the assailant.

The medical examiner advised that it took an hour after ingesting food for the stomach to empty. The medical examiner had advised the detective that poorly digested material was found in the digestive tract. The medical examiner concluded he likely did not eat at CDC between 7:35 and 8:05 when he signed out. More than likely he ate after he signed out at 8:05.

The defense counsel pointed to an area of the city near lower Rice Street that he called the Mt. Airy area and asked SGT Hartman if this area was considered as high a crime rate as the Dale-University area and he responded that they were both considered high crime areas. Counsel then asked the SGT about the west side of St. Paul. The Witness correctly pointed out that the west side was actually south of the Mississippi River. This was another one of the strange phenomenon with St. Paul and its make-shift street layout. The actual west side of St. Paul would be toward the boundary with the City of Minneapolis. The old Mississippi hooks around St. Paul in an arc running south and westerly. Once you get up and somewhat beyond Ft. Snelling the City of Minneapolis comes into play on the west side of the Mississippi and going northwest from the old fort. St. Paul likes to pretend that Minneapolis does not exist, but Minneapolis knows that St. Paul does not exist. Perhaps the founders did not want the "West Side" to be confused with that place called Minneapolis found further down the river. Another fun part of St. Paul is that the city is not laid out in numbered streets and avenues. The downtown area has some numbered streets, but the north and south streets are all names such as Robert, Wabasha, and St. Peter Streets. If you go elsewhere in the city, you better know where Grand or Cretin Avenues are located or have a good map. Now the problem has been solved by Google. St. Paul is an Irish town and Jesse Ventura blamed the street layout on a baseless charge that the Irish like to drink and they must have been into the old John Barlycorn when they were platting out the city roads. Jesse spouted out with this one when he was a guest on the Tonight Show with Jay Leno. Jesse caught a little heat for this one, but he was on his way out of politics so he did not care.

My wife, Phyllis, had an interesting meeting with Jesse Ventura when she was a candidate for the Public Utility Commission. She had been working as an ALJ for over twenty years until one day she got a call from the Ventura Administration and she was asked if she was interested in being on the PUC. She replied that she had never thought about it and in fact she had written a letter of recommendation on behalf of another candidate. She was told that she should let them know post-haste as the governor was anxious to get someone on board. Phyllis came down to my office and told me about it and asked me what I thought about a new job. It paid less than what she made as an ALJ, but I told her that should not be a major consideration. Her ALJ job was enjoyable, but it was a lot of work. She had done utility rate cases and jurisdictional dispute cases involving warring power companies so she was very familiar with the type of issues coming before the PUC. In rate cases, the administrative law judge does all of the heavy lifting. They review all of the testimony, both pro and con, regarding the pending case, and write up a decision with findings and a recommendation. The PUC Commissioners review the decision and criticize it and paw at it, but it is much easier to review someone else's work than to do it yourself.

Phyllis was aware that the commissioners did a fair amount of travel and that prospect was interesting as the judges used to get a trip to Reno every once in a while to take a course at the National Judicial College, but the trips got junked because of some claimed budget problem. I always thought the budget excuse was BS as the workers' compensation judge's salaries and expenses were paid out of the special compensation fund. In other words, we were not paid out of the general fund so the taxpayers should not get worked up if a judge gets a trip, once in a blue moon.

Another factor that came into consideration was our son, Cameron, and the increasing demands on our time that he required. He was eight and in school, but it would be nice to have a parent with a job that afforded more flexibility to attend an event at school or get him to swim practice. As an ALJ, Phyllis had to account for all her time and she would not have to do that as a commissioner.

The money was the only negative and that was outweighed by the positives. She quickly called the governor's office back and was contacted within hours and told that an interview had been scheduled with the governor. Phyllis always dresses nice and she was all decked out for her interview and showed up bright and early on Friday morning. She was met by John Wodele, the governor's administrative assistant and ushered into Governor Ventura's office. The first thing the governor did was apologize for his casual attire as he and Wodele were both wearing Jeans. He explained that they have casual Fridays at the governor's office and he usually does not dress in that manner. Phyllis said he was very polite and gracious throughout the process. He asked intelligent questions and was prepared for the interview. Phyllis hit it out of the park and was informed the following week that she got the job. She was given a leave of absence by the OAH and moved on to the PUC. She replaced Joel Jacobs who was on the city council when I was city attorney. Small world.

Before Phyllis was appointed, the governor had selected a particular candidate who had been beaten up badly by the press. This was about the time that Ventura began to call the press "the jackals." Jesse then went through a bunch of other candidates, rumored to be close to 100 in number and rejected them all. That is when he called Phyllis and inquired about her availability. Phyllis is exceptional, there is no doubt.

I had a couple interviews with two different republican Governors, Quie and Carlson. The interview with Quie went well, but I did not pass the religious test. I flunked that one many years ago. Carlson sat hidden away from me wearing his University of MN jacket and hardly said a word. He had decided in advance that I was not getting the job, and he did not want to waste his time on me. Phyllis also had an interview with Carlson and it did not go swimmingly. This was an earlier time when she was interested in the PUC. She had much the same experience with Governor Carlson that I did. I voted for the guy and did some campaigning for him and thought he was a decent governor. When he ran for a second term, I was not an enthusiastic supporter.

Back at the trial, we established that the "West Side" of St. Paul got its name because it was on the west side of the Mississippi river as determined by the directionally challenged St. Paulites, even though it is south of the river. The West Side was predominantly a Mexican or Hispanic area and had been a high crime area in the late 70's but by 1980 things had been pretty well cleaned up. There were no homicides on the West Side in 1984. The area where the Gibberd crime occurred was considered an ethnic black neighborhood, but as one proceeded toward Summit Avenue, the neighborhood was becoming more of a "yuppie" neighborhood.

We concluded with the testimony of SGT Hartman and the next witness called was SGT Whitman. SGT Whitman had been a cop for twenty five years, all with the St. Paul Police Department and had been an investigator with the sex/homicide division for the past five years. Prior to working homicide, he worked auto theft as an investigator for ten years. He worked patrol his first ten or eleven years.

Most recently he had worked on the Russ Sherer case and also on the Gibberd case. As part of the Gibberd investigation, he investigated Mr. Gibberd's background. Essentially, he did a background check of Mr. Gibberd. In the old days, the Army ran a background check on every officer before they were commissioned. I believe the actual leg-work was done by the FBI. The Bureau would give the file to an agent and they would talk to teachers, friends, and employers in an effort to dig up some dirt on a prospective officer. I had a friend of mine who processed a lot of the background information and maybe did some of the digging as well. He told me that the officer cadre was not without sinners. I had strongly suspected he was correct. I would speculate, however, that the officer corps would fare pretty well in comparison to judges, politicians, congressmen, or other low-life.

It was difficult to do a background check on Mr. Gibberd because he had only been in the country a short time. Probably the biggest difficulty in doing the background check in that era was that the officer did not own a computer or have an internet subscription. The computer and internet have certainly changed background check work and enable law enforcement personnel to gather information on a particular individual with a few keystrokes as opposed to hours of investigative work.

SGT Whitman was asked by Ms. Bjorklund if the eight grid area called the Summit-University area was a high crime area and he replied in the affirmative and knew of none higher. He also testified that the four grid area located near the WDC and Dale and University was as high a crime area as any in the city. That was a flat statement and not perfectly accurate. He was talking about grids, 109, 110, 129, and 130.

It turned out that the two investigators worked together on the case, but sometimes took parallel paths in their search for the killer. SGT Whitman gave personnel of the Special Investigative Unit (SIU) photographs of Mr. Gibberd that were made from the picture on his Control Data ID card and sent them back out to show to the workers and employees of the business establishments in the area of the killing (Ed. Note: This was previously done, but it appears they may have tried it again). This time, they found one person who identified Mr. Gibberd as being in that establishment from 7:00 to 8:00 p.m. The second time the same investigator talked to the PW (potential witness) the PW said that the person identified was on the premises from 7:00 p.m. to 7:40 p.m. Because of the time variance, SGT Whitman concluded that the PW was not reliable. I wondered what other information had been elicited from this witness? They certainly had to ask about how Mr. Gibberd was dressed and did they see a badge or ID on his person. Mr. Gibberd had not signed out until 8:05 p.m. so it seemed clear that the PW was misguided, at least with respect to time, but some people do have a poor sense of time, so I expected that they explored other angles with the PW.

SGT Whitman did conclude that Mr. Gibberd had gone to Wendy's and had eaten something containing lettuce and this was based on the autopsy report. He admitted that he did not know for sure where he had eaten as this was a working theory. I was beginning to get the impression that the police had worked very hard on the case and expended hours and hours investigating this heinous crime, but continued to come up empty as far as any concrete evidence tying the perpetrator to the victim. The police may have had two or three people they thought may have done the two crimes, but they did not have enough evidence to get any place. Mr. Sherer survived the ordeal, but must not have been able to make any sort of identification. This just seemed like one blind alley after another. The job of the investigator can be an all-consuming job. I can imagine that it is hard to turn it off at 4:30. Someone dear to others is dead and the survivors would like to get some sort of closure by knowing that the perpetrator has been brought to justice. A conscientious investigator gets to know the families of the victim and would like to help them in their time of grief. A lot of time in the shower or riding in the car is undoubtedly devoted to thinking about an unsolved case and asking oneself, "What have I missed?" Most of the time, one has probably not missed a damn thing, but there is always that haunting question.

SGT Whitman was not able to locate any motive for the attack. There was nothing personal between Mr. Gibberd and the attacker. He was not even sure Mr. Gibberd had eaten at Wendy's. He located someone in his office who was about the same height, age and weight as Mr. Gibberd and had the "double" walk from the WDC to Wendy's and it took about ten minutes and the odometer check in his squad car measured the distance at 7/10 of a mile (this was round trip time and measurement). This was undoubtedly hearsay testimony as the person who did the testing or measurement was not in court, but it was all being relayed via SGT Whitman. We were not even sure Mr. Gibberd was at Wendy's so the testimony probably lacked relevance, but the defense counsel was getting tired of objecting and it was theoretical in any event (we were not clear as to whether or not this was the same experiment as conducted by SGT Hartman). Attorneys love repetition as the more times they can put their case before the court, the better chance of having something stick. Usually the lawyers would object if the testimony was repetitious, but sometime it is hard to tell until the witness gets into the testimony and by that point the lawyer may decide to just let it come in as there may be no harm done. Sometimes I would object if it was clearly repetitious and especially if it dealt with a point or claim that was not very important.

The defense counsel asked SGT Whitman if one of the motives for the killing had anything to do with Mr. Gibberd working at Control Data Corporation and the officer was not able to make any connection to CDC. SGT Whitman described the way or manner of Mr. Gibberd's murder as being unusual. It was unusual in that a person walked up to the rear of him and shot him in the head, causing Mr. Gibberd to fall to the ground and as he was on the ground, lowered the gun and fired a second round into the back of his head. It was unique because of the deliberate manner in which the victim was murdered. It seemed to have been committed in a very dispassionate manner and without any display of emotion. This crime was different in that there was no robbery and there seemed to be nothing personal between the involved parties.

Mr. Wayne Hoff was next called as a witness by the petitioner and had joined Mr. Gibberd at CDC about six months before he died. He sometimes worked with Mr. Gibberd in the evening or after normal working hours. He described the decedent as a hard working individual who would continue to work as long as he seemed to be doing something constructive. If he ran into a major road-block, he would put the job aside and go home. Mr. Gibberd was working with a database that was written by a company called Bettyele. There were some problems installing the software and getting it tuned to run on the CDC machines. For what they were doing, it was often difficult to work during normal work hours as they often had to shut down the computer and start it up again and that was disruptive to other users. One has to remember that this was in the day before everyone had a personal computer and many workers were sharing a rather large machine. This was the era of the main frame. These were large machines. Your personal computer or even your cell phone can probably do much more than the computers available to Mr. Gibberd and his associates. Mr. Hoff did go to lunch on one occasion with Mr. Gibberd and they went to Wendy's. He said it was the closest place to the office. He would occasionally leave the premises at night to get a bite to eat and return to the office. He did not know whether or not Mr. Gibberd ever left the office at night to go to dinner and returned to the office thereafter. Mr. Hoff did go out in the evening with other coworkers and thereafter returned to work. He never went out with management people in the evening. There was food available in the vending machines at work and he described it as "hunger suppressant." There were times when the change machine did not work.

Mr. Hoff spoke with Mr. Gibberd around 6:00 p.m. on August 26, 1985 and they watched the balloons depart the fairgrounds. As the crow flies, they were only 3-4 miles from the site of the Great Get Together. I was always a big fan of the fair and loved to attend. I was probably 11 or 12 and did not have anyone to go to the fair with me so I went by myself. As I recall, my mother encouraged me to go by myself. She stressed that I was free to go and see what I wanted without interference from others. My dad dropped me off in the morning and picked me up at the end of the day. There were no cell phones so everything had to be pre-arranged. It is hard to believe that many parents nowadays would send a twelve-year-old off to the fair without a chaperone. It would probably be considered child endangerment. I can remember the event quite well because it was one of the few times my mother spent some time talking and discussing something with me. She was normally too busy or preoccupied with something else. I did not think there was anything wrong with a solo trip to the fair at the time, and still do not. Kids had a lot of freedom in those days. I do not recall seeing any balloons being released during my first trip to the state fair.

When I got a bit older, probably 13 or 14, my friend, Bruce, and I used to ride our bikes to the fair grounds and stay till dark and ride home. Bruce belonged to the Congregational Church in Falcon Heights and they ran a café or restaurant at the fair. Bruce and I would work an hour or two at the restaurant and would get free food. One day we put in our shift and we each grabbed a piece of blueberry pie on our way to the Midway. Bruce decided he was not hungry and tossed the pie in the front seat of a vacant convertible. I guess I was not that bold and preferred to eat pie more than throw pie.

Mr. Hoff returned to work on the morning of August 27 and learned that Ray had been killed the night before. He and Mr. Piper checked Ray's computer and determined that it had not been turned off or logged out. The implication was that Mr. Gibberd intended to return to work after getting a bite to eat. Also, his brief case was left open and books were scattered on his desk. Ray was tidy and always cleaned his desk before departing for the day. That was an admirable habit that I tried to cultivate, but when I was in the middle of writing up a decision, I usually let things sit overnight and got back to it the next day or sometimes not until days later. If one got on a run of cases, you could go a week before you had time to return to what you started. That was a little thing about the job that made it challenging. I usually tried to get as much done as I could before I left because I never knew for sure when I would get back to the case and it would usually take some time to get back up to speed.

It was evident that Mr. Gibberd had planned to be gone only a short time and return to work after a quick break. More than likely he went to Wendy's because it was close to the office and fast. Mr. Hoff was asked about the safety of the neighborhood and said he did not like the area and did not like walking in the parking lot at night. He said there were lots of kids out there at night. He was not aware of any incidents that occurred at the CDC plant that would have made him uncomfortable. He found Mr. Gibberd to be a kind and gentle person and not possessed of bad habits. Mr. Hoff found him to be a very trusting and naïve in that he could not comprehend some of the violence in our society. He was asked on cross about the kids in the parking lot and although they seemed rather rowdy, they had never bothered him. The parking lot was sufficiently lit to locate your car after dark.

At this point in time, we had completed a full day of testimony and we were all tired so we adjourned for the evening. It has always amazed me as to how tired one would get after a day in court. No heavy lifting is required and it is always warm and dry, but it is more work than digging ditches. Thinking is not easy. That is why we seek to avoid it. When you are in the courtroom, the wheels are constantly turning and that consumes energy and I guess work is the consumption and expenditure of energy.

After a hard day it is nice to relieve stress. Lawyers look for ways to ease the tensions and exercise is one of the best ways and probably the healthiest stress reliever. I got into jogging when I was in the Army and kept it up after I moved into civilian life. The advantage of it is that it takes no special equipment or expense and it does not involve all that much time. I ran winter and summer and almost liked the winter best as it was always cooler. I found that I could do a lot of thinking and pondering when I ran as the tensions would move on as I moved on and I seemed to be able to better focus in on a particular subject or problem.

I ran for probably thirty years and really enjoyed it and it helped me a lot. Some lawyers and judges look to alcohol to relieve the tensions of the courtroom and that probably explains the elevated rates of alcoholism in the trade. I managed to dodge that bullet, but I have been known to take a drink.

What finished my running career was my knees wore out. I was in my 60's when I began to experience pain in the medial part of both knees. I went back to see Dr. Frank Norberg, who I had seen earlier when I broke my arm. The cartilage on both knees was just about worn out on both medial sides. This is the part of the knee that cushions things at the knee joint where the tibia and femur come together. I went through most of the conservative treatment including an injection of Synvisc and cortisone. I actually had pretty good luck with the Synvisc injections in the left knee and achieved significant improvement. For some reason, I did not have nearly the same relief with the injections on the right side. Lately I have achieved some relief with Synvisc and it is easier to tolerate with one injection instead of the previous dosage of three injections.

I underwent surgery of the right knee in January of 2005 and they had planned on doing an autograft procedure. This was a transplant procedure and involved taking good cartilage from the outside of the knee and moving it and planting it on the medial side of the knee so that you had some cushioning. This was an arthroscopic surgery so there is only so much that can be done and when Dr. Norberg was able to look things over through his scope, he concluded that the area of damage was too large for a graft. At that point he went to Plan B. I had a meniscal tear and he cleaned that up and proceeded with drilling of the medial femoral condyle. This is what is currently called micro-fracture surgery. What he was doing was drilling on the femoral head of the knee and getting blood flow followed by scabbing and maybe some scar tissue. The hope was that when the scar tissue healed it would take the place of the cartilage. I was on crutches for three weeks and then limited weight bearing. I developed some swelling in my calf and went back to my regular doctor, Dr. Ivins, and he determined I had a clot and that necessitated taking anticoagulants or blood thinners. Part of that involved giving myself a shot in the stomach every day, which I did not enjoy.

At this point, I have daily knee pain, but usually get relief with ibuprofen or Advil. I could have a half knee replacement on either side, but basically I fear the surgery. I am afraid of the antiesthetic, possible infections, and a relatively long recovery. Hell, I do not even like a blood test so how would I put up with an involved and drawn out surgical intervention? I like my orthopedic doctor and he does not give me any hard sales talks and that I appreciate. I am not running, but I have an elliptical machine in my TV room and I get on that for a half an hour and do some floor exercise and I am pretty well good to go for another day. I am a big advocate of some sort of regular exercise. Walking is very good exercise. If you are not up to jogging or simply do not want to wear out your body parts, then walking is for you. Once again, there is no special equipment required and one can do it in any location. If you dress property, one can walk in just about any climate. Get a good pair of walking shoes. I would supplement walking with some floor exercises such as push-ups or sit-ups and some stretching moves. Do honest push-ups and not the Starchy variety.

Death in St. Paul

I still enjoy skating and try and do it outside, when possible. I move inside when the weather gets bad. I play hockey with my grandchildren about once a year. My son, Lars, has a pond in his back yard and he takes great steps to keep it clear and the ice in nice shape. Usually on New Year's Day we get together for the "World Pond Hockey Championship." My team is designated the U.S. Army team and is composed of myself and the other Army Vet in the family, my nephew, Erik. Assorted kids fill out both teams. The opposition is given the name, the Al Qaida terrorists. We have a very spirited game and I look forward to it more than the younger players. I played college hockey for two years at Hamline U and can still skate fairly well.

I initially met my orthopedic physician, Dr. Frank Norberg, after I broke my arm. Phyllis was out of town and I planned to run to the airport over the noon hour and pick her up. It was a gorgeous spring day and I was looking forward to seeing Phyllis. I finished a case in the morning so did not have to be in a big hurry to get back to work. I departed our office building located on Washington and Second Avenues in Minneapolis and moved down the public sidewalk probably forty or fifty feet when I suddenly found myself thrown to the sidewalk. I had been struck by a biker. Not the motorized biker, but the old-fashioned pedal biker. This biker was probably in his 30's and not prosperous looking. He was a mobile street person. Not exactly your rich target defendant type. He did stop and at first blush I seemed to be okay and he apologized and pedaled away. I had been carrying a work file and it was in a manila folder and was not heavy. I soon discovered that I could not lift that small file. Because I had no strength in the arm, the obvious conclusion was that it had to be broken. I did not have much in the way of pain, but almost no strength. At least there was no displacement. One advantage to my job is that you do pick up a fair amount of medical knowledge. We are like the guy that plays a doctor on TV. He is not a real doctor, but he does play one on TV. That is damn near as good as a medical license. I did not have any pain in the upper arm and I did not recall striking the humorous so it was pretty likely that I had a break in the radial or ulnar bone. I reached my car and was still able to drive with one arm, so I headed for the airport.

I reached the airport without incident and met Phyllis at our usual stop. Phyllis got in the car and we had our usual small talk and then she asked me, "How are you?" "I am fine, however, I do have a broken arm," was my reply. "Have you been to a doctor?" was her response. "I should know if my arm is broken, it's my arm." "What happened?" I told my story again and Phyllis agreed that I should at least go see someone. We headed down to Abbot Hospital and I did the waiting game until I was able to see a resident or intern on duty. They took an x-ray and confirmed that it was broken. They offered me the choice of seeing a staff orthopedic, the in house variety, or an outside orthopedic office, the so-called outhouse choice. I picked the outhouse variety and ended up with Dr. Norberg. He confirmed the radial head was broken in the elbow, but to my surprise, he did not cast it but gave me a splint to wear. He told me I did not have to wear it all the time, but left it to my discretion. That was judicial discretion if I ever saw it.

As fate would have it, Phyllis was very active in a group called MARC, the Midwest Area Regulatory Commissioners and we had the summer conference set for Bismarck, North Dakota. Phyllis was slated to be President of MARC in a year and the next conference would be in Minneapolis so it was important for us to get up to North Dakota. Susan Wefald of the North Dakota Commission was the current President of MARC and she was hosting the event. Her Husband, Bob Wefald, was a district judge up that way and a former State Attorney General. He was also a naval captain and a reserve officer so we had a lot in common. Part of hosting the MARC conference was keeping the spouses busy and Bob was helping out with the spouses' program. They had a canoe trip planned for the Missouri river on Sunday a.m. and Cameron and I had planned to enjoy the event. Fortunately, we were not planning on replicating the Louis and Clark canoe trip up the Missouri, but were only planning on about five miles. I had broken my arm about a week earlier in the bicycle break and I was not sure how I was going to go on a canoe trip with only one workable arm, but both Cameron and I had been looking forward to the trip so we had to give it a try. I had to try the same river that Louis and Clark had plied, even if it was only a five-mile trek.

We drove up to Bismarck and arrived on Saturday evening and checked in and went to a welcome reception at the hotel and went to bed early so we could get up the next morning and depart for the canoe trip. We met at the hotel and then caravanned out to the launch place at the Missouri River. The Missouri was quite wide at that point and was about a kilometer or half-mile wide. Cameron and I got in our canoe and I took the stern as I had more experience and was not going to provide a lot of power in the bow. My left arm was broken and I could do most of the power paddling with my right arm and use the left to guide the paddle. I had my splint secured with an ace bandage and as long as I did not strain the arm or subject it to excessive pressure, I figured I would be okay. I was right, the arm seemed to hold up and I did not seem to be in pain, except we fell way behind the other canoes. Cameron did not like to be trailing the herd and asked, "How come we are way behind the other canoes?" My response was matter of fact, "Because the other people canoeing do not have broken arms."

That evening I saw Bob Wefald at the cocktail party and I decided not to wear my splint and he asked where it was. I told him the protocol and he understood that and he did admit he was worried about me out on the river earlier today. I told him I have done a lot of canoeing, but I was also apprehensive, as I was wondering if I was going to make it. I was afraid I may end up getting towed. Bob has a brother, John Wefald, who used to be involved in Minnesota democratic politics, but moved on to become the President of Kansas State in Manhattan, Kansas. Bob and I both liked to talk about our military careers and Bob told me he tried to join the Army, but was turned down. He had just finished college and wanted to join before he got drafted. He started out with the Army with a view of going to Officer Candidate School (OCS). He was turned down because of acne. That did not sound like a deal breaker to me. Several of my friends had pimples and it never seemed like that big a deal. Acne was more serious and quite prevalent, but like crooked teeth, it seems to have vanished from the current scene. Bob became quite dejected as he did want to serve. He checked with the Navy and they showed the same reluctance. Bob persisted and ran across an elderly doctor who practiced up that way and the doctor told him, do not despair, he would fix things up. He wrote a letter to the Navy and they probably ran it by their own medical personnel and just like magic, he was in the Navy. I had experienced a kidney stone when I was in my 20's and before the Army would take me, I had my then father-in-law, Dr. Brick Hilger, write a letter to the military and tell them my kidneys were fine. My problem with the kidney stone occurred because I got sick and dried out. I did not drink enough water. I have never had any further problems since my original stone and Bob apparently worked through his acne dilemma and became a navy captain.

When I think back on my broken arm event, there were some similarities between my event and Mr. Gibberd's. I did not get shot, but was struck down while traversing a public sidewalk as was Mr. Gibberd. I did not assert a workers' compensation case, as I did not believe I had a decent case and I also doubted if I would have any permanent problems (I did not have any lingering problems with the arm, it healed nicely, for which I am thankful). In the old days, they put a cast on everything and that resulted in a lot of wasting or atrophy and that probably caused as many problems as the break because it took so long to get your strength back. Also, sometimes they got the cast on too tight and that could cause real problems. My arm was in a sling for a couple days and when I took it out of the sling and tried to straighten it, the pain was intense. I could imagine the pain if one's arm had been immobilized for a couple of months.

My accident occurred off the employer's premises and after I entered a public sidewalk. Mr. Gibberd was murdered on a public street or sidewalk. I was on a personal errand or mission and not on company pursuits. Mr. Gibberd had been eating. What I was doing was totally my own choice. I was not directed or asked to leave the premises by my employer. Mr. Gibberd made his own choice as to where or when he went to supper and was not asked or directed to go to a designated place by his employer. I was injured by a street risk, a bicycle driven by a careless biker, and that risk was not unique to me but

Death in St. Paul

was shared by everyone else on the street. Mr. Gibberd was assaulted and murdered and unfortunately the risk of street crime was shared by everyone else on the streets and sidewalks in the area. He was not a chaser or a drinker and there was no evidence that the crime was personal to him. There was no evidence that I was targeted or singled out for attack because of my status as an employee of the state. I did not recognize the biker as a disgruntled employee that I had stiffed. Likewise, there was no evidence that Mr. Gibberd was attacked because of his status as a CDC employee. Fortunately, I only had a broken arm, but Mr. Gibberd suffered a fate much worse.

We came back for day two of the trial and the petitioner called a gentleman I named Mr. Will Poster, who was Mr. Gibberd's manager from May of 1985 until his death in August. He saw Mr. Gibberd about once a week and they communicated regularly by a device they called electronic mail. No one in the courtroom recognized this term and Mr. Poster described it as a "system that we used that we send letters electronically. We have terminals and –and PCs and things and we can send communications back and forth." Email was used by the military to communicate and it spread to industrial users. It had not, as yet, been exploited for personal or home application as most folks did not have a home computer. If Control Data had only realized the commercial value of this communication medium, sitting right in front of them; they probably would still be around.

Mr. Poster testified that Ray was a database consultant and he was working on a new support database system. He was the only one working on that project. Essentially he was working on the basic structure of a new computer system. I am no computer expert, but thirty years ago this was big, cutting edge stuff. How close was he to a new system and who else knew about what he was doing? These are questions I have as I sit here at a much later time. Was there an issue or question of industrial espionage? This issue did not surface at the trial, but if Ray was on to something big, would a competitor wish to slow down or block that development? The police never were able to piece together a motive for Ray's demise, so perhaps it is not all that far-fetched to think about involvement by a competitor, foreign or domestic. Industrial espionage has always been around and it is still popular, but has become more sophisticated and moved into computer hacking and cyber warfare. When I did a follow up to this story, I asked SGT Hartman if he had thought about industrial espionage or a trade secret issue and indeed he did consider that angle. He talked to a couple executives from Control Data about that issue and they did not have anything for him to support that theory. I guess that idea was not as far-fetched as I thought.

Mr. Poster related that there were times that computer access was limited during normal working hours and Mr. Gibberd would have to use the computer after hours and the computer system he used was the only one available to him.

Mr. Gibberd was considered what CDC called an exempt employee in that he did not get paid for overtime and was not on a regular 9-5 schedule. Management had no objection if Mr. Gibberd and others went off premises to eat. It was in the employer's interest if Ray worked into the evening. Ray was a highly regarded CDC employee.

In June of 1985 there was quite a crunch going on at CDC as they were trying to install the new data system. They were awaiting a tape to come in from Bettyele systems and it finally arrived on August 8, 1985. Mr. Poster made it sound like the tape just turned up at the St. Paul facility as, "We finally found the tape in the building over in St. Paul." This was a crucial tape and it sounds like they mailed it ordinary first class mail. There had to be some sort of special delivery or special handling available. I believe that Fed Ex was around. No wonder that CDC was having some financial issues. They did locate the tape and they did install the new system. Mr. Poster got an electronic mail in August advising they had finished the installation at 4 or 5 in the morning. Occasionally Ray would work all night to finish a project. The poor guy had to work all night to make up for the incompetents who did not know how to deliver an essential element of the job.

Mr. Poster was asked if Mr. Gibberd would have had any business in the area where he was shot, apart from his employment at CDC and he responded "no." He did testify that Control Data did have a policy of building in so-called "depressed" areas.

On cross-examination, Mr. Gallegos clarified that Mr. Gibberd was not required to work after 5:00 p.m. He was only required to work a 40-hour week. The witness was never personally aware of Mr. Gibberd leaving the facility to eat and thereafter returning to work. It was common practice for all CDC employees to leave the work premises at all facilities in order to get something to eat. He was aware that Mr. Gibberd left the premises to eat, but that decision was Mr. Gibberd's and not the employer's decision.

I had taken a ruling under advisement and ruled that the statement to the daughter and to Mrs. Gibberd made by the decedent was not admissible in that it was hearsay and further was a statement of future intentions and usually such statements are of questionable veracity in the first place. I may say I am going to Willow River tonight, but I probably am not going anywhere. In other words, statements of future intentions are not inherently reliable. In fact, the opposite may well be true. The statements were made by Ray and were to the effect that he was going out to eat. We all knew he had gone out to eat and so this was not any crucial testimony. At this point in the trial, I still had little idea as to how I was going to find or who was going to prevail so I just made my ruling and did not worry about the final result. If I knew I was going to find for the defense, then I would have let the statements into evidence, as I did not want to get overturned on appeal because of an evidentiary ruling. I mentioned earlier in this writing as to how Judge Snyder from the Army Judiciary used to go back and change all his rulings to rule on all the objections and evidentiary rulings in favor of the defense. This was to secure the defendant's last minute preparations for Leavenworth.

At this point, the defense attorney gave a short opening statement. He called me Mr. Hearing Examiner, instead of judge, but I did not correct him, as it was not important. Some judges have such a big ego that they would have been inclined to make a big deal of it, but I do not like to embarrass attorneys, so I kept quiet. When the office first started it was called the Hearing Examiners Office as the judges were called hearing examiners. When the workers' compensation judges came over to the office in 1981, they were already called compensation judges and not too long after 1981 the hearing examiners became administrative law judges. Before they made the name change, every once in a while, someone would call the office and seek to make an appointment to have their hearing checked.

Mr. Gallegos outlined that he would show that the immediate neighborhood around the CDC Plant was not as crime-infested as we had been led to believe and it was misleading to compare it to the Summit-University area. The petitioner had relied on the police department grid system and the Summit-University area was a big footprint, it was two miles by one mile. That is a pretty large area and neighborhoods can change character in a hurry. The defense counsel also meant to show that Mr. Gibberd's practice when he went out to eat in the evening was not to go back to work. In fact, he seldom returned to the office after an evening meal. Lastly, he promised to bring in an eyewitness to the crime, who would testify somewhat differently than the testimony of the two police officers and would testify that Mr. Gibberd had some personal knowledge of the assailant. This last witness was shaping up to be a very revealing and possibly compelling witness.

Wendy Muck, a research analyst with the St. Paul Police Department was called and sworn and testified she kept crime statistics for the St. Paul Police Department and tried to spot trends or changes so that the police department could head off problems or get out in front of emerging criminal problems. She shared her information with the public and realtors or others in the market for a home who would call her and get information on a particular neighborhood. It was better to call Ms. Muck and check out a neighborhood before you moved into it rather than move in and then find yourself in the middle of a combat zone.

The WDC facility was in a two square mile area designated the Summit-University area. The larger areas were broken down into grids and the Gibberd shooting was in grid 109. Grid number 109 had University on the north, Marshall on the south, Western on the east, and Dale on the west. It turned out that the WDC facility was also in grid number 109, but on the south side of Interstate 94. Ms. Muck advised us that in grid number 109 for 1985 there were 299 offenses reported. I asked what constituted an "offense" and that included just about any reportable crime, excluding traffic. For example, shop-lifting would be included in the term. The overall crime ranking for grid number 109 for 1985 was 19th in the City of St. Paul. Grid 129 was directly to the south of grid 109 and that grid had a ranking of 7th for 1985. Grid number 108 had 283 offenses and came in at 30th place. It was her testimony that the downtown area of St. Paul was the highest crime area with 806 offenses. The overall Summit-University area was high crime area number two during 1985.

Ms. Muck was asked about criminal trends in the area of the WDC facility and reported that the area around the facility seemed to be in a decreasing crime area. There was not a lot of available housing in grid 109, but in grid 129 to the south there seemed to be a lot of people interested in moving into the area. In terms of national crime statistics, it seemed that St. Paul ranked about in the middle of the pack when compared to similarly sized cities. The six cities with more crimes were Birmingham, Sacramento, Tampa, Newark, Rochester (N.Y.), and Charlotte. Those with less crime included Louisville, Wichita, Omaha, Virginia Beach, and St. Petersburg, Florida. On a more current level the most recent comparisons were for 2001 and St. Paul had moved up to 4th place and Minneapolis appeared at 9th. These were crimes per 1,000 people. On the face of it, it appeared that Minneapolis, in 2001, was a safer place than St. Paul, but comparing major crimes between the Twin Towns it was Minneapolis leading on all counts: Homicide 43-9; Rape 399-221; Robbery; 1943-680 and Aggravated Assault; 1713-1326. Statistical comparisons can be misleading. In 2014 St. Paul had 11 homicides whereas the Mill City had 38. Which is the safest place?

Ms. Pat Robertson, the personnel manager at the WDC facility was called and testified there were about 400 people working on the day shift at the facility and about twenty five people employed during the second and third shifts. Most of the twenty five second shifters worked in the warehouse. She had been at the WDC facility since January of 1984 and none of the employees had expressed any concern to her with their personal safety or the safety of others while working at the facility. This seemed to be telling testimony. This was supposed to be a crime infested area, but no one was complaining, at least before the August 26, 1985 murder.

The racial component of the work force at the WDC facility was 20 percent, black, Hispanic, and oriental or Asian. The balance of the work force was white. Control Data also had another facility in the area called the Bindery. It was located on Selby and Grotto and had been around for 5-6 years.

This was interesting in that the Bindery was located close to Selby and Dale and that area had enjoyed the dubious reputation for many years as the worst area in St. Paul. Control Data had somehow selected a facility location in a bad area of the city, but managed to make it work. The employees did not complain about the neighborhood or crime problems in the vicinity of the Bindery.

Ms. Robertson was a native of St. Paul and had lived in the general area around the WDC facility for almost thirty years. She lived 8-10 blocks from work and to the south toward Summit Avenue. She and her family did not seem to have any special concerns over personal safety or crime. She had previously traveled from the WDC facility to Clark's Sub Shop on University Avenue. Clark's is located about a block west of Wendy's on University Avenue. It turned out she drove. I was not sure if she drove because she was lazy or in a hurry or if she was in fear of her life to walk. Her office was located with a good view of the street and she observed some of the employees would walk up the street toward Wendy's, but many drove. She concluded that most of the workers seemed to be drivers instead of walkers. This was certainly inconclusive testimony. About the only thing I could conclude was that Ms. Robertson spent too much time looking out the window. About 65 percent of the workers were so called non-exempt workers and I think she was talking about workers who are subject to the minimum wage and overtime pay laws. These are typically workers paid by the hour and on a 40-hour week. They were granted a half hour to eat and consequently most of them ate in the cafeteria. The folks that were exempt from the minimum wage or 40 hours per week requirement were the professional or salaried workers. The exempt workers were the ones who could take an extra few minutes for lunch because they did not have to return to work and bang on a time clock.

On cross-examination she testified that management had never issued any bulletins or policy statements that encouraged workers to remain on premises during lunch or other breaks. After the murder the employer did institute an escort service for those working the second shift to be escorted to their cars.

The escort service that was instituted after the murder was for those working the second shift. Those working the shift generally got off around 11:00 p.m. It was certainly dark at that time and some of the employees were apprehensive about going out to the parking lot alone. It turned out that the escort service was only used sparingly and was subsequently discontinued. Life around the WDC gradually returned to normal.

Ms. Bjorklund asked about a lay-off that occurred about the same time Mr. Gibberd was hired by CDC. Apparently about 5 percent of the work force was jettisoned. She asked the witness if many people who were separated would be upset by that development. Ms. Robertson responded that a significant number had volunteered to be let go. Some were involuntarily terminated. They were all afforded a severance pay package. This was testimony that was of questionable relevance and very speculative. Some of the employees were glad to leave and thus volunteered to hit the door. Others may have been upset, but they still

Death in St. Paul

took the severance package. By 1984, the economy was much better than it had been going into the 80's and people were getting jobs and buying houses and cars. It seemed to be a stretch that a disgruntled worker had committed murder. Then again, maybe not.

Ms. Busby was next called and her job was Manager of the Engineering Function at the WDC for the past month and a half. She was not present at the WDC in August of 1985. Her title sounded like she was watching the heating boilers or checking out the water pipes at the WDC, but in reality, she was a security supervisor. As part of her job, she kept or was custodian of company records called incident reports and these were reports that were usually prepared by the security guards, describing any crime or event that was out of the ordinary and occurred on their watch. This was in the days before every business used computer records, and even though Control Data was a computer giant, they were still keeping their incident reports on paper in an old metal file cabinet. Apparently the cabinet was stuffed full of papers, but she managed to wade her way through the piles of paper and came out with three major events that had occurred around the plant. One referred to a theft of petty cash within the building. She described it as a robbery, but it was not clear if the money was taken by force or threat of force. By definition, robbery involves the taking of property by force or threat of force. Robbery combines two crimes, theft and assault. The director of security did not seem to differentiate between the two crimes. It was left to me to figure out if it was petty theft or robbery. The difference is about five to ten years as many criminals have learned the hard way.

One of the incidents involved an assault of a female employee near the WDC building in August of 1982. A white male had approached her and said, "I'm going to kill you lady" and her response was to scream and run toward the building. The assailant did not follow, but chose to leave.

The so called "rock incident" occurred on the intercity freeway or I-94 where they have walkways over the freeway and some youths had thrown rocks from the walkway and hit the windshield of a car driven by the wife of a CDC worker. She had apparently dropped her husband off at the WDC facility and gotten on the freeway and proceeded a couple blocks when her car was hit. She turned around and came back to the WDC and reported it to the guards. This event happened in January of 1983.

The "rock incident" was not particularly new or unique and still happens even today in the same vicinity of the footbridge or over one of the vehicular bridges. Periodically some little delinquent urchin will grab some rocks and toss them off the bridge. They do have the top of the footbridge enclosed in wire mesh so it is probably much more of a challenge to power a rock through the wire and down to the freeway. I imagine wire cutters or other such stolen tools will probably make a sufficient opening. The Dale Street Bridge has wire mesh running up about eight feet. It takes some arm muscle, but a pretty good rock could be hoisted over the top. If only that energy and ingenuity could be channeled into a job. The rock throwing can be deadly as a few years back a car was hit in the windshield by a large rock and the driver lost control and struck a concrete abutment and was killed.

I had a rock throwing case back in the 70's and it involved a younger boyhood friend who contacted me and advised he was charged with criminal damage to property arising out of a rock throwing incident in the same vicinity as the WDC. He had been picked up in the vicinity of the Dale Street Bridge extending over Interstate 94. My client was in the area, but no one could put him on the bridge with a rock in his hand. The case was dismissed without having to put Mr. Client on the stand. I do not think he did it, as he denied it, but I suspect a prosecution witness failed to show and they had to dismiss the case.

The petty cash "robbery" occurred in February of 1981. Apparently the thieves came in the front door and proceeded down a hallway and grabbed the cash and exited the back door and the alarm sounded, but they were soon in a waiting "getaway car" and sped away. Quite the master plan and it sure appeared as someone on the "inside" planned the move and a couple buddies executed the plan. If the security people or the "engineering function" could find out who knew where the money was located and who was the custodian of the funds and check those people out, they would probably find the perpetrator. We do not know if the WDC security force followed up on that crime, but somehow I had my doubts.

Ms. Busby had spoken to the other guards and they were not aware of any other incidents that would constitute a major infraction of the law. There were no other assaults or significant incidents.

This certainly was not the picture of a crime-infested workplace. At the time this case was heard, our offices were located in the "Historic Flour Exchange Building" located on 4th Avenue South in Minneapolis, just a few blocks distant from the courthouse. I would venture to guess that we had more "incidents" at our workplace than occurred at the WDC facility. The Flour Exchange Building was owned by real estate magnate, Diehl Gustafson. The great George Mikan, known as "Mr. Basketball" of the first fifty years of the sport, had an office on the top floor of the building. George had "basketball knees" and moved slowly. George was said to be a friend of Mr. Gustafson's and perhaps did some legal work for him. George seemed like a good fellow and always greeted me when we passed while going in and out of the building. In the lobby was housed a giant polar bear that Diehl had shot a few years earlier while on an expedition to Alaska. Judge Bernie Dinner, an ex-Marine, was an animal lover and objected to the bear being displayed in the lobby, but the objection was duly noted by Gustafson and "overruled." Judge Dinner did not prevail on that ruling. Our office had courtrooms on the third floor and offices on the fourth floor. We were short of office space on the fourth floor so the

Death in St. Paul

administration fashioned three offices off in a corner of the third floor. I shared the space with Judge John Janssen and Judge Jeanne Knight. John was a JAG and a former Washington County Attorney. He was a good guy and we always got along well. Jeanne was moody and sometimes temperamental, but I eventually learned to work around that obstacle. Jeanne was an occasional smoker and she usually had a pack in her desk and if I was working late or had a tough day, on occasion I would filch a cigarette and light up at my desk. The trials were usually wound up by midafternoon so we had the place to ourselves. We could light up when we felt like it and no one knew or cared. With the current anti-smoking hysteria, that would probably be classified as a major crime.

The office had a system for assigning cases at the last minute, called a back-up case. Backup cases were extra cases not assigned to a judge and on the day of trial, if your case settled, you stood a decent chance of getting a backup case. One might show up in the morning dressed rather casually and suddenly be called into the courtroom. I kept an extra tie and sport coat and a pair of black shoes in my office, just in case I needed a last minute change of clothes. The judges were like Clark Kent, ready to find a room to change and spring into action. One day I was assigned a backup rather unexpectedly so I adjourned to "my judicial chambers" and grabbed my extra clothes and prepared for trial. I reached for my black shoes and did note that they seemed rather dusty. I looked inside and found a dead mouse. I disposed of the critter and dusted out my shoes and away I went.

I was a bit disturbed by the dead mouse and thought I should at least report it to our crack management team. The Chief Administrative Law Judge was Duane Harves. I was in law school with Duane. He was not sympathetic to my story and got a good laugh out of it. In fact, someone called him when I was in his office and he shared the story with some political friend of his. They had a big yuk-yuk. The call was not unusual, as Duane always seemed to be talking with some politician when I was in his office. I did not care, as I knew he was looking for a judgeship, but thought maybe we needed an exterminator. I did a lot of extra things around the office, but decided not to set up a trap line.

Duane was something of a rarity in State Government in that he liked to save taxpayers money. He had us quartered in low rent buildings and unfortunately for us, they were not always the fanciest quarters. Duane eventually got himself appointed to the district court in Dakota County and Rudy Perpich's nephew Bill Brown replaced Duane. Bill was a good guy and good chief and he relocated us to a nice building on Washington Avenue called the Washington Square Building. Our lease at the Flour Exchange expired about the time there was a glut of office space in Minneapolis and I think we ended up paying less money for nicer space. Jim Otto was a veteran property owner and he helped out in negotiating much better space at less money.

The administration kept track of the judges almost exclusively by the paper trail. We initiated the paper trail by filing a simple report on every case assigned. If it settled, we kept the file until the stipulation for settlement came in the door. If it did not show up, it was our job to send a "where in the hell is it" letter to the attorneys. Actually, we called it the "hate" letter and all of the secretaries knew it by that name.

If the case went to trial and all of the evidence was submitted and the case concluded, then we had sixty days to submit or complete the written decision. If we could not get the decision out in sixty days, then we had to get an extension of time from the chief judge. There were cases when a witness could not appear or there were scheduling problems and necessary evidence was not submitted and in that event we had to advise the administration if the record was to be open and the expected date of closure. If the file was to be open beyond thirty days, then we had to get the concurrence of the assistant chief to keep an open record. I did not have that many open records so do not recall having a big problem getting the concurrence of management to keep an open record. I was not real excited about having open records so I did what I could to discourage it and if the record had to be open, I tried to make sure that it closed as soon as possible. The further you got away from the trial the harder it got to write up the decision. My preference was to start writing the case within a day or two of trial. I have a fairly good memory, but like most people, my memory does not improve with time, it gets worse. It is much easier to write up the decision while the facts are still fresh in your mind. I tried to follow this method, but occasionally one got a run of cases and there was no avoiding the fact that you were going to be working on a cold record.

The statute directing that we had to issue our decision within sixty days contained a harsh penalty for non-compliance. The statute provided that if we did not get the decision out then we did not get paid. The chief judge could extend the sixty-day period for up to thirty days if "good cause" was shown. I never had much of a problem getting my cases out within sixty days and seldom, if ever, asked for an extension. Some of the judges were habitually running short on time and were constantly seeking extensions and bumping up against the time limits. I heard that a couple judges missed a paycheck, but do not know the details. I am not sure if the pay was suspended and then they received it at a later time or if the pay was forfeited and they did not receive it at all. I could see some legal issues with the forfeiture system. If one was working and not getting paid for it, it seems to me there is a provision in the constitution called the 13th Amendment that prohibits requiring one to work for another without pay. We fought a war over that same question. It was not my paycheck that was at issue and fortunately I did not have to wage another war to collect my check.

The district judges have a similar rule requiring cases be issued within ninety days or they do not get paid. Those folks are such hot shots that there is no one that has the temerity to enforce the rule so it is largely ignored. We have a chief judge that acts as the hammer. I do not know why the chief judge in district court could not do the same thing. Doing that job may interfere with the jolly little fraternity existing among the banditos.

When this case was completed, it did take some time to complete and unfortunately the sixty-day period was up during the time I was in summer camp with the reserves. I was due to spend two weeks at the JAG School in Charlottesville, VA and the sixty-day period was ending during that two-week period. The Assistant Chief was Myron or "Mickey" Greenberg and I went in and asked Mickey if I could get an extension. Mickey asked why I needed an extension and I told him where I was going and I told Mickey I was going to classes for two weeks at Charlottesville and may not have time to write it up while in that location. He asked about my evenings and weekends and I was honest and told him I could probably write it up then but it would "seriously interfere with my beer drinking." Mickey told me to try and write it up, so I did and mailed dictaphone tapes back to the office from Charlottesville and it got transcribed and it was issued while I was on military leave. I did have the University of Virginia Law School at my disposal and spent most of the middle weekend at the library researching the law before issuing the decision. While some of my comrades in arms, were living it up in Virginia Beach or Washington D.C. I was having fun in the law library. Actually, I did not mind it a bit. I wanted to do a good and thorough job and I had access to a wonderful law library so that gave me access to the latest death cases from all over the country.

My friend, Joe Reyhansky, from active duty days was stationed in Charlottesville and I busted out of the law library for a couple hours to spend an evening with Joe and Katy. They picked me up and we went to Hardwick's Restaurant or as Joe called it "Hard On's" and enjoyed a meal followed by some fireworks. It was over the 4th of July. The fireworks were at a local park in Charlottesville. Katy was wearing a tee shirt that said "Participant in S.E. Asia Land Games - Second Place Finisher." Joe was an enlisted soldier in Vietnam and this was a droll reminder of that service. After the fireworks, we piled in Joe's car and drove back to his place to have a beer. Joe's young son, Tommy, almost bailed out of the car, but other than that near tragedy, we made it back to his house. Joe threatened to break the kid's arm, but I knew he was not serious so I did not call child protection. Bailing out of a moving car is serious stuff. I asked Joe where he was planning on retiring when he finished his military career and he pointed to the couch I was sitting on and said, "Right there." Actually he moved on to Chattanooga, TN where he secured a position as a prosecutor in the local DA's Office.

I was not mad at Mickey for denying my request for an extension as I had to do the decision at some time or another so why not do it when I had the facilities to do a good job? I believe that was the only time I asked for an extension in twenty six years and it was turned down. I did try and avoid interaction and especially conflict with management. Some of the judges were continually fighting with management. I recall Dan Gallagher remarking to me on one occasion that "Our Lord could be chief judge and some of the judges would still find fault with him." A true commentary on our feisty little group. The judges were a tough audience to please. I recall on one occasion early in my career when for some reason I put together a decision outline that I thought might be helpful to the judges. This was before computer days. I showed it to the chief, Duane Harves, and he decided to share it with the other judges at a staff meeting. After the meeting, I was talking with Cathy Quintero and Joe Murray came up to me with the outline and asked, "What am I supposed to do with this thing?" I replied, "As far as I am concerned, you can use it to wipe your ass." Joe persisted, "No, no, what is this supposed to be about?" I responded, "It is only a suggestion, but if you want to use it to wipe your ass, I do not care." I guess Joe thought I was trying to force something upon him and I wanted to make it clear, I did not care what he did with the piece of paper; it was his choice.

When Mickey Greenberg was assistant chief we were still having annual evaluations. That was later scrapped as too much work for management or not worth the time. Mickey called me in one year for my evaluation and he gave me the statistics and we sat and talked. I was getting most of my decisions out in 35-40 days and Mickey said the office was shooting for a thirty-day standard. I asked Mickey, "We already have a sixty-day standard, why do we need another standard?" Mickey responded that it was a matter of public perception and not having people wait for a decision any longer than necessary. I could understand that and also knew that Mickey was bucking to get on the district court bench and this may help his cause. I remarked to Mickey that I had the lowest appeal rate in the office and people must be pretty satisfied with my work. Mickey dismissed that and said, "We do not worry too much about the appeal rate." All seemed to be well and thus concluded my annual review.

A year later I was back in Mickey's office for another annual review. Mickey looked things over and did comment that my appeal rate seemed high. I responded, "A year ago I had the lowest appeal rate in the office and you told me that was not important." Mickey moved on with the rest of the interview. It was not long afterward that Mickey moved on to the district court.

We had quite a few folks in the office who moved on to the district court. Some of the judges seemed to have as their "second job" the promotion of themselves as a future district judge. This seemed to hit high gear when we had a democrat in the governor's office. The republicans would elect some boy scout like Al Quie and he would push for non-partisan appointments and proceed to appoint a bunch of democrats. In his case they were religiously oriented democrats. A lot of democrats and republicans seemed to acquire a religious

Death in St. Paul

fervor when Quie was governor. He used to have prayer breakfasts and those wanting a judgeship were well advised to show up for the prayer breakfast with Al. I could not get out of bed on Sundays to go to church, so how in the world could I get up and venture to a breakfast to pray with Al?

When Al Quie was running for governor against Rudy Perpich back in 1978 I remember talking to my father about the coming election. He told me that Minnesota had only elected one non-Scandinavian governor in the history of the state and we were not about to change that practice and Quie would win in a walk. I think the non-Scandinavian may have been Harold Stassen. My dad was correct in that prediction as Quie did not have any problem in upending Perpich. The old man was actually not too bad a politician. He ran for the legislature on one occasion as the republican candidate up in Aitkin County. He lost and did not try it again. Any elected position is so dependent on name recognition that unless you happen to be a public figure or a publicized second story man, it is most difficult for an unknown to win on an initial try. My father should have stuck with it and may have prevailed on the second or third try. The old man seldom listened to me or anyone else for that matter, but on one occasion he did listen to me and he was better for it. Nelson Rockefeller was the VP for Gerald Ford and "Rocky" was in town for a fundraiser so I urged the old man to attend and he did and he received a nice photograph of himself with the vice president. It landed in the Aitkin paper.

One time the old man ignored what I told him and he eventually had to get it corrected. He was complaining of pains in his lower abdomen almost near his groin. He said it was his gall bladder. The old man had a lot of gall, but I knew that was too low for his gall bladder. I told him it was probably his colon. A year or two later, he went in and had part of his colon cut out. He was 85 at the time and it did not seem to slow him down. He had the surgery done by a surgeon in a small town in Idaho and I told him that might be a mistake, he should head for a bigger medical center. It turned out the "country surgeon" did a good job and he recovered nicely.

Quie was a decent guy and all that stuff and he had this wonderful idea to make non-partisan appointments of judges. In other words, he would appoint democrats or republicans. The democrats used to proclaim that their appointment process was non-partisan, but they have finally stopped that spurious claim, as it is even too much bullshit for them to swallow. What would an ambitious young lawyer do if they aspire to be a judge? In which political camp should one choose? If you go with the republicans, you may end up with a non-partisan "Dudley Do Right" in the governor's mansion and your work and contributions to the republicans have not even given you an edge. In fact, it may be a disadvantage, because the republicans can concentrate on your faults. They know you better. On the other hand, if you support the democrats, you know that the democrats are going to be loyal to the party when there is a favor to pass around. So many of the lawyers are now lefties that the field can get over-crowded, so that is another thing to consider. If I was a woman or minority, I would probably go with the republicans as the field is less crowded. If you do not fit into the later categories, then take your pick.

One other little thing to consider in making your political choice is which party, if any, is likely to support you when you get in office. The democrats are usually quick to close ranks and support their person if trouble develops. When Bill Clinton was lifting skirts back in the 90's the party leaders got behind him and told us it was only sex. When Trump got in trouble over a tape, the party leaders ran for the hills and yelled back over their shoulders that he should quit.

Currently there is another push for so-called non-partisan judges. The current proposal is sometimes called the "Quie Plan" and the people do not get to choose their judges. This is a great deal for lazy and incompetent sitting judges. The sitting judges do not run against a real person. They run against themselves. The issue on the ballot is should Judge Dimwit or Judge Dipshit be retained? If the people vote "NO" then the appointment goes back to the governor and they can appoint one of the holy ones. The great flaw in the system is, "Who in the world is going to mount a campaign against Judge Dimwit and spend thousands of dollars and hundreds of hours getting a no vote against Judge Dimwit and then not end up with the job? Under the current system, the candidate who gets off the couch and challenges Judge Corruption is motivated to undertake the task, because if they prevail then they get the job. This is the only way to get rid of corrupt judges. Who is going to undertake the herculean task of unseating a dead-beat judge, if someone else is going to be rewarded for your hard work? The answer is so self-fulfilling that even the blokes pushing for the change cannot provide a decent answer to that simple question. The motivation behind the "Quie Plan" is to benefit incumbent judges and poor ones at that. Folks, please do not get suckered into this change. Quie voted no on me a couple times, I would certainly vote no on his half-baked plan to short the Minnesota public.

Shortly after Quie was elected, two openings for the Workers' Compensation Court of Appeals opened up and Quie had a screening committee formed and their job was to review the applicants and pick five names to give to the governor. The chair of the committee was Judge Gillespie out of Cambridge. I had tried a couple cases in front of Gillespie when I was practicing up in Anoka County and we got along fine so I think that helped my cause and I was one of the five picked for the finals. As I recall, three of the other finalists were Paul Reike, Jim Otto, and Candi Hektner. This was my first shot at the appointment process and I had done nothing to prepare for it. I did not solicit any letters of support or otherwise do any sort of campaigning to get the job. I stupidly concluded it was a merit system. I was an extreme long shot.

I did get an interview with Governor Quie and he was active in the inter-

Death in St. Paul

view and we seemed to get along okay. One of the last questions was, "What do you like to do with your free time or personal time?" Had I been smarter and a serial liar, I would have used that question to proclaim my faith and extoll the virtues of my church affiliation. The truth of the matter was and still is that I have no church affiliation. I do have beliefs and am spiritual, but prefer to keep my beliefs to myself. I was not able to fulfill the governor's religious litmus test and did not get the appointment. Paul Reike is a good friend and smart guy and he did fulfill the religious test and Paul was appointed along with another friend, Jim Otto. Candi Hektner had been one of the favorites, but was not picked. Candi stands as an example of a woman that would have been selected if there was a democrat making the choices.

    I had known Jim Otto for quite some time and he hired me twice as a compensation attorney. I think Jim's wife, Beth, had been active in republican circles and that gave him the inside track on appointments. Jim did a good job on the WCCA but ran into some trouble over a statement he made in a decision. The petitioner had been described as "morbidly obese" by one of the doctors involved in the case and Jim repeated the line in one of his decisions. This was somehow determined by the petitioner's bar as "insensitive" and they organized a force of lawyers to oppose Otto's confirmation by the senate. They portrayed it like Jim had called the guy a fat ass. Low and behold, Otto was not confirmed and a more cautious individual was appointed in his place. I believe I was still an applicant for the position, but I heard not a word and sometime later I saw where Jack Wallraff was appointed. Jack did fulfill all of Quie's criteria for the job.

    Governor Quie's chief of staff or administrative assistant was a lawyer named Buzz Cummins. Years later Buzz became involved in the workers' compensation system as he had an administrative position with one of the insurance companies. Buzz had been present during my interview with Governor Quie. A continuing education event was in Tucson and Phyllis joined me for the event, and one evening we went out with Judge Patty Milun and her husband Tim. I always liked Patty as she had a lot of spunk and was good on her feet. We went out to a local restaurant and somehow got connected up with Buzz, who joined us for dinner. We got to reminiscing with Buzz about the "good old Quie days" and I remarked that the Quie administration seemed to like democrats better than republicans. Buzz responded that most people do not realize how hard it is to find "qualified republicans." My response was a simple, "Bullshit." My simple one-word reply was echoed by Patty. We did not get into the Quie definition of "qualified." Obviously, I did not meet the definition of "qualified." Buzz tried rather lamely to sell us on the idea that there were no qualified republicans in the state of Minnesota, but he realized he was pushing that boulder up a hill.

    As I have gotten older, I am wary of both parties. Approach them with caution and do not count on a lot of support, particularly from the elephants.

Back at the trial, we continued with the testimony of Ms. Busby. Mr. Gallegos wished to offer the sign-in and sign-out sheets to show that while Mr. Gibberd frequently signed out after normal working hours, he seldom signed back in. Either he forgot to sign back in or he did not return to work. Counsel believed it showed an inference that Mr. Gibberd had left the office for the day on August 26, and was on his own time. The law was pretty clear that for most people in the work-a-day world, we were not covered by workers' comp when we were commuting back and forth to work. That risk was borne by our auto carriers or perhaps another carrier if we were traveling by bus or mass transit. The exception to the rule was the traveling salesperson who was always in his car and always on the way to a call. Those folks were covered practically 24-7. If you employ a salesman or an estimator or a worker who is in a car a lot, the reason your workers' compensation rates are high is because the coverage extends practically as far and wide as their car can carry them.

Ms. Busby was requested by her counsel to obtain sign-in, sign-out sheets for 1985 from April through August. She was only able to locate two sign-in/out sheets for July. Ms. Busby related that there had been a high degree of turnover in the "security engineer" position and that may explain some of the record problems. Ms. Bjorklund objected to the records coming into evidence as the records were incomplete. I received the records and pointed out that the records could be received, but the absence of July records had a bearing on the credibility of the records and not on their admissibility. Mr. Gallegos represented that they would continue to search for the missing records and Ms. Bjorklund added sarcastically, "I wouldn't doubt it for a minute." I added that I was not going to wait for you to complete your search, but would close the record. That got a laugh from the peanut gallery.

The sign-in/out sheets were only used during work times during non-traditional hours. This would be after 6:00 p.m. on weekdays and all day on Saturday and Sunday. There were six sheets produced for April and only one set showed a sign out and sign back in. On April 10th Mr. Gibberd signed in at 7:50 p.m. and signed out the next day at 1:05 a.m. There was only one sign-out sheet for May and that was May 20th and he signed out at 10:35 p.m. In June he was putting in some long days. He worked late or after hours on nine different evenings. On some evenings he was working until 1:00 or 2:00 a.m. He was on the big push to finish the project. The July record was MIA but the August records seemed to be intact.

Turning to August of 1985 since this was the month of the murder, I will include all of the logs for that month. On August 1, he signed out at 8:32 p.m. August 2nd he signed out at 6:34 p.m. On August 6 he signed out at 8:38 p.m. On August 8th the pattern was somewhat different in that he signed out at 8:05 p.m. and then signed back in at 10:52 p.m. He was gone for almost 3 hours. On the 9th of August he signed out at almost midnight. On August 13th he signed back in between 6:00 and 7:00 p.m.

The sign-in and out log was often confusing, as is not unusual. On August 15th he signed out twice, around 10:00 p.m. and then again after midnight. After some discussion the first entry for the 15th of August, actually should have been on the 14th. On August 16th he signed in at 6 p.m. and on the 17th he signed out the next morning at 8:00 a.m. (he pulled an all-nighter). On the 18th he signed in at 6:43 p.m. and on the 20th he signed out at 6:10 p.m.

Based on the paper trail it seemed evident that Mr. Gibberd frequently left the premises in the evening and did not return. At least based on the paper work, he was more likely not to return to work as opposed to cycling back. Miss Bjorklund made it clear on cross that Mr. Gibberd may have left the plant before 6:00 and returned before 6:00 and it would not have shown up on the records. Also, the prior testimony indicated that he usually did not leave his office in a disheveled mess and consequently he likely meant to return to his office on the evening of the murder. The records were introduced under the theory of past practice to show what people typically do. We are all creatures of habit or at least most of us, and we tend to repeat patterns. We tend to drive to work over the same roads and we go to bed and get up at the same time, day after day. Mr. Gallegos was showing a pattern and thereby trying to prove that Mr. Gibberd left for the evening on the 26th and once he departed he had no further connection with his employer. The records were clearly admissible for that purpose and Ms. Busby was the keeper of the records and the law calls her the custodian of the records, so she was the proper person to call in order to get the paper work into evidence. It was persuasive testimony, but it still looked to me that I had to find that Mr. Gibberd did intend to return to the office on that fateful August night. His custom or habit was to always clean up his desk at the end of the day and he was never one to have a disheveled work area. That custom seemed to me to be more persuasive or stronger than the practice indicated by the work records or sign-in sheets. For one thing the sign-in sheets were not complete. We were missing some months. Moreover, they did show that on occasion he did sign-out and then sign back in during the same evening. He usually signed out and left for the day, but that was not a hard and fast rule as the records established.

Mr. Gallegos had a couple more witnesses to call and I was at the end of the tape so it was time for a change. When I first started out, the judges always used court reporters and when the judges were located at the Department of Labor and Industry, the court reporters were part of the program. When the judges were moved to the Office of Administrative Hearings, the chief judge, Duane Harves, determined that we did not need them and they were too expensive so they were laid off. It was a controversial decision and not popular with the judges, particularly the older judges. Judges are usually slow to change and hesitant to do anything different. The tapes actually did a pretty decent job. The attorneys had the option in all cases to hire their own court reporter. As long as the reporter was certified or approved by the office, then we used the supplied reporter and did not worry about the tapes.

I recall my colleague, Dan Gallagher, had some trouble with the tapes in that on a couple of occasions he forgot to turn the machine back on after a break. He had to repeat some of the unrecorded testimony. I got in the habit of pushing the record button when I got back from a break and always saying something like, "This is Judge Ronald Erickson and we are back on the record with the case of Summons v. Savage manufacturing company, social security number …" I was also reminding myself that we were back on the record and it was time to push the record button. The Army taught me the value of having a standard procedure and following that procedure. Everything in the Army has a standing operating procedure (SOP). If there is a fire extinguisher in the hallway, then there is an SOP telling you exactly where to place the extinguisher and how to operate it. In the event of fire, you likely will not have time to chase down the SOP, but not to worry, short-hand instructions will be posted near the device so that you will be able to properly operate it in the event of an emergency. This is all as provided in the SOP.

I never had to repeat a hearing because the tape was so bad, but we did hear from time to time that it had occurred. One of the laid off court reporters was Joe Andert and Joe continued doing some hearings when retained by one of the lawyers and also typed up records of hearings when the case was appealed. Joe was a friend of mine and would tell me if I was not speaking up or talking over people and I was able to avoid problems with the record. The last thing any judge wanted was to have to retry a case because of an indistinct record. Sometimes the court administrator would relay a comment or two from the court reporter or person who had transcribed the record of trial from the trial tapes.

Joe had done well in real estate and other investments and lived in North Oaks. For a time, he lived next door to Vice President Mondale. He said he was a good neighbor and I am sure he was. Joe had built several houses including the one he lived in. He had decided to sell the place and put a price on it but for whatever reasons it did not sell. Usually, when a place does not sell you probably have it over priced, but of course, sometimes there are other reasons. Joe spent years trying to sell his house. He would list it with an agent and have it on the market for a time and then after the listing expired he sometimes took it off the market for a short time. When it came back on the market, he would invariably raise the price. Joe concluded that it was under priced. He persisted in this procedure for some time until finally the market did heat up and the rising tide lifted all boats, including Joe's.

Joe then bought another home in North Oaks. He did very well on the purchase and bought it at a bargain price. I was out to his place and looked it over and it was indeed a great deal. Joe used to stop in the office frequently and

Death in St. Paul 233

have coffee with myself, Jim Otto, and Bernie Dinner. Bernie was a dear man and one of my favorite people in the world. As a young man, Bernie had been an enlisted Marine and during the Korean War had spent a year in the state of Washington guarding an ammo dump at Port Townsend, Washington out on the Olympic Peninsula. He must have done a good job as the ammo dump was never attacked or sabotaged. Bernie spent some cold and lonely nights out on the peninsula when he drew evening guard duty. He had some close calls when he was about to nod off and the staff duty officer would show up out of the blue to check on him. Bernie finished his tour and went back to UMD and completed his degree. He went into ROTC and was commissioned a Second Louie, but I do not think he pulled active duty as an officer. Bernie went to the U of M Law School and eventually got a job as an attorney with the Department of Labor and Industry. He got appointed a Comp Judge (Referee in those days) and eventually did a term or two on the WC Court of Appeals. He had done his time as a foot soldier with the DFL and got rewarded for his efforts. As I told you before, the republicans were likely to reward you for your efforts by telling you they could not find qualified republicans.

Despite his liberal background, Bernie was a sensible guy and was not about to reward cheaters and liars. He looked his cases over carefully and did a good job. Over the years, as a result of our daily coffee klatch I became familiar with his family. He was Jewish by background and practice and had a loving wife and three devoted daughters. He lived up near Robbinsdale and was forever painting his house. Most people would just get a painter or bite the bullet and take a couple weeks and devote it to painting the outside of their abode. Bernie would do it himself, but painted one side of the house a year. Over the course of four summers he would have the task completed, only to discover it was time to start over again on side number one. He was the perpetual painter.

Bernie continued to work into his 70's as he liked the job and knew that if he retired, his life would descend into numerous errands and he would miss the daily contact with Otto and myself. One day, Joe Andert came to me and told me he was worried about Bernie. I asked why and he had recently reported a case for Bernie and Bernie frequently called for testimony to be repeated and seemed to have difficulty keeping up with the hearing. I did not know for sure how to approach such news, but I was certainly glad to receive the information.

It was not too long after that revelation when Otto told me that Bette Baily, our secretary, had told him that management had requested that she forward a few of Bernie's decisions up the ladder for review. Otto and I asked Bette to send us a bunch of decisions for review and then we read through them and picked out the best four or five decisions and asked Bette to forward those up the line and not to mention that we had cherry-picked the cases for review.

Management obviously had Bernie in its cross hairs and they were intent on moving him along. They had presumably gotten complaints on Bernie and also it was during this period that the work load was down and they had too many judges. We were in the early 90's and the dot com boom was surfacing and the stock market was good and the economy was heating up. When jobs are plentiful, people are more likely to return to work following a work injury as there is frequently a job waiting for them that they are physically able to perform. When the economy is lousy, that old job may have disappeared while they were off work and on the mend. Also during a down turn, many an old injury is blamed for absence from work and that old claim is reopened. In Minnesota, once payment is made on a claim, the claim is open to the end of time with no real statute of limitations in force as payment is said to toll the statute of limitations.

With the work load diminished, management was eager to move judges off the rolls and spread the work among the remaining judges. A lot of the judges did not like that plan, and I was not nuts about it, but foolishly thought they would implement it by attrition. Some of the annual case counts failed to support an allegation that we were overworked.

We thought management may forget about Bernie after we had forwarded his well-reasoned decisions for review, but that was not to be. One evening I was working late (that was not an unusual event despite what my detractors may allege) and Bernie had just met with management and was visibly shaken. Management had accused him of drinking on duty and being half in the bag at a hearing. This was serious stuff and I did not believe such spurious allegations and told him it was likely a bluff and so don't do anything hasty until he had time to investigate the charges. Bernie was shaken, but decided to hold on for the time being. I have seen plenty of drinkers while in the military and while a member of the legal profession. The legal profession has done a good job of meeting the problem head on and organizations such as Lawyers Concerned for Lawyers did a good job of intervening in cases where lawyers needed help and making sure that help arrived. Several lawyers who practiced in the compensation field had been assisted by the program. I did not believe that Bernie was a candidate for their assistance or I would have been on the phone with a request for some advice and assistance.

As I look back on it, I do not believe that management made up the drinking story. Joe had told me that Bernie was becoming confused at the hearings and frequently asked for repeat testimony. Such behavior can easily be confused with drinking and I suspect that some lawyer or employee had come to the conclusion that "the damn judge is drunk" and so advised management. Management had a duty to investigate and boy did they take it seriously. Just recently I spoke with Tim Manahan about Bernie and his absent minded professor role during hearings. Tim had remarked to his witnesses following a trial in front of Bernie that he seemed confused and in disarray during the hearing. There were three or four witnesses gathered for the post mortem of the trial and they all agreed that it was an act. Bernie was playing the role of the absent minded professor or judge. Bernie had been an amateur actor, so maybe they were right. Tim told me the written decision was clear and cogent.

Sometime when all this drama was going on regarding Bernie, management retained Steve Simon, law professor from the University of Minnesota to check out Bernie. Steve spent some time talking with Bernie and I am sure he read some of his decisions. He must have read the ones that Otto and I had hand-picked. Simon was a good guy and did not sneak around or try and make things up. He also sat in on some of Bernie's hearings. He must have been satisfied that Bernie was okay, or at least not any crazier than the rest of the judges, so Bernie soldiered on as the good Marine that he was.

Management had tried almost everything in their arsenal to flush Bernie and had been blanked at every turn. Management was persistent and in desperation turned to the court of last resort; the legislature. Management was able to get a statute passed requiring that judges retire at age 70. There was no "grandfather provision" and it applied to all judges over 70, even if you were over the magic age when the law was passed. Suddenly both Bernie and Jim Otto were to be history. Jim Otto was a terrific judge. He was bright, energetic and knowledgeable. He was patient and popular with the lawyers. The law seemed like age discrimination on its face and I told Jim to fight the thing. Jim was one of these people that wanted to work till he dropped. He was convinced that if he retired or quit that he would die. Dan Gallagher called that a strong motivation to keep on working.

Management once again proved that you can get rid of civil servants. The truth is that management can get rid of just about anyone they wish. The key is to document everything and issue plenty of warning letters. Have a series of progressive punishments and document everything you do. If you have a paper trail, then anyone can be let out of the asylum. With Army officers they use the efficiency report, which becomes an inefficiency report.

Later on after I retired at age 65, Judge Arnold up in Duluth challenged the Dinner statute in court and somehow remained on the job. He and Judge Ellefson continued to work after age 70 as a result of the ruling. The statute may have been repealed for all I know. The so-called Bernie Dinner statute may or may not live on. I did not want to continue after age 65 as that was enough for me and Cameron was 12 or 13 and taking up more and more time. I was able to get him back and forth to swim practice and make a daily run to school to pick up or drop off what he had forgotten. I also had plenty to do as manager of our rental properties. Phyllis was very busy with her elderly mother and I was able to help out on her end. I was approaching the point where I did not think I could keep it up with the job and other demands and do the kind of job that I should. Knowing when to go is hard to do, but sooner or later we all have our time.

Meanwhile back to the good old courtroom. Let us find out what Attorney Gallegos has in his bag of tricks and if he can produce the famous surprise witness that he has promised.

Mr. Gallegos called his next witness, Ms. Gayle Darter. Ms. Darter lived in the area, about a mile from the WDC and she happened to be out and about and in the vicinity of Dale and I-94 on August 26, 1985, in the evening, just as the street lights were coming on. She had been in a car and had exited I-94 at Dale Street and turned left and headed north on Dale Street. She was in the passenger seat in the car and saw some couples apparently on foot coming toward them in the vicinity of Fuller Street She heard something that sounded like a firecracker and then she saw one man fall and the other man step near him and shoot him again. They had been walking close together. She testified that initially, she thought the man-victim was a woman as they were walking like a couple.

The witness was holding the map of the area, but unfortunately, she was holding it upside down so north became south and it was confusing. I helped her get the map straightened out as we did not need any extra confusion in court. There already was enough of that. Witnesses are nervous and somewhat in awe of the courtroom setting. My job is not to trade on that wonder, but calm people down and try to get an accurate version of what they know. My job was to facilitate testimony and not to headline the proceeding.

Ms. Darter got the map straightened out and continued. She first saw the walkers near the intersection of Dale and Fuller Streets. The first couple was a male and female and the second couple was the shooter and Mr. Gibberd. They were walking very close and she thought they were hugging. The shooting occurred north of Fuller and on the public sidewalk on the east side of Dale Street. The shooter was identified as a black person and he shot Mr. Gibberd and then took another step and discharged a round into the victim's head as he lay helpless on the ground. She made eye contact with the assailant and watched him as he walked briskly across Dale Street and continued in a southwesterly direction. The shooter did not run as he seemed to realize that he would attract less attention if he walked in a normal fashion.

Ms. Darter testified that she had lived in the area for 5-6 years and did not experience undue fear or apprehension. She did testify that she did not care for the area around University and Dale Streets because she did not like the Belmont Club or the Faust Theatre. The Belmont Club featured ladies dancing nude and the Faust Theatre showed dirty movies. Ms. Darden did not care for that area because if men saw you walking down the street in the area, "they think you are working." Mr. Gallegos followed, "As a prostitute?" Ms. Darden replied, "Right."

On cross-examination, Ms. Bjorklund asked Ms. Darden if her recollection of the events of August 26 were better two days after the event, when she gave her statement to the police, or months later when she was testifying. Ms. Bjorklund was trying to show that the witness had come up with something new and different other than what she had told the police.

Ms. Bjorklund followed with a question as to where she was when she first saw the shooter and victim. I suggested we show her the exhibit and have her mark it. She testified that the shooting may well have occurred by Fuller Street where the numbers 6 and 7 appeared, although it could have been a bit north closer to the driveway into Wendy's and the Uni-Dale Mall. Ms. Bjorklund tried to get the witness to say she only looked once or saw the victim once before the shooting, but she was insistent that she looked at them as they were walking down the street.

Question: "So it is possible that one man had his arm around the other man right before he fell to the ground, is that true?" Answer: "Yes." Question: "And you didn't see them prior to that?" Answer: "I seen them walking. I couldn't say how far I seen them walking, but I did see them—they were together. They had taken a few steps together that I noticed before the shot." Question: "A few steps?" Answer: "A few steps." It certainly seemed like the witness had a good look at the events and was in a good position to describe what happened. Her testimony was really unshaken.

I asked Ms. Darter about the first couple that she observed and whether or not they were a male and female. She replied with a "uh-huh." I usually ask if "that is a yes", but I failed in this case. I asked if they were white or black and white or what were they? She responded that they were both white. I asked her if she knew what became of couple number one and she did not know. They must have scurried away and it is unclear as to whether or not the police obtained their statements. Someone was shot twice and killed within a few feet of them so there is no doubt they were scared to death.

The next witness was Mary Bayberry. Ms. Bayberry worked at the World Distribution Center (WDC) at 304 North Dale as a manager for the past five years. She had been with her sister, Ms. Darter, and had been to Knox Lumber, then located at Prior and University. I think there is a Menards currently located at that site. They took I-94 back in an easterly direction and exited on Dale Street and made a left and headed north on Dale. She got close to Fuller and pulled into the far right lane. At that point she saw a couple gentlemen that appeared to be walking together. She thought she heard what sounded like a firecracker and her sister, Ms. Darden, was in the passenger seat and let out a big gasp of air. The witness gasped for effect. She said or thought "you certainly do overreact to fireworks" and her sister immediately replied, "He shot that man." This was hearsay testimony because Ms. Bayberry was relating what her sister said. This is a classic example of the excited utterance exception to the hearsay rule. Certainly her sister was excited by the events and in those circumstances one does not have time to make up stories or fabricate testimony.

One simply blurts something out and it is usually accurate. Ms. Bjorklund did not even bother to object as she realized it was a classic example of an excited utterance.

Ms. Bayberry had been going at a slow speed, about 20 mph. She pulled over at the Wendy's drive in and looked back and saw the killer crossing Dale and heading west on Fuller Avenue. He was not running.

She has lived in the area since she "moved up here in the summer of '62." She spent four years at Macalester College and did not live in the Summit/University area, but still considered it home. She was active in the community and served on the Board of Directors of the Summit/University Planning Council. Apparently this group functioned as some sort of planning board or commission. They looked over proposed new development in the area and had public hearings on proposals. She described the Summit-University area as being very active in terms of development over the past couple years. Some expensive homes were being built including townhomes ranging in price to $125,000. She was asked if people were expressing concerns over their personal safety while they were contemplating development in the area. She said that concerns over crime did not seem to be significant. In particular, none of the developers had expressed concern over crime or personal safety. It seemed that every month the council reviewed a monthly police report containing crimes in the area and most of the crimes reported seemed to be of a minor nature. She mentioned garage break-ins and that type of thing.

On cross-examination, Ms. Bjorklund made the point that Ms. Bayberry had just glanced at the two walkers and focused on the two people after the shot was fired. I asked her if she could provide a description of the two people. She responded that the black guy was taller than the while male and "they just looked like two guys walking down the street." I asked her how the white person was dressed and she described him as "nothing outstanding" and nothing negative, "Just a shirt and slacks." She then volunteered as to how neatly dressed the other person appeared. I asked her if she was talking about the black person and she replied that he was neatly dressed. She did not recall the second couple being in the area. She described a green car coming up and I interrupted her and said I was asking about any other pedestrians on the street. She responded with a no. I asked her during her observation of the two people how far the two people walked together. She was not able to tell, but did offer that the shooting occurred just beyond (south) of the Wendy's driveway.

I asked her if she noted the time of the shooting. She responded that it was between 8 and 8:30 p.m. because it was not dark enough to turn the lights on, but she had her lights on. She was driving during a period when one had to manually turn on and off car lights. One had to turn a dial or push or pull a knob to activate car lights so it was a conscious act and one was more likely to recall the time when the act was done. Modern day cars have lights that run all

Death in St. Paul

the time so we are not as conscious of nightfall. I always liked nightfall during Minnesota summers, as it seemed to stretch out for hours. I asked if counsel had any questions based on my questions and Ms. Bjorklund did have some follow up questions.

She was asked if she had given a statement to the police. She responded in the affirmative and had given a statement the next day. In her statement she said she did not see the victim until she heard the shot. She re-visited the area on several occasions and re-checked the visibility from various points as she proceeded north on Dale Street. She did not tell the police about spotting the two walkers before the shot, but she did talk to the police on several occasions and may well have mentioned it in one of her conversations with the authorities.

On re-direct, Attorney Gallegos, asked her about her mental condition during the immediate period after the shooting. She testified she was "shook up" because of the shooting and at 11:30 p.m. the police called and advised there had been another shooting in the area and they think it was the same guy. She was very frightened and left her house to spend the evening with her sister. The next day, she was concerned that her car had been seen by the shooter, and she was troubled by the possibility of the assailant looking for her. Attorney Gallegos pretty well established that her mental state was such, immediately following the shooting that she may have left something out. She affirmed that her trial testimony was accurate and true. Despite the fact that the assailant may have seen her, she still resided in the area.

Usually, the statement given right after the event is likely to be the most accurate rendition of the facts. This is a general rule and the exception always makes the rule. In this case it was obvious that she was in a troubled state when she gave her statement. People in those conditions are likely to leave something out. Also, the police officer that took the statement may well have been working the case for several hours and may have been dog-tired. Under those conditions, the person taking the statement can certainly make mistakes.

I had no doubt that the testimony of the two sisters was fairly and honestly given. They struck me as good hard working honest people. It is hard to shake the testimony of those types of witnesses. They offered very important testimony, but whether or not it I was going to accept their main conclusion that the shooter and the victim were acquainted was another question.

At that point in the trial, the defense rested. They had succeeded in raising some doubt as to whether or not this case was in fact a personal attack and was not totally random. The testimony of the two sisters had certainly raised the inference that the victim and the assailant may have known each other. On the other hand, the assailant may have spotted the victim on the street and called out to him and some sort of brief street confrontation may have preceded the shooting. At this point in time, this seemed to me the most likely explanation for the events immediately before the shooting.

Ms. Bjorklund wished to recall SGT Hartman for rebuttal testimony. She wished to recall him to rebut the testimony of the two sisters. Mr. Gallegos objected because he had not had a chance to review the statements. Ms. Bjorklund correctly pointed out that the police would not allow anyone to review the file because it was an ongoing case and the information was confidential under the Minnesota Data Privacy Act. She was correct about that, although disclosure under the privacy act was allowed if ordered by a judge. At least that was my very limited view of one of the most complicated statutes on the face of this earth. The Minnesota Privacy Act is and was one of the most complicated pieces of legislation in this or any other world. I did not get a request for an order, so I did not grant one.

Ms. Bjorklund recalled SGT Hartman and I reminded him he was still under oath. Once the oath is administered it did not have to be re-given during the same trial. It was a one shot wind-up. At least something I did had some real staying power.

SGT Hartman was aware of only two witnesses who saw the victim and the assailant prior to the shooting. The first witness, being designated as witness number 1, on Appendix Exhibit No. 2, saw the assailant walking south on the sidewalk to the east of Dale Street. The assailant was just to the north of the driveway into the Uni-Dale Mall and Wendy's. The victim was walking in the same direction ahead of the assailant. The assailant was walking faster than the victim. They were described as just two men walking down the street with one man walking faster than the other man.

The other person that saw the parties before the shooting was described as being a passenger in an automobile and going north bound on Dale and in the vicinity of Fuller Street and slowing down to change to the right lane and preparing for a right turn on University. This witness was obviously Ms. Darter, one of the sisters. SGT Hartman said this witness number 7 had described two couples or one or two other people in the immediate vicinity of the shooting. Witness 7 described the assailant and the victim as if they were in an embrace. On the drawing was placed a "circled x" with the designation "1st Shot" and this was in the east portion of the intersection of Fuller and Dale. This is where the sister was when she observed the first shot and the victim dropped to the ground. The time frame between the embrace and the shot was very short, possibly a second. The witness was talking about the 1st Shot mark immediately to the left of circled witnesses 8 and 9. From her vantage point the shooting was directly in front and to the right of Ms. Darter. She had the best seat in the house.

SGT Hartman was asked, "For purposes of your investigation, how are you interpreting that embrace? SGT Hartman responded that the medical examiner described it as a neck hold and the firearm was held to the back of the head and discharged. The medical examiner described it as a contact wound. The police were interpreting the embrace as a hostile action.

SGT Hartman was then asked about his conversations with witness number 6. She was Ms. Bayberry, the sister, who was driving the vehicle north on Dale Street. According to the police investigation, the first time the driving sister saw the two parties was after the first shot had taken place.

The driving sister gave testimony that was at variance with what she told the police. Was the variance crucial? Probably not. The passenger sister had a better chance to view the parties because she was not occupied with driving the car. Her testimony was pretty steady. The driver may or may not have seen the two pedestrians as they drove down the hill, but it did not seem to be a crucial point in the case as her sister did have a good look. SGT Hartman had talked to Ms. Darter on two occasions.

SGT Hartman was asked if it was common or not for witnesses to tell a slightly different story six months removed from the fact. He acknowledged that it was common. This was objected to by Mr. Gallegos as a conclusion, and although it was a good objection, I did not sustain it. Much of the testimony of SGT Hartman was hearsay and objectionable, but we had to remember that this was not a criminal trial. If it was, the petitioner would have had to bring in the medical examiner to testify as to why he thought the victim was in a choke or neck hold when he was shot. This was a civil case and nobody was going to go to prison at the conclusion of the trial. I did not want to force the petitioner to bring in a parade of witnesses. Mr. Gallegos did not wish to force such a conclusion and for that reason, he did not object to much of SGT Hartman's testimony as hearsay. As it worked out, I let all of Mr. Gallego's offered testimony into evidence and although I admitted the testimony, I did not follow the offered conclusion that there was some sort of personal relationship between the shooter and the victim. I found this was not a personal attack, but a random street crime. I went along with SGT Hartman and the medical people, who concluded the embrace of the victim was a hostile act.

Sometime after this trial was concluded, the legislature passed a statute providing that the compensation judges did have the authority to allow hearsay testimony. The judges seemed to allow a lot of hearsay testimony in any event. I can recall when I was in Law School, back in the dark ages, that my classmate, Web Hart, predicted that eventually there would be no hearsay rule. The hearsay rule is founded in the principle that witnesses should be subjected to cross-examination. If a person in court is attempting to speak for someone out of court and not present, then that defeats the chance of cross-examining the out of court declarant. If the out of court declarant cannot show up for court, then the hearsay exceptions are designed to attempt to insure that the out of court declaration is at least accurate. For example, medical records are supposed to be accurate, because someone's health and welfare is at stake and presumably all people involved in a patient's care are doing their level best to make an accurate accounting of medical events as they occur. For that reason, the law allows the one who retains the records, called the custodian, to bring the records to court and introduce them, despite the fact she did not even make any entries in the records. The alternative would be a parade of witnesses.

SGT Hartman testified to a lot of things and some of the testimony dealt with what others did, but for the sake of getting through the trial without spending a week, we allowed some leeway with the testimony and finished the trial in two days. Mr. Gallegos realized that I was allowing most of the offered testimony so there was no point in wasting a lot of time objecting.

SGT Hartman was asked about investigation procedure and if he gave more credibility to the first statement taken after the incident than to a later statement and he said the first statement is usually more reliable. He made it clear, that he would not disregard anything that a witness told him. This was in reference to Ms. Bayberry's testimony where details seemed to surface at a later time.

On cross-examination, SGT Hartman testified that he did not take the statement of the driving sister, Ms. Bayberry. It was taken the day after the murder, by another investigator. The procedure that SGT Hartman used in interviewing witnesses was that he let the witness tell her story and then went back with questions and asked the witness to repeat the story. He may ask some further follow-up questions and then he had the witness write out the statement in her own hand. I thought back to when I was city attorney and how all of the statements were hand written. I think that they were usually written by the police officer. Many of the witnesses simply could not write well enough to get anything down on paper that made sense. Writing skills are hit and miss, I found that out when I was in the Army. Maybe SGT Hartman did let the witness write out their own statements, when he had a witness that could write. One reason that 45 years ago the Coon Rapids PD started requiring two years of college for beginning patrolmen was they needed people that could write a coherent sentence. If the public and the cops could not put words together, then we were in trouble. Prosecutors rely on what is in the statements to put their cases together. Normally they will follow up with personal interviews of any important witness.

SGT Hartman was asked about Ms. Bayberry's testimony and he could not say for sure that she did not better recollect events at a later time as opposed to statements she had given at an earlier time. He was not prepared to say that her testimony was less reliable today than it was the day after the event. This is where I come in and get the big bucks. It is up to the judge as the fact finder (when there is no jury) to sort out the conflicts in the testimony and determine the most accurate view of what happened.

On re-direct, SGT Hartman was asked where witness number 6, Ms. Bayberry worked and she did work at Control Data. Mr. Gallegos objected to the question on relevance, but I allowed it. The witness did work for Control Data, but I already had the impression that all of the witnesses gave honest testimony and I could not see any liars in the courtroom. I was pretty sure that I would be able to find the facts in this case. However, the ultimate decision was going to turn on a question of law.

Mr. Gallegos asked SGT Hartman if he knew SGT Whitman and he certainly did. The counselor then asked SGT Hartman if it was true that in an interview with the St. Paul Pioneer Press that SGT Whitman had said it was not hard to become personally involved in Betty Gibberd's plight. Attorney Bjorklund objected as how was he supposed to testify as to what SGT Whitman told a reporter? It was hearsay, but I responded that it was also outside the scope of the witnesses' knowledge. I sustained the objection.

It was certainly true that Mrs. Gibberd was a very nice person and one would have to have a banker's heart not to become personally involved with her plight. It is easy to see how the investigators wanted to bring the perpetrator to justice to afford some sort of closure to Mrs. Gibberd. I also wanted to help her out, but I also had an obligation to follow the law and those two obligations were leading me to a fork in the road.

SGT Hartman reaffirmed his desire to bring the perpetrator to justice and with that the case was concluded. This was certainly a righteous goal and we all wanted the same thing.

The parties were given a week to submit proposed findings and legal briefs. I was looking for case law that would guide my way to the result. It was a rare case where I actually wanted legal briefs from the attorneys involved. Most of the cases involved fact questions and the law was not at issue. For example, a common case was an employee with a back injury and the question was whether or not the employee was currently disabled and could not work. This was a fact question and I did not need legal briefs to come to grips with that issue. I was not going to find the answer to a factual dispute in a legal brief. Joe Murray used to call the law we practiced "street law or ghetto law." I think he meant that it was a practical type of law and the resolution of most of our cases did not turn on an esoteric point of law. Joe was not a book pounder, but had a good practical sense. Joe was a WWII vet and most of those people had acquired a good dose of common sense.

I looked forward to receiving the legal memorandums of the parties, but most of the time I relied on my own research and thinking. I did not spend a lot of time hashing cases over with the other comp judges, as I preferred to deliver my own product. Some of the judges did spend a good deal of time discussing their cases with other judges and gathering opinions on how to proceed. My thinking was that this was not some kind of "collective" so we had to do our own work. My name was on the bottom of the decision and not Daniel Kelly's, so the case should represent my thought and product. The decision may not be perfect, but at least it was mine.

Once in a while, I would talk to Jennifer Patterson about a pending case. Jennifer was very bright and knew a lot of law. We had known each other before we became judges and Phyllis and I were dating when I first met Jennifer. Jennifer and her husband invited us over for an evening and we had a nice dinner. Shortly after that meeting, Jennifer stopped in my office and said, "Phyllis wants to marry you." I was somewhat surprised and responded, "I am not so sure, it might be just puppy love." Jennifer assured me that she was right on these matters and women usually could sense these things. What I knew about women would fit in a thimble so I was in no position to argue. Jennifer turned out to be a sayer, as Phyllis and I were eventually engaged and married.

Jennifer was always interested in my life and we would socialize with her and her husband on occasion. Eventually they divorced and she re-entered the dating and relationship scene. I think Jennifer liked to get a man's view of the world and for that reason she would solicit my advice on relationship issues or other personal issues. I am not sure I gave her any decent advice, but she seemed to think so, as she kept coming back. She eventually married prince charming and more recently retired, to the state of Washington.

On a couple occasions over the years Jennifer did surprise me. I do not like to waste a lot of time talking or complaining about my parents as Lord knows, just about everyone has a gripe or two about parents, including our own children. One day we got on the parental issue and I mentioned my parents unending list of flaws and Jennifer said, "They must have done something right as you are one of the nicest people I have ever known." I was taken aback and stunned and correctly told her that this was one of the better things that anyone has ever said to me.

The case had been heard on May 6 and 7 of 1986 and the record closed on May 14 and the sixty days for submitting a decision ended on July 13, 1986. The decision due date coincided with my reserve time in Charlottesville, VA and it looked like I had a reservation at the UVA Law Library. Mickey had curtailed my activities.

At this point, I had a couple thoughts on the case, but did not know in which direction I was headed. For starters, the injury or death did not occur on the employer's premises as it took place on a public street or sidewalk some 2-3 blocks from the work place. Did the injury (death) arise out of and in the course of his employment? There has to be a causal connection between the injury (death) and the employment activity. This was not a coworker doing the shooting or someone settling a score over a work dispute. I was hard pressed to see a connection between the death and the work place. Mr. Gibberd had gone off the premises because he was working after normal hours and needed a bite to eat. It was his choice as to whether he should leave the work place and where he should go. Did it make any difference where he dined? What if he had decided to get in the car and motor to Minneapolis and get a bite to eat and he had been shot coming out of a restaurant on Washington Avenue? Is he covered for workers' comp or not? Let us suppose he did not eat beef and did not like fast food. If he is covered while in St. Paul when eating an evening meal, then should he be covered while dining at his favorite place in Minneapolis? Everything seems to have a boundary or end point and I was looking for a signpost or guide to show me the boundary, but I think I was going to have to find my own boundary.

These were tough questions to wrestle with and I had to get to work. The first thing I always did was sort out all the facts and get them down on paper and then try and apply the law. A policy question lurked over this whole case and that was by finding for the employee was I somehow making the employer responsible for street crime? That was a big burden to attach to any employer. The cities and counties were already responsible for the effects of street crime as the police and fire fighters were frequently injured as a consequence of street crime, but they were in the business of fighting street crime so it was a necessary by-product of that business. Control Data's business was trying to make some computers and as it worked out, they did not do a good enough job at that endeavor.

The May 7, 1986 issue of the Pioneer Press Dispatch had a front page story featuring a picture of Mrs. Gibberd and her six-year-old daughter, Anna. It had been nine months since her husband's murder and the INS was leaning on her to deport her and force her back to England. She did not want to leave, but it was looking like she had no choice. Thirty years later it strikes me as out of place that she was actually deported. I am not sure we deport people anymore. Raymond's green card had expired and Betty Gibberd had to either leave or be deported. The article said that killings in St. Paul were considered rare as only fifteen had occurred in St. Paul during 1986 and seventeen in 1985. The Paper must have been talking to the same people that we were engaging. The article did point out that SGT Whitman had become personally involved in the case in that he took one of the Gibberd daughters to the police haunted house that they sponsor on Halloween. Mrs. Gibberd acknowledged that the police had worked "really hard" on solving this murder. There was no doubt in my mind, that lack of effort was not the reason this case was still pending.

In yet another strange irony to this case, Russell S. Sherer and his wife, Patty, reached out to Mrs. Gibberd after Mr. Sherer had recovered somewhat from the wounds he received when he was shot near William Mitchell Law School about an hour after Mr. Gibberd. It was still believed that the same assailant committed both crimes. Patty Sherer was in attendance at the first day of Mr. Gibberd's workers' compensation trial. There were some people in attendance at the trial, which is unusual in workers' compensation cases. Usually, we entertain the parties and maybe a spouse and that is about it. In my time on the bench, I only had a couple of cases that made the paper.

I soon got to work on the decision, but one small problem with our job is that we were not given any specific time for decision writing. We had cases assigned every day and we had to hope that something would settle so we could borrow some time to work on a decision. As I look back on this time frame, I was very busy and wanted to finish the case before I went to Charlottesville, but that was not possible. I did finish it within the sixty-day time requirement and kept my record intact. All of my cases were issued within the sixty-day deadline. That never changed.

My decision was almost fifteen pages, which was about twice as long as my usual decision. This is a summary of that decision. Mr. Gibberd was born in 1952 and only 32 years old at the time of his death. He and Elizabeth, or Betty, got married in 1974 and had two children. Mr. Gibberd was an exempt employee in that he was salaried and not paid for overtime. He did not have set hours but frequently worked beyond the regular 9-5 shift as that was necessary in order to get the job accomplished. The last three or four weeks before his death involved a lot of overtime as he was working to install a new software package. There was a cafeteria on premises that provided noon meals, but the employee frequently went off premises to eat lunch and sometimes for an evening meal. Management was aware that the employee and others left the premises to eat and there was no policy prohibiting this practice. On August 26, 1985, the employee signed out of work around 8:05 p.m. and walked to Wendy's and had a hamburger and walked south adjacent to Dale Street on his way back to work, when he was shot and killed by an unidentified assailant. There was no apparent motive for the killing and there was no credible proof of any personal connection or background between Mr. Gibberd and the assailant. There was no credible proof that the assailant was cognizant or aware of Mr. Gibberd's employment activity or that Mr. Gibberd's employment had anything to do with the assault. There was no evidence of any alcohol or drugs in Mr. Gibberd's system when he died. The employee worked for Control Data Corporation (CDC) at the World Distribution Center (WDC) and they maintain their own security force. Over the past four years there have been approximately 75-100 incidents reported to the security force. The two most serious incidents prior to August of 1985 involved an armed robbery in 1981 and a knife wielding youth in the parking lot. No one was injured in either event. The WDC is located in St Paul Police Department grid number 109 and this area ranked 19th in terms of reported crimes during 1985.

I found that the petitioner had failed to establish by a preponderance of the evidence that there was any causal connection between the employee's death and his employment with CDC. Further, the employee failed to establish that he was pursuing any errand or business on behalf of the employer at the time of his death. He was not in a place where his services were required by his employer. There was simply no evidence that at the time he died, the employee was doing anything to advance his employers interest. The employee had argued that the employer was required to provide safe ingress and egress to the property. This did not extend to an area some 3 1/2 to 4 blocks from the WDC. Based on the foregoing, the claim was denied.

This was a very difficult case, but unfortunately by all intents and purposes, this appeared to be a situation where Mr. Gibberd found himself to be in the wrong place at the wrong time. This could have happened to me or any of my loved ones. Control Data had nothing to do with it. They located their plant in an area that some considered marginal. Should all industry be in Edina or Eagan? If we are going the make employers pay for crime near their plants, obviously they will not bring business into poorer neighborhoods. Will that decision improve those neighborhoods? Obviously not; it will simply accelerate a decline. This was an unfortunate street crime and I could not determine that this should be the employer's burden.

As everyone expected, this case was appealed to the Workers' Compensation Court of Appeals. (WCCA) Eventually, the WCCA made their decision and they reversed me. Leslie Altman wrote the decision and Paul Rieke and another judge joined her in a unanimous decision. Paul told me that he talked Leslie into deciding the case for the petitioner and Leslie never forgave him for it. I am sure he was exaggerating as Leslie was also a friend of mine and she was an ally on the court of Mick Hanson.

Leslie totally agreed with my findings of fact, but simply drew different legal conclusions based on those facts. She concluded that his employment had placed him at risk. The employer did not provide meals for its workers after 3:00 p.m. so he had to leave the premises to eat. He was returning from his evening meal at Wendy's and under the circumstances this was considered the employer's premises. Leslie was extending the employer's property by a few hundred meters. A further provision of the law provided that assaults are not covered unless there is a connection between the employment and the assault. Purely personal assaults are not covered. She said the assault was not personal so it must be connected to his employment. The fact was that no one knows to this day, the reasons behind this tragic death.

The WCCA opinion was quite short, covering only three pages. I realize that length is not the test, but I was looking for more discussion. After the decision was issued, Phyllis and I ran into Leslie at a gathering and I said that she must be worried about getting re-appointed. There had been a change in the governor's office and the court seemed to be moving to the left. Leslie got kind of excited about what I said and it took a few minutes for Phyllis and I to calm her down. Leslie was always very serious and I probably should have kept my mouth shut. I found out that she had been a Minneapolis Park cop and her former partner was a brother of my neighbor, Susie. Susie's brother had good things to say about Cop Leslie. I am willing to bet she was a hard assed cop and did not hesitate to make an arrest or do what was necessary.

After Leslie tipped me over, the case went up to the Minnesota Supreme Court. Justice Kelley wrote the opinion for the court and concluded that the compensation judge had made the right call in this case and they over-ruled the WCCA. The court cited the 1983 law change that provided if there was substantial evidence supporting the findings of the compensation judge, then the findings could not be overturned on appeal. This was good for the compensation judges as it limited the authority of the WCCA to overrule us just because they felt like it. Another change that the legislature made in 1983 was they repealed the statute that said that the Workers' Compensation Law was remedial in nature and was to be liberally construed. In other words, in a close case, the employee should win because the law is to be liberally construed in their favor. After the 1983 statutory change, the law no longer was to be liberally interpreted. This was an important change affecting the Gibberd case as before 1983 the WCCA may well have justified its decision by giving a liberal construction to the law and finding compensability.

The Supreme Court noted that at the time of his death, there were no facts supporting a conclusion that Mr. Gibberd was performing a service to his employer. The court also pointed out that the injury occurred while Mr. Gibberd was on a public right of way and he was not subject to any greater risk than other members of the public at large, and consequently the case is not compensable. This is the so-called street risk doctrine. If he had been performing some service for his employer, then the street risk doctrine would not apply. The court also supported my finding that the employee was not subjected to any special hazard by his employment. The court pointed out that to be compensable, the special hazard is one that originates on the employer premises. I had found that if the special hazard rule is extended in this case, there is nothing to prevent it from applying to, or being extended to, injuries occurring blocks away and totally unrelated to one's employment activity. Lastly, there was no evidence linking the assault with his work activity. One could not even establish it was personal to Mr. Gibberd. The evidence was that it was a random attack.

That was the end of the line for the Gibberd case. The Supreme Court issued its decision about two years after my decision went out. By that time, I had a lot of other cases to worry about and for the most part, I try not to worry about what a reviewing court does with my work. I do take pride in my work and like a lot of other people, I would rather be validated than vilified.

Chapter 9
Russell Sherer Lives

The Gibberd murder and its aftermath took its toll on just about all who came in contact with the case. SGT Hartman put in hundreds of hours on the case and still came up with no killer. Betty Gibberd had come over with Ray and their small children with the idea of staying in the States. Ray was on a work visa and Betty was on a visitor's visa. When Ray died, the Immigration people became very interested in Betty's continued presence in the US and took steps to see that she went back to where she came from, England. Betty gradually became resigned to returning to England and made her peace with that decision. Ray's parents were in England and her parents were in her native Ireland. She had decided to join Ray's parents in England. A day before she was to leave, she was contacted by Senator Rudy Boschwitz' Office and advised they were preparing a special bill to speed through congress so that she could stay. The senator could arrange to have her stay pending the passage of the special bill. She had been through so much and had made the necessary arrangements to return home and thanked the senator for his efforts but she had made her decision, she was going home.

Betty Gibberd had made a number of friends while in the USA and among them were Russell and Patty Sherer. Russ Sherer was the William Mitchell student that was shot shortly after Ray was gunned down. When Betty found out about the shooting, she sent flowers to Russ Sherer's hospital room at Ramsey Hospital (Now Region's Hospital). Patty Sherer contacted Betty to thank her for her kindness and a friendship was born. Russ also received hundreds of cards and well wishes during the time he was in Ramsey.

Russ was a local kid and grew up in Minneapolis and graduated from South High. He attended the University of Minnesota for two years and decided to drop out and work for a time and shore up his sagging finances and then return to school. All was blissful with Russ until the draft board came calling. Russ decided he did not want to be a ground pounder and did not like SOS so he joined the Navy. He served in the Navy for four years and spent his first two in Morocco. I asked him if he played the male lead opposite Ingrid Bergman in Casablanca and he assured me he was not Humphrey Bogart. I told him he looked just like Bogey. He did not deny that, but instead told me he never got to Casablanca. Russ worked in communications during his time in the Navy.

Russ got out of the Navy and returned to his studies at the University of Minnesota. In fact, he got out a couple months early as the good folks in the Cracker Jack suits told Russ he could take his leave to return to school. Russ returned and did very well and graduated with a degree in mathematics from the University of Minnesota in 1968.

Russ got a job with Unisys in St. Paul and did computer work. He spent a dull decade during the 70's working at Unisys and doing logarithms in his spare time. He met Patty in 1979 and life became interesting again. Russ and Patty were married in 1983 and shortly thereafter Russ started law school at William Mitchell. At that point in time Russ was 41 years old. By this time the law school had relocated from the small quarters across from St. Thomas to the spacious quarters down Summit Avenue at Victoria Street. They purchased the former girls catholic school called Our Lady of Peace. It was known by the antonym OLP or by the female students as "Old Ladies Pension." It was a beautiful building with marble floors and rich paneling throughout. Except for some paint here and there and installing male bathrooms, the "new law school" was soon ready to accommodate aspiring lawyers.

Russ had done well with his studies at the U of M and also tested well on the Law School Admission Test (LSAT) and had been accepted at the University of Minnesota and Hamline Law Schools. Russ was older than the average law school student and picked Mitchell so he could attend the night program and continue to work during the day at Unisys.

Patty had been working for an airfreight company and started out throwing freight around and had worked her way up to supervisor. It was her job to oversee the loading of freight on the planes. The freight had to be carefully distributed because if you had too much weight on one side of the plane, you might not get off the ground or if you did get airborne it might be a short trip. The plane frequently transported chemicals or hazardous materials and these had to be carefully loaded and packed.

On August 26, 1985 Russ went off to school in the late afternoon and Patty went off to oversee the airplanes. The law school parking lot was very small and was limited to faculty members and handicapped students and women students. The women enrollment must have been small in 1985 as eventually there came to be more women in the law school than men. Russ parked on the public streets around the law school, as he had no other choice.

William Mitchell fronted on historic Summit Avenue, known for its stately homes and tree lined boulevards. Portland Avenue also ran east and west and bordered the north part of the law school. Russ had parked on Ashland Avenue, also an east-west street located a block north of Portland. On the corner

Russell Sherer Lives

of Ashland and Victoria was a small neighborhood fire hall that was to play a prominent role that evening. Victoria Street ran north and south and formed the eastern boundary of the law s`chool. Russ got out of class on the evening of August 26, 1985 and proceeded to walk, by himself, to his car. Russ exited the rear or Portland side of the law school and cut over to Milton Street, a north-south street on the west side of William Mitchell. Russ lamented to himself that it was only 8:45 p.m. and it was already nearly dark. Russ walked north to Ashland Avenue and took a right turn and walked to his car parked on the south side of Ashland, some 60 to 80 feet down the street. The State Fair was going, but he had no time for fair fun. The fireworks would start in a little over an hour at the fairgrounds. Fireworks for Russ were much more imminent. Fall was almost here. Winter would not be far behind.

Russ had only traveled a couple car lengths or so and he suddenly saw someone slip out from between parked cars and he was struck over the frontal skull by an object and he slumped to the ground and landed face up. His assailant was on him and one shot was fired to his forehead. Seconds passed and he heard someone say, "That was brain matter on the ground." Actually, Russ had thrown up. Things happened so fast that he did not get a decent look at his assailant. Russ was only a block from the school and was about a half block away from the fire station. The fire station still stands and is in use at Victoria and Ashland Streets a block north of the law school.

Fortunately for Russ, a young woman had been in the area and was only about a half block away when the shot was fired. The shooter came toward her and terrified, she hunched behind a parked car as the shooter ran by her vehicle. The woman then ran toward Russ and checked on him and ran to her apartment to retrieve some towels and asked her roommate to call the authorities. One of the local fire fighters soon appeared and he and the good neighbor attempted to stop the bleeding with the towels until the ambulance arrived.

The name of the good samaritan woman was never released to the public and SGT Whitman kept it confidential, not even releasing her name to the Sherer's. The Sherer's, ever thoughtful, purchased her some towels to replace the ones she used to help Russell and SGT Whitman acted as the deliveryman. One can imagine the shock when the witness saw SGT Whitman show up at her doorstep with an armload of bath towels. The mystery witness stuck around the area for only a short time, as she was afraid for her safety. After the shooting, she departed the area, but kept her whereabouts private. Her forwarding information was provided to SGT Whitman; otherwise she vanished. The good firefighter returned to the fire hall and for him it was another day's work.

Russell was rushed to Ramsey Hospital arriving around 9:30 p.m. and taken directly to emergency intensive care. Russ came under the care of a skilled neurosurgeon named Dr. Bingham. When Russ got to the hospital, he was able to ask the nurse to call his wife. Russ tried to tell them his wife was at work, but wives didn't work at late evening hours in those days so they called home and got no answer. Russ was able to give them his mother's name and number and they called her. They told Russell's mother that he had been shot and was in the hospital. Russell's mother called Patty at 10:00 p.m. and told her Russ was at Ramsey Hospital and had been hurt and could not talk. Patty was beside herself with fear and apprehension as she was driven to Ramsey in the late hours. A kindly coworker drove her and assured her that all would be fine. Fortunately, she arrived shortly before Russ was taken to surgery. His head was swollen up like one of the cone heads on Saturday Night Live and she marveled that the head could get that big. She kissed Russ as he was wheeled off to surgery.

    Dr. Bingham had to remove a portion of Russ' skull to access the area of damage and then go in and remove bone fragments and bullet fragments from the right side of his brain. After the surgery, he advised Patty that the operation had gone well, but that Russell would likely have paralysis in his left side. He would likely have limited use of his left arm and left leg. They were also concerned with the vision in his left eye.

    During the surgery or before, they determined that Russ had been shot with a smaller caliber weapon and most likely a 22-caliber pistol. Toward the middle and top of the skull was an entry wound surrounded by powder burns. Next to that wound was a horseshoe shaped deep laceration that was down to the bone. This is where Russ had been struck over the head, likely by the gun that shot him. The slug went through the upper part of the right side of Russ's brain and came to rest in the area behind his right ear that is called the mastoid area. It must have diverted somewhat from a straight path as Dr. Bingham determined that it was not doing significant damage where it landed, so he wisely determined to close Russ up and leave the slug where it came to rest. The slug was determined to be about a centimeter in size. Scar tissue would apparently form around the bullet and serve as natures' wrapping and thus bundled, it would do no harm. Russ cannot undergo an MRI because of the metal fragment in his head. One thing that was somewhat difficult to account for was there was a small puncture type wound in the back of the neck about 1/2 centimeter in size. There was no evidence of powder burns on the exterior of the wound. Most likely this puncture type wound was an exit wound penetrated by bone fragments and smaller pieces of metal fragments.

    When Russ came out of surgery practically three hours after going in, he spent time in the recovery room and it was 8:00 a.m. the next morning before Patty saw Russ. She had spent part of the night in the lobby sleeping between two chairs. The hospitals were not family friendly in those days.

    To Patty's great relief, when Russ was asked to move his left arm, his arm responded and when he was asked to move his left leg, he raised it almost a foot off the bed. It looked like Russ may avoid paralysis after all. To Patty it seemed that she had just seen a miracle.

Russ remained in intensive care for almost a week following the surgery and was taken out of intensive care on the Friday following surgery. When Russell was still in intensive care, he had some visitors he wanted to see so he got out of bed and rolled his transfusion bottle with him and went out to see his guests. He likely put his charge nurse into therapy, but Russ was a gritty and determined guy. When he did get out of intensive care, he was started on physical therapy and occupational therapy. He also had speech therapy. When Russell started on occupational therapy they gave him a cognitive test to establish some sort of base line and Russ tested at a third grade math level. That would have been a pretty good test score for me, but Russ was a math major at a major university. Russell never experienced any seizures. He did not experience a visual loss.

The physical therapy was directed toward the extremities on his left side and overall coordination. The occupational therapy was directed at improving Russell's cognitive functions. He had speech therapy, as he needed work on some word pronunciation and speech patterns.

While Russell was in the hospital he had an armed policeman posted outside of his hospital room every night from 8:00 p.m. to 8:00 a.m. the following morning. Russell and Patty had no idea who had done this or what was motivating the shooter. Russell was not robbed as his wallet and watch remained on his person following the assault. Russell was wearing a wide whale corduroy sport coat with the professor patches on the elbows and chocolate brown slacks with a cream colored shirt when he was attacked, so there was nothing in his attire that would have made him stand out. I would have considered him a sharp dresser.

When Russ was in the hospital, he and Patty each celebrated a birthday. To mark the occasion, Russell baked a cake. He had never baked, but he and Patty had something to celebrate. He was alive and making slow progress. After less than three weeks in the hospital, Russ was released to return home. They lived in Inver Grove Heights, and the first thing they did was install a security system in the house. Russ had physical therapy 2-3 times a week and most of the time Patty drove him back and forth. If she was not able to drive, then a friend or neighbor would transport Russ to the session. Russ needed a lot of care and he was still in the recovery phase. Patty eventually came to the realization that it was too much for her to get Russ back on his feet and work full-time. Her shift was from 4:00 in the afternoon until 2:00 in the morning. By the time she got home and grabbed a few hours' sleep it was time to help Russ with his recovery or take him to therapy sessions. By April of 1986 Patty was forced to leave her job with the air freight company as there was simply not enough time to do everything that had to be done. Later on she did return to the work force, taking a position with a local school district.

Shortly after Russ was shot, Dean Hogg at William Mitchell called Patty and asked what they could do to help. Patty asked him why they did not have enough parking to take care of the students as it was putting students at risk and especially with evening classes they should have a safe place to park near the school. The Dean responded that they would love to have a bigger parking lot, but community opposition to losing green space had prevented them from getting the necessary permits. It was odd that the people in the neighborhood did not seem to object to cars being parked in front of their houses and coming and going at all hours of the day and night. They probably did object to the traffic and cars in their neighborhood, but somehow could not make the connection between cars parked on the street and the lack of parking at the law school.

As one would expect the double shootings in St. Paul did generate a lot of interest from the press and the public at large. When Russ was in the hospital, Patty was continually contacted by members of the press, and she initially chose not to talk to the press about the shooting. Patty had a fear of the press and was concerned that what she said may not be accurately reported. She had a healthy skepticism. Finally, she spoke to the people in the hospital about all of the publicity and she was encouraged by the hospital administration to have a press conference. They pointed out that they had people that were used to press conferences and they would help her to make sure that things did not get out of control. This was good advice as otherwise the press would have resorted to reporting rumors and leaks and all sorts of inaccurate information may have gotten out. She did have a press conference at the hospital and it went well and one thing she was asked about was the lack of parking at William Mitchell. She told the press that the dean of the law school wanted more parking but they could not get it accomplished because of neighborhood objections to losing green space. Patty continued, "Why would people support green space when doing so was putting people at risk? Is it important to allow students to be safe?" Patty turned out to be a great politician as the law school went back to the city fathers and this time the parking lot sailed right through the city's labyrinth of hoops. Patty was on hand for the ribbon cutting at the William Mitchell parking lot. The lot should have been dedicated to Russell and Patty Sherer.

During her press conference, Patty did thank all those who had sent cards and get well messages to Russell when he was in the hospital. He received over two hundred messages and it was impossible to respond to everyone. This is one astounding thing about my home state, that people would sit down and write letters of encouragement to a perfect stranger. I am sure it still happens every day.

Over the years I have gathered a pretty healthy skepticism of the press. For a time, I almost quit reading the papers as I got the feeling I was not getting any news. I adopted the view of my friend, Jack Meyer, that one gets enough news

Russell Sherer Lives 255

just walking by the newsstand. At times it gets disgusting as the papers are so shallow. Recently when I was writing this, on a recent edition of the Minneapolis Tribune the headline was, "Condom use falls at U." This was supposed to be news.

As Russell and Patty were concentrating on his recovery, things were happening with the criminal investigation of Russell's assault. The Sherer's soon became acquainted with SGT Richard Whitman the lead investigator on the Sherer case. SGT Hartman was leading the investigation on the Gibberd case and periodically they would compare notes. Both of the investigators had started as street cops and worked their way up through the ranks. SGT Whitman was a St. Paul kid and went to Washington High over on Rice Street. Upon graduation he moved on to the University of Minnesota and spent a couple years and decided to drop out and earn some money and like magic, he was drafted. Russell Sherer could relate to that experience.

When SGT Whitman was discharged from the Army he went to work as a patrolman with the St. Paul Parks Department. He spent a couple years keeping the parks safe and moved over to the St. Paul Police Department. He again was a patrolman and after ten years on patrol he moved on to SGT and investigated auto thefts for ten years and spent his last seventeen years in homicide. He retired in 1995 at age 62 with forty years of police work under his belt. He told me he missed the job for the first five years but got over it. I had the same experience when I left the bench as I missed it for five years as well. I also got over it.

When I called SGT Whitman and asked for him he responded, "It has been a long time since someone called me that." Indeed, it had as he had been retired for almost twenty years. He still lives in his home on St. Paul's West Side.

Russ and Patty Sherer met SGT Whitman shortly after the shooting. Two days following the shooting the police thought they had their man. The suspect was a black person who seemed to fit the description of who they were looking for. The arrest did not hold up as the man had an alibi and not one of the witnesses to either of the two shootings was able to identify him. The suspect was released.

When SGT Whitman appeared in my courtroom he was an articulate and bright witness. He was self-assured in court. He took a personal interest in the case and took Mrs. Gibberd and her two daughters to a Halloween haunted house that the police department was sponsoring for St. Paul youth. He also maintained contact with Russ and Patty over the years. They went out to eat on a couple of occasions and exchanged Christmas cards.

The Sherer's also maintained a friendship with Betty Gibberd through the years. In 1988 the Sherer's took a trip to England and spent a few days with Betty and Ray's parents who lived in the same vicinity. Upon arriving at the Gibberd's, Russ and Patty were invited to evening tea. They found out "Tea" was supper. Betty had built a home in England and it was called Pike's Peak at Fishbourne. Fishbourne was the name of the local village. Ray Gibberd had been a big fan of Pikes Peak and had flown a private plane over the top of the mountain. After Ray died, Betty chose to return him to the peak so she chartered a plane and had his ashes scattered over the Colorado mountain.

A few years after the visit to England, they again heard from Betty Gibberd and the girls had been doing some Irish step dancing and apparently had shown some skill and were invited to Boston for a step-dancing event. Boston has a large Irish population so it seemed like a natural place for this event. St. Paul would have been another possible venue, but people around here do not dance. There are too many Scandinavians living here and they fish and build stuff. I have always struggled on the dance floor. Phyllis is going to get me into square dancing and hopefully I can stay off her toes.

As fate would have it, Russ's best friend from the Navy, Tom Reha and his wife Majella, resided in a small town outside Boston called Stoughton, Massachusetts and when they called Tom, he insisted they stay at his home. In yet another bit of coincidence, My wife's last name is Reha. There are not many Reha's around so this was a surprise. It is a Czechoslovakian name and means farmer. Phyllis' paternal grandparents both were born in Slovakia.

Russ and Patty had a great trip reuniting with an old service friend and Betty Gibberd and her two daughters who were around ten and twelve at that time. They maintained contact with Betty after the step dancing, but eventually after the girls reached adulthood, Betty made the decision to sell her home and she returned to her native Ireland. She had a sister still living in Ireland. The Sherer's have not had contact with Betty Gibberd since she returned to the Old Sod.

The Sherer's still live in the northern suburbs in the same home in which they moved some two or three years after the shooting. They adopted a girl and she is now 28.

Russ returned to Unisys in January of 1986 and also went back to law school at the same time. He started back to law school on a limited schedule. He limited his schedule to one class. Russ had returned to driving at that time after avoiding the steering wheel for several months. He gradually got back to full-time law school and graduated in January of 1988. Russ took the bar exam and passed on the first time through.

Russ returned to work at the same job, but at least for a few months, he was not the same Russ. He found he was nervous whereas before the shooting he was always calm. He lost confidence and found himself second-guessing himself on many occasions. He could not recall the names of some of his coworkers. Russ was fortunate as gradually his memory function recovered and he slowly began to calm down and return to his former self.

By a year or so after the shooting, Russ had made remarkable progress with some of his memory difficulties and other issues and made a full recovery. He got back to full-time status at law school. After he passed the bar, Russ continued to work at Unisys. He returned as a code writer for computers and worked in that capacity until he retired in 2006. Following his retirement, Russ did volunteer legal work assisting low income clients with their legal disputes. He did that for 2-3 years until he retired from his retirement job. Russ does have some memory difficulties these days and there is really no way of knowing whether or not there is any connection between the current problems and the events of August of 1985.

SGT Whitman enjoyed a good retirement until four years ago when he fell in his basement and fractured his ankle. He had a displaced fracture and was forced to undergo surgery to install a plate and surgical screws. Unfortunately, during the surgery, he threw up and some aspirated materials entered his lungs and he almost died. He has had a slow recovery from that ordeal and does claim to have some memory problems. When I first showed him the crime scene in the Gibberd case, he insisted it was not the scene of the murder. It took some time to explain to him that this was the crime scene and he gradually came around and realized we had the right place. I found with SGT Whitman that it seemed to take him some time to focus or direct his attention to a new idea, but once he got himself acclimated, then everything was fine.

A few years following the shooting, the Sherer's were out for an evening with SGT Whitman and his wife and SGT Whitman confided in the Sherer's that they think they had the person that did the shooting and he was currently in the prison at St. Cloud for committing another crime, and was going to be in that venue for a time.

SGT Whitman did relate that they had a composite picture or drawing of the suspect in the Sherer shooting and showed it to the mystery witness and she determined that the shooter was not black. SGT Whitman was quite emphatic on that point. On the other hand, Patty saw the police drawing and thought the person in the sketch had Negroid features. SGT Hartman also remained convinced that the shooter was black. My view is that SGT Whitman was mistaken on this particular point. Certainly the race of the perpetrator in the Sherer case is more difficult to determine as there was only one witness and it was darker at the time of the second shooting.

Although the police were never able to establish a motive for either shooting, there was considerable evidence connecting the two shootings. The evidence seemed to point to a conclusion that a 22-caliber weapon had been used in both crimes. The method of the shooting was similar, being an execution style shooting to the head. The sheer boldness of the crimes indicated a connection as did the lack of motive or reason behind the shootings. The perpetrator of both crimes seemed to be black.

The question remains, was it the same shooter? The Gibberd crime occurred around 8:25 or 8:30 p.m. and the shooter left on foot. According to the Sherer's time line, Russ was shot only fifteen or twenty minutes later or at 8:45-8:50. The Pioneer Press Dispatch article of May 7, 1986 said the shootings were an hour and a half apart. The papers certainly make mistakes and SGT Hartman cautioned me that when it comes to criminal reporting, they are frequently wrong. The time of the Gibberd shooting seems to be pretty well fixed as there were several witnesses who had the time fixed and it was so close to nightfall that it is easy to remember the time. The Sherer time line is also fixed because of the hospital records. Russ is clear that he left the law school around 8:45 and walked to his car and was shot and was in Ramsey Hospital by 9:30 p.m. He was shot between 8:45 and 9:00 p.m. or only a half hour *or less* after the first shooting.

The Gibberd shooter would have had to hurry to pull off a second shooting. The shooter in the Gibberd case was deliberate and diabolical when he shot Ray and then calmly put another round in his head. No second round was fired in the Sherer case. People being in the area did not bother the shooter in the Gibberd shooting. Only one person was in the area during the Sherer shooting and this person would likely have difficulty in making an identification given the hour of the evening. The presence of the one person in the area was probably what saved Russ Sherer's life. If no one was in the area, then there is a strong probability that the assailant would have fired another round. His first shot was a kill shot as it was directed at a vital organ and if the shooter had not become alarmed by the presence of a witness in the area, he likely would have expended another round. The outline of a person down the street was likely enough to make a difference, as the shooter did not linger for a second shot, but fled on foot.

The shooter in the Gibberd case was calm and deliberate. The presence of no less than nine witnesses and cars moving along a busy street did not cause him to panic and flee in haste. He deliberately expended another round and then calmly walked away from the scene. He did not run. The Sherer shooting was after dark with no significant traffic in the area and only one potential witness some distance down the street. The Sherer shooter did not expend another round, but instead ran from the scene *and ran in the direction of the witness!* This does not seem like the same shooter. Given the short time sequence and the different mode of operation, it seems highly likely that there were two shooters on the evening of August 26, 1985 in St. Paul, Minnesota. SGT Whitman may have been correct, they were not the same shooter.

Chapter 10
Police Business

I contacted SGT Dale Hartman by phone and he was very receptive to what I was doing. He was living outside One Horse, Texas on a ten-acre tract of land. It was essentially a horse ranch that he had set up to save horses retired from the St. Paul Mounted Patrol from a trip to the glue factory. Dale told me that when he was a pink-cheeked officer at the Police Academy an instructor told him that when they retire they should buy ten acres of land and hollow out a spot in the middle of the acreage and this is where you want to retire. At that point in your life, "you will need nothing else because you will have seen it all." Dale had seen it all and wanted to retire in the south because he grew up in Oklahoma and never did like Minnesota winters. He missed the Minnesota State Fair and Minnesota fishing. I could relate to that as I always go to the fair and fish every summer whenever I can get to my cabin or when I can fit in a fishing trip to Lake of the Woods. I would also add family to the reasons I am still in this place. I do manage to tolerate high taxes, big mosquitos, and long cold winters.

I exchanged email information with Dale and we planned to arrange a meeting. I am old school and much preferred a face-to-face meeting with Dale as opposed to emailing or some sort of video-conference. When I phoned Dale, I called him SGT Hartman and he soon advised me to call him "Dale." I always start out on a formal basis with people I do not know. On my first job after I graduated from college, I worked for an elderly gentleman named Ward McMaster and Mac told me to always use "Mister" when you are talking with someone you do not know or just met. Good advice, I took it to heart.

We emailed back and forth and agreed to meet on a Sunday morning at the Lone Gonad Café located south of Dallas and off the freeway on the way down to Austin. Phyllis had a business trip planned for quite some time and her business was improving as she had a client foot the bill for her trip down to Austin, Texas for the semi-annual National Association of Regulator and Utility Conference (NARUC). I was originally not planning on going along, but I realized I could tag along and also line up a visit with Dale during the same trip. The last minute tickets on Delta going into Austin were getting expensive so I saved money by flying into Dallas instead of Austin. I rented a car so that I was able to meet Dale and continue on to Austin. I also had a car available to me while I was in Austin. I planned to see my Army Reserve friend, Jim Mahoney, while I was there. I would have to drive back to Dallas, but that did not cause me any heartburn. Mahoney is conservative and loves the Texas way of doing things.

I had flown into Dallas-Ft. Worth Airport when I was in the reserves and knew it was a sprawling place and just hoped the car rental location was in the same terminal so I did not have to transfer to another terminal. I had to meet Dale at ll:00 and did not have a ton of time to waste. It turned out the cars were not in the terminal but were at a central rental center so the terminal you arrived at did not matter. The first time we went down to Ft. Hood, the Army Reserve flew us into Dallas and then put us on a connecting flight via Reo Airlines into Killeen, Texas, a flight of about sixty miles. Those connecting flights are very expensive. We got into Killeen and still had to get cabs to get out to Ft. Hood. The next year I suggested we rent a car at the Dallas Airport and drive a bunch of us down to Hood. That saved the Army the expense of purchasing expensive connecting flights. We saved a ton of money for Uncle Sugar and had a car to use when we were at Ft. Hood. As a JAG, I knew there was no law against saving the taxpayers some money.

I picked up my rental car near the Dallas Airport and asked the clerk for instructions to Hillsboro as that was where Interstate 35E and 35W came back together to form plain old I-35. For some reason, he routed me around the long way. I did not tell him I was a lawyer or judge so I was hard pressed to figure out why he did such a thing. I guess I should have used Google maps as the Google does not know or care what you do for a living. Google is damn smart, though.

I got down to our meeting place at the Lone Gonad Café with about ten minutes to spare and the place looked Texas all the way as it featured a big bar and a slightly smaller restaurant. I picked out a booth way in the back of the restaurant and in an out of the way corner. As per my usual practice, I sat in the booth with a view of the whole room.

I always liked Texas and the people. Phyllis did not share my view as she thought they were all shit kickers and racists. Dale was running late so I was becoming concerned. Cops were usually early. Dale showed up about 11:15 and was wearing a Texas hat and an "Army" sweatshirt. We shook hands and I told him, "I like the sweatshirt." I followed up with a question asking about his military career and thus began the interview.

Dale's father was in the military during WWII and served in the Army Air Corps and stayed in the Army after the war and later transitioned to the Air Force when they gained Force status. Dale was born in Minnesota and moved on when he was three. He lived in Northeast Minneapolis right up near where

Police Business 261

my Aunt Vera resided near St. Anthony Boulevard. He mentioned the soapbox derby sight on the St. Anthony Hill and I knew it well. His parents must have liked it around here as they came back at a later time. When Dale was 9 or 10 he lived in Ardmore, Oklahoma and this is when he developed an affinity and love for horses. He lived out in the countryside and a nearby neighbor had a ranch of sorts and kept the horses pastured near Dale's home. Dale and his younger brother would go over to the ranch two or three times a week and ride the horses. The horses were described by him as, "just ranch horses." I asked him if they had saddles or bridles or anything like that and he said, "Hell no, we just rode them bare back and hung on to the mane as we had no saddles or bridles." He said the ranch owner and Dale's parents knew they were riding the horses, but no one seemed to care and the owner probably thought that the horses needed the exercise. Nowadays the place would have been surrounded by fences and razor wire and signs advising all to stay away. If the child welfare people found out about the riding, Dale and his brother would have been tossed in a foster home. The other day on the radio, the child "nannies" became all excited because a brother and sister aged 12 and 8 walked back and forth to a park to play and have some fun. It has become neglectful parenting to send your brats down to the park for a couple hours to blow off some steam. They should have sent them to the state fair.

After bouncing around a couple more air bases, Dale found himself back in Minnesota. His parents located in Fridley and he went to the local high school. I asked him if it was Friendly Fridley or Fertile Fridley and it turned out to be both as he was married at 17. When he was in high school he got a job at Ding's Riding Stable located out that way. A friend of his asked if he wanted a job and Dale was an experienced rider so he was hired. One of their principal jobs was to go out in the pasture and retrieve the horses and get them back to the stable. I did the same thing with cows when I was 5 or 6 but did not ride them back. My older brother told me that he and my Aunt Phyllis would roll some cigarettes with grandpa's cigarette roller when the grandparents went to town. He and Aunt Phyllis then stashed some cigarettes out in the woods and puffed away when they went out at night to get the cows. The Erickson's have always had this thing over tobacco. Dale did not stash any smokes, but he would take three or four bridles along with him and would bridle three horses and then hop on a favorite, and ride it bare back and drag a couple of the horses with him back to the stable. He said the horses were not real smart, but they were devious. Sometimes they would run toward a tree and try and brush you off. I have been given the brush off by many people, but never by a horse.

Dale graduated from Fridley High in 1964 and started out at the University of Minnesota. He was married in the fall of 1964 at age 17. He lived in his parent's basement and lasted one quarter at the U. He wanted to join the Army or one of the uniformed services but they would not take him because he was married. In those days, the Army did not want to take on any dependents unless they came along later. When I was stationed in Germany, the enlisted personnel had to get the military's permission if they were going to marry a German National. Dale was persistent and found his way to the Minnesota National Guard and they took him into the guard and sent him off to Ft. Knox for basic training. He followed up with Advanced Individual Training (AIT) down at Ft. Sill in Artillery School where he specialized in radar and communications. He had a wife and child and spent most of his first year of marriage in the military. This was a rough way to commence married life and this union already had a limited life expectancy.

The military schools are some of the best around and when Dale returned to Fridley he got a job as an electronic technician with the Applied Science Division of Litton Industries. They had a big presence in the Twin Cities in those days, but are long gone. They did a lot of military contracts and his time in the guard proved useful. They had a decontamination unit and one of their projects was figuring out how to decontaminate a General Purpose (GP) medium tent following chemical or airborne contamination. I spent my share of time in GP mediums, as that was my home for two weeks when we went to Ft. McCoy for summer camp. My tent could probably have used decontamination after a couple weeks in that place. Actually, the GP medium seemed like the Ritz Carleton as the prior summer I had gone to Camp Ripley at Little Falls and spent my time in a shelter half, sleeping on the hard Ripley ground.

Dale was working in applied science and one of the jobs he focused on was implanting small electronic sensors in body parts. An example of this type of implant was a pacemaker or an implantable insulin pump. One of his jobs was to go over to the U of MN medical school to pick up body parts. This likely was good training to prepare him for the blood and gore of being a homicide detective. A lot of people could not work homicide as it takes a strong stomach to handle some of the gristly cases they encounter. For one thing, one cannot be afraid of dead bodies or body parts. Dale would go to the medical school and pick up the body part and put it in a cooler and bring it back to Litton. Sometimes He used a super-sized cooler when he was bringing a torso or leg. He would usually throw the parts in the back seat of his car and head back to Litton. Fortunately, he did not have any police encounters when he was making those trips. When Litton had finished using the body parts, a dilemma was presented, as the University had a no return policy on body parts. They did not run the place like Dayton's department store where you could take back damn near anything.

One of the local brain trusts out at Litton Industries finally hit upon an idea for parts disposal. There was plenty of vacant land out hear the Anoka County Airport and the University of Minnesota had an airport out that way as well. They were either adjacent to each other or maybe even overlapped. Dale

Police Business

located a large hanger that was no longer being used. He took the parts out that way and dug a hole in a part of the vacant land near the hanger and buried the spare parts. He was able to park in the hanger and stay out of sight while he conducted his spare parts disposal. Years later, the parts may have resurfaced when the owners sold off part of the adjoining land for residential use. At one time, the second Metro Airport was going out that way, but eventually that idea was buried along with the Dale's used parts.

When I was city attorney, I found that most of the police force was prior service. Military service teaches one weapons training, discipline and self-reliance, and these are the key ingredients of becoming a good cop. The police departments are organized along military lines, so the veteran also understands that aspect of the job. It was not surprising that Dale began to give some thought to police work.

Dale remained in the National Guard and he was bright and ambitious and he soon made E-5. He was serving as a platoon sergeant when he signed on for Officer Candidate School (OCS). The guard ran their OCS as a part-time and full-time mix with some of the courses conducted while in a drill status, but he was activated for thirty days for the "in residence" portion of the course. He was commissioned a second lieutenant or "butter bar" in the Military Police Branch. He followed up with the MP Basic Course, which was two months. He was spending a lot of time in the military. He could have gone to Vietnam, but changed his mind when the prospect of becoming a full-time policeman materialized.

As an MP in the guard, he became acquainted with several guard members that were cops when working at their day jobs. He began to talk with them about pursuing a career in law enforcement. This search for a new career was accelerated by the cut back in research money by the military. He sensed that his days at Litton Industries may be limited. He talked to cops from both the St. Paul and Minneapolis Police Departments and they all advised him to go to St. Paul.

Dale had taken the tests for police acceptance and had passed and was on the waiting list for a job with the St. Paul, Minneapolis, and Brooklyn Center departments. He thought the Brooklyn Center department was too small and afforded less opportunity. Most people told him that the St. Paul department seemed to enjoy the backing of the community and the political leaders. St. Paul has always had a real sense of community and the locals realize they need the police and are often willing to cooperate and assist the force. Dale said that the Minneapolis department had more of a "them verses us" mentality as the department was frequently at odds with City Hall. This seems to coincide with my perception of the two departments over the years. The St. Paul department was deemed less political by all of those in the industry. In March of 1970 Dale started as a St. Paul cop.

Dale had been with the St. Paul Police Department for a couple years when the Vietnam protests began to sweep through the University of Minnesota. The protesters took over the ROTC building and some of the other campus structures. The threat of violence and burning and destruction seemed to be real. The governor activated the guard to maintain the peace and restore order. Dale was a fairly new lieutenant with the 47th M.P. Company and was serving as a platoon leader. It was an ugly time and protest. He had feces and urine thrown at him. Racial taunts filled the air. In one sort of bizarre moment, one of the protesters removed the blouse and brassiere from his girlfriend and proceeded to fondle her breasts while the protest moved on. Dale managed to resist the urge to cop a feel.

Dale carried an M-16 with him as did the members of his platoon. Most people did not realize that Dale and his platoon sergeant had been issued live rounds for their weapons. It was a serious matter and deserved a serious response. All of the other platoon leaders and platoon sergeants were similarly armed.

When they were a day or two into the confrontation, they managed to regain control of the ROTC building without any bloodshed. The protests still continued without abating. The guard leadership determined that they needed more weaponry so they sent a deuce and a half (two and a half ton) truck over to the ROTC building. The bed of the truck had struts or metal frames that could be covered with a canvas. Tarps are frequently used to cover any freight. This truck was sent over uncovered and in the back of the truck was a conspicuous gun rack decked out with M-16's. The crowd spotted the weapons and went bezerk and only the quick thinking of a young lieutenant named Don Sterner saved the day. Sterner jumped in the back of the truck and promised the crowd that if they would get out of the way, he would send the truck back to where it came from. The crowd backed away and Sterner was as good as his word and a potential disaster was avoided. Sterner was also a cop with one of the local departments. Dale did not know if the clips for the rifles or the ammunition were in the cab of the truck, but no one asked.

Dale was on the police patrol for the first eight years and then promoted to sergeant and worked as a patrol supervisor for three years. He shifted over to detective SGT and worked in the theft unit for a couple years. This was theft of all kinds from shoplifting to grand theft auto. During the same time period he was promoted to lieutenant. When he joined the department, there were three female officers in the department. Political pressure being what it was, there was growing sentiment among the politicians that one of the women sergeants should have gotten the promotion to lieutenant. There were also five other male SGT's that were promoted to lieutenant at the same time as Dale. Litigation and a court case quickly ensued and the result of that encounter was that the original promotions to lieutenant were all tossed out. The PD then re-opened

Police Business

265

the lieutenant's examination and everyone had to re-take the examination. The examination consisted of 850 questions. The graders went through one of the women's examination forms and they allegedly tossed out all of the questions that the female examinee missed so the result was that she had a perfect score and went to the top of the list. This method of scoring was not public information, but Dale had a good friend in the civil service or personnel section and she told Dale what had supposedly happened. Dale could not go public with the news, as that would get his friend in trouble. She was not supposed to be telling tales involving the inner workings of the fair and unbiased civil service system. I asked him if it was a girlfriend and he said, "No, just a friend." Dale was soon replaced as patrol lieutenant and bumped back down to sergeant. The other five SGT's who had originally been promoted, were again promoted under the second test. The test may have been rigged, but since he was the only one affected by the decision, he did not seek police union support, and he did not pursue the matter any further. He probably took the best course he could; he did nothing. He went back to work and forgot about the whole incident.

After starting in the homicide unit, Dale worked four or five cases as an investigator, but his first case as lead investigator was the Raymond Gibberd case. Dale was at home when he received word from the police desk person that a homicide occurred in the Summit-University area. Dale showed up at the crime scene and examined the body. It was on the sidewalk at Dale and Fuller and had not been moved. Dale examined the face and abrasions were evident on the face. There was no blood or bleeding from the abrasion site. This told Dale that Mr. Gibberd had died instantly as his heart had stopped by the time he hit the ground, as there was no blood circulating through his system. He confirmed his courtroom testimony that Mr. Gibberd was wearing his Control Data identification badge at the time of death. The badge issue is one that I missed as I found he was not wearing his badge. Judges miss stuff, even when we do our best to get everything correct. One thing to remember is that the assailant approached Mr. Gibberd from the rear and walked in a brisk manner to close the distance to the victim. He came up behind Mr. Gibberd and grabbed him and fired a fatal round. It seemed doubtful he even saw the badge prior to the killing. Dale did tell me that Mr. Gibberd had a Wendy's paper bag with him. This did not come out at the trial and was a pretty good indication that Mr. Gibberd had been to Wendy's. I found as a fact he had been to Wendy's but the paper bag eliminated any reasonable doubt as to where he had dined. There was a lot of skirmishing over where Mr. Gibberd went to dinner and had we known of the Wendy's bag it may have saved some time and argument.

A suspect soon developed and he was picked up within two days. He was also a suspect in the Sherer shooting. He did have an alibi and although it was not air-tight, it did seem to check out. They circulated a photo of the suspect among the staff at Wendy's and checked with their witnesses, but no one in that area was able to identify him. SGT Hartman thought that they got this lead through the St. Paul Police Department Intelligence Unit. The head of the homicide unit was a captain as was the head of the intelligence unit and the lead came down through Dale's captain. At that time, the intelligence unit kept its leads on 3 x 5 cards and they had a large room in police HQ filled with file cabinets loaded with cards called Field Interview Cards. Many of the cards were generated by patrol officers who would write up a card when they ran across a criminal who could be of future interest to the department. When an arrest was made, the information was already on its way to the card file, but if there was no arrest and future information would prove useful, a card was generated. The Gibberd and Sherer cases had generated considerable media attention so that everyone in the PD was anxious to move on the case.

The initial suspect did not have the kind of past record that seemed to fit this particular crime. He had a history of being a relatively petty criminal. He had a domestic assault that involved a sibling. He struck Dale as a small-time bully and bullies are usually cowards. Had someone been able to make an identification of suspect number l, Dale would have picked him up.

Eventually a couple of other suspects surfaced. The second suspect was the one that ended up in St. Cloud reformatory. This was the individual that SGT Whitman thought was the perpetrator and advised the Sherer's that he was in custody on an unrelated charge. Dale got permission to go up to St. Cloud with SGT Whitman to interview the suspect or person of interest (PI). The two investigators drove up and got the perpetrator in an interview room, but after 3-4 minutes the PI started yelling for the guards. Dale did not control the interview in prison as the guards had the final say. He said that was why he liked to have interviews at the police station. SGT Whitman had spent most of the time working this suspect so Dale did not have a lot of insight or time invested in this man. This suspect had some violence in his past, but Dale did not get the impression that this was his man.

A third suspect was an artful dodger. It took SGT Hartman quite a bit of time to track him down. His name surfaced through Crime Stoppers. This was a community source for individuals to provide anonymous leads on criminal activity. One of the Crime-Stoppers provided the name to check out and it took a few weeks to run him down. Over the next 3-4 years "The Dodger" was picked up 3-4 different times and Dale talked to him each time he was brought in. He circulated his picture to all of the witnesses, but came up empty. This guy happened to be a real "loose cannon" or "loose bolt" and that seemed to be the type of individual that Dale was looking for. Each time Dale encountered him the non-verbal communication was telling Dale that this person did not want to communicate, but likely knew something. He presented as hunched up and arms folded and a slouching posture. The physical description that he had been provided fit this person very well. Dale's cop sense or cop's intuition was

Police Business

telling him that this is a person that knows something. Dale checked out the picture of the dodger with his witnesses and no one could identify him. If he had received any kind of identification, he would have picked up the dodger. He remained convinced that the dodger was his best suspect.

Later the dodger was busted in Wisconsin and sent to the Wisconsin State penitentiary at Waupun, Wisconsin. Waupun is located about 260 miles from St. Paul and about 60 miles northwest of Milwaukee. It is the oldest prison in Wisconsin. Most recently the prison received some notoriety when a woman witch or wiccan was named prison chaplain. Her name was Jamiyl Witch and she changed her last name to Witch in honor of her chosen religion. The appointment caused quite a ruckus among the more religious members of the legislature and GOV Scott Walker did not like the appointment at all. The Witch managed to ride out the storm and in 2011 she was taken hostage by a prisoner who barricaded himself in her office. Reverend Witch was blamed for engineering the whole event and also was charged with sexual assault for some kind of alleged forced sexual act. None of the charges held up and were all dropped. This information is all thanks to Witchipedia, or rather Wikipedia.

He was serving time in Waupon for a robbery or assault. It was a crime against a person and this coincided with a violent past. This was before the Reverend Witch was chanting or serving at the Waupun Pokey. Dale asked permission to go up to Waupun and interview the suspect. At that time, they were short of money and the police department did not approve the request. Dale thought that this was a strong suspect, but there was no assurance that the PI would talk to him. This was probably four or five years after the murder. St. Paul must have thought it was nothing but a witch hunt. Dale had made prior efforts to get something from the dodger and the department probably believed that nothing would change during another round with him. He would likely still stonewall any questions.

Dale did secure permission to go down to Gary, Indiana to interview one of the witnesses. He would not tell me who it was but I do suspect it was the sister who was riding in the passenger seat of the car driven by her sister. This was the witness number 7 that I called Ms. Darter. She had the best look at the killer. Dale flew to Chicago and rented a vehicle and drove to Gary. Before seeing his witness, he checked in with the Gary Police Department, as that is a custom that police usually follow. They do not plunge into another police jurisdiction without putting the local department on notice. Dale went to the local department and told them where he was going and they asked him, "What kind of equipment do you have with you?" Dale responded that he had his usual 357 magnum. This was a good solid weapon and had replaced the 38 as the police weapon of choice. The Gary department contact then told Dale, "That is not a very good place to go. You better take a shotgun with you." Dale told the local cop that he did not think he needed the shotgun, but when the local cop insisted he take the weapon, he took it and locked it in the trunk when he got to his destination, but kept his 357 magnum handy. The witness had moved to Gary a year or so after the murder. She was very concerned for her safety in St. Paul as she had gotten a direct look at the killer and their eyes had locked. I did wonder why if she was concerned over her safety, she had landed in Gary? It seemed an odd choice for one seeking safety. Dale told me that she had moved there to take a new job and it did not have anything to do with the Gibberd case. Dale had a photo set up or photo line-up and at that time was using either six or ten photos in his groupings. He had two suspects and put both of them in the same grouping and it did not make any difference, as the witness could not identify either one of the suspects. It was yet again another blind alley.

Dale and SGT Whitman looked long and hard for a possible motive for the killing. Dale assured me that the obvious motives of money, sex, and jealousy were not present in this case. I asked him if he had given any thought to the possibility of industrial espionage. He had discussed just such a possibility with some of the executives of Control Data. He was a thorough detective.

Dale remained convinced that the same shooter was responsible for both of the shootings on August 26th, 1985. The close proximity of the offenses was one factor. The similar method or manner in which the crime took place was a second reason. Both victims were shot at close range to the same vital area. Dale did relate that the ballistic information indicated a similar weapon. The Sherer case involved a 22 caliber round and the Gibberd case likely involved a similar slug. Neither case involved a round that was larger than a 22 caliber. They would never recover the Sherer slug for close ballistic examination as most of it was still lodged in Russ Sherer's skull.

Dale did retrieve a couple of slugs from the Gibberd autopsy and they remain on file with the department. One of the slugs had a couple good barrel marks and he was hoping to find a weapon match. He had a number of small arms sent to him by the St. Paul department and other departments in the area, but nothing matched.

Another source that told Dale it was the same shooter was the "street talk." This is what they were getting from the small time criminals and usual suspects that the cops rely on for information. A few bucks to purchase a cheap wine was passed to a street derelict in exchange for information on who was doing some big talking. Dale dismissed the idea that the Sherer shooter was a white male. He was convinced he was looking for a black male in both crimes.

As far as motives or reason for the shootings, Dale thought it was a "wacko wanna be" or a "gangster wanna be." In other words, it was someone trying to build their criminal credentials or gangster resume. The acts were carried out in a professional manner so the shooter was careful about avoiding the appearance of being an amateur killer.

For the first few days Dale and SGT Whitman were of the view that they

Police Business

were dealing with a professional hit man. Both crimes involved shots to a vital area and were conducted at close range. In the case of the Gibberd shooting, the perpetrator worked methodically and did not run from the scene. A professional job seemed to be the answer. That view was to change.

Shortly after the two shootings, street talk seemed to surface and it appeared that someone had been shooting off their mouth. This was not characteristic of a professional killer. Those types usually do not talk.

Dale eventually settled on the most likely scenario was that the killer wanted to get in a gang or establish his criminal bono fides. He was likely a violent and unstable individual. Dale used the expression a "loose bolt." He was likely too chaotic or unpredictable for the gangs as they could not control him and did not pick him up or take him into the group. He was too violent and unpredictable for the gangs. That is a bad ass.

Dale never did talk to SGT Whitman's "mystery witness." SGT Whitman managed to keep her under wraps during the entire investigation. SGT Whitman was known as a "character" around the police station. He was looked upon in St. Paul as the local Columbo. He sometimes wore baggy suits and tattered hats, but the main thing was, he was effective and got results.

Following his work on the Gibberd case, Dale continued with homicide for another five years but he did live close to the station and for that reason he seemed to always be the one called in during the middle of a Saturday night for a criminal investigation. One Saturday evening he had been to a wedding and had quite a bit to drink and refused to come into the station. He explained he was at a wedding and in no shape to investigate much of anything. He caught some stuff for not coming in, but was not disciplined. Eventually, he grew weary of all the late night calls and moved to arson.

Dale did hear from Betty Gibberd a couple of times after she returned to England. She called a couple times to check on the investigation, but unfortunately he did not have any words of encouragement for her.

Dale always loved horses and was an experienced horseman and that accounts for why the chief of police called Dale into his office one day and asked him if he was interested in starting a mounted patrol. Dale responded that horses were a ton of work and he did not think he wanted to get involved in it. The chief was a friend of Dale's and suddenly changed his tone and said, "I am not asking you to do this, Dale." Dale understood what an order was and responded with a "Yes Sir."

This was around 1994 when Dale set up the mounted patrol. This was a herculean effort on his part. He contacted over fifty community organizations involved with the city and worked with them to gain their approval. Once he had the community support, he then took it to the city council for approval. The community support proved vital. As he got the program going, the Kiwanis club and some of the other organizations made contributions to maintain the horses. Horses get expensive to board and feed and community contributions were essential.

He went to the Mounted Qualification School in Omaha and then wrote the training standards for the mounted patrol. The patrol consisted of six mounted officers and seven horses were authorized. Individuals would donate horses to the unit, so at times they had around thirteen and sometimes as many as eighteen horses. The chief would ask Dale how many horses he had and Dale would reply, "Seven." The chief would then lean in and ask, "How many horses do you really have?" I recall seeing the mounted horses at events such as the winter carnival parade. The mounted unit was always impressive and served as a good method of crowd control and could provide security over a far-flung parade route when patrol cars would not be at all useful. A parade route was always bumper to bumper but a horse could get around that kind of logjam.

When he first started out with the mounted patrol, one of Dale's first areas of responsibility was the overall supervision of the park rangers who patrolled the city parks. One of Dale's officers was given the assignment of managing the park rangers. These were not mounted officers, but were non-sworn, full-time rangers who functioned as a force with limited powers to patrol the city parks. They wore uniforms and ran around in cars or motor vehicles, but were not certified peace officers. The City of St. Paul has some large parks such as Crosby Park and Battle Creek and it was too much ground for the regular police force to cover and moreover the duties likely did not call for sworn officers.

Dale functioned as the over-all supervisor of the mounted unit and had four regular officers assigned to work full-time in the mounted unit. He liked to work his mounted officers in pairs, if possible. The officers spent about 60 percent of their time working regular patrol and about 30 percent working special events. About 10 percent of the time was spent on training. The amount of time that any officer spends on training is quite astounding. Weapons training is a regular event, as most police seldom handle their weapons unless they are out on the shooting range. The old saw is that the cop never takes his gun out unless he is prepared to use it. As new threats emerge, the police have to be trained to deal with it. We have new groups of people moving in such as the Somali or the Hmong and the police officer must have some awareness of their culture and belief system. Why do or say something that will offend or anger a Muslim or minority when it can be avoided? You have to be trained in these things. It just does not happen by chance. Street smarts or street experience certainly helps.

One thing about the mounted patrol that I overlooked was the great visibility that being on a horse provides. Dale was working a parade up on Rice Street with his four mounted officers and they encountered a younger male who had too much to drink and was creating a disturbance. Dale and one of the other officers closed ranks on the individual so they could confront him and quiet things down. The mounted officers would close ranks on a suspect so that he was "sandwiched" between the two mounted officers. From Dale's vantage point, he looked down and saw that the individual had a sword under his coat. Dale moved to grab the sword, but the individual dropped down and scrambled out from under Dale's horse. He managed to stay on his mount and chase the swordsman down and make a bust.

Most police departments publish a monthly status report or productivity report. This document is usually internal and lists arrests, stops, and other activity for each officer over the past month. Dale and his fellow officers called it "the funny papers." Dale's four mounted officers were consistently among the top producers in the department.

The mounted patrol functioned year round. In the winter, they usually did not work when it was below zero. When the mercury was between 0 and +10 the work was at the officer's discretion. There was always plenty to do back at the stables, so a cold winter day could be spent caring for the horses and equipment.

Dale retired from the force in December of 1999 at age 53 with close to thirty years on the force. Earlier, he had "retired" from the National Guard under the rules of qualitative management. Dale had advanced to major and was the Minnesota Guard Provost Marshall. That was the "Sheriff" or top MP in the State. To get promoted to lieutenant colonel, one has to complete the Command and General Staff Course. When Dale came up for consideration for LTC, the board looked at his file and he had not taken the course. He was passed over as non-qualified and when that happens twice, you are out. Dale was very busy with his civilian job and just did not have the time to complete the course work. He had his twenty years in so he qualified for a pension at age 60.

I can fully understand why he did not have the time for the school because it takes a lot of time as the course is interesting, but challenging as well. The military sets up these hurdles as a means of thinning the heard. Whether or not it works out to be in the best interest of the service is above my pay grade to determine.

Dale did various consulting work after leaving the force and worked for some lawyers after he retired doing background work on criminal cases. He crossed to the dark side. He kept raising his hourly rate and eventually he priced himself out of business. He was weary of criminals and criminal lawyers by that time so he decided to move on to Texas and get his ten acres in the middle of nowhere as he was told to do when he was a rookie cop.

Dale has three horses on his ranch. These are mounts that are retired from the mounted force. He also has some of the horses that were donated to the mounted patrol. He rescues horses.

Dale and his third wife, Barbara, have been happily married for twenty five years. They each have four children from prior unions. Dale has three children from his first marriage and one from his second. His second marriage was to a professional woman who worked in the county welfare system. When they married, they both had decent incomes and drove nice cars and took great vacations. Wife number two then decided she wanted to go back to school and get a degree as a registered nurse. This meant the end to the nice cars and exotic vacations. It was an old clunk and a beer in the back yard. She managed to get a nursing degree and when this was accomplished she gave Dale an ultimatum: either they have a child or she was leaving. Dale became a father again. Later on that marriage did not work and Dale moved on. Dale loved the woman and has no regrets about any part of the relationship.

Dale has managed to maintain good relations with his three wives and four children. All three of the wives have shown up for all of his children's weddings. When he married Barbara, his first wife walked him down the aisle and gave the groom away. Dale and his first wife both realize they were too young at seventeen to raise a family, but Dale told me "he would not change a thing." Each move he made along the journey was the best decision, at the time, that he could make.

Dale's story enfolds as does many others. I could not help but recognize similarities in the paths that we had taken. I hope I had made the best decisions, at the time, that I could make.

After the trial back in 1986, Control Data continued to make computers, but they were nearing the end game of the computer business. They were making the big computers and some of the other folks were making them a little smaller as well as better and faster. By 1988 they were pretty well out of the computer manufacturing business. The surviving portions of the business eventually transitioned into Control Data Systems and Ceridian. There likely have been books written, or perhaps should be written, tracing the demise of CDC. Some will claim that CDC became too involved in trying to solve social problems by building plants in poorer neighborhoods or that they got involved in too many divergent business ventures. Somehow they lost their way.

The World Distribution Center (WDC) formerly located up on Dale Street on the southeast corner of Dale and I-94 is long gone. Most of the site has been replaced by the Hallie Q. Brown Community Center. A Soccer field looks down over the freeway. Houses along Iglehart Street have displaced some of the former WDC parking lot. Down the street to the south a few blocks, Sweeney's is still offering food and drinks to the neighborhood crowd. Going to the north and over I-94 it is only a couple of blocks to Fuller Street and a block beyond Fuller to University Avenue. The Wendy's restaurant is still in the same place as is the Uni-Dale Mall. The driveway exiting the mall and Wendy's will still show one the way to Dale Street. This portion of the area is unchanged since Ray Gibberd exited that driveway over thirty years ago.

If one travels south on Dale Street from the Gibberd crime scene it is only about a mile south to either Ashland or Portland Avenues and if one makes a right turn and proceeds west for four or five blocks to the vicinity of Hamline Mitchell Law School (formerly William Mitchell), one will approach the Russell Sherer crime scene. The distance is about a mile and three/eights. It can be covered in 2-3 minutes by car. One would have to be in good shape to cover it on foot in less than ten minutes. I did compose a drawing of the Sherer crime scene and have marked the location of the crime as determined by the Sherer's and Dale Hartman (see Appendix Exhibit No. 4).

Similar crimes occurred on that same evening back in August of 1985. One ended in tragedy and by a miracle or Divine Providence, one survived. It is hard to account for these things.

Dale Hartman made the right choice when he picked the St. Paul Police Department over the Minneapolis Police Department. I would have made the same call, but that would have been easy for me to pick my hometown. St. Paul's strength rests with its strong neighborhoods and hopefully that can continue.

Dale has gotten to be a friend and he has promised to come back next summer and do some fishing and tell me the story of "Dead Ted." He tells me there is another book there for me someplace.

EPILOGUE

Last year I went north to Duluth with my two sons, Kyle and Lars. We spent some time with my grandson, Andrew, who has just started at UMD. We stayed out at Park Point and walked over to the Amsoil Center and watched the Bulldogs play Western Michigan. We topped it off with a beer at the Canal Brewing Company. I finished reading a book on the Norwegian home front during World War II that my grandson Griffin had loaned to me. Norway had an active resistance force throughout the German occupation.

Last winter, my Grandsons, Matt and Bill, joined me in a hike through Ft. Snelling State Park. The deer abound in the park and they are so used to people that one can walk within 20-30 meters of the animals. They have little fear of humans. Winter is the time to do the deer watching as they do not have tree and ground cover.

This winter the weather is mild and we are concerned that the skating pond behind Lar's place may not be frozen. Lars and Sue host the annual pond hockey game. I am not sure how much longer I can play as I am fast closing in on 76. 75 may sound old, but I took my friend Dan Gallagher to lunch last week and he is looking in the rear view mirror at 86. Age is somewhat relative.

Two summers back, I moved our son, Cameron, out of Chicago as he moved on to Israel to undertake religious studies for a year. We all missed Cameron and are glad he is back. My granddaughter, Hallie, is going to the University of Chicago and had an apartment near campus on the south side. In the process of moving Cameron, we hauled some extra furniture over to Hallie's place and she helped me unload the SUV and get the stuff placed in her dwelling. When we were done I asked her if she could scare up a heater for me someplace in her apartment. She produced a cigarette and I puffed away and talked with her on the back porch. Faye will also occasionally produce a smoke or lately she is vapping and shares a puff or two. I can still smoke occasionally and not be burdened by the habit. I realize I am better off without it.

I guess these last few paragraphs explain why we do not live in Phoenix or Miami for all or part of the year. There is still too much going on back here.

Phyllis and I still get along well. I still am in love with her and enjoy being around her. She has started her own consulting business and it is quite successful. I try and help out with managing the business and the accounting aspects of her employment and do what I can to advise her on some of the substantive issues. We still have some rental property and some of which we own and some I manage for family members. I have been involved with rental property over the past forty years. It keeps me productive. I think as one becomes older, we slowly become invisible. If we are productive, we maintain visibility.

I think back often on certain aspects of my life and I have made good and bad decisions. Hopefully the good ones outnumber the bad. Unfortunately, we do have a tendency to remember the bad decisions longer than the good ones. I could go with what my new friend, Dale, told me, "I made the best decision, at the time, that I could possibly make." I wish I had experienced a better launch or start but perhaps my parents did what they had to do. They took their parental pride in proclaiming that I had been instilled with a work ethic.

Many people in our midst are working at jobs they do not like or they are ill-suited to perform. I was very fortunate in that I ultimately got a job that I liked and one that I was good at doing. Going to work for me was not all that much like work. Jim Otto used to say that he was "going down to the club." Otto loved the place and at well over age 80 would still be working, but for the "Bernie Dinner Rule." Someone once said that when you do what you like it is not work.

Not everyone was in love with my work as I did receive one death threat. I knew who it was and did not consider it credible, so did not bother to report it. It would have just wasted a lot of my time and I never had much to waste. I received two very nice hand written notes from employees who thanked me for my courtesy and patience and thought I was fair. I had the letters posted in my office for many years, but they probably got lost in a move. I ran into Carol Hooten at a party after she had been elected to the district court and she told me that I was "fair." It was a nice compliment and I hope it was not an isolated view.

I hope you enjoyed traveling with me on this trip. It was an adventure and had its moments. Most of what I have said has been the truth. It likely has not been completely and wholly truthful because frankly I am not sure I can handle the complete and unwashed truth. Who do you know that can?

CERTIFICATE OF NON-ACHIEVEMENT

IS PRESENTED TO

CAPTAIN RONALD E. ERICKSON

UNITED STATES ARMY

CAPTAIN RONALD E. ERICKSON distinguished himself by exceptionally mediocre service during an indefinite period while serving in a position of absolutely no responsibility. During this period he was confronted by a variety of inconsequential challenges. His reaction to these trivial matters was to clutch completely. Unlike his cooler, more level headed contemporaries, Captain Erickson repeatedly crumbled under the slightest pressure. His flaccid standards could not fail to be attained by even the most indolent individual, although he had difficulty maintaining them himself. He has consistently displayed a total lack of knowledge of, or interest in, any facet of his position. During his tenure, because of his lackadaisical and indifferent approach, the position rapidly deteriorated to utter shambles. His inability to produce acceptable results under any circumstances characterized the insignificant effort he put forth. His selfish and uncooperative personality soon permeated his entire section to the extent that all with whom his section dealt were treated with hostility and contempt. His complete failure to accomplish even a single given task stands as a tribute to those who wish to do away with the military establishment. His inebriated appearance, sloth, lack of ambition and odious traits of character, coupled with his "to hell with it" attitude have brought the utmost disgrace to his superiors and contemporaries alike. His ineffectually substandard performance of duty is in keeping with the lowest traditions of humanity and reflects discredit upon himself, his country, and society as a whole.

JEROME X. LEWIS
LTC, JAGC
Staff Judge Advocate

APPENDIX EXHIBIT NO. 1

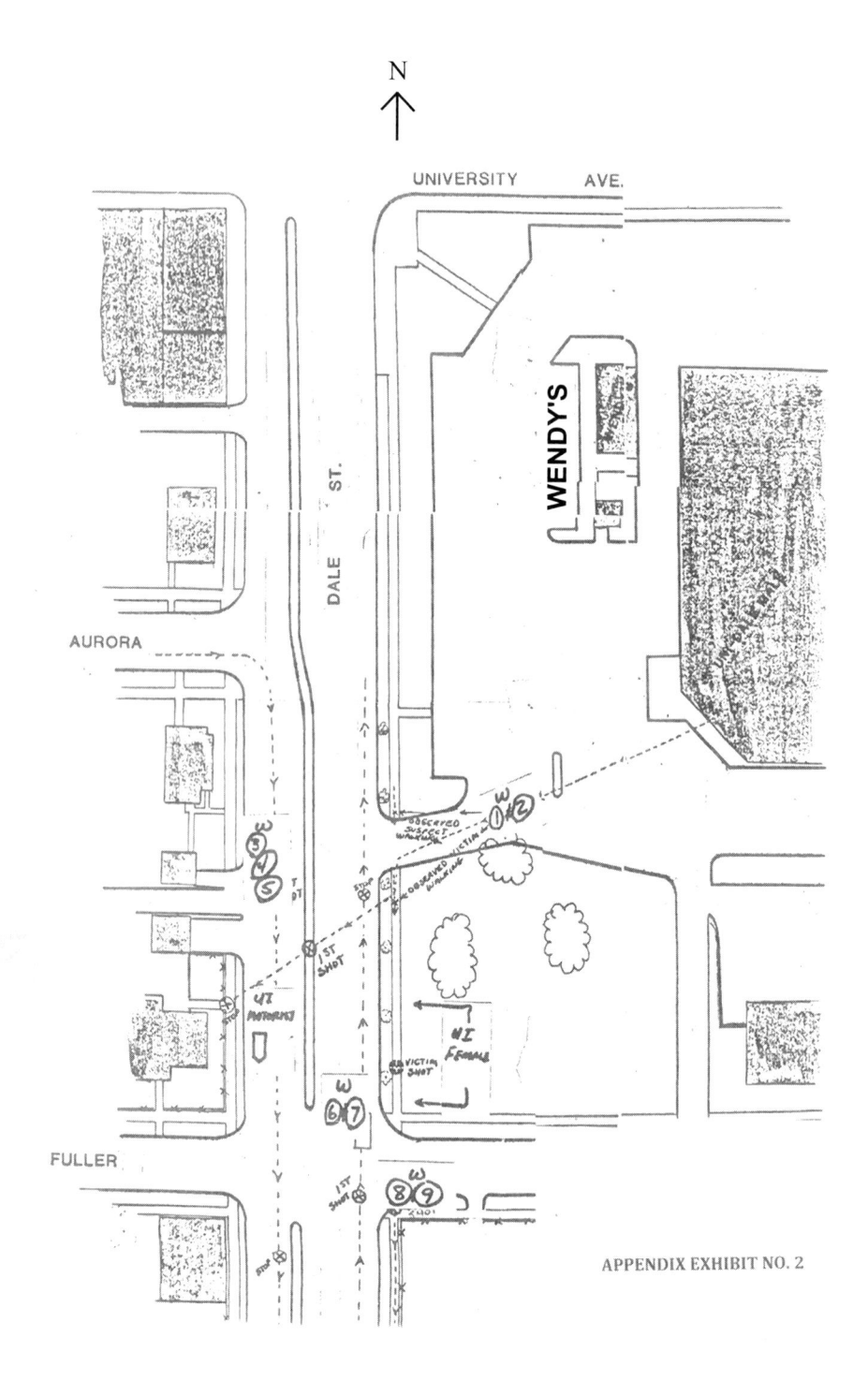

Appendix 278

APPENDIX EXHIBIT NO. 2

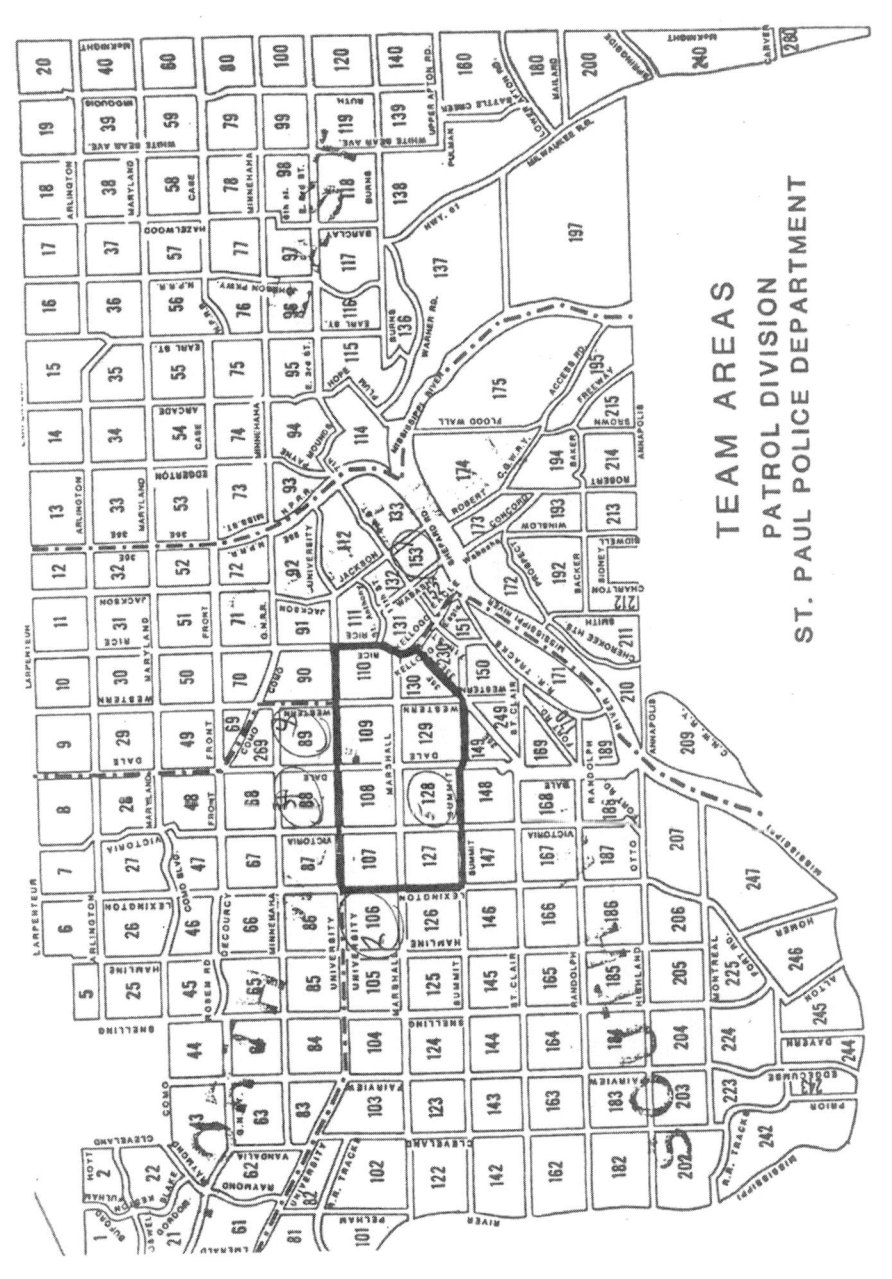

Appendix

TEAM AREAS
PATROL DIVISION
ST. PAUL POLICE DEPARTMENT

APPENDIX EXHIBIT NO. 3

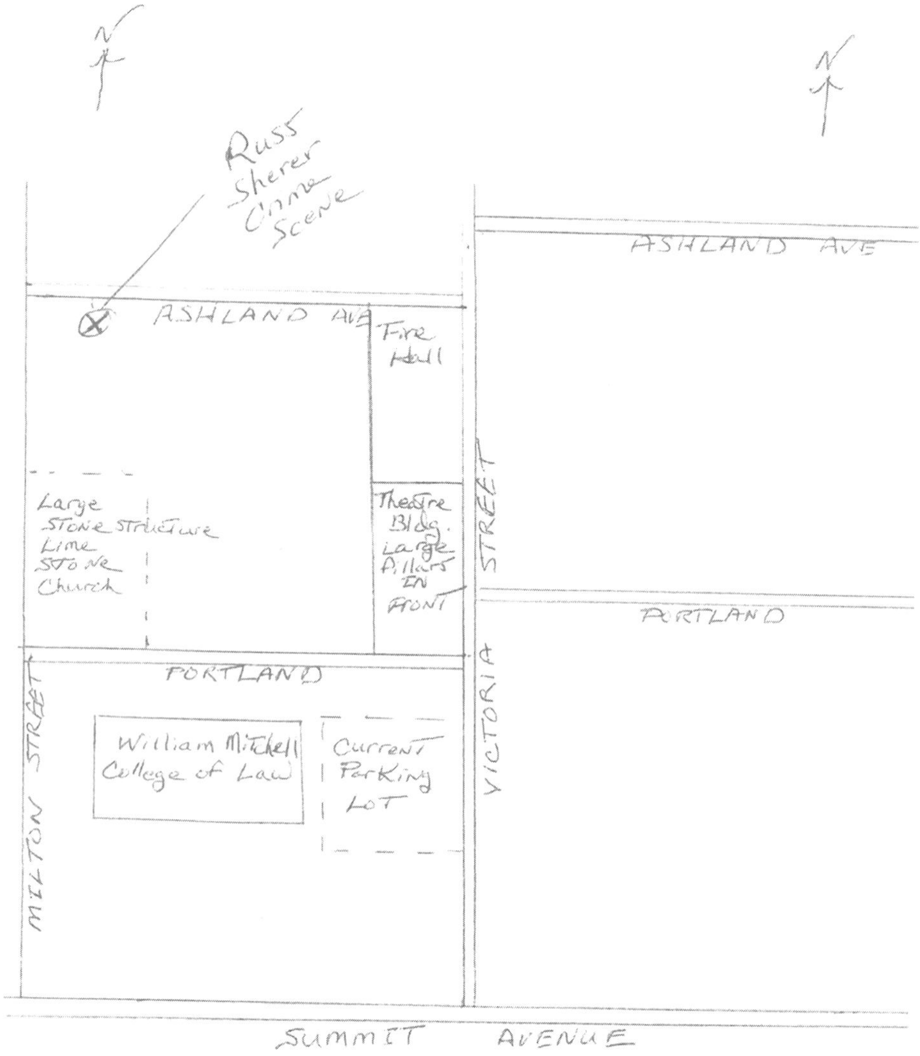

Appendix

APPENDIX EXHIBIT NO. 4

About the Author

"He is a veteran and a father," Captain Thorpe Nolan piped-up in his defense. This was in response to a charge hurled by one of his numerous detractors when he was a JAG defense counsel stationed in Europe. Occasionally, line officers had to get in a dig or two at those who were defending "guilty bastards" or telling colonels they could not bomb churches. Erickson was in the old Army when only males were present, but fun was still permissible. Prior to joining the Army, he had been a city attorney and prosecutor. Someplace along the way, he learned to pound a nail and built a wilderness cabin. After all that, he became a judge and did that for 26 years.

Ron Erickson attended Hamline University and graduated, without distinction from the University of Minnesota. He went on to William Mitchell College of Law and graduated with honors sometime during the previous century. He resides in Eagan, Minnesota with his wife and their cats called Ito and Kato, named after characters from the O.J. Simpson trial.